THE
SEAL OF THE SPIRIT

A STUDY IN
THE DOCTRINE OF BAPTISM AND
CONFIRMATION
IN THE NEW TESTAMENT AND
THE FATHERS

G. W. H. LAMPE

*Ely Professor of Divinity
and Fellow of Gonville and Caius College
Cambridge*

SECOND EDITION
WITH
CORRECTIONS
A NEW
INTRODUCTION
AND
ADDITIONAL
BIBLIOGRAPHY

LONDON
S·P·C·K
1967

First published 1951
by Longmans, Green and Co Ltd

Second edition 1967
by *S.P.C.K.*
Holy Trinity Church
Marylebone Road
London N.W.1

Made and printed by offset in Great Britain by
William Clowes and Sons, Limited
London and Beccles

CONTENTS

INTRODUCTION

FIFTY years have passed since Bishop Westcott prophesied that
the next great theological controversy would be centred upon
Baptism. There are many signs that the controversy which he
expected is now developing. 'We believe', says the second
report of the Joint Committees of the Convocations of Canterbury and York,[1] 'that there is emerging a considerable cleavage
of theological opinion about the meaning of the sacrament of
Baptism', and at no point is there likely to be a wider cleavage
than on the problem of the relationship between Baptism and
Confirmation, particularly in regard to the sacramental reception of the indwelling presence of the Holy Spirit. No aspect of
the doctrine of Baptism is more difficult to define than this, or
more likely to evoke radical differences of opinion.

The question is emphatically not one which concerns the
academic theologian alone; its solution is a matter of urgency
for the parish priest, now confronted with the grave problems
presented by the practice of what is sometimes called the
'indiscriminate baptism' of infants in an increasingly non-
Christian society, and by the widespread failure of the traditional discipline of catechism and Confirmation to achieve its
purpose. The pastoral difficulty is of particular concern to the
Church of England with its very large numbers of merely
nominal adherents. It is the Church of England, too, which is
especially vexed by the theological problem of the nature of
the Holy Spirit's activity in Baptism and Confirmation, for the
past century has seen a great change of emphasis in much of its
teaching on this subject.

'It is emphatically the teaching of the Prayer Book', says
Professor A. M. Ramsey,[2] 'that in the rite of Holy Baptism we
are made members of Christ and of the Church which is His
body', and it follows that the baptized person participates in

---

[1] *Baptism Today*, p. 24.
[2] 'The Doctrine of Confirmation', *Theology*, Sept. 1945, p. 195.

the Holy Spirit, as indeed many Anglican theologians have
affirmed even in the case of infants.[1] Confirmation, according to the Articles, is not a sacrament in the strict sense of the
term,[2] and the Prayer Book clearly regards it as the occasion
when the response of conscious faith required of the candidate
for Baptism, and, in the case of infants, vicariously made by the
godparents, is openly affirmed, and the candidate receives in
his turn the bishop's blessing with the outward sign of the laying on of hands and prayer that he may be strengthened by the
Holy Ghost, that His seven-fold gifts may be increased in him,
and that he himself may 'daily increase' in the Holy Spirit.
With the Catholic revival there came a notable shifting of emphasis to the sacramental aspect of Confirmation. Great prominence was given to the idea that in the laying on of hands
there was conferred either, as the 1928 rite affirms, 'a special
gift of the Holy Spirit', or even, as many Confirmation addresses assert, *the* gift of the Holy Spirit. This tendency was
carried to extreme lengths by Fr. F. W. Puller,[3] who distinguished the reception of the indwelling Spirit in Confirmation
from His regenerating activity in Baptism, and held that in
Baptism we receive the gifts of grace, in Confirmation the
Spirit Himself. This doctrine, laying the main weight of theological emphasis not on Baptism but on Confirmation, was
further developed by Dr. A. J. Mason in his famous book,
The Relation of Confirmation to Baptism, published in 1890 (and in
a fuller edition in 1891), in which the activity of the Spirit *ab
extra* as the agent of baptismal regeneration was distinguished
from His inward presence mediated in Confirmation, and an
array of patristic texts was marshalled to support the prior importance of Confirmation over water-baptism in the initiation
rite of the early Church.

Their theories involved what is, so far as the 'believers''
Baptism of the primitive Church is concerned, the difficult and
highly artificial isolation of one mode of the Spirit's activity
from another (a criticism which applies to the distinction which
H. J. Wotherspoon later attempted to draw between the grace

---

[1] See Ramsey's small catena of Anglican writers, *ibid.*
[2] Article XXV.
[3] *What is the Distinctive Grace of Confirmation?* 1880.

of the Spirit in Baptism and His gifts in Confirmation) ;[1] they also separated the status of sonship by adoption and of being 'in Christ' from the gift of Christ's Spirit. In effect they treated Baptism as no more than a preparatory rite for the great Christian sacrament of initiation, Confirmation. They did not pass unchallenged. Dr. Bright replied with damaging criticism of their 'incoherent anomalies',[2] and Dr. A. T. Wirgman matched Mason's patristic citations with an even larger collection of *testimonia* to prove that the Fathers in fact took the opposite view to that which Mason had ascribed to them.[3] He succeeded in demonstrating, if not his own case, at least the important truth that the Fathers had no consistent doctrine on the matter.

This controversy did not, however, develop fully in the time of Mason and Wirgman. The latter's book received a very favourable review from Dr. Darwell Stone,[4] who also defended the traditional doctrine against the 'modern view' of Puller and Mason both in an article, 'The Relation of Confirmation to Baptism',[5] and in his book, *Holy Baptism*, published in 1912, but few other writers took up the question (Dr. Wirgman had already been moved to complain in a letter to the *Church Times*[6] that the Mason school of thought had vouchsafed no answer to his book) and the controversy died down. Although on the Continent somewhat similar views to those of Mason, magnifying the importance of Confirmation in Christian initiation, were expressed by, among others, J. B. Umberg, S.J., in 1920,[7] the matter rested until recent years.

The practical aspect of the problem, however, never ceased to disturb pastoral clergymen. Adult Baptism has often presented as difficult a question, when considered in relation to Confirmation, as the Baptism of infants. As many war-time Chaplains in the Services found, unbaptized adults who seek admission to the Church usually ask in the first instance not for

---

[1] *Religious Values in the Sacraments*, 1927.
[2] *Morality in Doctrine*, p. 91.
[3] *The Doctrine of Confirmation considered in Relation to Holy Baptism as a Sacramental Ordinance of the Church*, 1897.
[4] *The Guardian*, Dec. 1, 1897.
[5] *Church Quarterly Review*, 45, Jan. 1898, pp. 357–82.
[6] Nov. 19, 1897.
[7] *Die Schriftlehre vom Sakrament der Firmung*.

Baptism but for Confirmation. They are often surprised to hear that Baptism is first necessary; and they frequently treat the great sacrament which makes a man a Christian as though it were a mere preliminary, a formality to be complied with somewhat hurriedly and casually so that the really important rite of Confirmation can take place. Such a misconception would never arise unless our liturgical practice and popular instruction reflected a confusion in theology.

Within the last twelve years the theological aspects of the problem have been reconsidered and debated from several conflicting points of view. In 1936 Dom Gregory Dix revived the theory that in the teaching of the New Testament and the Fathers Baptism is no more than a prelude to Confirmation (given with the external sign of unction) which is the decisive moment in a single rite of initiation. The latter comprises both water-baptism and the 'baptism in oil' which is the sacrament whereby the believer is sealed with the Holy Spirit 'unto a day of redemption'. Making much use of the evidence obtained from his study of the *Apostolic Tradition* of Hippolytus, he advanced the remarkable opinion that 'Confirmation was in the Apostolic Age regularly administered *before* baptism in water, that the original matter of the rite was a baptism by affusion in oil, . . . and that Confirmation originated as the Christian equivalent of the circumcision imposed on proselytes to Judaism, and had the same importance and significance for Christians that circumcision had for Jews—i.e. *Confirmation* constituted the effective rite of admission to the New Covenant.'[1] As Dix was candid enough to remark, 'Doubtless this appears sufficiently fantastic'; but his paradoxical thesis was argued with his usual brilliance and ingenuity, and compelled a fresh examination of the biblical and patristic evidence from which such remarkable conclusions had been drawn. Thus from the point of view of academic study Dix's revolutionary theories had the healthy effect which a radical challenge to accepted opinions produces in any field of historical investigation.

It was a different and much more serious matter when theological conclusions began to be drawn from these theories as

[1] 'Confirmation or the Laying on of Hands?' *Theology, Occasional Papers No. 5,* 1936, p. 1.

though they had been firmly established upon a solid foundation of evidence. In 1944, Dr. Kirk, criticizing the first Interim Report of the Joint Committees of the Convocations upon the administration of Baptism and Confirmation, pursued the Dix–Mason line of thought to its disastrous conclusion when he asserted that a baptized but unconfirmed Christian has not received the Holy Spirit sacramentally or within the orbit of the Church's ordinances.[1] 'Thus', as Professor Ramsey comments, 'if baptized children are partakers of the Holy Spirit before their Confirmation they are so, like some of the heathen, only through His uncovenanted activity.'[2] Dr. Ramsey himself, though he disagrees with Dr. Kirk's conclusions about Confirmation as a distinct rite separated from Baptism, accepts the view that in the undivided initiation rite of the early Church it was through Confirmation that the indwelling presence of the Holy Spirit was mediated.

In 1946 Dix again entered the debate with his lecture on *The Theology of Confirmation in Relation to Baptism* in which he reaffirmed that 'the teaching of the New Testament [is] that Baptism in the Spirit is *not* Baptism in water, but something else which follows closely upon it';[3] that in the Scriptural teaching it is 'the "Baptism of the Spirit" which "seals" a man to eternity and for which "Baptism in water" is only a preliminary';[4] that 'the seal' is given in the earliest liturgical forms by a ceremony very like Baptism but carried out by affusion with oil, and that this rite of Confirmation is 'the Baptism of the Spirit'.[5] The change in Western terminology from *consignatio* to *confirmatio* reflects a change in the theological significance of the rite: 'A document which needs "sealing" is not valid until the seal has been affixed. The "confirmation" of a document, though it may add to its authority, implies that it was already operative before it was "confirmed". This is precisely the change of emphasis which was now taking place in the West.'[6] When the ancient single rite of initiation had split up into Baptism and Confirmation, the influence exerted by certain fifth-century and later writers, especially the 'pseudo-Eusebius of Emesa' whose *Homily on Pentecost* found its way into

---

[1] *Oxford Diocesan Magazine*, Nov. 1944, p. 99. [2] *Op. cit.*, p. 195.
[3] p. 22. [4] p. 27. [5] p. 14. [6] p. 21.

the False Decretals, resulted in the growth of the typical mediaeval theory of Confirmation, namely, that it bestows an *augmentum gratiae* of the Holy Spirit; it was, so Dix argues, upon the foundation of this late and misleading conception which had abandoned the primitive notion of the eschatological 'seal', that the traditional structure of Anglican as well as modern Roman doctrine was erected.

Unfortunately, these highly controversial and unproven assertions have been adopted in certain quarters as a basis upon which to attempt a reconstruction of the teaching and practice of the Church of England. In an address to the Diocesan Synod of St. Albans in 1946,[1] Fr. L. S. Thornton took exception to a statement in the Joint Committees' Report which stated that 'it is surely difficult to believe that any of the gifts needful to fulfil the blessings conferred by Baptism are withheld until the later rite of Confirmation has been received. We cannot but believe that they are . . . operative from Baptism onwards.' To this Thornton objected that 'the statement happens to be in glaring contradiction to the solid weight of Church teaching in the age of the Fathers. The evidence will be found in Mason's well-known book on *The Relation of Confirmation to Baptism.*'[2] He repeats Dix's assertion that the seal of Confirmation corresponds in the Christian dispensation to the seal of circumcision in the Old Covenant. 'First comes Baptism for the remission of sins; then the promised circumcision of the heart in the seal of Confirmation. When these two stages are completed, then and not till then the indwelling of the Spirit takes place.'[3]

Apart from the fact that this doctrine is entirely strange to traditional Anglican teaching, it contains the most startling implications. 'The promise of the Spirit', says Thornton, '. . . is implemented for us only when through the Apostolic ministry we are sealed by that same Spirit "unto the day of redemption". Unconfirmed Christians, it would seem, have not yet entered into the full mercies of the Covenant; for they have not yet received that "first instalment" of the indwelling Spirit which prepares us for the day of our final redemption.'[4] The reason for this withholding of the Spirit until Confirmation is said to be found in the fact that 'as the members of the body

---

[1] *Confirmation Today.*   [2] p. 7.   [3] p. 9.   [4] p. 9.

are connected with the head through the central nervous system, so the members of Christ are brought into full relationship with him by their contact with the episcopate'.[1]

Theology, however, claims in part to be an empirical science, and, if the test, 'By their fruits' (in this case the fruits of the Spirit) 'ye shall know them', is to be taken seriously, this doctrine that no person unconfirmed by a bishop can be possessed of the Holy Spirit, unless it be by some uncovenanted act of mercy, is flatly contrary to all experience. It would require the plainest and most direct authority of Scripture, recognized and upheld by the constant and uniform testimony of the Church's tradition, to compel us to accept a doctrine apparently so much at variance, not only with the facts of experience, but also with the essential character of the Gospel. In the absence of such over-riding proof, we should apply to the views outlined by Thornton, Daniel Waterland's verdict on another theological doctrine: 'All sense, all reason, all Scripture, all antiquity and sound theology reclaim against so wild a thought.' The consequences of its acceptance, should we be persuaded of its truth, would be grave in the extreme. Christian Baptism would be reduced to the level of the baptism of John, a preparatory cleansing in expectation of a future baptism with Holy Spirit; Confirmation would become, not merely a sacrament in the fullest sense (which the Anglican Articles deny), but the great sacrament without whose reception no man could call himself a Christian; the New Covenant would be set on a par with the Old Covenant of the Law in so far as it too would have its outward sign and seal without which no one could be reckoned among the number of God's people, even though he had been baptized; and at a stroke the whole basis of the oecumenical movement for the unity of Christendom would be shattered. Progress in that movement demands a mutual recognition by the severed bodies that they are true parts of the internally divided Church of Christ; but on Thornton's view no non-episcopal body, and no church whose bishops cannot claim to represent the 'apostolic ministry',[2] possesses the Holy Spirit. Their members have never been 'brought into full relationship' with Christ,[3] for they 'have not yet entered into

[1] p. 10.   [2] pp. 9–10.   [3] p. 10.

the full mercies of the Covenant';[1] that is, they have not received the 'seal' which is the essential positive sacrament by which Christians are constituted. They are almost in the position of catechumens, and, since they lack the essential sacrament of union with Christ in His Body, the Church, effected through the power of the indwelling Spirit, they·can neither celebrate nor receive a valid Eucharist, and *a fortiori* possess no valid ministries.

When the acceptance of a doctrine could lead to the drawing of such monstrous conclusions, including the unchurching of an immense number of our fellow-believers, we should do well to examine its foundations carefully. The theories of Dix and Thornton, and, to a lesser extent, of Mason, make great use of the New Testament conception of the seal of the Spirit, in which Thornton sees 'an unmistakable reference to Confirmation';[2] much of their argument proceeds from this identification of the 'seal' with Confirmation, or from the theory that Confirmation is the means by which the sealing with the Spirit is received. It is therefore an urgent task to re-examine the use of the term 'seal' in the New Testament and the Fathers, and to consider its bearing upon the doctrine of the gift of the Spirit in Christian initiation.

In studying this subject we are entering upon a most difficult work. As every reader of the Bible and the Fathers is well aware, it is highly complicated, and the opinions upon it of the ancients often seem to be as confused as those of modern theologians. In undertaking this investigation, we shall therefore do well to imitate the diffidence of John the Deacon, who, when he was asked a question about the relationship between Baptism and Confirmation, replied: 'De qua re magis a doctis audire vellem quam ipse aliquid dicere. Quid tamen mihi videatur, salva meliore intelligentia, et maiorum plena sententia, quod in omnibus . supradictis volo tenere . . . breviter dicam.'[3]

---

[1] p. 9.   [2] p. 7.   [3] *ep. ad Senarium* 14.

INTRODUCTION
TO THE SECOND EDITION

THE fifteen years which have passed since this book was first published have been marked by a steadily growing concern in all parts of the Church about the doctrine and practice of Baptism. This intense interest has been focused primarily upon two issues, both of which lie mainly outside its scope. The first of these is the question whether or in what circumstances infant Baptism is theologically legitimate and pastorally justifiable, with attendant problems concerning the historical origins of infant Baptism and the degree, if any, of scriptural authority which may reasonably be claimed for it. This, despite certain strong tendencies on the part of some among both 'Baptists' and, especially, 'Paedobaptists' to modify their traditional attitudes, remains one of the principal controversial issues which still divide Christendom even in an ecumenical age. The second is the problem of the relation between the given unity, on the one hand, which all Christians possess or appear to possess through their participation in one mutually acknowledged Baptism and, on the other, the divided state of the Church which prevents them from joining together in a single Eucharist. The latter problem, however (as the Theological Commission on Christ and the Church strikingly discovered when preparing the report, *One Lord, One Baptism*, called for by the Commission on Faith and Order), immediately raises the prior question of what is meant by Christian Baptism. It is therefore itself inextricably involved in the theological problem concerning the relation of Baptism to personal faith, and so in the issue of infant Baptism.

The problem with which this book is concerned, namely the relation of the gift of the Holy Spirit to Christian initiation, and hence the theological relationship between Baptism and Confirmation, is at the same time a subject of continuing controversy. It is true that this is very largely an argument among Anglicans. Nevertheless considerable space has been devoted to

xv

it by Fr. Bernard Leeming, s.j., in his *Principles of Sacramental Theology* (pp. 184–225), and the adoption, in large measure, of the theological standpoint of the late Dom Gregory Dix and Dr. L. S. Thornton (decisively refuted, in my opinion, by Fr. Leeming) by Frère Max Thurian of the Taizé Community in his *Consecration of the Layman* may be said to have extended the discussion into Continental Protestant circles. In any case, the theological issues in this controversy possess an importance which transcends denominational boundaries.

It is this consideration which, I venture to think, warrants the reissue of this book in its original form. Despite the large amount of literature on the subject which has since appeared, little advance has been made towards the settlement of the theological issue with which it deals. On the one side there are those who, like myself, are convinced that the bestowal of the Spirit is one aspect of the single reality, salvation in Christ, which is sacramentally represented and effected in Baptism. This view has been ably presented by many recent theologians and, within Anglicanism, it underlies the majority report of the Joint Committees on Baptism, Confirmation, and Holy Communion to the Convocations of Canterbury and York in 1954. On the other side there still stands the theory which was advocated in different forms by Puller, Mason, and Dix that Baptism in water is a preparatory rite signifying repentance and, in some versions of the theory, regeneration by the 'external' action of the Holy Spirit, but that the principal positive element in Christian initiation, the efficacious sign of the bestowal of the indwelling Spirit, is to be found in the postbaptismal chrismation, or postbaptismal imposition of hands, by the bishop which followed water-baptism in the rites known to Tertullian and Hippolytus and in the Roman rite for many centuries, and which, in the medieval West, for various complex reasons, and at different times in different places, became in the end the separate rite of Confirmation. The most notable advocate of this view in recent years was the late Dr. L. S. Thornton in his book, *Confirmation : Its place in the Baptismal Mystery*. It was endorsed by the minority report of the Joint Committees in 1954, and it underlies the widespread desire to incorporate into the revised services of the Church of England the preface to the Order of Confirmation in the Prayer Book of 1928, with its reference to Acts viii. 14–17 as the scriptural authority for Confirmation—a passage which, if it taught anything concerning the normal and regular pattern of Christian initiation (which it almost certainly does not), would tell us bluntly that the Spirit does not 'fall upon' those who are '*only* baptized in the name of the Lord Jesus'.

Neither side has so far succeeded in convincing the other. One reason why this is so may be that the discussion has to a considerable extent been carried on within the field of the history of liturgy. Within this limited sphere much valuable work has been done. It has been shown quite convincingly that from the time of Tertullian and the *Apostolic Tradition* of Hippolytus onwards the Church as a whole, with an important exception in Syria, came to practise a complex rite of initiation, in which the central act of Baptism was followed both by a presbyteral anointing of the baptized and also by an episcopal consignation, together with, or identified with, an imposition of the bishop's hand, with prayer for the blessing of the Holy Spirit.

This outline of the rite of initiation, found in most parts of the Church during the patristic age from the time of Tertullian onwards, is described and discussed in this book, and I should not wish to modify greatly what is here said about it. I should not, however, wish now to lay so much emphasis upon the possibility of an important discrepancy between the text of the Latin version of the *Apostolic Tradition* and that of the oriental versions. I think it is probable that this work presents us with a rite of initiation similar in essentials to that which underlies Tertullian's *De Baptismo*. Nor should I wish to adduce the treatise *De Theophania* as evidence that elsewhere Hippolytus lays great stress upon the association of the Spirit with the water of baptism; whereas I remarked previously that this treatise is 'at best a dubious work of Hippolytus', I should regard it, on the internal evidence of its theological content, as spurious. The discussion of the liturgical history of initiation ought now to take into account the important contention of J. M. Hanssens[1] that the reconstructed *Apostolic Tradition* belongs to Alexandria rather than to Rome. I do not, however, find the argument convincing, and I should retain the *Apostolic Tradition*, so far as the baptismal

[1] *La Liturgie d'Hippolyte.*

rite is concerned, as evidence for Roman practice in the early third century. The progress of patristic studies necessitates certain relatively minor corrections : it is, for example, unnecessary now to hesitate about ascribing the *De Sacramentis* to Ambrose. These, however, are not such as to affect the argument.

Much more could now be said about what liturgical scholars often call the 'disintegration' in the Western Church of this early sequence of the single complex rite of initiation. The complicated history of the process by which the bishop's part in that rite (with the imposition of hands, as distinct from chrismation, acquiring a heightened importance in the Carolingian age) came at various times and places to be omitted, added after the baptized had received Communion, retained in its original place in the sequence, or gradually separated from Baptism itself to become the distinct sacramental rite of Confirmation, has been traced recently in J. D. C. Fisher's *Christian Initiation: Baptism in the Medieval West*. The same book discusses the changes and developments in the medieval Western doctrine of Confirmation which were consequent upon the changes in liturgical and pastoral practice. It is now clear that the frequent interpretation of the grace of Confirmation by medieval theologians in terms of 'strengthening' and of the 'arming' of the Christian warrior was by no means an invention of Faustus of Riez (pseudo-Eusebius) in his famous Pentecost sermon, but that it had much earlier precedents. The theory propounded by Dix and accepted by Thornton and Thurian that a 'depreciation' of the theology of Confirmation was brought about in the Middle Ages through the influence of the False Decretals, in which extracts from the sermon of Faustus were incorporated, has been shown by Fr. Bernard Leeming[1] to be 'based rather upon the supreme rhetorical skill of the late Dom Gregory Dix than upon an impartial assessment of the facts'.

Except at certain points, it can fairly be said that the liturgical history of Christian initiation from the end of the second century onwards, though complicated and sometimes obscure, is hardly a matter for controversy. It is otherwise with the question whether the sequence of initiation as we find it in the *Apostolic Tradition* and as it is reflected in the Fathers of the third and

[1] Appendix to *Principles of Sacramental Theology*, pp. 620–34.

fourth centuries represents a 'primitive wholeness' of baptismal doctrine and practice to which the Church ought to return.

This introduces the difficult problem of deciding whether this complex rite of initiation can properly claim to be primitive. Here, again, the results of historical inquiry are necessarily inconclusive. For the period from the earliest writings of the 'Apostolic Fathers' to Irenaeus, inclusive, there is no explicit evidence except in certain Gnostic groups that Christian initiation included any ceremonies additional to Baptism in water. No positive conclusions can be firmly based upon a negative inference from silence; but the absence of any reference during this period to the other elements in the complex rite is certainly very striking, and it is not only the silence of our admittedly scanty authorities but also such positive statements as the assertion of Hermas that 'the seal is the water' which strongly suggest that, whatever may have been the liturgical practice, Tertullian's association of the gift of the Spirit with a post-baptismal imposition of hands was unknown to the writers of the century or so following the Apostolic age. The evidence from this period has been usefully surveyed by A. Benoît in *Le Baptême chrétien au deuxième Siècle*. On the other hand, if, as seems probable, the Apostolic Fathers, Justin and Irenaeus, knew nothing of an elaborate rite such as Hippolytus describes, those who share the opinions of Mason, Dix, and Thornton have a right to ask how it came about that such a rite could suddenly make its appearance at the turn of the second and third centuries, and become generally accepted as traditional and hence as 'apostolic'. No clear answer can be given. The explanation proposed in this book, that its origins are to be sought in the initiatory rites of second-century Gnosticism, still seems to me probable, but it is far from being capable of being demonstrated and it can scarcely convince those who believe, despite the absence of any positive evidence, that at least in respect of its baptismal rites the *Apostolic Tradition* deserves its title.

Similar considerations apply to the evidence of the New Testament itself. It seems to me to be clear that except for the possible implications of Acts viii. 14–17, Acts xix. 6, and Hebrews vi. 2 the New Testament affords no basis for the view that initiation in the primitive Church included any rite besides

Baptism in water and that 'Spirit-baptism' was regarded, not as the reality signified and effected by 'water-baptism' but as a further stage of initiation, associated with unction or the laying on of hands or both, to which Baptism in water was merely preparatory. I should not now wish to alter substantially the arguments for this conclusion set out in this book. Certain further considerations, however, ought to be mentioned. One of these is the possibility that, as F. L. Cross argued in *I Peter, A Paschal Liturgy*, a very early baptismal rite can be discerned in 1 Peter. If this is so (but C. F. D. Moule[1] has shown it to be doubtful), it is significant that no trace of a distinct 'Spirit-baptism' appears in this 'liturgy'. The opinions of recent commentators on Hebrews vi. 2 ought also to be borne in mind. There is considerable support for the view, discussed by (among others) F. F. Bruce in his *Commentary on the Epistle to the Hebrews*,[2] that the washings (*baptismoi*) and laying on of hands to which the Epistle refers are Jewish rites and have no connection with Christian initiation. On the other hand, H. W. Montefiore, in Black's New Testament Commentaries, 1964, believing that the author of the Epistle is Apollos, associates the passage with the rebaptism and laying on of the hands described in Acts xix. 6. On the vexed question of the meaning of Acts viii. 14–17 and xix. 6 I should still wish to maintain the extraordinary and untypical character of the episodes there narrated. They are major turning-points in the Church's mission, at which the pentecostal manifestations of the Spirit, by which the apostolic mission to the world was inaugurated, are reproduced through the identification of certain particularly important new converts with representatives of the apostolate. It ought, however, to be added that a strong motive in these narratives is St. Luke's conception of the relation of the Jerusalem Church to the world-wide mission. The Spirit, in its missionary aspect as the Spirit manifested in 'tongues' and prophesying, is imparted to Samaritans through contact with the heads of the Jerusalem Church, the body which directs, controls, and supervises the progress of the entire mission, and to the nucleus of the Church in the great centre of Ephesus (where only the 'baptism of John' had hitherto been

[1] 'The Nature and Purpose of I Peter', *New Testament Studies*, 3, 1, 1956.
[2] *The New London Commentary on the N. T.*, 1964.

known) through contact with Paul, who, in Luke's view, was acting as a missionary authorized and approved by the Church at Jerusalem. The fact that the Lucan picture of this situation differs strikingly from that which we derive from the Pauline Epistles is irrelevant to a consideration of these passages. The fact remains that, as J. E. L. Oulton remarked,[1] 'the laying on of hands' in Acts 'is a confirmation of baptisms rather than a confirmation of the baptized', and that one thing which is plain in these obscure passages is that the laying on of hands is an action performed in abnormal circumstances, when the normal expectation that Baptism (in water) would be accompanied by an illapse of the Spirit had for some reason been unfulfilled.

Nevertheless, in the New Testament, as in the century following it, we are faced with the impossibility of proving a negative. It is possible, as L. S. Thornton has shown, to insist that throughout the New Testament there is to be discerned a duality in the operation of the Spirit, corresponding to two stages in Christian initiation. In his paper, *Confirmation Today*, published in 1946, Dr. Thornton maintained that unconfirmed Christians have not yet entered into the full mercies of the Covenant ; they have not yet received the first instalment of the indwelling Spirit. In *Confirmation : Its place in the Baptismal Mystery* this extreme position is modified : 'the Holy Spirit', he says, 'is the creative agent of all that is effected in baptism'. Yet 'the specific endowment of the neophyte with the gift of the Holy Spirit belongs to a second stage in initiation', 'the second part of the baptismal whole'. This duality in initiation corresponds to two distinct operations of the Spirit which in turn correspond to Christ's incarnation and anointing and to Easter and Pentecost ; the one relates to being, the other to mission. Thus Baptism 'is for the neophyte his entry into the new birth of the world through death and resurrection, whereas Confirmation constitutes his participation in the pentecostal gift of the Spirit'. Thus in his later work Dr. Thornton in effect revived the distinction, so trenchantly critized by Bright in his *Morality in Doctrine*, between an 'external' and an 'internal' operation of the Spirit in Baptism and Confirmation respectively.

[1] 'The Holy Spirit, Baptism and Laying on of Hands in Acts', *Expository Times*, 66, 1954–5.

My present purpose in calling attention to Thornton's contention is not to repeat Bright's criticism of its underlying theology, but to observe that the evidence of the New Testament cannot decide the answer to the question whether the sequence of initiation set out in the *Apostolic Tradition* represents primitive practice. I interpret the evidence as showing it to be highly unlikely that there was a duality in Baptism as this was administered in the apostolic Church. Thornton, on the other hand, comes to the opposite conclusion; though the exceedingly strange, not to say fantastic, exegesis which he is constrained to employ in order to reach it reinforces my belief that it is false.

The problem of the relation of Confirmation to Baptism cannot be solved by investigating the history of the baptismal liturgy. It must be approached by way of the theology of Baptism itself. We have to ask, not simply what sacramental sign the Church of the apostolic age or of the Fathers or of later centuries associated with the gift of the Spirit but rather what is meant by the 'gift of the Spirit'. To this question a sound Trinitarian theology based upon the teaching of the New Testament can give a clear answer. The work of the Spirit is to make the glorified Christ present to his people, to unite them with him through faith responding to grace, and so to assure them of sonship to the Father through the Son. To receive the gift of the Spirit[1] is to come to be, in the Pauline phrase, 'in Christ'. To be a Christian is to be indwelt by the Spirit: these are two ways of expressing one and the same reality.

Baptism, if it means anything at all, is the sacrament of union with the glorified Christ through grace and faith. It effectively signifies incorporation into Christ, and so death to sin and resurrection to newness of life in him. This is not to be understood individualistically : the believer is incorporated into Christ through membership of the Church which is the Body of Christ; the infant in a believing family is incorporated into Christ through being brought within the household of faith. The primary effect of Baptism is obvious and visible: it admits the baptized into the Church.

---

[1] The traditional language of 'gift' is itself unfortunate, and it may be better expressed in terms of the coming of the Spirit to the believer and his experience of the Spirit's indwelling.

All the gifts of grace which are associated with Baptism are aspects of the incorporation into Christ which Baptism signifies. Hence the theology of Dix and Thornton rests upon an impossible proposition : that we can be cleansed from sin and regenerated in Baptism, but that it is only through Confirmation that we receive the indwelling of the Spirit (which is identical with receiving Christ). It is impossible because remission of sins and regeneration are aspects, inseparable from all the other aspects, of the gift of sonship of God through Christ ; and the indwelling of the Spirit is another aspect of the same reality, not a further blessing additional to sonship, regeneration, and forgiveness.

The distinction which Puller and Mason made between the 'external' operation of the Spirit in baptismal regeneration and the indwelling presence bestowed in Confirmation is also impossible. So too, not to speak of the philosophical difficulties which it involves, is Karl Adam's distinction between a 'dynamic' presence of the Spirit in Baptism and a 'substantial' presence in Confirmation. This is all quite unreal. Fr. Leeming has well expressed the truth of the matter : 'There is no intermediary state between the state of sin and the state of being in Christ and in His Spirit. In baptism the Christian dies to sin that he may live the new life with Christ. . . . Now the life unto God in Christ is a life not merely caused by the Spirit, but a life with the Spirit dwelling in the soul. . . . It is theologically certain . . . that sanctifying grace involves the indwelling of the Holy Ghost.'

The worst theological error of all is that expressed by F. H. Elpis in his pamphlet, *One Baptism*.[1] In Baptism we first receive the life of Christ, 'but as we are united to the Second Person of the Holy Trinity, who told His Church to look forward to the coming of the Paraclete, so we need also that second act or stage, commonly called Confirmation, that we may be filled with the indwelling Spirit'. This is wholly false. The Church was not told to await the Paraclete after being already united with the Second Person of the Trinity ; the disciples were promised the coming of the Paraclete to be the mediator to them of the glorified Christ : to make them Christian believers, united with the Lord and receiving new life through him. The idea that we can be

[1] Baptismal Reform Movement, 1946.

Christians, united by faith with Christ, and yet be without the indwelling of the Spirit, is a basic Trinitarian error, resting on a tritheistic theology. It finds expression in the most regrettable prayer for Confirmation candidates in the Prayer Book of 1928. It was baldly stated by Fr. H. Cooper in a letter on Baptism in the *Church Quarterly Review* of January 1955 : 'I cannot agree that being incorporated into the body of Christ automatically bestows the gift of the Spirit, for that seems to confuse the Second and Third Persons.' The same tritheism appears in Thornton's assertion that 'as the Spirit in the Church is complementary to the Christ, so is Confirmation the complement of Baptism' ; and it was effectively repudiated by J. C. Sladden, reviewing Thornton's *Confirmation : Its Place in the Baptismal Mystery*:[1] 'The Spirit is not merely complementary to the Christ. He is the bearer of the Christ to the Church. . . . In whatever sense, degree or measure the Spirit does not dwell in us, in the same sense, degree and measure the Christ also does not dwell in us, nor we in Him.' This, and not any question of liturgical history, is to my mind the decisive point in the Baptism–Confirmation controversy.

Baptism is the sacrament of the whole gospel. As J. P. Hickinbotham puts it,[2] 'Salvation is an indivisible whole, received once and for all by receiving Christ Jesus as Lord, and must therefore be received in a single sacrament—that of baptism in which we are joined to the Lord Jesus and made partakers of his baptism of water and the Spirit and receive all the fruits of the mission to which he was then consecrated as Servant and Messiah. . . . Everything is given in baptism because God is given.' Nothing, therefore, can be added to what is given in Baptism. Its significance and its effects have to be unfolded and continually experienced afresh in the entire course of the Christian life, somewhat in the way in which what is sacramentally given in Christian marriage is 'explicated' and worked out in the whole subsequent course of married life ; but nothing can be added to its completeness. Confirmation is a *confirmation* of the baptismal gift ; Holy Communion continually renews and sustains it ; but it needs no 'second act or stage'.

[1] *Theology*, February 1955.
[2] 'Confirmation in the Early Centuries', *The Churchman*, June 1963.

This is not to deny that gifts of the Spirit are bestowed for particular purposes, or rather that the Spirit operates with special manifestations of his presence which correspond to particular vocations. 'There are diversities of gifts but the same Spirit.' Those who are called to particular functions within the one body of Christ receive those charismata of the Spirit which are appropriate to them. It is right that the words 'Receive the Holy Ghost for the office and work of a priest in the Church of God' should be pronounced in Ordination. No one supposes that they imply that the ordinand has not yet received the fullness of the indwelling Spirit; but the presence of the Spirit will now be manifested to him in new ways corresponding to his special vocation. Confirmation is the ratification of Baptism; it is also the moment at which, by prayer and the laying on of hands, the presence of the Spirit begins to be manifested in a new way corresponding to the tasks of responsible and active service as a layman in the Church which the newly confirmed person is undertaking. The charismata of tongues and prophesying, where these are manifested, correspond to the task of witness to Christ in the Church's mission; and, as the present rapid increase of pentecostal manifestations demonstrates, these special operations of the Spirit may take place independently of any sacramental ordinance. In no case do they imply that one becomes a Christian in successive stages or that there are 'higher degrees' in the process of Christian initiation.

Does the developed initiation rite of the patristic period, then, and the theology which accompanied it, represent a doctrinal wholeness, whether primitive or otherwise? I am inclined to think that the liturgical wholeness paradoxically exhibits a doctrinal disintegration. To surround the sacramental act of Baptism with subsidiary rites is a natural development which could be edifying. If Baptism, in itself a simple and not strikingly impressive ceremony (at least when not administered by immersion), signifies the whole gospel of salvation, it may be desirable to 'unpack' some of its rich load of symbolism and to clarify its meaning by means of subsidiary rites. In the practice of the Church of the third and following centuries, however, there can be little doubt that the effect was to dissolve the Christocentric wholeness of the sacrament of Baptism. Thus one aspect of Baptism, the repudiation of the world of sin, or (in mythological terms) deliverance from the powers of evil, came to be associated with the pre-baptismal exorcisms; on the other hand another aspect of the single sacrament, the reception of the indwelling Spirit, became especially linked with the post-baptismal con-signation; another aspect, that in Baptism we are made the people of the Messiah, similarly came to be attached to the anointing after Baptism.

It may be argued that so long as all these rites are held to-gether within the liturgical unity of Baptism no harm is done, and that the disintegration of baptismal theology did not set in until the liturgical wholeness had been broken up. This is true to some extent. The subsidiary rites of the ancient sequence of initiation could be not merely harmless but positively edifying; but only if they are clearly understood to be explicatory of the one gift given in Baptism alone, and not as additional sacra-ments. To restore the ancient sequence on this condition might be reasonably held to be desirable.[1] But it is very easy indeed for secondary ceremonies to be misunderstood and for the sacra-ment of Baptism to become depreciated. The confusion which beset the doctrine of Baptism in the patristic age, and which has since persisted, is evidence of this fact. So, in a much lesser de-gree, is the common popular misunderstanding of the post-baptismal signing with the Cross in the Anglican baptismal rite. This is undoubtedly an 'explicatory' ceremony, illuminating one aspect of what has been done in the Baptism which precedes it; but to the uninstructed it often suggests that this is what con-stitutes 'christening' and that Baptism itself is little more than a preliminary. To restore the ancient sequence would therefore be likely to prove theologically dangerous both on this ground and because the proper significance of Confirmation as a con-firmation both of grace and of faith would almost inevitably be affected adversely.

November 1966   G. W. H. LAMPE

---

[1] Confirmation, involving a vitally important addition, not to the divine gift in Baptism, but to the baptized person's response—namely, personal faith—would, of course, still be required.

NOTE

CITATIONS OF PATRISTIC TEXTS

EXCEPT in those cases where the chapters or sections of the older editions are short enough to enable a reference to be found immediately without further aid, the Greek Fathers are generally cited by the page and line of the 'Berlin Corpus' (*GCS.*) where that edition is available, and from Migne (*PG.*); the Latin Fathers are cited by page and line of the 'Vienna Corpus' (*CSEL.*), where available, or from Migne (*PL.*).

The Apostolic Fathers are cited from the edition of Lightfoot, the Apologists from Goodspeed, *Die Ältesten Apologeten*, the Apocryphal Acts from the edition of Lipsius and Bonnet, Chrysostom from the Benedictine text as reproduced in the Gaume edition (1834), Cyril of Alexandria from the edition of Aubert (1638), and Theodoret from that of Schulze (1769).

PART ONE

THE SEAL OF THE SPIRIT
IN THE NEW TESTAMENT

CHAPTER ONE

THE PAULINE CONCEPTION OF SEALING AND ITS ANTECEDENTS

THE natural starting-point for a study of the conception of 'sealing' in the New Testament and the Fathers is provided by three Pauline texts. In the first of these St. Paul tells his Corinthian converts that 'he that stablisheth us with you in (R.V. mg. 'into') Christ, and anointed us, is God; who also sealed us (R.V. mg. 'seeing that he both sealed us'), and gave us the earnest (ἀρραβών) of the Spirit in our hearts'.[1] In Ephesians there occur two similar allusions to 'sealing' with the Spirit. The former runs: '. . . in Christ: in whom ye also having heard the word of the truth, the Gospel of your salvation, . . . in whom, having also believed, ye were sealed with the Holy Spirit of promise, which is an ἀρραβών of our inheritance, unto the redemption of God's own possession, unto the praise of his glory';[2] the latter: 'grieve not the Holy Spirit of God, in whom ye were sealed unto the day of redemption.'[3]

On the interpretation of these passages the most diverse views have been advanced, of which four illustrations may be selected as being of importance. J. B. Lightfoot, for example, doubted whether St. Paul directly connected this sealing with the rite of Baptism.[4] J. C. Lambert,[5] on the contrary, refers the texts to Baptism, and interprets the 'seal' in the sense in which the word is used in Rom. iv. 11 to describe the circumcision of Abraham, that is, as an outward token and proof of a spiritual reality which has been already brought about by some other means. On this view St. Paul is maintaining that Baptism is a sign and proof of the justification of his converts by the faith which they possessed while yet unbaptized. Wirgman,[6]

---

[1] 2 Cor. i. 21–2.   [2] Eph. i. 13–14.   [3] Eph. iv. 30.
[4] *Apostolic Fathers*, pt. i. vol. 2, p. 226, n. 9.
[5] *The Sacraments in the New Testament*, pp. 167, 176, 182.
[6] *The Doctrine of Confirmation*, p. 75.

commenting on 2 Cor. i. 22, argues that, 'although we find some of the Fathers applying the term "seal" to Confirmation, a custom which left its mark in the Eastern formula of Confirmation, it must be remembered that "the seal of the Lord" is in its truest sense a synonym for Holy Baptism'. He quotes Pusey:[1] 'It is unquestionable that the primary use of the word "seal", both among the Fathers and the Liturgies, relates to Baptism.' Against this view, A. Seeberg,[2] Dix,[3] and others, follow the theory advanced by Mason[4] and Umberg[5] of the identity of the 'seal' with Confirmation, and Thornton[6] accepts as an undoubted fact that 'in 2 Cor. i. 20–22 St. Paul connects the seal with the anointing and with the gift of the Spirit. This is an unmistakable reference to Confirmation.'

Dix supports his contention with the arguments that 1 Cor. x. 1–4 implies a separation in St. Paul's view between baptism in water, typified by the crossing of the Red Sea, and baptism in the Spirit, typified by the 'cloud', which precedes the water-baptism; and that 2 Cor. i. 21–2, like 1 John ii. 20, 27, 'cannot without strain be interpreted metaphorically', but refers to an actual *rite* of sealing by means of unction. Having postulated a close similarity between the Jewish and the Christian sequences of initiatory ceremonies, he can go on to infer a correspondence between this rite of sealing and circumcision. As the latter was the actual rite of admission into the Old Covenant, so Confirmation, administered with the outward sign of unction,[7] is the seal of the Spirit and the primary rite of admission into the New Israel of the Church.

In the following chapters it is the present writer's intention, if possible, to justify the following contentions about these difficult texts.

First, that the connection between the 'sealing with the Spirit' therein mentioned and the sacrament of Baptism is so close that the one can be regarded as the thing signified by the

[1] *Scriptural Views of Holy Baptism* (Tract 67), p. 153.
[2] *Der Katechismus der Urchristenheit*, p. 230.
[3] *Confirmation or the Laying on of Hands?* pp. 10–11.
[4] *Op. cit.*   [5] *Op. cit.*   [6] *Op. cit.*, p. 7.
[7] On this point, of course, Mason and Dix differ; the former thinks that the imposition of hands was the regular medium of Confirmation; the latter, chrismation.

other. That St. Paul refers to a single specific moment in the spiritual history of his readers is evident from his use of the aorist tense, χρίσας, σφραγισάμενος, δούς, in 2 Cor. i. 21–2, and ἐσφραγίσθητε in Eph. i. 13 and iv. 30; that this moment is the reception of Baptism, or rather of the inward experience of which Baptism is the effective symbol, is made abundantly clear from a general consideration of St. Paul's baptismal theology (which should not be regarded as a peculiar product of his individual experience, unrelated to the earliest tradition and to the mind of our Lord, but rather as the unfolding in the light of his more profound spiritual apprehension of the teaching of the apostolic Church as a whole).

Secondly, that 'the equation of Confirmation=circumcision'[1] is by no means securely established so far as New Testament thought is concerned, and, further, that even the comparison between circumcision and Baptism in Col. ii. 11–13 (cf. iii. 9–11) implies not a correspondence between these institutions as *rites*, but rather a contrast between their respective spiritual efficacy. The real correspondence to which St. Paul points is between the Christian's possession of the Spirit as the result of his faith-response to the grace of God in Christ, and the inward 'circumcision of the heart' to which the great prophets had looked forward.[2]

Thirdly, that the view of Lambert and others is mistaken in identifying the meaning of the 'seal' in these three passages with that which we meet in Rom. iv. 11. In the latter case the use of σφραγίς is parallel to that which we find in 1 Cor. ix. 2, where St. Paul refers to his converts as σφραγίς μου τῆς ἀποστολῆς, i.e. the outward sign, token, and guarantee of the reality of his apostleship. In the texts which we are discussing, however, the word σφραγίζω is used in its primary religious significance, 'to set a mark of ownership upon', 'to stamp as the personal property (of God)'. St. Paul's meaning is not that Christians have received Baptism as an outward token or proof of the justification they have already obtained, but that through their response of faith to the saving act of God in Christ, symbolized and made effective to them in Baptism, they

[1] Dix, *op. cit.*, p. 13.
[2] Cf. Phil. iii. 3; Rom. ii. 28–9; Deut. x. 16; Jer. iv. 4.

have received the inward stamp of God's possession, the sign and mark that they are His people. This stamp is the presence and activity of the indwelling Spirit of God, the 'first instalment' of the ultimate total redemption which is yet to come at the Parousia.

Fourthly, that in these texts, explicitly in 2 Cor. i. 21–2, and less obviously in Eph. i. 13, iv. 30, St. Paul is not referring to any material unction or other rite of Confirmation, but is reminding his readers that by their incorporation into the Body of Christ, effected through Baptism into Him, they have become partakers in the effects of His own Baptism at the hands of John; they have been made sharers in the Messianic character, 'anointed' by God with the Spirit which stamps them for the day of redemption. We may notice the deliberate play on Χριστὸν καὶ χρίσας in 2 Cor. i. 21, which indicates that St. Paul is using Χριστός not simply as a proper name, but with the thought in his mind of that Messianic anointing which the New Testament regards as having been received by Jesus at His Baptism.[1]

The descent of the Spirit upon Jesus at His Baptism 'was a descent upon us because of His bearing our body; and it happened . . . for our sanctification, that we might share his anointing'.[2] 'Every baptism administered according to Christ's ordinance', says Wirgman, 'is linked to our Lord's Baptism in Jordan.'[3] As Cullmann, Flemington, and others have lately demonstrated, Christian Baptism is the application to each believer of the Baptism of Christ as it was consummated and fulfilled in His death and resurrection. The Christian who has sacramentally died and risen with Christ to the new life in the Spirit is 'anointed in the Messiah' upon whom the 'unction' of the Spirit came, and through whom the Spirit was poured out at Pentecost to make his followers Χριστοί.[4] Incorporation into Christ is emphasized by the phrases ἐν τῷ Χριστῷ (which in its

---

[1] Cf. Acts x. 38.
[2] Ath., Ar., i. 47 (PG. 26, 108C).
[3] Wirgman, op. cit., p. 52.
[4] Cf. οἱονεὶ γὰρ καθ'ἕκαστον ἅγιον Χριστὸς εὑρίσκεται, καὶ γίνονται διὰ τὸν ἕνα Χριστὸν πολλοὶ χριστοὶ οἱ . . . κατ'αὐτὸν εἰκόνα ὄντα θεοῦ μεμορφωμένοι, Or Jo., 6 (3) (GCS. p. 115, 17; PG. 14, 212C); Meth. symp., 8, 8 (p. 90, 17; PG. 18, 149C); Eus., eccl. theol., 3, 15 (p. 173, 3; PG. 24, 1029C); Mac. Aeg., hom. spir., 43, 1 (PG. 34, 772C); Proc. G., Gen., 39, 2 (PG. 87, 476A); etc.

context plainly means 'the Messiah') . . . ἐν ᾧ, of Eph. i. 12–13, and εἰς Χριστόν of 2 Cor. i. 21; in Eph. iv. 30 τὸ πνεῦμα τὸ ἅγιον τοῦ θεοῦ, ἐν ᾧ is seen in the light of Pauline theology to imply ἐν Χριστῷ. The presumption is therefore strong that St. Paul (and incidentally St. John in 1 John ii. 20, 27) is speaking of the spiritual anointing received by Christians as partakers and members of the Christ, that in 2 Cor. i. 22 it is this anointing which is described as a 'sealing', that the same thought is implied in Eph. i. 13 and iv. 30, and that the only rite which is here contemplated is the Baptism which the Church derived in its earliest days from John and which had been transformed in its significance by the baptism, death, and resurrection of Jesus. It may be observed in passing that nothing is said by St. Paul about the minister of this 'seal'; there is certainly nothing to indicate that to confer it was a prerogative of the apostles.

In order to establish these propositions we must first consider why St. Paul chose the metaphor of 'sealing', and then briefly examine the salient points of the New Testament doctrine of Baptism in relation to the bestowal of the Holy Spirit.

The Idea of the Seal

Any discussion of the term 'seal' in the context of Christian belief and practice is complicated by the remarkable diversity which we find in the use of the words σφραγίς, σφραγίζειν, signaculum, signare, and, to a lesser extent, in the related expressions χαρακτήρ, χάραγμα, χαράσσειν. The attempt of such writers as Dix and Thornton to find a simple equation between 'sealing' and 'Confirmation', and to proceed to use this equation as a principle by which to interpret the vast number of instances of the use of the term 'seal' in the Fathers, breaks down through their failure to take sufficient account of this bewildering variety of meaning. There is no single or obvious clue to the meaning of the term even within the relatively limited field of the doctrine of Baptism in its relation to the gift of the Spirit. Each instance of its use has to be considered individually on its merits, for there are few of the many meanings of σφραγίς, σφραγίζειν, signaculum, signare, which are not adopted by Christian writers to serve as baptismal metaphors, and in many cases the metaphorical application combines more than one of the literal senses of the term.

The various ways in which these words are employed in their ordinary secular meanings have been fully explained by F. J. Dölger,[1] and it would be out of place to reproduce here even a summary of his thorough account. If we leave out of our reckoning the use of these words by secular authors and consider only the meanings which they bear in the Fathers, we are left with the following list, which is by no means exhaustive. σφραγίς (*signaculum*) is used to denote a stone in a signet ring, the design or inscription which it bears, the stamp which is made with it upon wax, and hence a seal which is an authentication, guarantee, or proof; it signifies a token of agreement or affirmation, a mark of ownership, a seal set upon a letter, parcel, book, or other object as a mark of ownership, and also as a safeguard or protection against interference. Hence it comes to mean that which closes or seals up, and so can be equivalent to 'completion' or 'perfection', in the sense of that which completes and sums up a process or series.[2] σφραγίζειν (*signare*) means, among other things, to set a seal upon a document, and thus to give it authority, to ratify, affirm, attest, seal up or shut, fix in, assign limits or bounds to something;[3] to put a seal upon, in the sense of complete or make perfect; to set a mark of ownership upon something, stamp, or brand it.

Many of these meanings are applied metaphorically to the Christian experience of the Spirit in relation to Baptism, and to some extent they often overlap. Thus a mark of ownership, the sign of the believer being 'branded' as the property of Christ, a sheep of His flock, is also, when viewed from another angle, a proof or guarantee of his status, and a ratification or attestation of his faith and hope. For our present purpose, however, in seeking to establish the meaning of our three Pauline texts, there is one sense of 'sealing' which must especially claim our attention; for in these passages it is not the converts' faith which is being sealed, but their actual persons, and they are sealed 'with a view to a day of redemption'. It is therefore clear that we

---

[1] *Sphragis*, Paderborn, 1911.
[2] e.g. Cyril as the 'seal' of the Fathers, Anast. S., *hod.*, 7 (*PG.* 89, 113D).
[3] e.g. St. Paul 'seals', i.e. determines, the content of the Gospel, Cram., *cat. in Heb.*, 7, 1 (p. 545, 3).

have to do with quite a different use of the term from that which we have noticed in Rom. iv. 11, and which we find again in Rom. xv. 28 where St. Paul expresses his intention of 'sealing' his 'collection' to the Jerusalem Church. The meaning which will best help us to interpret his thought is that of marking with a sign of ownership, a use of σφραγίζειν which has a long and interesting history both in Jewish and in pagan religious usage.

This really consists in the application to religious ideas of the practices of branding cattle with the owner's name, the branding or tattooing of slaves, and the tattooing by which soldiers were signed as the emperor's men and easily recognized if they deserted the service. The latter custom is post-Pauline, but it illustrates the type of practice upon which his metaphor of 'sealing' is ultimately based. Branding an animal with a mark by which he can be instantly distinguished as his owner's property is, of course, a universal ancient and modern practice;[1] we read in Plutarch, for example, of the branding of cattle destined for sacrifice, as a sign that they were set apart for that purpose.[2] It is not surprising that the metaphor of the 'signing' of Christ's flock in Baptism or in its accompanying rites is one which was very generally employed by early Christian writers.

A similar marking was impressed upon slaves, primarily, of course, on runaways[3] with a view to preventing any further attempt to escape, but also on ordinary slaves in order that they should be 'stamped' as the property of a particular owner. Thus in the Jewish documents from Elephantine we read of a slave 'having a yod marked on the arm at the right of a marking in the Aramaic language'.[4] In some cases, at least, this sign was tattooed rather than branded.[5] The interesting inscription from Epidaurus,[6] which relates miraculous cures performed by Asclepios at his temple there, contains the amusing tale of a Thessalian named Pandaros. He had στίγματα ἐν τῷ μετώπῳ, and in a vision he saw the god binding a band around his

---

[1] Cf. *pecori signum* . . . *impressit*, Verg., *Georg.*, 1, 263.
[2] *Lucullus*, 24.
[3] e.g. Quintil, *inst.*, 7, 4, 14; Xen., *Hell.*, 5, 3, 24, στιγματίας τις.
[4] 28, 4 (ed. Cowley).   [5] Cic., *off.*, 2, 7.
[6] *IG.* 4, 951, lines 48–68; see P. Perdrizet, 'La miraculeuse Histoire de Pandare et d'Echédore', *Archiv. für Religionswissenschaft*, 14 (1911), pp. 54–129.

forehead; he was bidden consecrate this band in the temple, and when he untied it he discovered that his tattoo had vanished. His friend, Echedorus, who was in a similar plight, converted to his own use some money which Pandaros had given him to offer as a thank-offering to the god; he had a vision in which Asclepios asked for the money, and he replied that he had none, but that he would dedicate a picture of his cure if his tattoo marks were removed. A band was then tied round his head, but, on going out in the morning and removing it, the unfortunate man found, by looking at his reflection in a pond, that his own stigmata were still there and that he had acquired in addition the marks which Pandaros had lost.

If slaves were often tattooed, prisoners were frequently branded. The *Laws of the Homeritans*,[1] for instance, prescribe as part of the penalty for a convicted thief: σημείῳ τινί, ἤγουν σφραγῖδι σιδηρᾷ σφραγίσαντες πεπυρακτωμένῃ ἐπὶ τοῦ μετώπου. Similarly, captives taken in war were not infrequently branded; among many instances in classical authors there are the cases of the Theban deserters mentioned by Herodotus;[2] the Athenian prisoners who were branded by the Syracusans[3] with the pictorial sign of a horse; and the prisoners of whom Quintus Curtius writes: 'quosdam manibus auribusque amputatis inustisque barbararum litterarum notis in longum sibi reservarent.'[4] It is to this practice that a passage in the Psalms of Solomon refers: υἱοὶ καὶ θυγατέρες ἐν αἰχμαλωσίᾳ πονηρᾷ, ἐν σφραγῖδι ὁ τράχηλος αὐτῶν, ἐν ἐπισήμῳ ἐν τοῖς ἔθνεσιν.[5] We may recall the alleged branding by Ptolemy Philopator of Jews who refused to apostatize: τούτους δὲ ἀπογραφομένους χαράσσεσθαι καὶ διὰ πυρὸς εἰς τὸ σῶμα παρασήμῳ Διονύσου κισσοφύλλῳ.[6]

Here we are approaching the conception of 'sealing' in connection with religious cults; but before we discuss the pagan and Jewish cult-practices which form the immediate background of St. Paul's metaphor of the 'seal' we may glance at an extension of the secular use of physical markings which furnished many useful metaphors of 'sealing' for later Christian writers, and figures prominently in their theology of Baptism. This is the

---

[1] *Legg. Homerit.*, 5 (*PG.* 86, 584B).
[2] 7, 233; cf. Geo. Pis., *v. Anast.* (*PG.* 92, 1712B).
[3] Plut., *Nic.*, 29.
[4] 5, 5, 6.   [5] ii. 6.   [6] 3 Macc. ii. 29.

practice in the later Empire of tattooing soldiers as a sign of their service, a mark of recognition, and a precaution against desertion. Tertullian evidently refers to the use of this more permanent equivalent of the modern identity-disc when he compares the secular soldier with the devotee of Mithras: 'et, si adhuc memini, Mithra signat illic in frontibus milites suos.'[1] Cyprian derives from it a metaphor of the Christian *militia*: 'Tu tantum, quem iam spiritalibus castris caelestis militia signavit.'[2] We shall later have to consider the most interesting source of information about the 'signing' of a recruit, the *Acta Maximiliani*.[3] The purpose of the custom is made clear enough from the regulations laid down by Vegetius: 'Non statim punctis signorum scribendus est tiro dilectus, verum ante exercitio pertemptandus, ut utrum vere tanto operi aptus sit possit agnosci';[4] and, 'Nam victuris (v.l. picturis) in cute punctis milites scripti, cum matriculis inseruntur, iurare solent; et ideo militiae sacramenta dicuntur';[5] more explicitly, Augustine remarks that a military *character* 'ornabat militem, convincit desertorem'.[6] Ambrose indicates its nature thus: 'charactere domini servuli inscribuntur, et nomine imperatoris signantur milites.'[7] That the sign was sometimes imprinted on the hand is indicated by Gregory the Great,[8] and by Aetius who defines the στίγματα as τὰ ἐπὶ τοῦ προσώπου ἢ ἄλλου τινὸς μέρους τοῦ σώματος ἐπιγραφόμενα, οἷα τῶν στρατευομένων ἐν ταῖς χέρσιν.[9] (Aetius goes on to describe the method of performing the operation, and gives what must have been a popular recipe for the removal of the marks.) The *Acta Maximiliani*, however, show that it was sometimes imprinted on the neck.

Under the 'direction of labour' in the Lower Empire the members of public corporations might be subjected to a similar tattooing to that imposed upon soldiers and slaves.[10]

---

[1] *praescr.*, 40.   [2] *Donat.*, 15 (*CSEL*. p. 15, 15).
[3] Knopf, p. 86.   [4] *De re milit.*, 1, 8.
[5] *Ibid.*, 2, 5.
[6] *enarr. in Ps.* 39, 1 (*PL.* 36, 433A); cf. *ep.* 185, 6, 23; *ep.* 88, 9.
[7] *obit. Valent.*, 58.
[8] *epp.* 3, 65: 'qui in manu signatus est'.
[9] *tetrabibl.*, 8, 12 (Venice, 1534, p. 152, 43).
[10] Stigmata, hoc est nota publica, fabricensium brachiis ad imitationem tironum infligatur, ut hoc modo saltem possint latitantes agnosci, Cod. Theod., 10, 22, 4; cf. Cod. Justn., 10, 11, 43.

From this picture of the soldier or member of a guild 'stamped' with the emperor's mark upon his hand, brow, or neck, it is no great distance to the idea of the 'sealing' of a religious devotee with the sign or emblem of the god whom he serves. This seal may be a physical mark, or it may be some inward token by which he is assured of his status in relation to the god, and enabled to hope that in some future 'gathering in' of the god's people he will be recognized and admitted among the chosen.

The conception of the believer as bound, like a soldier or a servant, in loyalty, service, and devotion to his god is a striking feature of the pagan mysteries. 'La consécration à Isis du héros d'Apulée', remarks Cumont, 'est vraiment le resultat d'une vocation, d'un appel de la déesse, qui veut que le néophyte s'enrôle dans sa milice sacrée.'[1] Among Christians the idea of religious vocation as a *militia* is even stronger, and we shall find that it plays an important role in the history of Baptism and of the conception of the 'seal' by which a convert is enrolled, and, as it were, 'signed on' under the standard of Christ.

Besides serving his god like a soldier, the believer also stands before him as a slave; so we find the worshippers of Cybele described as 'Idaeae Matris famulos'.[2] It is therefore not surprising to discover that the practice of tattooing or otherwise setting a mark upon the body as a sign of consecration to a deity was common in many of the cults of pagan antiquity, especially in those oriental or semi-oriental religions in which the worshipper was brought into a personal relationship to his god like that of a servant to his master. Herodotus[3] describes a temple in Egypt at which a fugitive taking sanctuary might receive a physical mark which stamped him as the god's property and so as inviolable and sacrosanct. We have already cited the branding of recalcitrant Jews with the ivy-leaf of Dionysus.[4] Philo thought it necessary to utter a warning against imitating what was evidently a common custom among pagans, a visible token of their devotion to idols.[5] The kind of practice to which he was referring is illustrated by Lucian's description

---

[1] *Religions orientales dans le Paganisme romain*, p. 23.
[2] Cic., *legg.*, 2, 9, 22.   [3] 2, 113.
[4] 3 Macc. ii. 29.   [5] *spec. legg.*, 1, 58 (*monarch.* 8).

of religious tattooing in the cult of the Syrian Goddess: στίζονται δὲ πάντες οἱ μὲν ἐς καρπούς, οἱ δὲ ἐς αὐχένας, καὶ ἀπὸ τοῦδε ἅπαντες Ἀσσύριοι στιγματηφορέουσι.[1] For the Dionysiac cult there is the evidence of an inscription from the neighbourhood of Philippi,[2] and for the worship of Attis the more detailed account of Prudentius:[3] 'Quid, cum sacrandus accipit sfragitidas? Acus minutas ingerunt fornacibus, His membra pergunt urere, ut igniverint; Quamcumque partem corporis fervens nota Stigmavit, hanc sic consecratam praedicant.' Tertullian, as we have seen, knew that the 'soldiers' of Mithras were 'signed' in this way,[4] and we also hear of a similar marking which was practised by the Ethiopians in honour of 'Apollo'.[5] Finally, we may notice the significant comment of Primasius of Hadrumetum on Rom. i. 24 (ut contumeliis afficiant corpora sua): 'Dum sibi characteres et ustiones infligunt in consecrationibus idolorum.'[6]

In the Semitic world, as we might naturally expect, these devotional customs were widespread. We read of physical markings in connection with the cult of the dead, the Israelites being forbidden to 'make any cuttings in your flesh for the dead, nor print any marks upon you'.[7] That is to say, the Israelites were commanded not to follow the example of their neighbours, such as the Egyptians who, at any rate as worshippers of Isis in later times, 'in adytis habent idolum Osiridis sepultum, hoc annuis luctibus plangunt, radunt capita, ... lacerant lacertos, veterum vulnerum resecant cicatrices'.[8] Theodoret explains the Mosaic prohibition by saying: καί τινα δὲ τοῦ σώματος μόρια βελόναις ἐκέντουν καὶ μέλαν ἐπέβαλλον, εἰς θεραπείαν τῶν δαιμόνων.[9] The same custom is indicated by Jeremiah's πᾶσαι χεῖρες κόψονται.[10]

Among the Hebrews, too, there is good evidence that the

[1] De Dea Syr., 59.
[2] 'Nunc te seu Bromio signatae mystides at se
    Florigero in prato congregem uti Satyrum
    Sive canistriferae poscunt sibi Naides aeque,
    Qui ducibus taedis agmina festa trahas ...' CIL. 3, 686.
[3] peristeph., 10, 1076-80.
[4] praescr., 40.
[5] Lydus, mens., 4, 53 (Teub., p. 110).
[6] Primas., Rom. i. 24 (PL. 68, 420A).
[7] Lev. xix. 28; cf. Lev. xxi. 5; Deut. xiv. 1.
[8] Firm. Matern., prof. rel. err. 2 (CSEL. p. 76, 25).
[9] qu. in Lev. xxviii (Schultze, 1, p. 207).
[10] xxxi. 37 (LXX).

wearing of such a distinguishing badge was widely prevalent. In this case it was intended to be a token of Yahweh's owner-ship. B. Stade,[1] following Wellhausen, saw in Cain the epony-mous ancestor of the wandering Kenite folk, the people of Hobab the priest (of Yahweh), Moses' father-in-law, a tribe of which such fanatical Yahwist devotees as the Rechabites formed part.[2] The 'sign' of Cain[3] is then the distinguishing badge of the tribe, a religious mark (for it is given by Yahweh) which places its wearers under divine protection and proclaims their allegiance to him. R. Eisler[4] plausibly connects these Kenite nomads and their distinctive sign with the wandering 'Sleb' tinkers of the desert, who wear an X incised on the forehead. Whether or not this connection be admissible, the X sign, as we shall see, plays an important role in the history of religious sealing, for it is in this form that the sign of bond-service to God takes on an eschatological significance as the seal marking off the elect and saving them from the wrath of divine judgment.

Frequent instances are to be met with in the Old Testament of the wearing of a badge of divine ownership. That Yahwist prophets were tattooed or bore an incised mark on the forehead appears probable from 1 Kings xx. 41 and Zech. xiii. 6; the Second Isaiah looks forward to a time when 'one shall say, I am Yahweh's . . . and another write on his hand, Unto Yahweh',[5] a passage which Procopius of Gaza explains as denoting a tattooing on the hand or arm such as was practised by Chris-tians.[6] In later times the sign is not actually on the body, but is worn as a phylactery on the hand and forehead;[7] we may com-pare the seal, 'Holy to Yahweh', engraved on the *petalon* worn upon the mitre of the high priest.[8]

For the purpose of our present enquiry, however, the most significant Old Testament passage is Ezk. ix. 4–6, where the Lord says to the man with the inkhorn, 'Go through the midst . . . of Jerusalem, and set a mark (Heb. *taw*) upon the foreheads of the men that sigh and that cry for all the abominations that are done in the midst thereof. And to the others he said . . .

[1] *ZATW.* 14, 1894, pp. 250–318.
[2] 1 Chron. ii. 55.   [3] Gen. iv. 15.
[4] *The Messiah Jesus and John the Baptist*, p. 234, n. 8.
[5] Isa. xliv. 5 (R.V. mg.).   [6] *Isa.* xliv. 5 (*PG.* 87, 2401B).
[7] Deut. vi. 8; xi. 18; cf. Exod. xiii. 9.   [8] Exod. xxviii. 36.

Go ye through the city after him, and smite: let not your eye spare, neither have pity . . . but come not near any man upon whom is the mark; and begin at my sanctuary.'[1] This conception of a sign set by God upon His elect to mark them as His own and protect them from destruction is a frequent motif in Hebrew eschatology, and it exercised a profound influence upon the Christian theory of the sealing of the faithful 'for a day of redemption', and particularly, as we shall see, upon the 'sealing' of the neophyte with the sign of the Cross; for, as Jerome pointed out, the apparent prophetic foreshadowing of this rite in the Ezekiel text. is very striking: 'Antiquis Hebracorum litteris, quibus usque hodie utuntur Samaritani, extrema Thau littera crucis habet similitudinem, quae in Christianorum frontibus pingitur, et frequenti manus inscriptione signatur.'[2] The eschatological conception of the sign recurs in the Psalms of Solomon (where, at the divine vengeance on the ungodly, the flame of fire and wrath shall not touch the righteous because τὸ σημεῖον τοῦ θεοῦ ἐπὶ δικαίους, εἰς σωτηρίαν, but as for the sinners, τὸ . . . σημεῖον τῆς ἀπωλείας ἐπὶ τοῦ μετώπου αὐτῶν),[3] and in 4 Ezra, where we hear of the 'sealing' of those 'that have gathered faith for a treasure'.[4] It is, of course, in part this idea of a token by which God recognizes and acknowledges his people that underlies the practice of circumcision as the sign of the Covenant.[5] Circumcision, which acquires an immense degree of importance in the Maccabaean and post-Maccabaean epochs,[6] is itself in the nature of a 'seal for a day of redemption', for, according to *Jubilees*,[7] the uncircumcised 'belongeth not to the children of the Covenant which the Lord made with Abraham, but to the children of destruction; nor is there, moreover, any sign on him that he is the Lord's, but (he is destined) to be destroyed and slain from the earth, and to be rooted out of the earth, for he hath broken the covenant of the Lord our God'.

The uncircumcised is ἄσημος,[8] one who does not possess the

---

[1] The passage is to be compared with the similar 'sealing' at the first Passover; Exod. xii. 23.
[2] *Ezech.*, 3 (*PL*. 25, 88B ff.).   [3] xv. 8, 10.   [4] vi. 5.
[5] Gen. xvii. 11.
[6] 1 Macc. 1. 15, 48, 60; *Ass. Mos.*, 8, 1; Jos., *Ant.*, 12, 5, 1.   [7] xv. 26.
[8] P. Berol., 7820, see Deissmann, *Bible Studies*, p. 153.

stamp of the covenant which entitles him to be acknowledged by God as one of His people. The eschatological idea of the recognition is so prominent in the thought of circumcision, and so likely to be interpreted crudely, that Aphraates is constrained to point out that it was not really necessary to enable God to recognize His own, but that the Israelites might know one another and that an Israelite might have no excuse if he were detected as a transgressor of the Law.[1]

In the New Testament, the eschatological conception of the seal, such as we have seen in Ezek. ix, is most strongly emphasized in the Apocalypse. The locust-demons are commanded not to 'hurt the grass of the earth, neither any green thing, neither any tree, but only such men as have not the seal of God on their foreheads',[2] that is, who are not among the hundred and forty and four thousand who were sealed . . . the servants ($\delta o \hat{v} \lambda o \iota$) of God. The seal which they bear is the name of the Lamb and of his Father written on their foreheads.[3] By contrast, the followers of the 'beast' wear a mark on their right hand or upon their forehead,[4] which is his name or the number of his name. The rider on the white horse himself bears a mysterious name written (apparently on his brow),[5] and on his cloak and on his thigh, 'a name written, King of Kings and Lord of Lords'.[6]

It is against this background of the sealing of God's people with a sign which marks them as His own, assures them of salvation in the day of wrath and judgment, and protects them from divine condemnation and from the malignant powers of evil, that we must set St. Paul's reminder to his converts that they have been 'sealed for a day of redemption'. The seal is not, however, always thought of in terms of an outward sign, although, as we shall see later, Christian thought came to be greatly influenced by the notion of an external mark (in this case consignation with the Cross) set upon the people of God. The prophets looked forward to the giving of a spiritual sign of a better Covenant, the inward 'circumcision of the heart' linked with the bestowal on man of the Spirit of Yahweh; and, from a different point of view, Philo saw a more profound and

[1] dem., 11, 60.   [2] Apoc., ix. 4.   [3] Ibid., vii. 3.
[4] Ibid., xiv. 1; etc.   [5] Ibid., xix. 12.   [6] Ibid., xix. 16.

spiritual significance in the ancient notion of the 'seal', though he loses sight of the eschatological connotation which it acquired from the prophets' teaching. Making use of the familiar philosophic comparison of the archetypal idea with a seal which, while itself remaining entire and unchanged, makes many impressions of itself on perishable wax,[1] Philo describes the Logos as the divine seal;[2] it is the archetypal idea of ideas :

ἡ ἀρχέτυπος σφραγίς, ὅν φαμεν νοητὸν εἶναι κόσμον, αὐτὸς ἄν εἴη τὸ παράδειγμα, ἀρχέτυπος ἰδέα τῶν ἰδέων ὁ Θεοῦ λόγος.[3]

As the Creator's seal the Logos is impressed upon the universe :

‹ὁ Θεὸς› ἀσχημάτιστον οὖσαν τὴν τῶν πάντων οὐσίαν ἐσχημάτισε καὶ ἀτύπωτον ἐτύπωσε καὶ ἄποιον ἐμόρφωσε καὶ τελειώσας τὸν ὅλον ἐσφράγισε κόσμον εἰκόνι καὶ ἰδέᾳ, τῷ ἑαυτοῦ λόγῳ.[4] The seal is stamped upon the human soul, for the divine image is engraved upon it by the Logos : ὁ δὲ μέγας Μωσῆς οὐδένι τῶν γεγονότων τῆς λογικῆς ψυχῆς τὸ εἶδος ὡμοίωσεν, ἀλλ᾽ εἶπεν αὐτὴν τοῦ θείου καὶ ἀοράτου πνεύματος ἐκείνου δόκιμον εἶναι νόμισμα σημειωθὲν καὶ τυπωθὲν σφραγίδι θεοῦ, ἧς ὁ χαρακτήρ ἐστιν ὁ ἀΐδιος λόγος· ἐνέπνευσε γάρ, φησιν, ὁ θεὸς εἰς τὸ πρόσωπον αὐτοῦ πνοὴν ζωῆς, ὥστε ἀνάγκη πρὸς τὸν ἐκπέμποντα τὸν δεχόμενον ἀπεικονίσθαι· διὸ καὶ λέγεται κατ᾽ εἰκόνα θεοῦ τὸν ἄνθρωπον γεγενῆσθαι, οὐ μὴν κατ᾽ εἰκόνα τινὸς τῶν γεγονότων.[5] In this passage we are approaching the idea of a sealing with the Spirit, and we find traces of this conception elsewhere in Philo, as, for example, when he speaks of ὁ . . . τῷ κατὰ τὴν εἰκόνα θεοῦ χαραχθεὶς πνεύματι.[6] In the system of Philo, however, the doctrine of the Spirit is relatively unimportant, and he has little to say on it that is in any way original. For him the Spirit is a kind of divine substance, transmitted from God to man, making Adam the friend of God,[7] and indwelling man by nature. We do, nevertheless, find a rather more advanced conception in the description of Abraham as a type of the εὐγένης: τοῦ θείου πνεύματος, ὅπερ ἄνωθεν καταπνευσθὲν εἰσῳκίσατο τῇ ψυχῇ, περιτιθέντος τῷ μὲν

---

[1] Arius Didymus (Diels, Doxogr. Gr., p. 447) ap. Eus., p.e., 11, 23 (PG. 21, 908C). cf. Proclus, in Eucl., def. 1 (Friedlein, p. 90, 14), where the Deity impresses a seal upon the universe.
[2] leg. alleg., 1, 12, 31; 13, 42; opif. mund., 46, 134.
[3] opif. mund., 6, 25; cf. migr. Abr., 18, 103.
[4] somn., 2, 6; cf. fug. et invent., 2, 12.
[5] plant., 5, 18; cf. ebriet., 33, 133; q.r.d.h., 37, 181.
[6] plant., 11, 44.   [7] opif. mund., 50, 144.

σώματι κάλλος ἐξαίρετον, τοῖς δὲ λόγοις πειθώ, τοῖς δὲ ἀκούουσι σύνεσιν.[1]

In these developments we can already begin to discern something of the content which St. Paul gave to the 'seal of the Spirit'. Our next step is to consider why he related this 'sealing' to a single specific moment in the experience of his converts,[2] the moment of their initiation. In order to examine this relationship of the seal of the Spirit to the rite of initiation we must first consider briefly the origin and the significance of Baptism in the Church of the Apostolic age.

---

[1] virtut. (nobilit.), 2, 7.   [2] See above, p. 5.

CHAPTER TWO

THE BAPTISM OF JOHN

THE New Testament, it must be admitted, affords no such explicit evidence for the direct Dominical institution of Baptism as it provides in the case of the Holy Communion. The command of the risen Christ recorded in Matt. xxviii. 19, though there is no reason to deny that it is an integral part of the First Gospel, may represent a reading back into the time of the Resurrection appearances of what the Church of the Gentile mission found to be divinely appointed as its task. Yet St. Paul in his teaching on Baptism is clearly explaining, and interpreting more profoundly, a practice which was familiar to his readers and of which there is no hint that he himself was the originator. St. Peter, according to the account given in Acts,[1] told his audience on the day of Pentecost, 'Repent and be baptized, each one of you, in the name of Jesus Christ for the remission of your sins, and you shall receive the gift of the Holy Spirit.' Here again the suggestion of the author, whether or not his historical picture be correct, is that the actual command to be baptized is not something which caused any surprise to the hearers of St. Peter's speech. There is no indication that the rite itself needed any explanation, despite the fact that in pre-Christian use βαπτίζω is a rare word, being used in the LXX only of Naaman's dipping in the Jordan,[2] of Judith's nightly purifications in a spring of water during her sojourn in the camp of the unclean Gentiles,[3] and of ritual lustration after contact with a corpse.[4] The novel element in the command is not baptism as such, but the fact that it is to be undertaken 'in the name of Jesus Messiah', and that through it the astonishing fulfilment of Joel's hope of a general outpouring of the Spirit in 'the last days' will be extended here and now to those who repent.

[1] Acts ii. 38.   [2] 4 Reg. v. 14.   [3] Judith vii. 7.
[4] Sirach xxxi (xxxiv). 30.

The explanation is that fact which the Gospels make very plain and which has in recent years been brought to our notice by such writers as F. Büchsel,[1] O. Cullmann,[2] J. F. Leenhardt,[3] and W. F. Flemington,[4] namely, that Christian Baptism looks back to the baptism of John by way of the baptism received at his hands by Jesus.

The work of Jesus was a continuation, or rather a fulfilment, of John's mission, and there was evidently a most intimate connection between the movement initiated by John, on the one hand, and Jesus and His followers on the other. Christianity, in fact, sprang from John's mission of preaching and baptizing, a truth that the Synoptic Gospels clearly indicate. According to the Q tradition,[5] Jesus explicitly declared that the Baptist fulfilled the prophecy of Malachi and was the 'messenger sent to prepare the way'; the natural interpretation of the passage is that He regarded John as the 'forerunner' of Himself. Dibelius[6] is surely mistaken in thinking that this text does not represent an authentic tradition of the words of Jesus, for the saying which precedes it, 'Yea, I say unto you, and much more than a prophet', is scarcely intelligible without this explanation. A similar attitude to John's work on the part of Jesus is indicated in the Marcan tradition by the reply which He gave to the question about authority.[7] It is natural, therefore, to suppose that, since the first Christians were not instituting a novel ceremony, they were in fact giving a new significance to an existing practice, originated and made familiar by John and probably, to judge from John iii. 22, 26, iv. 1–2, continued by the followers of Jesus (some of whom had apparently been disciples of the Baptist), if not by Jesus Himself. 'Hätte Johannes nicht getauft, gäbe es wahrscheinlich keine christliche Taufe.'[8]

The first question, then, for our enquiry must be the significance of John's baptism, and the Old Testament background against which alone it can be understood. The Mandaean traditions, in terms of which Reitzenstein and others sought to

---

[1] *Der Geist Gottes im N.T.*
[2] *La Signification du Baptême dans le N.T.* (Rev. de Théol. et Phil., 30).
[3] *Le Baptême chrétien.*   [4] *The N.T. Doctrine of Baptism.*
[5] Matt. xi. 10; Luke vii. 27.
[6] *Forschungen z. Rel. u. Lit. der. A.u.N.T.*, 15 (1911), p. 11 f.
[7] Mark xi. 30 ff.   [8] Büchsel, *op. cit.*, p. 141.

interpret the Baptist, may safely be ignored for our purpose; at best they serve only to show how certain later developments of the Baptist's movement extended beyond the frontiers both of Judaism and of Christianity.[1]

For our evidence we must rely on the Gospels. Josephus[2] is of little assistance; he appears to be interpreting the Baptist's work in such a way as to attract the interest of Gentile readers, presenting him to the public in the guise of an ethical philosopher whose peculiar baptizing activities need not be considered very seriously. The real value of Josephus's account lies in its corroborative testimony that John was known as ὁ βαπτίστης, a word apparently coined to describe him, and that therefore, in spite of the attempt of Josephus to minimize this aspect of his work, the fact that John baptized stands out even in this narrative as the most notable thing about him. That this account is quite independent of the Christian tradition seems highly probable. Its terminology is not that of the New Testament. It includes the use of βαπτισμός and βάπτισις, of which the former is employed only of the 'washings of cups' in Mark vii. 4 and in two passages in Hebrews[3] (one referring to Levitical purifications and the other possibly to Christian Baptism), and the other does not occur at all. Both words are rare in the Fathers.

The Gospels show John to be a Spirit-possessed prophet[4] whose 'call' is reminiscent of that which came to some of the prophets of the Old Testament.[5] His eschatological preaching announces the approach of the Kingdom of Heaven,[6] and warns the people of coming wrath,[7] judgment on Israel (in the face of which the claim to belong to Abraham's seed will avail nothing)[8] effecting a 'weeding out' of the spiritually and morally dead,[9] and the coming of 'the stronger than I' who will baptize with Holy Spirit[10] and with fire.[11] The preparation for this 'purging' (cf. Mal. iii. 3) is repentance, manifested in

---

[1] Büchsel, op. cit., p. 137. [2] Ant. 18, 5, 2.
[3] Heb. ix. 10, vi. 2.
[4] Luke i. 15, 80; cf. Mark xi. 32; Matt. xi. 9.
[5] Luke iii. 2 (cf. Hag. i. 1, Zech. i. 1), (Luke i. 15, cf. Jer. i. 5).
[6] Matt. iii. 2. [7] Matt. iii. 7; Luke iii. 7.
[8] Matt. iii. 9; Luke iii. 8. [9] Matt. iii. 10; Luke iii. 9.
[10] Mark i. 7–8. [11] Matt. iii. 11; Luke iii. 16.

ethical reformation,[1] and symbolized by a purificatory washing 'for remission of sins'.

It is probable, though not certain, that John regarded this remission as actually effected through the inward repentance and outward cleansing, and not as something reserved for the 'mightier one' to bestow at his coming upon those who had undergone the rite. St. Matthew omits all reference to remission of sins in connection with John's baptism; it cannot be bestowed until Christ's 'blood of the covenant' is 'shed for many'[2] . . . a significant indication of the change in the meaning of the rite which was effected for Christians by the baptism of Jesus and its fulfilment in His saving work, the transformation, that is to say, of John's anticipatory symbol of preparation for future judgment into a sacrament of Christ's death and resurrection and the application to the believer of their saving efficacy.

We must make due allowance for the Evangelists' tendency to treat John simply as the conscious forerunner of Jesus, a tendency which leads Mark in particular to portray him as Elijah *redivivus*, and which may to some extent distort their historical picture of his work. It is possible, for instance, that in actual fact the Baptist was himself regarded by some of his followers as the Messiah.[3] Nevertheless, we are probably entitled to accept the biblical portrait of John as broadly accurate, and against the background of the strongly eschatological preaching which we have just considered John's baptism falls into line with the symbolical actions of his predecessors in the prophetic tradition. It is an 'acted prophecy', a tangible sign of the repentance which purifies the heart, allows the penitent to be numbered among the elect community in the approaching judgment, and prepares him for the reception of the general outpouring of the Spirit of Yahweh which was a part of the traditional apocalyptic hope of the 'last days'.

John's baptism signified spiritual cleansing and the entry of its recipients into the 'Remnant' community of the Messiah; it was a corporate rite, as the phrase in Josephus, βαπτισμῷ συνιέναι,[4] implies. It does indeed differ in one major respect

---

[1] Luke iii. 10–14.   [2] Matt. xxvi. 28.
[3] *Clem. Recog.*, 1, 54, 60; cf. Luke iii. 15.
[4] Jos., *Ant.*, 18, 5, 2; but cf. Thackeray, *Josephus the Man and the Historian*, p. 132.

from the prophetic symbolism employed by the ancient prophets; unlike their actions, it is not a single acted prophecy but a *rite* inaugurating a collective movement. The difference between their methods is not, however, really very great. The canonical prophets had their companies of disciples,[1] and their efforts were directed towards the building up of the corporate society of a renewed people of God. On the other hand, so far as each individual convert was concerned, John's baptism was a single unrepeated symbolic act. Moreover, in addition to a certain precedent afforded by the 'conversion' of Naaman after his dipping in the Jordan (in respect of which it is Elisha rather than Elijah who typifies the Baptist), the Old Testament is full of metaphorical language portraying under the imagery of water and washing the inward cleansing and the outpouring of the Spirit associated with Israel's eschatological hope. To translate these prophetic metaphors into symbolic action was a natural step for a new prophet to take, for they are vivid enough to lend themselves easily to this treatment. Windisch[2] is even tempted to consider whether in all cases the Old Testament language really is no more than metaphorical, or whether some kind of precedent for John's baptism may have existed. This is highly unlikely. As we shall see, John is far more concerned to enact the symbolical and metaphorical language of the Prophets than to imitate any already existing ceremonies. His baptism has no direct connection with the lustrations prescribed in the Law, which were often repeated and never signified an ethical purification in anticipation of a coming judgment; the most that can be said is that there may have been an indirect link between his baptism and the ceremonial washings in so far as the prophetic metaphors which he translated into action were themselves derived to some extent from ritual practice.[3]

It is most improbable that John's baptism was related to the ritual washings of the Essenes; it was a rite administered to each convert once and once only, and it was intended for the whole nation; the Essenes were remarkable for their frequent repetition of ritual 'baptisms', and their sect was highly exclusive.[4]

---

[1] Isa. viii. 16.
[3] e.g. Ps. li. 7.
[2] *Taufe und Sünde im ältesten Christentum*, p. 40.
[4] See Windisch, *op. cit.*, p. 78.

It is possible[1] that John was influenced by the practice of proselyte-baptism, which fairly certainly existed in his day. By the end of the first or the beginning of the second century A.D., the Hillelite school attached so much importance to that ceremony that it could be argued whether baptism or circumcision were the essential rite of entry into Israel;[2] this implies that the practice was already of long standing, and the view that this was so receives some support from an early instance of a baptism of converted Roman soldiers,[3] as well as from an apparent reference to the rite in Arrian's *Epictetus*[4] (though Reitzenstein holds that this passage relates to an unorthodox ascetic sect).[5] Jeremias[6] quotes Rabbinic evidence for the early association of the passage of the Red Sea with proselyte-baptism; the converted stranger must enter the 'promised land' as Israel had done, through water.[7] He believes that St. Paul in his comparison of Christian Baptism with 'baptism into Moses in the sea' is following the established exegetical tradition of the school of Hillel, and that already, by the time of the Baptist, proselyte-baptism was an initiatory rite based upon, or finding its justification in, a midrashic interpretation of the Exodus. John, it would then seem, went out into the desert like more than one first-century leader of a quasi-Messianic movement and inaugurated the community of the new and purified Israel in the river Jordan.

Nevertheless there are important differences between John's baptism and the normal Jewish rite; this is certainly true of its significance, and probably also of the manner of its administration. Though all Jewish baptisms were purificatory, John's is unique in its ethical significance. Apart from the doubtful allusions to baptism in the *Sibylline Oracles*,[8] there is little evidence that proselyte-baptism was connected with spiritual as opposed to merely ceremonial cleansing. The rabbinical comparison between the baptized proselyte and a new-born child[9] is a

---

[1] And strongly maintained by Jeremias, *Der Ursprung der Johannes-Taufe, ZNTW.* 28, 1929, pp. 312–20, and by Dix, *Confirmation or the Laying on of Hands?* p. 10.

[2] *Yeb.*, 46a.   [3] *Pesach.*, 8, 8.   [4] 2, 9.

[5] Yet we might expect a clearer allusion in Just., *dial.*, 14, 1; 19, 2; see Poster, *Tractate Gerim (Angelos* 2, 1926, pp. 1–38).

[6] *Op. cit.*   [7] Num. xv. 14 ff.

[8] 4, 165; 5, 478.   [9] *Yeb.*, 22a, 48b.

piece of rhetorical imagery and means little more than that the convert abandons his former ties and obligations, and enters upon a new status as an Israelite,[1] though it is true that by virtue of this new status the convert is freed from the guilt which he incurred by breaches of the 'Noachic precepts' during his heathen life. This notion is, however, essentially legalistic and bears little relation to spiritual and ethical renewal. The eschatological significance of John's baptism has no parallel in the theory of proselyte-baptism, and, although both rites were performed once and for all in the case of each individual and in both total immersion was probably employed,[2] the methods of their administration were probably otherwise dissimilar. The title, 'the Baptist', and the language of the Gospels,[3] together with the early pictures of Christ's Baptism, strongly suggest that John actually baptized his converts; the suggestion of B. S. Easton[4] that βαπτίζω, as used of John's work, means 'hold a baptism' rather than literally 'baptize' has no evidence to support it. On the other hand, Jewish baptism, according to the tractates *Yebamoth* and *Gerim* (the latter although of late date conserving early evidence), was always self-administered, the presence of other people besides the candidate being necessitated only for the purpose of witness.

The probability is therefore strong that John derived the conception of his prophetic symbolism not from any existing rite but from the Old Testament prophecies themselves; nor is it a matter for surprise that a prophet of the first century should receive his inspiration through the written text of the sacred books. Many prophecies pointed the way for him. A collective act of repentance at a crisis in Israel's history had its precedent in Neh. ix. 6–37 (cf. Dan. ix. 4–19). A symbolical outpouring of water was linked with repentance in 1 Sam. vii. 6, and there was such striking metaphorical language as that of Mic. vii. 17–20 with its allusions to the wrath and mercy of God, His casting of the people's sins into the depths of the sea, the

---

[1] Brandt, *Die judischen Baptismen* (*ZATW*. Beiheft 18), and Moore, *Judaism*, i, pp. 334–5, discuss this and kindred points fully.

[2] Cf. *Orac. Sib.*, 4, 165; but the evidence of early Christian art makes the assumption somewhat uncertain in the case of John's baptism.

[3] Apart from the Western reading ἐνώπιον for ὑπό in Luke iii. 7, and the omission of ὑπ'αὐτοῦ by some Old Latin MSS. in Luke vii. 30.

[4] *Self-Baptism*, *AJTh.* 24 (1920), pp. 513–18.

likening of trembling sinners to 'serpents', and the 'performing of mercy' to Abraham. The Scriptures and apocryphal writings were, moreover, full of passages which associated cleansing by water with repentance and coming judgment, with a future dispensation of the Spirit of Yahweh, and with that creation of a new heart and spirit in man which is the essence of Jeremiah's conception of the New Covenant.

Isaiah's prophecy that the rebellious will be devoured by the sword is preceded by the injunction, 'Wash you, make you clean . . . though your sins be as scarlet, they shall be as white as snow".[1] 'O Jerusalem,' cries Jeremiah, 'wash thine heart from wickedness that thou mayest be saved.'[2] The promise is given in Ezekiel that, 'I will sprinkle clean water upon you, and ye shall be clean . . . A new heart also will I give you, and a new spirit will I put within you: and I will take away the stony heart out of your flesh, and I will give you an heart of flesh. And I will put my spirit within you, and cause you to walk in my statutes. . . .'[3] 'In that day', we read in Zech. xiii. 1, 'there shall be a fountain opened to the house of David and to the inhabitants of Jerusalem for sin and for uncleanness', and it is to be noted that this prophecy occurs in the middle of a passage which exerted a profound influence on the thought of the Evangelists (and probably of our Lord Himself), about the Passion and the Atonement.

An even more striking prediction, which John may well have had in mind, is the famous picture of the healing and life-giving waters issuing from the Temple and going 'down into the Arabah . . . from En-gedi even unto En-eglaim'.[4] The LXX reading, ὕδωρ ἀφέσεως,[5] certainly suggested Baptism to Christian commentators, and the whole passage was regarded as having found its fulfilment in Christ.[6] It may have been from this prophecy that John drew his parable of trees bearing fruit or being cut down,[7] and it may possibly have influenced his choice of the Jordan as the scene of his acted prophesying, though the most important factors in that decision were prob-

---

[1] Isa. i. 16–20.   [2] Jer. iv. 14.   [3] Ezek. xxxvi. 25–7.
[4] Ezek. xlvii. 1 ff.   [5] verse 3.
[6] John vii. 38–9; cf. Jerome, ad loc. (PL. 25, 467). Justin had already seen a direct prophecy of Baptism in the language of Isaiah (dial., 14. 1).
[7] Matt. iii. 10; Luke iii. 9; cf. Ezek. xlvii. 12.

ably Israel's entry into Canaan and Hosea's vision of a renewal of God's people in the wilderness.[1]

Similar metaphorical allusions to cleansing occur in the post-canonical literature.[2] Negatively, water, in the form of a renewal of the Flood (which is turned into fire), is associated in Enoch with the final judgment and the destruction of the ungodly;[3] and it is the expectation of judgment and of a baptism of fire which form one of the most prominent features of John's preaching. It is possible that the connection and contrast frequently made between baptism in water and the Flood of destruction[4] may have been anticipated by the Baptist. However that may be, his prediction of a coming baptism by the fire of Messianic judgment probably has its roots in Num. xxxi. 23: '. . . everything that may abide the fire, ye shall make to go through the fire, and it shall be clean; nevertheless it shall be purified by the water of separation: and all that abideth not the fire ye shall make to go through the water'; it may also have been suggested by the purificatory fire of Mal. iii. 3. It is on the whole unlikely that the reference in John's preaching to 'fire-baptism' represents a reading back into the Baptist's time of ideas of fire and Spirit suggested by the events of Pentecost, for it is an aspect of John's teaching which disappears from view in the later writings of the New Testament[5] and seems to rest on early and good tradition. It is also improbable that the connection between water, fire, and wisdom to be found in 4 Ezra[6] represents earlier beliefs and has any bearing upon the teaching of John.

Besides signifying a cleansing in preparation for judgment, John's baptism was also a preparatory rite for a future baptism with Holy Spirit.[7] A general outpouring of the Spirit of Yahweh was an important part of Israel's eschatological hope. Although there are periods when little is heard of it, and although the conception of the Spirit varies greatly, the Old Testament, the apocryphal literature, and the Rabbinical comments thereon are full of allusions which indicate the importance in the thought of many Jews of this hope of the outpouring of the

---

[1] Hos. ii. 14.
[3] Enoch, lxvi. 1–2, lxvii. 8–13.
[5] Acts i. 5, xi. 16, xiii. 25; John i. 26.
[7] Mark i. 8; Matt. iii. 11; Luke iii. 16.

[2] e.g. *Orac. Sib.*, 4. 165.
[4] Cf. 1 Pet. iii. 20–21.
[6] xiv. 39–40.

Spirit. They enable us to understand why the bestowal of the Spirit upon those who had faith in the crucified, risen, and ascended Christ, and who were baptized in His name, was recognized as the fulfilment of prophecy; the Spirit that descended at Pentecost was the 'Holy Spirit of promise'.[1] Thus Isaiah[2] foresees a time of destruction to last 'until the Spirit be poured upon us from on high, and the wilderness become a fruitful field . . . then judgment shall dwell in the wilderness, and righteousness shall abide in the fruitful field'.

This hope of a general renewal by God's Spirit is strongest in Ezekiel. Whereas the Spirit had hitherto possessed only certain chosen individuals such as prophets, Ezekiel[3] hopes that the entire community may partake of God's Spirit as the life-principle of a people who know God and are truly and inwardly His people. The Second Isaiah expects a similar blessing and outpouring of the Spirit.[4] It is a hope which sometimes takes the form, primarily if not exclusively, of a renewal and universal diffusion of the Spirit of *prophecy*,[5] which had as it were 'gone underground' since the days of the ancient prophets, and in Zech. xii. 10 the Spirit is qualified as 'the spirit of grace and supplication'. It is comparatively infrequently found to signify (as in Isa. lxiii. 10, Hag. ii. 5, Zech. iv. 6, Ps. li. 11, cxxxix. 7) the immediate presence and activity of God. Nevertheless the expectation of Ezekiel is strongly reaffirmed in *Jubilees*,[6] and in much later times R. Acha (*c*. A.D. 320) cites Isa. xxxii. 15; lxi. 1, and Lam. iii. 49 ff. as evidence for the direct connection between the bestowal of the Spirit and the age of the final redemption.[7]

In several of these passages the Spirit is associated with cleansing, and is itself likened to water. This symbolism rendered John's baptism an appropriate prophetic action to be undertaken in preparation for the Spirit's outpouring. It also made the rite of Christian Baptism appropriate as the sacrament through which that outpouring actually takes place. Cullmann[8]

---

[1] Eph. i. 13.
[2] Isa. xxxii. 15.
[3] xxxix. 29.
[4] Isa. xliv. 3.
[5] Num. xi. 29; Joel ii. 28–9; for the understanding of St. Luke's interpretation of the Christian experience of the Spirit, it is important to notice that it is the latter passage that he regards as fulfilled at Pentecost.
[6] i. 21–5.
[7] *Midr. Lam.*, 3, 50 (73A), cited Str. Bill., ii, 134.
[8] *R. Th. Ph.*, 30 (1942), pp. 121 ff.

holds that water-baptism must have seemed to the Christians to be less suitable as a sacrament of the Spirit than as a symbol of purification, and that it was partly on this account that other rites tended to be added to water-baptism, so that even at a very early date the baptismal ceremony was in danger of breaking apart.[1] It must, on the other hand, be remembered that in a hot country the analogy of water to the Holy Spirit would appear perfectly natural. The transformation of the desert into a garden by the action of rain is, in a sense, parallel to the action of the divine Spirit in changing men's stony hearts into hearts of flesh. The general tendency of Scripture to liken the Holy Spirit to water was often pointed out by Christian writers on baptism.[2]

With this aspect of Israel's hope the idea of the new Covenant stands in close connection. Even where it is not expressly alluded to,[3] its effects (namely, knowledge of, and fellowship with, God, divine blessing, peace, and salvation) are an essential element in an expectation which in the later writers becomes genuinely eschatological.[4] It is closely related to the notion of a 'circumcision of the heart', the inward sign of a new spiritual relationship to God, corresponding to the outward seal of the old covenant of Sinai. Both these conceptions, of a spiritual covenant and of its seal in men's hearts, are of the highest importance for the understanding of the sealing with the Holy Spirit of which Christian Baptism is the sacrament; the fundamental New Testament doctrine that the true covenant-relationship with God involves the bestowal on man of His Spirit is by no means foreign to the thought of the Old Testament.

John's baptism could furnish no such sacrament of the Spirit. The hope still lay in the future, though the Baptist believed that its fulfilment was swiftly approaching. The 'last days' had not yet dawned, and his mission was only one of preparation. For the outpouring of the Spirit in the times of the 'end' the coming of the Messiah had to be awaited.

A general bestowal of the Spirit had long been associated

---

[1] Cf. Acts x. 44, xix. 1.
[2] e.g. Cyr., *Zech.*, 6, 106 (Aubert 3, 801D).
[3] As it is in Jer. xxxi. 34; cf. Ezek. xxxiv. 25, xxxvii. 26; Isa. liv. 10, lv. 3, lxi. 8.
[4] Cf. Enoch i. 8, v. 7–8; *Jub.* i. 16, 21 ff.; 4 Ezra vi. 26–8, viii. 52; etc.

with the Messiah, who was to be pre-eminently the bearer of God's Spirit. 'Es wird Aufgabe des Messias sein', remarks Bousset, 'den Geist auf alle Gläubigen auszugiessen.'[1] Isaiah's ideal Davidic king was expected to be characterized by the fullest endowment of the Spirit of Yahweh[2] (the seven-fold form in which this endowment is described has played a part in the Christian theology of Baptism and Confirmation out of all proportion to its importance in its Scriptural context, for the prophet describes an ideal figure of an inspired ruler in the language of an Eastern court-poet, not in that of an exact dogmatist drawing up a formal and exhaustive catalogue of the 'gifts of the Spirit'). It seems to be highly probable, in spite of the contrary assertion of some authors,[3] that the actual title of the Messiah connotes his possession of, or rather by, the Spirit of Yahweh. When Samuel 'took the horn of oil, and anointed him in the midst of his brethren, . . . the Spirit of Yahweh came mightily upon David from that day forward', and 'the Spirit of Yahweh had departed from Saul'.[4] The king of Israel, by virtue of his anointing with oil, was supposed to receive the inward unction of the Spirit to endow him with the peculiar gifts needed by a just and wise monarch; and the Messianic hope was of the coming of a ruler who would be in fact as well as in theory the anointed of the Lord, the true bearer of His Spirit. This interpretation of the significance of the royal unction is borne out by the Psalmist's ideal picture of David:[5] 'I have found David my servant; with my holy oil have I anointed him: with whom my hand shall be established; mine arm also shall strengthen him.' The 'hand' and 'arm' of Yahweh are often virtually synonymous with His 'Spirit'.[6] The link between the ideas of anointing and of Spirit-possession is more clearly demonstrable from the metaphorical language of the prophet who declares that the Spirit of the Lord has come upon him, 'because he hath anointed me'.[7] Christ's own interpretation of His mission, and of course the primitive Church's conception of His Messiahship, owed much to this passage. It is powerfully reminiscent of the Servant poems and would have been read as

---

[1] *Die Religion des Judentums*, p. 375. [2] Isa. xi. 2.
[3] e.g. Michaelis, *Reich Gottes und Gottes Geist nach dem N.T.*
[4] 1 Sam. xvi. 13–14. [5] Ps. lxxxix. 20–21.
[6] Cf. Isa. lxiii. 11–12. [7] Isa. lxi. 1.

part of the same work and perhaps as referring to the same person. It may possibly have been already connected with the Messiah in the pre-Christian expectation.

Apart from this probable connection of the royal unction with Spirit-possession, a notion which exercised an enormous influence upon Christian doctrine and liturgical practice, the idea of the Messiah as the bearer of the Spirit plays little part in the canonical Old Testament. In the apocalyptic literature, however, the thought becomes more explicit. Enoch[1] echoes the Isaianic prophecy of the Messiah's seven-fold endowment: 'The Lord of Spirits seated him on the throne of his glory, and the Spirit of righteousness was poured out upon him.' With the transference of the Messianic hope to the sphere of eschatology, the idea that the Messiah would be the bearer of the Spirit becomes fused with the expectation of the universal outpouring of the Spirit at the end of the present age. In the Psalms of Solomon[2] the belief that the Spirit will rest upon the Messiah is associated with the general blessings of the future age; of the 'High Priest' of the Testament of Levi[3] it is said that he will open the gates of Paradise, remove the threatening sword, and give the saints to eat of the tree of life; then the Spirit of the Lord will be upon them. In a haggadah on Gen. i. 2 it is said that the Spirit of God will be manifested in the spirit of the Messiah, and will spread his wings and bestow his grace upon Israel.[4] That the Messiah was expected to be the agent of the ultimate outpouring of God's Spirit, and that the Messianic hope was already connected closely with the thought of a general purification of Israel, is shown by the fact that John, according to the Fourth Gospel,[5] was taken for the Messiah, or at least for Elijah or 'the prophet', because he baptized and spoke of the Spirit's coming. Similarly, Jesus was hailed by some as the Christ because he spoke, in words recalling Ezek. xlvii. 1 ff., of the future outpouring of the Spirit.[6] In the preaching of John the various lines of Israel's eschatological hope converge. The expectations of the cleansing and purifying of a renewed People of God, ready for the New Covenant, the

---

[1] lxii. 2; cf. xlix. 3.   [2] xvii. 42.
[3] xviii, which is probably genuine except for the very obvious Christian interpolations in the passage.
[4] *Gen. Rabbah*, 2 (Buber, p. 153).   [5] John i. 25.   [6] John vii. 38–41.

constituting of the faithful Remnant to await the advent of the Messiah, and the preparation for the final judgment by which the elect should be winnowed out from the *massa perditionis* of the ungodly and gathered into God's storehouse[1]—all these eschatological visions of the prophets are set forth visibly in the symbolism of John's rite of baptism.

So far as John's own work was concerned, these visions remained eschatological and unfulfilled. He was the voice that cried 'Prepare'; but the events to which he looked forward, the coming of the Spirit-possessed Messiah and the baptism of his followers in the Spirit which should rest upon Him were nearer at hand than he realized. The expected baptism with Holy Spirit actually happened, so far as one of John's followers was concerned, when Jesus came to be baptized by him. When John has received from his messengers the news that the Messianic signs are being visibly enacted he recedes from the forefront of the Evangelist's scene. Although the advent of the New Covenant and the general outpouring of the Spirit still await the death and resurrection of Jesus by which alone they can be brought into being, the age of hope is already giving place to the age of fulfilment, and in the light of that fulfilment the Christian interpreter can look back upon John's mission as 'the beginning of the Gospel'[2] and John himself as one who 'proclaimed the Gospel to the people',[3] and recognize why a necessary qualification of the apostles who were to guarantee the truth of that Gospel by their testimony must be that they were 'men which have companied with us all the time that the Lord Jesus went in and out among us, *beginning from the baptism of John*'.[4]

[1] Matt. iii. 12; Luke iii. 17.   [2] Mark i. 1.   [3] Luke iii. 18.
[4] Acts i. 21-2.

CHAPTER THREE

THE BAPTISM OF JESUS

'BAPTIZATUS est Dominus baptismo Iohannis, et cessavit baptismus Iohannis.'[1] The baptism of John, as we have seen, was an act of prophetic symbolism expressive of the cleansing of a faithful Remnant in preparation for the expected 'baptism' of Spirit and fire in the Messianic age. The Christian rite, as we meet it after Pentecost, is still a baptism of water accompanied by repentance, but it is administered in the name of Jesus and through it the Spirit is actually bestowed.[2] It is still an eschatological rite, for it looks forward to the final redemption which is still to come at the Lord's return in glory; but, considered in relation to John's baptism, it represents a realization and fulfilment of Israel's hope. Hence the emphasis in Christian thought is shifted from the prophecy of a coming baptism of fire to the realization of a present baptism of Spirit.[3]

The great event which changed Johannine into Christian Baptism was, as von Baer,[4] Cullman,[5] and Flemington[6] have shown, the Baptism of Jesus regarded first, as the Synoptists and the Fourth Gospel both imply, as the foreshadowing and symbolical summing up of His mission as Son and Servant of God, of His death, resurrection, and ascension and of the New Covenant to be inaugurated in these events, and, secondly, as an event which prefigured and made possible the Pentecostal fulfilment of the ancient hope of a universal outpouring of the Spirit upon the people of God.

Through their insistence on the centrality of the Baptism of Jesus in the thought and practice of the early Church, these writers have restored to us a most valuable key to the understanding of the origin and meaning of the Christian rite. That

---

[1] Aug. *tract.*, 4, 14, *in Jo.*   [2] Acts ii. 38.   [3] Acts i. 8.
[4] *Der hl. Geist in den Lukasschriften.*   [5] *Op. cit.*
[6] *The New Testament Doctrine of Baptism*, to which the present writer, as will be easily recognized, owes much in this and the previous chapter.

this key had to be sought and rediscovered is not due to any obscurity on the part of the New Testament writings. The witness of all four Gospels testifies to the high importance which the tradition of the primitive Church attached to the Baptism of our Lord, and each Gospel contributes to the elucidation of that tradition. The apostolic preaching, as recorded in Acts, supports their evidence, for a most explicit reference to the Baptism is contained in the speech of St. Peter at Caesarea,[1] a passage which, more than any other speech in Acts, bears the stamp of an authentic early tradition of what the first preaching really did emphasize; it is, moreover, implied elsewhere in the book.[2] The reason for the need to recover the biblical teaching lies to a large extent in the tendency of the Fathers to distort the significance of the Baptism. In spite of the very great prominence given in popular devotion from early times to the Epiphany feast, at which Christ's Baptism was commemorated, and despite the importance for early Christology of the Spirit-anointing, the Fathers are too often content either to moralize on the humility shown by our Lord in receiving Baptism, or to enlarge upon the theme of the sanctification of baptismal water effected by His immersion in the Jordan—a theory for which there was no warrant in Scripture. They were, however, right in a sense when they saw in Christ's Baptism the agency by which water and the Holy Spirit were brought into union for the purpose of the Christian sacrament, for, though the Spirit descended on Jesus and not upon the water (a fact which many patristic writers forgot, thus betraying the materialistic decadence of much of the post-biblical theology of Baptism) it was this descent of the Spirit which turned a purificatory lustration into a sacrament of the Holy Spirit's approach to men.

Whereas the multitudes were baptized by John as a Remnant elected to await the dawning of the age to come, Jesus received the promised descent of the Spirit, and the association of water and Spirit which had been prefigured in the metaphorical language of the Prophets became translated into reality. Hence, when the death and resurrection of the Christ had established the New Covenant, and the Spirit could be bestowed on all

---

[1] Acts x. 38.　　　　[2] Acts iv. 27, xiii. 24–5.

those who responded in faith to His saving work, the union of water and Spirit as the outward sign and the inner reality of the sacramental rite became normative for the baptismal theology of the early Church.

The descent of the Spirit was directly connected with the heavenly proclamation of the Lord's divine Sonship; indeed, His possession of the Spirit, which fulfilled the traditional expectation of the Messiah,[1] has as its immediate consequence the declaration and realization of His status as the Son of God; sonship and Spirit-possession are in effect identical. This 'resting' of the Holy Spirit upon Jesus is sharply distinguished by the Evangelists from the 'enthusiasm' of an ecstatic prophet's inspiration. Since it is so intimately bound up with sonship, it is not a possession by an impersonal force, but a state of personal union with God the Father. The ancient prophecies of the bestowal of *ruach* on the Messiah find their realization in something far more profound, a permanent condition of unity with the Father, discernible throughout the earthly ministry and illustrated with special clarity in the prayer at Gethsemane.[2] It is true that the state of being permanently 'anointed' with the Spirit has its moments of particularly high spiritual exaltation;[3] it is not, if we may for convenience use the quantitative language which ought properly to be avoided, uniformly present in the same degree—a fact which it is worth while to bear in mind when we consider the indwelling of the Spirit in the primitive community[4] and in the baptized and confirmed Christian. Nevertheless, this 'resting' of the Spirit is of a different quality from the temporary and partial Spirit-possession of a prophet. It is a continuous and enduring endowment of Jesus with the 'authority' and 'power' (greater than that of scribes and prophets) which are manifested in his teaching and mighty works, the Messianic σημεῖα of John iii. 2.

This distinction is expressed in the imagery of the dove. The Spirit is not a prophetic inspiration; it descends from heaven, 'in bodily form', as Luke pictures it,[5] resting upon the Christ

---

[1] See above, pp. 30, 31.
[2] Cf. Luke iv. 14; Matt. xii. 18, 28; Mark iii. 29 (Matt. xii. 31; Luke xii. 10); Acts x. 38.
[3] Luke x. 21.   [4] Cf. Acts iv. 31, in relation to Pentecost.
[5] Luke iii. 22. For the dove as a covenant sign cf. *TWNT. s.v. ἁμαρτία*.

with the fullest endowment of divine power. We cannot be certain whether or not any further symbolism is involved in the picture of the dove. If the Spirit's descent is to be portrayed in a material likeness, a winged creature is an obvious choice; it clearly could not be depicted as an angel, for this would suggest that a divine being, an aeon or 'heavenly Christ', such as the Valentinians were later to imagine, had supervened upon the man Jesus. There are examples from the Rabbinic literature of the likening of the Holy Spirit to a dove,[1] and Philo's interpretation of Gen. xv. 9[2] is often cited as an instance of the symbolizing of Wisdom by a dove (but it is to be noted that in this passage the περιστέρα (the word used in the Gospels) represents only human wisdom, whereas it is the τρυγών which stands for the divine Wisdom that differs from the former as archetype from copy). There remains the possibility that the description of the dove coming upon Jesus as He comes up from the water is intended to recall Noah's dove going out, as the water dried up, to be the harbinger of the first covenant; the Spirit now comes upon Jesus as Messiah, and opens the way towards the new covenant in which all Israel will 'know the Lord' through the indwelling presence of His Spirit. Whether or not this interpretation be correct, we shall certainly be mistaken if we follow Leisegang[3] and Heinemann[4] in seeing in the appearance of the dove an indication of pagan influence upon the tradition. The background of thought is the Old Testament, and the portrayal of the Spirit as a dove evidently caused no surprise or difficulty to the early Christians, who made considerable use of this imagery.[5]

The heavenly voice which followed the Spirit's descent proclaimed Jesus (according to the Marcan version and the Alexandrian text in Luke) as ὁ υἱός μου ὁ ἀγαπητός, ἐν ᾧ εὐδόκησα.[6] Whereas in the 'Western' reading in Luke Jesus is greeted in the purely Messianic terms of Ps. ii. 7 (which was a regular proof-text for the Messiahship of Jesus),[7] the version

---

[1] Str.-Bill., i. 123. [2] q.r.d.h., 126. [3] *Pneuma Hagion*, pp. 89–91
[4] *Die Lehre vom hl. Geist im Judentum u. in dem Evangelien* (*Monatschr. für Geschichte u. Wiss. des Judentums*, 66, 1922, pp. 169–80, 268–79; 67, 1923, pp. 26–35.
[5] *Protev. Jac.* 9; *Mart. Polyc.* 16 (surely *not* a 'Pionian' interpolation).
[6] Mark i. 11; Matt. iii. 17; Luke iii. 22.
[7] Cf. Acts xiii. 33; Heb. i. 5.

given by Mark strongly suggests that Jesus is designated God's
Son in words which indicate that His Sonship and Messiahship
are to be interpreted in terms of the role of the Second Isaiah's
Servant of Yahweh. The Messianic 'Thou art my Son' of
Ps. ii. 7 is combined with an echo in the words ὁ ἀγαπητός, ἐν
σοὶ εὐδόκησα of the first Servant poem (Isa. xlii. 1) together
with a passage (Isa. xliv. 2) which would be read in the first
century as an integral part of the Servant prophecies.[1]

It is worth noting that, even though Luke may perhaps omit
(if the 'Western' reading be adopted) this allusion to the
'Servant' character of Jesus' Messiahship, his use of ἐκλελεγμένος
(v. l. ἐκλεκτός) in his account of the similar episode at the
Transfiguration[2] brings out at that point, more strongly than
the language of the other Evangelists, the fact that Jesus was
expressing His Sonship and working out His mission in and
through the character of the suffering Servant. Moreover, if
the reading ἐκλεκτός be preferred in John i. 34, the Fourth
Gospel expresses the same point very clearly: 'I have seen
(the Spirit descending and abiding upon him) and I have
borne witness that this is God's chosen one'—that is, 'my servant . . . my chosen in whom my soul delighteth.'

In his participation in a general baptism of sinners awaiting
judgment it is hardly fanciful to see a symbol of the Servant's
role as the bearer of 'the sins of many', and I am inclined to
agree with the suggestion advanced by Flemington that the
difficult saying of Matt. iii. 15, οὕτω γὰρ πρέπον ἐστὶν ἡμῖν
πληρῶσαι πᾶσαν δικαιοσύνην, contains an allusion to Isa. liii.
11, . . . 'my righteous servant shall make many righteous: and
he shall bear their iniquities'. Though the passage appears to
be a relatively late development of the Baptism story, designed
to explain the problem of Jesus' participation in a baptism
of repentance, the actual words attributed to Him may be
related to His other saying, ἦλθεν γὰρ Ἰωάννης πρὸς ὑμᾶς ἐν ὁδῷ
δικαιοσύνης,[3] which also finds a certain echo in the Lucan
tradition,[4] and may perhaps be authentic. It may not be
too much to claim that this saying shows that Jesus is regarded
by St. Matthew as interpreting His Sonship and Messianic

---

[1] Possibly also with an echo of the ἀγαπητός ("only") applied to Isaac.
[2] Luke ix. 35.   [3] Matt. xxi. 32.   [4] Luke vii. 29.

3

anointing in such a way as to identify Himself with the righteous Remnant of Israel and, as its representative, to unite Himself with those who are undergoing John's baptism in order that they may be constituted a renewed community of the 'saints'. Perhaps we may go even further and see a deeper meaning in the words of Jesus; the Servant who is to suffer vicariously and 'bear the sin of many' will procure a general justification, or declaration of righteousness, for His people. This sacrificial motif is perfectly explicit in the Fourth Gospel. It is as the 'Lamb of God which taketh away the sin of the world' that Jesus is revealed to John by the descent of the Spirit.[1] The view of C. F. Burney[2] is worth remembering, whether or not we follow it, that there is here a direct allusion to the Servant. He held that ἀμνὸς τοῦ θεοῦ represented the Aramaic *thalja d^e elaha*, which would be susceptible also of the interpretation *servant of God*. The view that this passage indicates that the Baptist, or the primitive Aramaic-speaking community, thus spoke of Jesus in the light of Isa. liii, was maintained by J. Jeremias;[3] it was rejected by C. H. Dodd,[4] but subsequently defended at greater length by Jeremias.[5] If this interpretation be rejected, it is unlikely that the Fourth Gospel is making any allusion to Isa. liii at this point, for the remainder of the Gospel shows that by ἀμνὸς its author intended a reference to the Passover lamb, and not to the lamb of Isa. liii. 7.

If we are right in our exegesis of the heavenly voice and the 'fulfilment of all righteousness', our Lord at His Baptism was designated the anointed Son whose mission of bringing in the new covenant of the Kingdom of God was to be worked out in terms of the Servant's task of intercession and of reconciliation through suffering. In the actual Baptism, however, the work of the Servant is only prefigured, and symbolized by anticipation. Like the Church's Baptism, the Baptism of Jesus is proleptically effective. The role of Servant which He undertakes at His Baptism is fulfilled, not in the Jordan, but at Calvary.

Jesus looks back to His Baptism more than once as His

[1] John i. 29–33.
[2] *The Aramaic Origin of the Fourth Gospel*, pp. 107–8.
[3] Art. ἀμνὸς in Kittel's *Wörterbuch*.
[4] Review of Kittel's *Wörterbuch*, Lieferungen i–viii, *JTS.* 34, 1933, pp. 284–5.
[5] *ZNTW.* 34 (1935), pp. 115–23.

ministry proceeds. In one instance He attributes to what there took place the source of His ἐξουσία (if we are right in finding this underlying significance in Mark xi. 30 and its parallels), and on two occasions He links the thought of His Baptism with His death.[1] In the first case, recorded by Mark,[2] the context strongly reminds us of the thought of the suffering Servant. Within the setting of that thought Jesus speaks of His coming death as τὸ ποτήριον ὃ ἐγὼ πίνω, and as τὸ βάπτισμα ὃ ἐγὼ βαπτίζομαι. The former metaphor looks forward to the Last Supper cup of the blood of the Covenant, the latter backward, in the first instance, to the Baptism by John, but also forward to the Servant's atoning death in which the symbolism of that Baptism finds its fulfilment.

In the sacrifice of Calvary and in Christ's resurrection the new Covenant prefigured in the Baptism by John and the Last Supper is effectively established; in the atoning work of Christ the 'Gospel sacraments' of Christian Baptism and Eucharist have their common ground and become the effective signs by which the Servant-Baptism of Christ and His sacrifice of the New Covenant are applied through faith to His followers.

This thought is implicit in other parts of the Gospels besides this passage of Mark. In the second of the texts to which we referred above, βάπτισμα δὲ ἔχω βαπτισθῆναι, καὶ πῶς συνέχομαι ἕως ὅτου τελεσθῇ[3] (if any text gives us an authentic word of Jesus it is surely this), Jesus probably refers to the Baptism of the Servant-Son, already undertaken in a figure and shortly to be actually manifested in His death. The passage is admittedly difficult; the fact that the heretic Marcus,[4] MSS. read by Tertullian,[5] the De Rebaptismate,[6] and Hilary,[7] inserted ἄλλο, aliud, before the word βάπτισμα, indicates that its difficulty was felt in ancient times. Nevertheless, we shall probably be right in connecting these two Marcan and Lucan texts with each other, and in seeing therein a proof that our Lord interpreted His Baptism as foreshadowing His death. This view, already propounded by Flemington and others, runs counter to the common theory that Christ's words in these two passages are

---

[1] See Flemington, op. cit., p. 31.   [2] Mark x. 38.
[3] Luke xii. 50.   [4] Iren., haer., 1, 21, 2.   [5] pudic., 22.
[6] 14.   [7] Tract. in Ps., 118, 3, 5 (PL. 9, 519B)

purely metaphorical and contain no reference to the actual Baptism. C. F. D. Moule,[1] for instance, explains the βάπτισμα of Luke xii. 50 in the sense of the 'flood' of trouble which is to overwhelm Jesus, but to this it may be replied, in the first place, that, while βαπτίζειν is fairly commonly used in the LXX and the Fathers in the sense of *overwhelm* or *sink*, the noun βάπτισμα appears to bear an exclusively religious meaning; secondly, it may be argued that the interpretation of these texts which we have followed goes far towards explaining how it came about that St. Paul could, without apparently arousing surprise or opposition among older disciples, lay immense emphasis upon the connection of baptism in water with the Christian's participation through faith in the death and resurrection of Christ. It may also afford us a clue to the understanding, not only of the association of 'the Spirit, the water, and the blood',[2] but also of the Fourth Evangelist's substitution of the *Pedilavium* for the institution of the Eucharist in his account of the Last Supper. In this narrative, the sharing of the cup of the covenant in Christ's blood is replaced by the acted symbolism of the Servant—a dramatization of such sayings as those recorded in Luke xii. 37, xxii. 27, and Mark x. 42–5[3]—in which Jesus associates His disciples with Himself in His cleansing and atoning death, and for that end makes use of baptismal symbolism that corresponds to the Eucharistic symbols of bread and wine in the Synoptic narratives. Christ's Baptism as it was completed and given its full significance in His death, is therefore most intimately linked with the Last Supper, and we conclude that neither the 'cup' nor the 'baptism' of Mark x. 38 is an accidental metaphor. The consequent association of the two Christian sacraments of the Gospel must never be forgotten in any formulation of the theology of Baptism; it is in fact possible for patristic writers to ascribe to one sacrament the effects generally attributed to the other, as, for example, when Firmicus Maternus speaks indifferently of regeneration, rebirth, and renewal as obtained through participation in the Eucharist and through the water of Baptism.[4]

---

[1] *Baptism and Confirmation*, by J. R. S. Taylor and others, p. 31.
[2] 1 John v. 8.
[3] The context of this saying refers to the 'cup and baptism'.
[4] *prof. rel. err.*, 18, 8; cf. 2, 5.

It was said of the Servant, 'I have put my Spirit upon him';[1] the prophecy was fulfilled, as we have seen, at the Baptism of Jesus, and Matthew and Luke remind us of this fact in other passages besides their narratives of the Baptism itself. The former quotes the Second Isaiah's prophecy in connection with our Lord's ministry;[2] the latter pictures Jesus' inauguration of His ministry (after the Baptism and the Temptations) in the words of Isa. lxi. 1–2,[3] which would naturally be taken by his readers to refer to the same Servant of Yahweh who is described in Matthew's citation.

During Christ's earthly ministry, however, the general out-pouring of the Spirit remains an unfulfilled promise reserved for the future,[4] when through the death, resurrection, and ascension of Christ there will be brought into being that new Covenant with which in the Old Testament expectation the imparting of God's Spirit had been so closely associated. It is as clearly implied in the Synoptists as it is explicitly affirmed by the Fourth Gospel that before the saving work of Jesus was completed, He 'spake of the Spirit which they that believed on him *were to receive*: for Spirit was not yet, because Jesus was not yet glorified'.[5] It is for the same reason that we are told that Jesus did not Himself baptize,[6] until in His death He 'baptized' all men.

So far as Christ's followers were concerned, therefore, it was the completed βάπτισμα of His death, and not merely His Baptism in the Jordan, which enabled them to receive the 'Holy Spirit of promise'. Indeed, for Jesus Himself the Spirit-baptism at the Jordan was in a sense proleptic, anticipating His 'reception' of the 'promise of the Holy Ghost' when He had been exalted at the right hand of God.[7] That the risen and ascended Lord received the Spirit to impart to His followers is most clearly stated in the Lucan writings, but the thought is familiar to St. Paul,[8] and may perhaps be symbolized in the Marcan and Matthaean accounts of the Baptism. The former tells us that Jesus, εὐθὺς ἀναβαίνων ἐκ τοῦ ὕδατος εἶδεν . . . τὸ πνεῦμα ὡς περιστέραν καταβαῖνον εἰς αὐτόν.[9] In the latter we

---

[1] Isa. xlii. 1.   [2] Matt. xii. 18.   [3] Luke iv. 18.
[4] Cf. Luke xi. 13, xii. 10, etc.   [5] John vii. 39.   [6] John iv. 2.
[7] Acts ii. 33.   [8] Eph. iv. 4–10.   [9] Mark i. 10.

read, βαπτισθεὶς δὲ ὁ 'Ιησοῦς εὐθὺς ἀνέβη ἀπὸ τοῦ ὕδατος καὶ ἰδοὺ . . . εἶδεν πνεῦμα θεοῦ καταβαῖνον . . . ἐρχόμενον ἐπ' αὐτόν.[1] Much argument has been devoted to these texts on the assumption that they may be intended to indicate a time-interval between Christ's Baptism in water and His reception of the Spirit, and so throw light on the relation of Confirmation to Christian Baptism. Wirgman,[2] for example, follows a common line of patristic interpretation[3] when he emphasizes the 'distinct actions' of our Lord's Baptism and of His reception of the Spirit on His emergence from the water, and maintains that their separation in time corresponds to the distinction between Baptism and the subsequent Confirmation. Dix, who holds that a pre-baptismal rite of chrismation was practised in the apostolic age as the sacrament of sealing with the Spirit, adduces the circulation of the Synoptic Gospels (containing these texts) as a possible reason for an alleged transference of 'Confirmation' so as to follow Baptism instead of preceding it.[4] J. C. Sladden, on the other hand,[5] is at pains to show that according to Mark i. 10 Jesus received the Spirit at, and not after, His Baptism, as He was in the act of emerging from the water, and not after any significant interval of time. On this view the Matthaean and Lucan accounts of the Spirit's descent might perhaps represent an early dissociation in the Church's theology of Spirit-baptism from the water-baptism with which it had originally been united. E. C. Ratcliff,[6] discussing Justin's description of the Baptism,[7] suggests that his words, ἀναδύντος αὐτοῦ ἀπὸ τοῦ ὕδατος . . . τὸ ἅγιον πνεῦμα ἐπιπτῆναι ἐπ' αὐτόν may indicate that he conceives the 'gift of the Spirit' to come to Him subsequently to water-baptism, but Ratcliff recognizes that ἀναδῦναι may simply mean emerge (from immersion in the water, not from the river; the dove could not be seen to alight on Jesus while He was submerged in the water), and may not imply any separation at all between Spirit- and water-baptism.

The latter view is probably correct so far as Justin is concerned, but as regards the New Testament passages it is conceivable that these arguments are beside the point. The

[1] Matt. iii. 16.　　　　　　　[2] The Doctrine of Confirmation, p. 42.
[3] e.g. Hil. Mt., 2, 6.　　　　　[4] Confirmation or the Laying on of Hands? p. 15.
[5] CQR. 146, 1948.　　　　　　[6] Theology, April 1948, pp. 133–9.
[7] dial., 88, 3.

description of Christ *ascending* from the water, which represents His death, may possibly point forward to the Ascension, when the Spirit bestowed by anticipation upon the Servant-Messiah at the Jordan was received by Him from the Father so as to be poured out on all those who should henceforth be baptized in His name. The New Testament use of ἀναβαίνω supports this exegesis. It is not the most obvious word to use in describing a person 'emerging' from water, despite its employment to describe a fish being 'landed' (Matt. xvii. 27); as we have observed, Justin slips into the use of ἀναδῦναι in his version of the story. It is employed most frequently to denote a solemn ascent to Jerusalem and its Temple, and is used seven times with reference to Christ's Ascension,[1] one instance being in Eph. iv. 8–10, a passage whose thought of the Ascension as the prelude to the sending down by Christ of the blessings of the Spirit is closely parallel to the Marcan picture of Christ ἀναβαίνων and the Spirit καταβαῖνον. That this allusion to the Ascension should occur in Mark is in no way surprising. That the Lord had been exalted into heaven was an integral element in the apostolic preaching; we may compare Acts ii. 33, iii. 21, v. 31; it is implied also in 1 Thess. i. 10, iv. 16; Rom. viii. 34; Phil. ii. 9. The adaptation of Ps. lxviii. 18 (and its application to the Ascension) which we find in Eph. iv. 8–10 probably represents, not St. Paul's original exegesis, but an interpretation of a well-known proof-text which had already become traditional.

In Luke there is no such hint of the Ascension in the narrative of the Baptism. This fact in itself is corroborative evidence for our interpretation of the Marcan ἀναβαίνων; for Luke no doubt omits it deliberately in view of the fact that he has reserved for Acts a full account of the Ascension and the descent of the Spirit which were adumbrated in the events of the Baptism.[2] Instead of the picture of Christ's 'ascent', he presents us with another picture—of Christ receiving the Spirit

---

[1] John i. 51, iii. 13, vi. 62, xx. 17; Acts ii. 34; Rom. x. 6 (cit.); Eph. iv. 8–10; cf. *Asc. Is.* 2. 16; in paganism it describes the ascension of Dionysus. Or. *Cels,* 4, 17 (p. 286. 15, *PG.* 11, 1048).

[2] That Luke knew the Marcan description of the Baptism (even if he is not following it) seems likely from his echo of it (ἀνέβησαν ἐκ τοῦ ὕδατος) in Acts viii. 39, where he may be drawing a parallel between a typical Christian baptism and that of Jesus (see below, p. 64).

while praying; thus Luke applies to Christ's reception of the Spirit his repeated doctrine that the grand object of prayer is the gift of the Spirit, and points to a similarity between this initial bestowal of the gift upon Jesus at prayer and the later outpourings upon the praying Church.[1]

Christ's own Baptism with the Old Testament background of the Servant prophecies, the Messianic unction with the Spirit, and the New Covenant, with, in addition, its anticipation or proleptic summing up and symbolizing of the new relationship between God and man established through His saving work, is the ground and origin of Baptism as we find it practised in the apostolic Church, the sacrament of participation in the Spirit-anointing of the *Christos* through the response made by faith to His work of reconciliation. When, therefore, the completion of that work made it possible after Pentecost for believers to be baptized in the name of Jesus Christ, the Baptism by which they were made partakers of the Christ corresponded in many respects to that which the Lord Himself received. Baptism was still a symbol of repentance for remission of sins, and this aspect of it had, of course, no parallel in the case of Jesus, except in so far as a 'renunciation of Satan' had taken place *after* His Baptism in the rejection of the Temptations; but the rite had also acquired a positive significance. It was the medium of the bestowal upon those who were baptized into Jesus Christ of the Spirit which had rested upon Him.

As His own Baptism prefigured His death, so the Christian rite looked back to it and applied its saving efficacy to the baptized convert who in a symbol died and rose again to the new life of the risen Christ. As the Spirit had descended from heaven upon Jesus, so the rebirth of the baptized consists (as the Fourth Gospel terms it) in γεννηθῆναι ἄνωθεν.[2] The declaration by the heavenly voice was, 'Thou art my Son'. In Baptism the believer in his turn enters into the status of a son in relation to the heavenly Father, a relationship and status of which the indwelling of the Spirit is the proof and assurance. The New Covenant, as O. C. Quick points out,[3] is more than a covenant

---

[1] Acts i. 14; cf. iv. 31.
[2] John iii. 7. Cf. the connection of Ascension and Spirit in John vi. 62.
[3] *The Christian Sacraments*, p. 167.

in the ordinary sense; it is the realization of our filial relationship to God, and in this realization through Christ of God's
Fatherhood towards us we are 'born again'.

Jesus entered into the baptism which John administered to
'all the people'.[1] Christian Baptism is also a collective rite by
which the people of God is constituted; it is a sacrament not
only of the individual's membership of Christ, but also of his
incorporation by virtue of his union with Christ into the community of the Church. Finally, an important point which has
too often been neglected in theology, the Baptism of Jesus was
proleptic, signifying and summing up in a single action the
entire mission and saving work of the Servant-Messiah, which
was to be unfolded and revealed gradually in the course of His
life, death, resurrection, and ascension; the Baptism of His
followers is also proleptic, signifying and summing up in a
single moment all the consequences of their faith-union with
Christ, which will be gradually unfolded in the course of their
lives and fully realized only at the Parousia. This fact is of great
importance for the proper apprehension of Baptism as the
sacrament of the bestowal of the Spirit. For the present, however, it is sufficient for us to note that the fact that Christian
Baptism is a re-presentation of the Baptism of Jesus implies that
it is through Baptism in water, and not through any other
ceremony, such as a physical anointing, that the believer enters
into the possession of the Spirit which is imparted through his
membership of Christ.

[1] Luke iii. 21.

3*

CHAPTER FOUR

BAPTISM IN THE APOSTOLIC CHURCH

IN the Baptism of Jesus, as we have seen, the preparatory rite administered by John was, so far as the Lord Himself was concerned, transformed into the expected Baptism with Holy Spirit. After the Resurrection the Lord told His disciples that the same fulfilment of promise would soon be extended to them as well. The baptism of John would be completed for them, too, by a baptism of the Spirit[1] It may be assumed from the connection (which Luke's narrative makes explicit) between Pentecost and the Johannine baptism that the disciples had already participated in the latter, and that the promised Spirit-Baptism was to transform the preparatory water rite into the same complete Baptism which Jesus had Himself received at the Jordan. There is thus implicit in Acts a direct correspondence between Pentecost and the Baptism of Jesus. Later legend endeavoured to depict this correspondence more graphically; examples of this tendency may be seen in Justin's story of the kindling of fire, reminiscent of Pentecost, at the Baptism,[2] and perhaps in the Ebionite Gospel's account of the shining of a 'great light'.[3] The Lord's promise meant that the disciples were to participate in the Baptism received by Him as Servant-Messiah, and that therefore the nationalist hope of the restoration of the kingdom to Israel was at an end.[4] Nor was the Parousia already at hand; Christ ascended into heaven and the gift of the Spirit, in whose power the disciples were to become witnesses to the uttermost parts of the earth, was at once a fulfilment of the prophetic hope of the last days and the ground of a new eschatological expectation. The outpouring of the Spirit marked the community of believers as belonging to

[1] Acts i. 5. [2] *dial.*, 88, 3.
[3] Epiph., *haer.*, 30, 13 (*GCS.*, p. 350, 13; *PG.* 41, 429A).
[4] Acts i. 6.

46

the interim period between the Resurrection and the final consummation, of which possession of the Spirit was the token and
pledge, when Jesus should 'so come in like manner as ye have
seen him go into heaven'.[1]

Whatever may be the historical value of the details of the
Pentecost story, the New Testament as a whole makes it abundantly clear that the great turning-point came when, after the
completion of the work of Jesus, His followers were enabled to
share in the Spirit which had been exclusively His own. The
conviction that the Spirit-baptism, which in the Baptist's
preaching had been no more than a part of the eschatological
hope, had now, through the resurrection of Jesus, become a
piece of 'realized eschatology', is not confined to the Lucan
writings. In the Fourth Gospel, where Luke's conception of
Pentecost is entirely absent and its place has been taken by
another narrative of the Spirit's bestowal, the same truth is
expressed which the Lucan narrative embodies: the hope of a
general outpouring of the Spirit has been fulfilled by the action
of the glorified Messiah who is the Spirit's source. An apparent
difference between the Lucan and Johannine conceptions,
namely, that in Acts the whole company of believers receives
the Spirit, and in the Fourth Gospel only the Apostles (in the
first instance), is of no major significance; for the Apostles, even
if they are to be exclusively identified with the $\mu\alpha\theta\eta\tau\alpha\acute{\iota}$ of
John xx. 19–23 (which is by no means certain), are the repre-
sentatives of the community as a whole, and nowhere does the
New Testament imply that some Christians possess the Spirit
while others do not.

We cannot say precisely how or when the new dispensation
of the Spirit was inaugurated. Luke's conception of it, expressed
in terms of Pentecost and its phenomena, is coloured by his
constant preoccupation with the Gentile mission as the climax
of the Gospel. The power of the Spirit bestowed at Pentecost
inaugurates that mission, which it continues to guide and
direct, by inspiring the Apostles to confess the exalted Jesus as
$\kappa\acute{\upsilon}\rho\iota\sigma$ and $X\rho\iota\sigma\tau\acute{\sigma}s$.[2] The mighty acts subsequently wrought
by or through the Spirit all serve the progress of the Gospel.
Hence at Pentecost the Spirit is conceived in 'missionary'

[1] Acts i. 11.   [2] Acts ii. 36.

terms; the visible appearance is in the form of 'tongues as of fire' distributed among the Apostles; the gift bestowed upon them is the power to 'speak with other tongues as the Spirit gave them utterance'; and the fulfilment of the ancient eschatological hope is demonstrated by Peter's appeal to the prophetic testimony of Joel and his expectation of a universal outpouring of the Spirit of *prophecy*. The fact that the chief interest of Luke is in the advent of the Gospel to the Gentile world must be borne in mind later when we consider his notions of the gift of the Spirit and the manner of its bestowal, for it goes far towards explaining certain puzzling features of what Acts has to say about the relationship between the Spirit and Baptism. Nevertheless, we have no evidence except Luke's upon which to form a judgment on what Baptism came to signify in the light of the new dispensation which had just begun at Pentecost. We may, however, expect some illumination from a comparison between the version of the primitive Church's beliefs which is afforded to us by Acts, and, on the other hand, the general witness of the New Testament to beliefs which seem to have been more or less universally diffused throughout the early community.

The first and most impressive fact which emerges from such a comparison is that the distinctive characteristic of early Christianity was the conviction that the community of believers possessed as a matter of present reality the indwelling of the Holy Spirit which had been hoped for by the prophets as the primary blessing of the future age of God's new covenant with man. The narrative of Acts is full of the idea of the Church as a Spirit-possessed society; to such an extent, indeed, is the activity of the community regarded as directly inspired and guided by the divine Spirit that the so-called 'apostolic council' can in all sobriety put forward the astounding claim that its decisions represent what had 'seemed good to the Holy Spirit and to us'.[1]

The conception of the Spirit-filled body of all Christian people is developed by St. Paul and raised, as we shall see, to a higher level of spiritual insight. 'Ye are not in the flesh, but in the spirit, if so be that the Spirit of God dwelleth in you';[2] it is

---

[1] Acts xv. 28; cf. v. 3, 9, ix. 31, xx. 28.   [2] Rom. viii. 9.

the inspiration of the Spirit which enables every ordinary convert to declare his belief in κύριος Ἰησοῦς.[1] The conception is
not, however, merely Lucan and Pauline; it is diffused through
almost all the New Testament writings, and it is certainly
primitive. It is attested in such different books as Hebrews,
James, 1 Peter, and the Fourth Gospel. The progress of the
Gospel was marked, says the writer to the Hebrews, by πνεύματος
ἁγίου μερισμοί[2] which are associated with the powers of the
age to come; apostasy from the Church is an insult to the Spirit
of grace.[3] Even the epistles of James and 1 Peter, which in
general pay relatively little attention to the conception of the
Spirit, speak of 'the Spirit which he made to dwell in us',[4] and
'the Spirit of the glory and of God' which 'rests upon you'.[5] It
is only natural that the Johannine literature should develop
this theme at a far more profound level of reflection and
interpretation.[6]

The second main conception which emerges from a comparison of the early Church's beliefs reflected in Acts with the evidence of the New Testament as a whole is that the Spirit
comes from God the Father through the risen Christ. To pour
out the Spirit upon the faithful community was expected, as
we have seen, to be the function of the Messiah; that this function had been actually fulfilled by the crucified and risen Jesus
was proved by the experience of the primitive Church, as the
apostolic writings testify with impressive unanimity. Indeed,
the cardinal proof adduced in the early preaching to demonstrate that Jesus was actually the Messiah was simply the obser-
vable fact that through Him the Spirit had in fact been bestowed
upon the whole body of His adherents. That 'He hath poured
forth this, which ye see and hear' is the inescapable fact of
experience by which 'all the house of Israel' may 'know
assuredly that God hath made him both Lord and Christ, this
Jesus',[7] and the 'Holy Ghost, whom God hath given to them
that obey him' is a witness, through the Apostles, that God
exalted Jesus at His right hand to be a Prince and a Saviour.[8]
For St. Paul, as we shall see later, the Spirit is the Spirit of

---

[1] 1 Cor. xii. 3.   [2] Heb. ii. 4.   [3] Heb. x. 29.
[4] Jas. iv. 5.   [5] 1 Pet. iv. 14.   [6] John xiv–xvi, xx. 22.
[7] Acts ii. 33, 36.   [8] Acts v. 31–2.

Christ, virtually identical with the risen Christ Himself in respect of His activity within the Church which can be described either as the Body of Christ or as the temple of the Spirit. 'God sent forth the Spirit of his Son into our hearts, crying, Abba, Father.'[1] St. Paul's missionary work and its successful accomplishment of its object are dependent upon the 'supply of the Spirit of Jesus Christ',[2] and his converts can be reminded in the same breath that the Spirit of God dwells in them, that they have Christ's Spirit, and that Christ is in them.[3] The same insistence that it is through Christ that the believer receives the Spirit is repeated in the Fourth Gospel. The 'Spirit of truth' will be given to the disciples in response to the prayer of Jesus;[4] the Paraclete is sent by Christ from the Father,[5] and he 'will take of mine and shall declare it unto you'.[6]

In the thought of St. Paul and St. John the vitally important difference between the Old Testament hope of the Spirit's outpouring and its actual fulfilment lies in the fact that the Spirit which was really bestowed upon the renewed Israel of God was the Spirit of Jesus, in whose offered life the new Covenant had been constituted. This conception is not so profoundly expressed in Acts. There are, however, certain considerations which explain this difference. In the first place there is Luke's rather undeveloped 'ruach' conception of the Spirit; and secondly there is his paramount interest in the Gentile mission, which makes him look for the operation of the Spirit chiefly in terms of prophecy, speaking with tongues, and evangelistic preaching. It would not be true, however, to suggest[7] that the early Church thought of the Spirit as a power operating independently of the person of Christ and manifested chiefly in ecstatic experiences, and that it was only recognized as the inner principle of life 'in Christ' after St. Paul had effected a synthesis between the traditional idea of the Spirit and his own Christ-mysticism through his discovery that 'the Lord is the Spirit'.[8]

In point of fact, the intimate connection of Christ with the believer's possession of the Spirit and its presence in the Church is at the heart of the entire apostolic tradition of preaching. The

---

[1] Gal. iv. 6.   [2] Phil. i. 19.   [3] Rom. viii. 9-10.
[4] John xiv. 16–17.   [5] John xv. 26.   [6] John xvi. 15.
[7] As Bousset (*Kyrios Christos*, pp. 112 ff.).   [8] 2 Cor. iii. 17.

Spirit which comes upon converts to the faith is the same Spirit which descended upon Jesus at His Baptism and with which he was anointed;[1] its bestowal is implicitly connected with the Baptism of Jesus;[2] and it is in virtue of the Spirit-anointing of the 'Servant' that the Spirit's charismata are granted to the Church's members.[3]

That the Holy Spirit is the bond which unites the ascended Lord to his followers and the agency through which they become His members, sharing in His Messianic unction, is the general teaching of the New Testament as a whole; the thought is clearly implied in Acts, and it reaches its highest expression in 1 John: 'And hereby know we that he abideth in us, by the Spirit which he gave us'; 'Hereby know we that we abide in him, and he in us, because he hath given us of his Spirit.'[4] Because the Spirit is the link between Christ and the believer, it is through the κοινωνία of the Spirit that there comes into being the fellowship of the Church which is so strikingly portrayed in the early chapters of Acts—chapters which prepare us, as it were, for the developed teaching of St. Paul that the greatest gift of the Spirit is ἀγάπη.

Finally, as we have already observed, possession of the Spirit is at once a present reality and an eschatological promise. The believer lives in partial realization of the age to come, and the indwelling of the Spirit is, as St. Paul was to explain, a first instalment or token of the ultimate total transformation of the entire personality.

The great Pentecostal climax of the Gospel of redemption (as Luke believes it to have been) is the original starting-point of the Church's Baptism. The Johannine rite received a new meaning as soon as the Apostles had experienced the coming of the Holy Ghost. The Spirit had descended upon them immediately; but the case of their converts was different. They had to be brought to faith in Jesus as the Christ by the apostolic ministry of witness and preaching of the word, and their union with Christ, attained by faith, is sacramentally mediated to them by Baptism. The Baptism of Jesus, as the Servant who makes atonement for His people, having been completed in His

---

[1] Acts x. 38, 44.   [2] Acts i. 8.   [3] Acts iv. 27.
[4] 1 John iii. 24, iv. 13.

death and resurrection, those who accept Him as the Christ are baptized in the name of Jesus the Anointed for remission of sins.[1] By undergoing Baptism the new converts come to belong to the Christ; they are made His property, entered in the name of the Messiah as members of His people;[2] and through their participation in the Anointed they receive a share in His anointing, the gift of the Holy Spirit, the sign that the Messianic age has already dawned.

Viewed against the background of Christ's Baptism and its symbolism, even the Lucan picture of Baptism in Acts ii. 38 contains latent within it the idea that through the old symbolical rite, transformed through the Pentecostal outpouring of the Spirit, there is effected an incorporation of the believer into Christ's death and resurrection. St. Paul need not have looked outside the primitive tradition for the basic elements in his mystical theology, though it required his personal experience and spiritual insight to enable the Church to arrive at a conscious realization of much that it had previously perceived but dimly. Nor does Luke antedate the practice of Baptism. The outward rite was ready to hand from the outset; early Christianity was never a religion without cultus, and, from the time when, at Pentecost, the old ceremony became the means of enlistment in the name of Jesus Christ and reception of the promised Spirit, the Church was linked with the risen and ascended Lord through the two interrelated sacraments, Baptism and the Eucharist, in both of which the action of God in Christ, accomplished once for all, is represented and actualized for the believer. Whatever the tradition of the baptismal formula in any part of the Church, whether the Trinitarian form was employed or Baptism was strictly and literally 'in the name of Jesus Christ', this Christocentric significance of the sacrament seems to have been constant.

Certain aspects of what Acts goes on to tell us about Baptism must be considered later, but for the present we shall gain a clearer conception of the baptismal theology of the apostolic age if we move directly from Luke's account of the origins of the rite in Jerusalem and briefly consider the developed teaching of St. Paul. Before we do so it is worth repeating that,

[1] Acts ii. 38.   [2] Cf. Jer. vii. 10 on the significance of the 'Name'.

although it seems that the essence of the Pauline thought on Baptism was implicit in the primitive tradition, Luke's own theory differs widely from St. Paul's.

For the former, as we have remarked, the Spirit is the power which rested upon Jesus, in which He carried out his ministry and performed His mighty works, and which became as the result of Christ's death, resurrection, and ascension, and the climax of Pentecost, the power in which the missionary Church extended its activity to the ends of the earth. It is therefore primarily thought of as the Spirit of prophecy and of 'tongues', making its presence obvious to all and sundry.

Hence, there is little appreciation of the Spirit as personal, or as other than a gift of God, something 'poured out', as Joel had foretold, in the last days, whose operation often appears as a quasi-physical phenomenon.

St. Paul, on the other hand, identifies the Spirit with the risen Lord's presence in His Body, the Church, and so comes nearer to a true conception of the Spirit as personal, though he too is dangerously ready to think of the Spirit as 'something given' rather than as the personal God in His approach to man —as a gift rather than the Giver. The long failure of the Church in apostolic and much later times to arrive at a satisfactory understanding of the Holy Spirit, and the fact that baptismal thought and practice became firmly set along certain definite lines well in advance of the progress of dogmatic theology, had an unfortunate effect on the doctrine of Baptism. No very clear lead towards such an understanding of the Spirit was given by St. Paul, and, as we shall see, there was a lamentable retrogression in the sub-apostolic age from the position which he had reached. In ancient times, as in modern, unsatisfactory conceptions of the Holy Spirit lie at the root of much theological confusion about Baptism and are a fruitful source of superstition. St. Paul's Christocentric doctrine of the Spirit and His activity in the Church is naturally connected with the fact that he differs from the Lucan teaching in making the Atonement, and the justification and sanctification of the sinner through faith in Christ, central to his theology of Baptism.

St. Paul's teaching does not represent a wholly new conception of Baptism; it consists largely in the explicit and detailed presentation in the light of his profound personal experience of what had been implied in the words and actions of Jesus and in the primitive preaching. It is significant that what he brings before his converts as the foundation and focus of Christian living is not his private revelation on the Damascus road, but the initiation which they, no less than he, had received in the already existing society of the Church. It is true that it is through the response of faith to grace that a man is justified, and that it is the hearing of the word which elicits this faith,[1] so that he rightly reminds the Galatians that they have received the Spirit through the 'hearing of faith';[2] and it follows that faith is in a sense prior to Baptism and to all else except the prevenient grace of God. Nevertheless, it is impossible to separate the reception of the word from the Baptism which is its visible sign and the effective symbol by which the saving act of God in Christ is brought to bear upon the convert. The rather testy language in which St. Paul declares that Christ has not sent him to baptize, but to preach the Gospel,[3] has behind it the obscure ramifications of Corinthian party-strife and some acute sensitiveness on his part about his own status and apostolic commission vis-à-vis Cephas and the rest. What he really meant we can only guess. One thing is certain; he is not disparaging Baptism as such. The only question here is who baptizes, and what is the effect of party-strife on the meaning which Gentile converts attach to their Baptism. This very passage is evidence of the indissoluble connection in Pauline teaching between Christ's atoning death and the Baptism by which its effects are applied to the believer and he is 'entered up' in Christ's name as belonging to Him and as being 'in Christ'. The answer to the party-cries, 'I am of Paul', and 'I of Apollos', is 'Was Paul crucified for you, or were you baptized in the name of Paul?' The true effect of Baptism should be that every believer could cry, 'I of Christ', that is, justified in Christ and through the re-presentation of His saving work a sharer in His character as the Χριστός, anointed with the Spirit and declared to be, like Him but in a different way (by adoption), a son of God. There could be no baptism in the name of Paul

---

[1] Rom. x. 8–10.   [2] Gal. iii. 2–5.
[3] 1 Cor. i. 17.

or Apollos or any other than Jesus, for He alone was the anointed and He alone had reconciled the world.[1]

By virtue of the effective sign of Baptism, faith of course being always presupposed, the application of the Atonement to the believer implies his forgiveness; Christian Baptism therefore effects the cleansing for which the prophets had hoped.[2] But the 'washing away of sin' takes place only because Baptism is the sacrament of that union with Christ, and consequently that state of being 'in the Spirit' (or of possessing the indwelling Spirit) which justifies and sanctifies.[3] As the Israelites were 'baptized into Moses in the cloud and in the sea', so the Christian who is baptized in Christ's name is thenceforth 'in Christ'.[4] This experience is, in a sense, a re-enactment in every convert of Christ's own Baptism as a symbol setting forth His death and rising again: 'As many of us as were baptized into Christ Jesus were baptized into his death'; we are 'buried with him by baptism into his death, planted together in the likeness of his death', and are confident of living with Him in the resurrection life of freedom from sin.[5] We were buried with Christ in Baptism and raised together with Him.[6]

By virtue of our participation through faith in Christ's death and resurrection, we, like Jesus, receive the 'promise of the Spirit'; but the Spirit is now recognizable, as it were, as the Spirit of Christ and it is as being 'in Christ' that we are 'in the Spirit'.[7] The bestowal of the Spirit, again, brings to the convert (as to Jesus at His Baptism) the assurance of sonship, enabling us to cry, 'Abba, Father',[8] freeing us from bondage, and giving that freedom of approach to God which is the privilege of His sons.

This transformation of the ordinary human personality by union with Christ in His death and resurrection[9] involves nothing less than a new Creation,[10] for to be 'raised together with

---

[1] On similar lines the author to the Hebrews (vi. 6) argues that a second Baptism, which he regards as the logical consequence of post-baptismal sin, would be impossible, since it would be equivalent to crucifying Christ afresh.
[2] 1 Cor. vi. 11; Eph. v. 26–7.   [3] 1 Cor. vi. 11.   [4] 1 Cor. x. 2.
[5] Rom. vi. 3–14.   [6] Col. ii. 12.
[7] Rom. viii. 15–16; 1 Cor. xii. 13.
[8] Rom. viii. 15 (in baptismal context; cf. Gal. iv. 6).
[9] εἰς ὑπὲρ πάντων ἀπέθανεν· ἄρα οἱ πάντες ἀπέθανον, 2 Cor. v. 14.
[10] εἴ τις ἐν Χριστῷ, καινὴ κτίσις, 2 Cor. v. 17; cf. Gal. vi. 15.

Christ' means the putting off of the 'old man' and the putting on of 'the new man which is being renewed unto knowledge after the image of him that created him'.[1] The indwelling Spirit is thus the ἀρραβών of the eschatological hope of the putting on (or being 'clothed upon') of the incorruptibility of the οἰκητήριον τὸ ἐξ οὐρανοῦ[2]—a thought which recalls the 'clothing' of the Apostles with 'power from on high' in Luke's narrative of the preparation for Pentecost.[3] From another point of view, the 'baptized into Christ' may be said to 'put on Christ';[4] and with this putting off of the old man and putting on of Christ all human distinctions are put away, even the barrier between the circumcision and the uncircumcision. Against the arguments of Judaizers who would recall his converts to the practice of circumcision, St. Paul maintains that, in contrast with the rite of the old Covenant, Baptism signifies the putting off of the entire 'body of the flesh'[5] through burial and resurrection with Christ; and in the experience of the Spirit there is the fulfilment of the prophets' predictions of the New Covenant's token, the inward circumcision of the heart.[6]

Union with Christ, effected through Baptism, necessarily implies incorporation into His Body, the Church. In language recalling the Old Testament metaphors in which the Spirit's action is likened to that of fresh water irrigating the stony desert, St. Paul combines the inward 'watering' of the Spirit with the outward washing of Baptism as the means whereby each believer, irrespective of his earthly status and condition, is grafted into the one Body: 'For in one Spirit were we all baptized into one body, whether Jews or Greeks, whether slaves or freemen, and were all "watered" with one Spirit.'[7] The Church as the Spirit-possessed community is the sphere of the κοινωνία of the Spirit. It is entered by Baptism, not because this is a rite which has been arbitrarily appointed as the Church's method of recruiting its members, but because Baptism into Christ is synonymous both with reception of

---

[1] Col. iii. 9–10.   [2] 2 Cor. v. 1–5.   [3] Luke xxiv. 49.
[4] Gal. iii. 27. Cullmann (*Die Tauflehre des N.T.*, p. 31) sees a military metaphor here of putting on a uniform. If so, this is an early instance of an idea common in later baptismal theology.
[5] Col. ii. 11–12.   [6] Rom . ii. 28–9; Phil. iii. 3.   [7] 1 Cor. xii. 13.

the bestowal of His Spirit, and with entry into the spiritual fellowship of His Body, whose distinctive characteristic is ἀγάπη.[1]

The Pauline conception of the Spirit, and hence of Baptism, is, however, always eschatological. The Spirit is still the Holy Spirit of promise, the token first-instalment of the ultimate redemption of that which God has sealed as His own.[2] Possession of the Spirit is a guarantee and assurance of the hope of the age to come, for it is a partial fulfilment of that hope within the present order. It is a pledge that in the final consummation 'what is mortal' will be 'swallowed up of life'.[3]

Summing up some of the conclusions which emerge from St. Paul's teaching, so far as we have traced it in this brief study, we can affirm that Baptism, whose reception by the believer is his visible act of trusting response to the prevenient grace of God in Christ, is a re-presentation of Christ's own Baptism and its application to each convert. This fact alone can afford any convincing explanation why the apparently rather unsuitable rite whose very title indicates that it was a 'dipping' (whether it included anything else is a question we must reserve for later discussion) was retained when it had come to signify so much more than a Johannine 'cleansing'. It is Christ's Baptism, illuminated by its fulfilment in His death and resurrection; hence it is the effective sign of the application of His saving work to the believer, and it is into Christ's βάπτισμα of death that the believer is incorporated.[4] Through his membership in the 'Anointed' the believer shares in Christ's 'unction' with the Spirit.

The various effects of Baptism which we have been considering are of course inseparable except in the theologian's analysis. They are simply different aspects in which we may view what is in fact a single creative act of God in Christ. Pauline thought affords no ground whatever for the modern theories which seek to effect a separation in the one action and to distinguish a 'Spirit-Baptism' and a 'water-Baptism', not as the inward and outward parts of one sacrament, but as independent entities.

---

[1] 1 Cor. xiii. 13.   [2] Eph. i. 13.   [3] 2 Cor. v. 4.
[4] In the light of this teaching we can understand why the martyr, who *literally* shared Christ's death, was regarded as having been baptized even if he had not received the sacrament, and was believed to be pre-eminently *spiritualis*.

When, for example, Mason[1] distinguishes the effects of Baptism (regeneration and cleansing from sin) from the bestowal of the indwelling Spirit which he holds to be the effect of Confirmation, when J. Behm[2] and others distinguish water-baptism, as signifying something negative, from a positive baptism of the Spirit, when Dix maintains that 'Baptism into the death and Resurrection of Christ and the Pentecostal Baptism of the Spirit are not one thing but two, both of them inseparably and necessarily connected, but not the same',[3] when Thornton will allow to water-baptism only the effect of blotting out sins and the *preparation* of a temple for the Spirit,[4] and when, to take an extreme example of this type of thought, G. C. Richards expresses the astonishing opinion that New Testament Baptism 'does not carry with it full Church privileges, but is the intermediate stage between the catechumenate and full membership',[5] we can only infer that these writers have totally misunderstood the Christological heart of the Pauline teaching, which is simply that Baptism effects incorporation into Christ. If we are *in* Christ, we are in the Spirit, or the Spirit is in us, we are in the organ of Christ's continuing earthly activity, the Church, and our sins are forgiven. So far as the inward part of the sacrament is concerned, there is no temporal sequence of gifts. Temporal process is involved only in the believer's realization and growth into what he has received in the moment of his incorporation into Christ. He has to realize what he has become, but not to acquire any additional status. Hence there is no room for any other full sacrament of the Gospel in addition to the two complementary sacraments which look back in time to the Cross, re-present to us the Atonement, and look forward to the Parousia of which they are a pledge.

Before we proceed to relate this teaching to St. Paul's texts on the 'seal', we must briefly consider the contributions of other writers to the sum of the New Testament doctrine. I Peter, the greater part of which is in all probability a baptismal homily, underlines certain aspects of the Pauline

---

[1] *Op. cit.*, p. 143, citing with approval Pacian of Barcelona.
[2] *Die Handauflegung im Urchristentum*, pp. 166 ff.
[3] *The Theology of Confirmation in Relation to Baptism*, p. 30.
[4] *Confirmation Today*, p. 9.
[5] *Baptism and Confirmation*, p. 14.

teaching, notably the centrality of the Cross in the context of Baptism,[1] emphasis on the Resurrection,[2] and the thought of the baptized as a covenant people partaking of Christ's priesthood and royalty.[3] We may notice a certain difference of tone, as compared with the Pauline letters, in the use of the expressions ὁ . . . ἀναγεννήσας ἡμᾶς, and ἀναγεννημένοι οὐκ ἐκ σπορᾶς φθαρτῆς, ἀλλὰ ἀφθάρτου.[4] Here we seem to be approaching a change of outlook; the Pauline eschatology is giving way to a more immanentist conception; the stress is being laid on the idea of a present rebirth rather than of a future redemption. Nevertheless, although it is expressed in Hellenistic rather than Hebraic terms, the thought is not far removed from that of the Pauline 'new creation' and in any case there is no need to see in this language the influence of the mysteries.[5] We may perhaps compare the Philonic notion of Noah inaugurating man's δευτέρα γέννησις after the Flood. There may even be a connection of thought in 1 Peter between the Flood as a type of Baptism, and the 'rebirth' begun by Noah as a type of the spiritual regeneration of the Christian.

The παλιγγενεσία of Titus iii. 5 is probably synonymous with the eschatological 'renewal' of Matt. xix. 28, but the eschatology seems distinctly to be more fully 'realized' than in the Pauline theory. It appears highly probable that the common interpretation of this passage is mistaken which translates διὰ λουτροῦ παλιγγενεσίας καὶ ἀνακαινώσεως πνεύματος ἁγίου as though the text read διὰ λουτροῦ . . . καὶ διὰ ἀνακαινώσεως. This text is of considerable importance, for it has often been adduced in support of the view that in the New Testament Baptism in water for remission of sins is distinct from Baptism of the Holy Spirit; we must accordingly pause for a moment to examine it.[6]

The following points seem to tell against the above interpretation. In the first place, the Greek will hardly admit of the two genitives being other than co-ordinate, and alike dependent on λουτροῦ; the variant reading, καὶ ἀνακαινώσεως διὰ πνεύματος bears out this rendering; παλιγγενεσίας and ἀνακαινώσεως

[1] ii. 24, iii. 18, iv. 1.   [2] i. 3,   [3] ii. 9.   [4] i. 3, 23.
[5] See additional note, p. 93.
[6] See further, J. Dey, Παλιγγενεσία, pp. 133 ff.

represent co-ordinate and almost synonymous ideas; and it is not surprising to find λουτρόν used, as it is so frequently in later writers, as a synonym for βάπτισμα. We should also observe that the 'regeneration' and 'renewal' are connected here with the idea of the Covenant,[1] and that 'washing, Spirit' (of which the Christian 'washing' is the effective sign), and the 'regeneration' and 'renewal' which are effected by the Baptism of water and Spirit, are all aspects of the promised New Covenant. Further, it would be wholly misleading to suggest that there can be regeneration without the gift of the Spirit any more than there can be 'renewal'—at any rate in New Testament theology. We miss the point of the text either if we accept Usener's conjecture ἀνακοινώσεως,[2] or if, in an attempt to exalt a supposed 'Spirit-baptism' at the expense of the sacrament of Baptism, we follow the curious rendering of the passage by Richards: '. . . the bath-water of regeneration, and the renewal of the Holy Spirit.'[3]

We are again carried further from Pauline eschatology in the γεννηθῆναι ἄνωθεν of John iii. 7. Here if the thought is still not greatly divergent from that of St. Paul, the accent is different, and more suggestive of Hellenistic ideas of rebirth, though there is as yet no such idea of a quasi-magical and unethical rebirth as we meet in Gnostic and semi-heretical popular literature in the second century.[4] In this passage the inward and outward aspects of Baptism are clearly defined, and here, once more, the wording ἐξ ὕδατος καὶ πνεύματος indicates a single experience, and not two 'baptisms', one of water and one of Spirit. The act of Baptism and the reception of the Spirit are simultaneous.

For the rest, the Fourth Gospel, as we have already seen, underlines truths hinted at elsewhere. In the Pedilavium[5] baptismal symbolism replaces the institution of the Eucharist,

---

[1] κληρονόμοι, v. 7.   [2] Das Weihnachtsfest, pp. 160 f.
[3] Op. cit., p. 22.
[4] In this connection Philo's description of the call of Moses is interesting: 'Sursum vocatio Prophetae secunda est nativitas (sive regeneratio) priore melior; illa enim commixta per carnem, et corruptibiles habebat parentes; ista vero incommixta simplexque anima principalis (vel spiritus principis) mutata a genita ad ingenitam, cuius non est mater; sed pater solus qui est universorum. Quamobrem et sursum vocatio . . . divina nativitas,' qu. in Ex., 46 (Aucher's rendering of Armenian text), Aucher, Philonis Judaei Paralipomena Armena, 1826, p. 502, partly cited by W. L. Knox, Some Hellenistic Elements in Primitive Christianity, p. 94.
[5] John xiii. 1–11.

and points to the Servant by whose death the disciples will find that they have been cleansed. It seems unlikely that the story of the blind man's illumination[1] when he is washed in Siloam, ὃ ἑρμηνεύεται ἀπεσταλμένος,[2] could be read by the early Church without conveying a clear reference to Baptism into the Christ, whom the Fourth Evangelist constantly asserts to have been 'sent' by the Father;[3] and it is in this Gospel that the Baptism and self-offering of Christ are linked together and become the source of the Gospel sacraments in the water and blood of the Cross. It is the same writer (unless we adopt the unlikely theory that the Gospel and the First Epistle are by different hands) who speaks, in language directly recalling Christ's 'anointing', of Christian believers possessing an 'unction from the Holy One', which teaches them concerning all things and is the truth, and which distinguishes them (as χριστοί) from the πολλοὶ ἀντίχριστοι of heresy.[4] It is patently clear that the unction referred to is the Messianic unction of the Spirit.

We may now return once more to consider the 'seal' of the Pauline texts from which we started our enquiry. In 2 Cor. i. 21–2 the 'earnest' of the Spirit in our hearts is the token and pledge of final redemption, the first instalment of the eschatological transformation of the whole man. As we have seen, this presence of the indwelling Spirit is one aspect of the state of being 'in Christ' which we receive through faith in Baptism. This bestowal of the Spirit is therefore equivalent to putting on Christ, or becoming members of Christ, and, in becoming united with Christ in His death and resurrection we share, as it were, in His baptismal anointing;[5] in faith-union with Him we, too, receive an unction from God, the descent of the Spirit whose presence is the sign and token of our status as the people of the New Covenant in Christ's blood, the true Israel of God. The mark of God's ownership, the sign that we are part of His περιποίησις, is not, as in the case of the old Israel, an outward

---

[1] Cf. Eph. i. 18; Heb. vi. 4. [2] John ix. 7.
[3] Cyril so interprets the passage (Jo. vi. 1; Aubert, 4, 602).
[4] 1 John ii. 18, 20, 27.
[5] For the believer as a χριστός cf. Or., Jo., 6 (3) (GCS. p. 115, 17; PG. 14, 212C); Meth., symp., 8, 8 (p. 90, 9; PG. 18, 149C); Eus., d.e., 4, 16 (p. 190, 24; P.G. 22, 317B); Cyr., ep., 1 (Aubert, 5, 7A); etc.

token in the flesh, but this inward experience of the Spirit, which represents the 'circumcision of the heart' and is the Holy Spirit of promise, the pledge to us that we are assured of a 'day of redemption' and the sign by which at the Parousia the Lord 'knoweth them that are His'.

St. Paul is clearly not thinking in the first instance about a rite, but about the consequences of faith-union with Christ, or rather, he is thinking about certain aspects and implications of such a union. It is as one such aspect that he treats the inward seal which is marked, as it were, on the faithful. Nevertheless, as we have already noticed, his use of the aorist tense indicates that this union and its logical consequence of participation in the Spirit are thought of as directly related to a particular moment in the experience of the believer. In the light of what we have seen to be the New Testament doctrine of Baptism in relation to the Spirit, there can be no doubt that the decisive moment to which St. Paul refers is Baptism. Our investigation has shown that in Pauline thought possession of the Spirit is one aspect of the condition of being 'in Christ'. It follows that if Baptism effects union with Christ, as St. Paul certainly claims that it does, then it is Baptism which also effects the bestowal of the Spirit. There is one Baptism, because it is Baptism into the one Christ and incorporation into the one Body. There cannot be a baptism for some aspects of membership of Christ (such as regeneration or remission of sins) and another for the other aspect of the same experience (reception of the indwelling Spirit) by which we are sealed.

The question remains whether the ceremony of the one Baptism in the apostolic Church consisted solely of water-baptism, as we have hitherto assumed, and as the evidence we have considered would certainly appear to suggest, or whether the sacrament of Baptism normally included some kind of rite of 'Confirmation'. We must also consider the less likely possibility that a distinct ceremony of Confirmation preceded or followed Baptism, though in view of what has been said we shall not expect the meaning assigned to such a rite in the New Testament (if it existed at all) to be that of a sacramental medium of the seal of the Spirit. The further question will arise whether Confirmation, if it was practised, was administered by an outward sign of laying on of hands or by an anointing. Our answers to these questions may be considered together as we examine the New Testament and, particularly, the confusing and perhaps actually confused data presented to us in the Acts of the Apostles.

CHAPTER FIVE

CONFIRMATION IN THE APOSTOLIC AGE?

MANY of the most acute theological problems which have beset the relationship of Baptism to Confirmation in the course of the Church's history take their origin from the difficulty of interpreting St. Luke's apparently inconsistent account of the practice of Baptism in the apostolic age. Not only does the picture which he draws of the method by which converts were initiated appear at times to be self-contradictory, but it also seems to be at variance with the evidence of St. Paul on the subject. Consequently, commentators on Acts and dogmatic theologians alike have produced a remarkable variety of theories to account for these supposed inconsistencies, and drawn totally divergent inferences for baptismal theology.

At Pentecost, we are told, St. Peter's converts were baptized,[1] but there is no indication that any other ceremony took place than the baptism in water such as had been familiar from the practice of the Baptist; they were promised the gift of the Holy Spirit through this rite, and we are certainly intended to infer that they did receive it. The situation which Luke's narrative presents to us on this occasion is, in fact, parallel to that which St. Paul envisages in what he says to his readers about Baptism.

The Ethiopian eunuch converted by Philip the deacon is baptized, but the Spirit, mentioned immediately after the description of the emergence of Philip and the candidate from the water (perhaps we should see here a deliberate reminiscence of the Baptism of Jesus), snatches away Philip instead of coming upon the convert as we should expect.[2] The Western text has it that the Spirit fell upon the eunuch and an angel caught away Philip, a reading which suggests that the Western scribe or

---

[1] Acts ii. 41.   [2] Acts viii. 39.

editor was puzzled by the story (as we are) and improved it in the obvious fashion. It is conceivable, however, that the eunuch is described as going on his way rejoicing (χαίρων), not as a mere piece of 'padding' to the narrative, but to indicate that he was in fact possessed of the Spirit after his baptism. χαρά is associated with the Spirit in Acts xiii. 52 and 1 Thess. i. 6; it is a 'fruit of the Spirit',[1] and the Kingdom of God consists in χαρά among other spiritual virtues;[2] St. Peter describes it, in a baptismal context, as a product of faith.[3] The verb is used to describe the exultation with which Christians may suffer for Christ and greet the Parousia.[4] Clearly, the thought underlying χαίρειν in this context is not far from that of Spirit-possession. I am inclined to think, however, that Luke has an insufficient appreciation of the Spirit as the inner principle of the ordinary believer's life in Christ to make him interested in whether or not the average convert partakes of it. For him the Spirit is essentially, as we have observed, the power guiding the missionary expansion of the Church and assisting the progress of the Gospel by signs, prophesyings, and speaking with tongues.

There is plenty of evidence in Acts that converts were regularly baptized, as, for example, Lydia, and the Philippian jailer. Here, again, there is no mention of their reception of the Spirit, though in the latter case we may notice the significant phrase, ἠγαλλιάσατο πεπιστευκώς.[5] ἀγαλλιᾶσθαι and its substantive always in the New Testament signify spiritual joy, which is a divine endowment, and is, indeed, a part of the expected blessings of the 'last days';[6] again, therefore, the thought of 'joy' is close to that of reception of the Spirit. Crispus and the Corinthian converts are said to be baptized[7] without any mention of the Spirit, and also without any indication that St. Paul did more than simply baptize them, which is the impression we

---

[1] Gal. v. 22.   [2] Rom. xiv. 17.   [3] 1 Pet. i. 8.
[4] 1 Pet. iv. 13.   [5] Acts xvi. 34.
[6] For the eschatological significance of ἀγαλλιάομαι, cf. Apoc., xix. 7; Matt. v. 12; 1 Pet. iv. 13; Jude 24; and perhaps Luke 1. 14, 1. 44, i. 47; John viii. 56; Mart. Polyc., 19, 2. For its connection with the Spirit, cf. Luke x. 21; in Barn., 1, 6 'joy' is the fruit of the ἀγάπη which is the Spirit's supreme gift, and a direct link between joy and the presence of the Spirit appears to be indicated by the phrase of Hermas (sim. 9, 24, 2), πάντοτε ἀγαλλιώμενοι ἐπὶ τοῖς δούλοις τοῦ θεοῦ καὶ ἐνδεδυμένοι τὸ πνεῦμα τὸ ἅγιον. It is noteworthy that Luke, whose allusions in Acts we are considering, is the writer who most strongly emphasizes spiritual joy.
[7] Acts xviii. 8.

receive from St. Paul's own remarks on these Corinthian conversions.

On one occasion Baptism follows the direct, unmediated, bestowal of the Spirit;[1] but this episode is in no way typical; it is a major turning-point in Luke's narrative—a second, purely Gentile, Pentecost, reproducing in the case of the Roman centurion, Cornelius, the immediate descent of the Spirit upon the original company at Jerusalem (a fact to which Peter himself calls attention).[2] There is also the peculiar instance of Apollos who, having received, not full Christian Baptism, but 'the Baptism of John' (which suggests Baptism as it was administered by Christ's disciples before Pentecost), was nevertheless ζέων τῷ πνεύματι,[3] and who apparently was not given any other Baptism or sign of the bestowal of the Spirit. We can only guess at the reason for this last peculiarity: possibly the Spirit is regarded by Luke as normally, but not universally, imparted through Baptism; possibly a direct commission from the Lord was deemed to have conferred upon him the Spirit, for he ranked very high among the apostles, being regarded by the Corinthians as standing approximately upon the same level as St. Peter or St. Paul.

There remain three passages in which, though converts are baptized, their reception of the Spirit appears to be mediated through the imposition of hands. Of these the most striking is in the account of the visit of Peter and John to Samaria when Philip has there preached the Gospel and baptized converts (Acts viii. 4–19).

In the opinion of most ancient commentators, and of very many modern writers, such as Mason, Wirgman, Umberg, Coppens, and Richards,[4] the narrative means simply that no one but an apostle could administer the rite by which the gift of the Spirit was conferred (the gift being regarded either, as by Mason and Umberg, as the initial gift of the indwelling Spirit, or, as by Wirgman and Richards, as a special 'strengthening' gift to those who already possess the Spirit as the principle of the Christian life), that the rite in question was the imposition of hands with prayer, and that this sacrament of

---

[1] Acts. x. 44.
[2] Acts x. 47, xi. 15.
[3] Acts xviii. 25.
[4] See Bibliography.

Confirmation was practised in the apostolic Church as a regular part of the initiatory ceremony, or, at any rate in such exceptional cases as that of the Samaritans, as a distinct rite administered at some time after Baptism.

To this theory there is an obvious objection. If this was really the indispensable sign of the gift of the Spirit, it is exceedingly odd that, in all the space which he devotes to baptismal teaching, St. Paul never once alludes to it (for we have seen that to suppose an allusion to Confirmation in 2 Cor. i. 22—and in any case this would be to unction and not to the imposition of hands —is quite arbitrary). It is also very strange that the performance of the rite is not one of the many ministerial charismata described by St. Paul in 1 Cor. xii. 4–10, and it is impossible to believe that he, as an apostle, confirmed those Corinthians whom he thanks God that he never baptized. There is, moreover, not the slightest indication that apostolic hands were laid upon the three thousand converts added to the Church after St. Peter's Pentecost sermon; indeed, it is not easy to envisage the practical possibility of such a proceeding.[1] On the contrary, in this instance the gift of the Spirit, as we have already remarked, appears to be bound up with the actual ceremony of Baptism as the inward 'thing signified' with its external sign. Nor were hands laid upon the Ethiopian; yet, even if we ignore the suggestion made above that the allusion to his 'rejoicing' implies that he had received the Spirit,[2] we cannot suppose that he went on his way without that gift of the Spirit which differentiated Christian Baptism from Johannine, especially as he would apparently have had no further opportunity of obtaining it.[3] We have already noticed other instances in Acts where no sign is afforded of any other ceremony being added to the Baptism of converts, and the Pauline Epistles certainly give no indication of such a rite having been practised when they speak of the baptized as possessing the indwelling Spirit of God.[4]

Many explanations have been advanced to account for this

---

[1] But see Lowther Clarke, *Liturgy and Worship*, p. 445.
[2] p. 65.
[3] Chrysostom, who did not read the Western text of Acts viii. 37, certainly held that the Ethiopian received the Spirit (*hom.* 19, 1, 2 *in Acts* (9, 154A–155B)).
[4] Rom. v. 5, viii. 9; 1 Cor. xii. 13; etc.

apparent contradiction in Acts. The authors mentioned above have for the most part taken the view that Luke regards the laying on of hands for the reception of the Spirit as so regular and indispensable a complement to Baptism that he does not always feel called upon to mention it. Of this theory Dr. Rawlinson justly remarks that it is unconvincing.[1] It certainly fails to account for what would on this view be the odd case of the Ethiopian. To bring his baptism into line with this interpretation it would presumably be necessary to suppose that Philip laid his hands upon him; but if that were the case, the narrative of the visit of Peter and John to Samaria becomes well-nigh inexplicable. The other difficulty often alleged against the above hypothesis, namely, that St. Paul received the laying on of hands from one who was not an apostle, does not, I believe, really arise, for, as we shall see later, Ananias *was* commissioned as an apostle for this particular task.

A variant of this theory maintains that the words βάπτισμα, βαπτίζειν, in their Christian use signify more than water-baptism, and that in fact they stand for the entire initiatory rite and its performance, this rite being held to include the imposition of hands. To this it may be replied that there is absolutely no evidence to support it, so far as the New Testament is concerned; on the contrary, if our view be correct of the relation between the Christian rite, the Baptism of Jesus, and John's baptism, it follows that the meaning of βάπτισμα and βαπτίζειν remains constant in all three, so far as the outward ceremony is concerned. We shall see later that there is some, though relatively little, evidence of a comprehensive use of these words from time to time by the Fathers to denote a complex rite of initiation, but for the apostolic age there is none to make us believe that the etymology of the words was ever so far strained as to admit of a wider significance than that of dipping in water.

Leenhardt[2] suggests that the Church found ready to hand in the Old Testament the ceremony of laying on of hands as a sign of benediction and of the transmission of the Spirit for the purpose of the accomplishment of a particular task, that it was thought desirable to bring this rite into connection with

---

[1] *Christian Initiation*, p. 19.   [2] *Le Baptême chrétien*, 1945, pp. 38–9.

the baptismal bestowal of the Spirit, that it began to be assumed that it constituted a separate rite of the gift of the Spirit,
especially when the Spirit was conceived in terms of external
manifestations, and, that if on particular occasions such as at
Samaria these manifestations did not appear, this rite would be
put into effect in the hope that, to put it crudely, it would
'work' where Baptism had failed to produce the expected
result.

Cullmann[1] believes that the imposition of hands was introduced as a symbol of the bestowal of the Spirit because the
ceremony of water-dipping, at any rate when considered apart
from the Baptism of Jesus, seemed inappropriate for this particular purpose. Hence Christian initiation soon came to be
in danger of breaking apart into two separate rites, namely,
Baptism itself, signifying purification from sin, and the laying
on of hands, denoting the positive gift of the Spirit. This tendency, an anticipation of what was to happen later, reached
its highest point of development in Acts viii. 12–17, and xix. 1–7.
The Johannine literature, on this view, exhibits a counter-
tendency towards a unification of the rite once again.[2] Büchsel[3]
holds that the laying on of hands is a very early part of the
initiation ceremony, but that it is relatively unimportant and
must not be regarded as a separate rite for the bestowal of the
Spirit, as opposed to Baptism, the symbol of cleansing.

Behm[4] is inclined to fall back on the somewhat desperate
expedient of a two-source theory of the composition of Acts viii.
1–25, one representing a story of Philip baptizing in Samaria,
and the other a narrative of a visit to the same area by Peter and
John, a visit which was accompanied by manifestations of the
Spirit and the rebuke of Simon Magus. The editorial link
between the two sources would then be formed by Acts. viii. 14.

A possible explanation of the difficulty lies in the great
importance which the conversion of Samaritans possessed for
the development and further expansion of the Church. At this
turning-point in the mission something else was required in
addition to the ordinary Baptism of the converts. It had to be
demonstrated to the Samaritans beyond any shadow of doubt

[1] *Rev. de Phil. et Théol.* 30, pp. 121 ff.   [2] John iii. 3–5; 1 John v. 6.
[3] *Op. cit.*, p. 262.   [4] *Op. cit.*, pp. 24 ff.

that they had really become members of the Church, in fellowship with its original 'pillars'. They could not be sure that they had indeed been accepted into the Christian body until the Jerusalem Church had sent down its two chief leaders on a mission to inspect the new work, just as it later despatched Barnabas on a similar visit to Antioch to examine, and, if he approved of it, to give its official blessing to the evangelism of Gentiles.[1]

Until the fact had been demonstrated that the leaders of the Church were in full accord with Philip, and that the Samaritan converts were really acknowledged and accepted by the heads of the original apostolic body, the gift of the Spirit which was received through membership of the Spirit-possessed community was withheld. An unprecedented situation demanded quite exceptional methods.

This theory has the advantage of explaining how it came about that, though we are given to understand that the normal convert in other places received the Spirit in Baptism, no manifestation of the Spirit's presence took place at Samaria until the people had been granted this most certain sign of their genuine acceptance into the fellowship. The imposition of hands is then primarily a token of fellowship and solidarity; it is only secondarily an effective symbol of the gift of the Spirit; it becomes such a symbol solely in virtue of being a sign of incorporation into the Church of the Spirit.[2]

We must, however, look a little further than this for our explanation, for, although this hypothesis may account for the events at Samaria, it will not help us to explain the imposition of hands by Ananias upon St. Paul, nor that which he himself administered to 'certain disciples' at Ephesus. Dix suggests a possible clue when he interprets the evidence of Acts as showing that what was really being done in the laying on of hands was an ordination of prophets.[3] The use of this symbol in commis-

---

[1] Acts xi. 22 ff.

[2] Mr. N. Q. King points out that this interpretation provides a 'psychological' explanation of the delay in the Spirit's manifestation. Until the great Apostles arrived in person, the long-standing prejudice and bitterness of Samaritan against Jew may have hindered the converts subconsciously from entering into the possession of the Spirit and its accompanying 'joy', in spite of the preaching and miracles of Philip.

[3] *Confirmation or the Laying on of Hands?* p. 18.

sioning men for an office, particularly as deputies or successors of those who already possessed the office in question, was perfectly natural.[1] It was frequently employed in the Old Testament as a sign of blessing,[2] and, especially in the sacrificial ritual,[3] of identification (in some sense at least) of the offerer with the victim; so it could come to be used in the commissioning of a person to be the representative or successor of another.[4] This commissioning might involve a transference of the Spirit by contact from the Spirit-possessed ordainer to the ordained.[5] The use of this practice as a sign and means of establishing contact and personal identification is clearly the reason for its employment by Jesus and others in performing healings. It also signifies contact between an individual and a corporate body which commissions him or gives him an official status as one of its members, so that we are not surprised to meet it in the ceremony of the appointment of a Rabbi. It is found in the pagan world with a not dissimilar significance in the coronation of the ancient kings of Rome.[6] In the New Testament, in addition to its use in healing and blessing, the laying on of hands is employed in the delegation of a particular office or the commissioning of men to do a particular task on behalf of some person or persons.[7]

I believe that Dix is correct in connecting these passages of Acts with some kind of 'ordination' or with something akin to ordination, at least in certain respects: it is not, however, likely that they refer to an ordination of prophets. If prophets were commissioned by the Church, which seems improbable (the charisma of prophecy was an obvious and unmistakable manifestation of the Spirit, which a man either did or did not possess; if he did possess it, nothing remained to the Church but to test his moral character and receive him with all honour), the form which their ordination would naturally assume would be anointing with oil, in accordance with Old Testament precedent.[8] It might be argued that the parallel adduced by Dix (the imposition of hands with which in the *Ascension of Isaiah* (vi. 3–5) the disciples of Elisha are incorporated into the

---

[1] e.g. Acts vi. 6.   [2] Cf. Gen. xlviii. 13–14.   [3] Lev. iii. 8, xvi. 21,
[4] Num. xxvii. 23.   [5] Deut. xxxiv. 9.   [6] Livy 1, 18, 7.
[7] Acts xiii. 3.   [8] 1 Kings xix. 16.

prophetic body and receive the Spirit of prophecy) suggests that a prophet might 'transfer' his charisma to another by this means; but Peter and John are not prophets, and it would in any case be unsafe to rely upon this relatively late book as a guide to first-century practice. Further, neither the Samaritans nor St. Paul are explicitly said to have prophesied, as the Ephesians did, when hands had been laid upon them, although in the former case it is certainly true that the Spirit is manifested in visible signs which are sufficiently striking to impress Simon Magus as a first-class piece of magic.

We must bear in mind, once again, that for St. Luke the Spirit's primary work is the furtherance of the Church's worldwide mission; charismata such as prophecy and 'tongues' are bestowed for that purpose. The original nucleus of the Church received the Spirit in the most striking and dramatic way at Pentecost, and at every turning-point in the missionary enterprise something in the nature of a Pentecostal manifestation of the Spirit recurs. The key to the interpretation of these episodes seems to lie here. The preaching of the Gospel in Samaria represented a crucial moment in the advance of Christianity. Hence, after the Baptism of the first Samaritan converts, the leaders of the Church's mission come down from Jerusalem and, by the sign of fellowship and 'contact' incorporate them into the apostolic (i.e. missionary) Church, with the result that there occurs a Samaritan 'Pentecost', at least to the extent that visible signs are manifested of the outpouring of the Spirit. It may not be too much to assert that this event is meant to demonstrate that a new nucleus of the missionary Church has been established, and to suggest that Luke's readers are intended to infer that the Gospel proceeded to radiate outwards from this new centre of the Spirit's mission.

Similarly, St. Paul is given the sign of fellowship and 'identification' from Ananias who, having seen the Lord and been 'sent' by Him,[1] is, for the purpose of meeting Paul, a duly commissioned Apostle. In this case, it is true, one purpose of the imposition of hands was the healing of St. Paul's blindness; but this was clearly not its sole object. St. Paul receives the Spirit, and that Luke as usual conceives this as the 'missionary' Spirit

[1] Acts ix. 10, 17.

is shown by the fact that he tells us that Paul immediately *preached with power*.[1] He is, in fact, associated, through fellowship with an apostle, in the missionary or apostolic work of the Church.[2] That the baptism of Saul of Tarsus was a critical moment in the history of the Gentile mission is scarcely in doubt, nor yet that as a convert he proved to be a new centre and focus of that mission and an agent through whom the Spirit was to achieve fresh advances. The conversion of St. Paul and his incorporation into the Pentecostal mission of the Spirit in the Church is therefore parallel, in its own much greater degree, to the conversion of Samaria.

We know, of course, that St. Paul himself regarded his assumption into the apostolic body as directly effected by the Lord without any human intermediary at all. Had he not been commissioned by the Lord as a missionary of the Gospel? The Jerusalem Church, however, no doubt viewed the matter in quite another light, and St. Luke's conception of St. Paul's apostleship is very different from that with which we are confronted in the Epistles. It is possible that the episode recorded in Gal. ii. 9 when Paul and Barnabas received the 'right hands of fellowship' from the 'pillars' of the Jerusalem Church may have looked from the Jerusalem side like another formal association of these two missionaries in the apostolic task for which the Spirit had been poured out. We might almost have expected that the 'right hands' would have been laid on their heads instead of clasped in their own hands, for as a sign of greeting and fellowship the handshake was uncommon among Jews, and so rare among Christians that it came to be adopted as a secret sign by the Manichaeans;[3] but this was a solemn pact or agreement, and not an ordinary bestowal of a blessing, commissioning, or an act of identification. The laying of hands on these same two leaders of the mission by the prophets and teachers at Antioch does, on the other hand, represent a formal act of association in the missionary enterprise; in this case they are commissioned as representatives of a Church for a particular task.

---

[1] Acts ix. 20, 22, 27.
[2] How far Luke's account is historically accurate does not here concern us.
[3] Hegem., *A. Arch.*, 7 (*GCS.* p. 11, 2).

It therefore seems probable that the laying on of hands by Ananias, which preceded St. Paul's baptism (partly, at least, because the action was in one aspect an act of healing, and St. Paul had to recover his sight before he could well be baptized) and, to a lesser extent, the imposition of hands upon him and Barnabas at Antioch, represent association and 'personal contact' between the possessors of the Spirit which operated in the Church's missionary task and the new missionary who was beginning to take part in it. It is an action parallel in its symbolism to the imposition of hands upon the Seven.[1] In the latter case, the men who are thus formally associated with the apostles as their representatives are already 'full of the Spirit';[2] the laying on of hands therefore does not convey 'the gift of the Spirit' in the baptismal sense, but the Seven evidently receive (or rather, Stephen and Philip evidently receive) what Luke regards as the distinctive mode of the Spirit's activity in the missionary enterprise—the Spirit of power which confirms the word of God with signs and wonders.[3] The imposition of hands upon St. Paul may also be parallel to the use of the rite mentioned in the Pastoral Epistles. The meaning of χεῖρας ταχέως μηδένι ἐπιτίθει, μηδὲ κοινώνει ἁμαρτίαις ἀλλοτρίαις[4] remains most obscure. It is, however, conceivable that it refers to association in the apostolic or missionary labour, in the sense that Timothy is not to associate men with himself hastily and indiscriminately to be his representatives in his evangelistic work. Such conduct could result only in Timothy's own identification with their sins. A commissioning of this sort had been given to Timothy himself with the laying on of the hands of the senior men of the Church (the πρεσβυτέριον), 'through prophecy'.[5] No doubt prophets, who, like the apostles, possessed the Spirit of the missionary endeavour, played a large part in commissioning preachers of the Gospel in the name of the missionary Church.[6] In Timothy's case the charisma of the Spirit takes the particular form of reading, exhortation, and teaching; that is to say, it expresses itself in the exercise of a function midway between those of an apostolic preacher and an *episcopos*. In 2 Tim. i. 6 the charisma which is in Timothy through the

[1] Acts vi. 6.　　　[2] Acts vi. 3.　　　[3] Acts vi. 8, viii. 6.
[4] 1 Tim. v. 22.　　[5] 1 Tim. iv. 14.　　[6] Cf. Acts xiii. 1–3.

imposition of St. Paul's hands is again mentioned, being described as πνεῦμα δυνάμεως καὶ ἀγάπης καὶ σωφρονισμοῦ, which is to give him confidence for the μαρτύριον of our Lord.

We may therefore be right in seeing in the laying of hands on the Samaritans and St. Paul something more akin to Ordination than to Confirmation, but which takes the particular form of the association with the missionary, apostolic, ministry of new members to join in the work. It is at these two important turning-points in the Gentile mission that Luke draws attention to the practice.

There is one such turning-point, however, which is, in Luke's eyes, of such supreme importance as to demand a direct and immediate descent of the Spirit. Two special revelations were necessary to bring St. Peter to the house of the Gentile Cornelius; to remove all doubt that it was the will of God that these Gentiles should be brought into the Church, something more than the normal reception of the Spirit in Baptism was needed. Nor would an outward sign of the identification of the Gentiles with the leader of the apostles through the laying on of hands be sufficient to mark this climax of the mission; there could be nothing less than a direct descent of the Spirit, producing the unmistakable external sign of 'speaking with tongues'.[1] The situation is unique, and, as we remarked previously, in no way typical of the relation of the bestowal of the Spirit to Baptism; in this case it appears likely that no baptism would have been administered unless there had first been this divine intervention.[2]

The episode of the 'disciples' at Ephesus[3] is rather more difficult to understand. That they were Christian disciples seems highly probable. The absolute use of the word μαθητής (in view of its many occurrences in Acts) can scarcely indicate anything else, nor, despite the alleged support afforded by John i. 20–23 (the 'Ephesian Gospel'), is there any real reason to suppose the existence of a Johannine sect at Ephesus or indeed anywhere else outside Palestine in the first century. In all probability these men were converts of Apollos, who was presumably

[1] Acts x. 44–7.   [2] Acts x. 47.
[3] Acts xix. 1–7; the interpretation of this incident is somewhat confused by Luke's desire to draw a parallel between the activities of St. Paul and St. Peter—in this case St. Peter's dealings with the Samaritans.

a very early follower of Jesus, 'knowing only the baptism of John'—i.e. the baptism of expectation of the period before Pentecost. When the disciples are baptized by St. Paul in the name of the Lord Jesus they receive from him the laying on of hands, and the Holy Spirit comes upon them.

Once again, the solution to the apparent contradiction between this procedure and the normal practice of Baptism is perhaps to be found in the fact that this is another decisive moment in the missionary history. Next to Antioch, in fact in succession to Antioch, Ephesus is the centre of the Gentile mission, the headquarters where St. Paul makes his longest stay, and the centre from which missionary activity radiates into Asia Minor and St. Paul's emissaries visit his churches at Corinth and elsewhere. The planting of the Faith in this centre is clearly an event of immense importance, and it is natural that the first converts (who were already 'disciples', but so far from receiving an endowment of the Spirit for participation in the mission had never yet heard that the eschatological expectation of the Spirit had been fulfilled) should become a nucleus and focus of this new Church, the strategic centre of the Pauline preaching. They are accordingly given the token of their incorporation into the apostolic ministry represented by St. Paul himself, and the Spirit which guides and directs the Church's mission is manifested in them by the visible signs of 'tongues' and prophecy. They are made sharers in the active 'apostolicity' of the Church as soon as they have been incorporated into Christ by Baptism.

The laying on of hands, then, is a sign of association in the apostolic or missionary task of the Church. We are left in ignorance whether such non-missionary ministries as local presbyters, episcopi (unless Timothy be reckoned as such), or deacons, received this token in the apostolic age. The ordination of the Seven is no real guide in the matter of deacons, for in actual fact they, or at least the only two of whom we hear anything, perform the function, not of deacons, but of apostles. Indeed, the κοινωνία expressed in the imposition of hands seems, so far as our explicit information goes, to have been confined to 'apostolic men', including the 'first-fruits' of the great new advances in the Church's progress. It may be compared with the blessing given to the original apostles by the 'lifting up of hands', when the risen Lord commissioned them for the apostolic task of witness. In the latter case, of course, the manifestation of the Spirit did not take place immediately, but had to await the completion of the number of the apostles and the final exaltation of the risen Lord.

A mention of the same rite, of a rather different character, occurs in the Epistle to the Hebrews.[1] Here it is alluded to in very close connection with βαπτισμῶν διδαχή. Unless the imposition of hands should be referred to some kind of ordination ceremony (which in this particular case is unlikely to be correct, since ordination would scarcely figure in a list of the first principles of Christian doctrine and practice) we must assume that what had been a special ceremony of the commissioning of new members for the missionary work of the apostolic Church, carrying with it, as its inward effect, a particular endowment of the Spirit for that work, had become, at any rate in certain circles, a common practice associated with the ordinary rite of Baptism. The passage is, however, hard to understand. The meaning of βαπτισμῶν is something of a puzzle; it certainly does not refer to separate 'water' and 'Spirit' baptisms; and the word for the Christian sacrament in the Bible is elsewhere always βάπτισμα, and not βαπτισμός. Probably Dr. Rawlinson is right[2] in his suggestion that it denotes many kinds of lustration, Jewish, Johannine, and pagan, as well as the Christian Baptism which the διδαχή enabled catechumens to learn about and to distinguish from the other rites which might appear to the uninstructed to be very similar.

If the allusion to the laying on of hands is really to be connected with Baptism, as the Greek suggests, we may perhaps suppose that the ceremony of fellowship and identification in the apostolic task has come to be applied to ordinary converts to indicate their association with the existing society of the Church by the symbolism of the laying on of the hands of the congregation's leaders or leader.[3] Although there is no hint that

[1] vi. 2.   [2] Op. cit., p. 20 n.
[3] If this ceremony was carried out in early times by a collegiate episcopate, each 'bishop' would presumably lay one hand only on the candidate's head. It would be physically difficult for several men to lay two hands at the same time. The use of the singular manus in most Latin references to the rite may represent a survival of

the ceremony was believed to be directly related to an endowment of the Spirit, and although it would be entirely subsidiary
to Baptism, the essential rite of incorporation into Christ, it
would be a highly significant piece of symbolism, signifying the
converts' entry, through their baptismal union with Christ,
into the community of His Body, and marking their fellowship
with the brethren in the active tasks of Church life. The ceremony would be a most natural one, almost corresponding to
the handshake with which a new member would be received
by the president of a modern society.

If we now pause to consider what light the New Testament
references to the laying on of hands throw upon the nature and
history of the rite of Confirmation, we may conclude, first, that
there is little evidence to be found there for the belief that the
imposition of hands was a regular ceremony universally employed in the apostolic Church, either in the form of a separate
rite distinct from Baptism, or as a particular moment in a complex ceremony of initiation. Secondly, after making all due
allowance for the fact that almost all our information about the
practice comes from St. Luke, with his own individual conception of the Church's mission and the activity of the Spirit in
relation to it,[1] we may reasonably infer that its meaning is
related to that of ordination, but that this particular ordination
is of a peculiar kind; it is a ceremony of laying on of hands
accompanying prayer, by which a man is constituted a sharer
in the apostolicity of the apostles of Christ; it is the sign by
which he receives a special endowment of the Holy Spirit who
guided and directed the Church's activity in carrying out the
Lord's command to bear witness to the Gospel throughout the
world. It is a commissioning for active service in the missionary
enterprise, through which there are bestowed the special
missionary charismata of prophecy, 'tongues', and the power
to perform signs and wonders, to which may be added, if it is
legitimate to associate the imposition of hands referred to in the

old terminology. It is possible, if Apollos (cf. Manson, *Bull. John Ryl. Lib.* 32. 1,
1949) or someone connected with his converts wrote Hebrews, that Heb. vi. 2 is
related to Acts xix. 1–7.

[1] It is, however, over-pessimistic to conclude with B. S. Easton that 'the only
answer (to the problem of Luke's conception of the Holy Spirit in relation to
Baptism) is that Luke never thought about the matter at all' (*The Purpose of Acts*,
p. 40).

Pastoral Epistles with that which is described in Acts, the gifts of exhortation and teaching.

The obscure language of the Epistle to the Hebrews, more-over, might afford some ground for the belief that the rite was in regular use in some places, that it was connected with Baptism, and that it was sufficiently firmly established in some quarters to become included in the basic elementary features of Christianity in which converts were instructed. The total lack of evidence for such a ceremony in the century following St. Paul's death[1] must, however, tell heavily against the view that it was generally practised in the apostolic age as a regular rite of 'Confirmation' throughout the Church Catholic. We must not, of course, expect to find uniformity of baptismal practice in the primitive Church, or, indeed, in the Church of the second century, and it is always possible that a rite such as the imposi-tion of hands may have been employed in a local church with-out becoming widely accepted; but the evidence of the New Testament, with the possible exception of Hebrews, does not suggest that this happened in the case of this particular cere-mony. Acts has the peculiar missionary situation of the primi-tive Church always in mind, and must be read in that particular context; it is most unlikely that its account of baptismal prac-tice is really self-contradictory, or that St. Luke has simply reproduced information contained in different sources emana-ting from divergent local church traditions; he shapes his material with far too great care to allow discrepancies to remain in his narrative. It is when Acts comes to be read outside its missionary context by late second century writers who try to relate it to the changed circumstances of their own day that its account of the laying on of hands is misinterpreted as a description of Confirmation. The importance attached to the imposition of hands at Baptism by such authors as Tertullian is directly due to their reading of Acts, and their assumption that it taught that the Christian experience of the Spirit, in the full sense in which St. Paul had spoken of it, was really mediated

[1] Representations in early Christian art of an imposition of hands (Wilpert, *Die Malereien der Katakomben Roms*, pl. 39, 57, 223.2, 240.1) seem to show the baptizer holding his hand on the candidate's head *during* the baptism; they thus have no bearing on Confirmation, but may exhibit a resemblance between Chris-tian and Jewish practice (cf. *Yeb.*, 46a).

to the faithful in every case through the imposition of hands. They felt obliged to try to reconcile what they took to be the meaning of Scripture in these texts of Acts with the entirely different doctrine of the Spirit's bestowal which they found elsewhere in the New Testament and, in the main, embodied in the accepted baptismal tradition. The reason why the confusion of thought which was thereby created arose only at this relatively late period is due to the fact that Acts was apparently little read during the greater part of the second century.[1]

As we shall see later, when subsidiary ceremonies come to be attached to Baptism as part of an increasingly complex rite of initiation, and some sign other than Baptism itself comes to be regarded as the special channel of the gift of the Spirit, the particular ceremony which acquires this significance is chrismation, and not primarily the laying on of hands, although the latter often comes to be artificially identified with chrismation in order that the established rite of anointing may be able to claim the Scriptural warrant of those passages which mention the imposition of hands.

The conclusion would seem to follow that the laying on of hands described in Acts has little or no direct connection with the use of the same sign in Confirmation today, nor has it anything to do with the Pauline 'seal of the Spirit'. On the other hand, the ceremony is by no means confined by the Bible to its use as a sign of fellowship in the evangelistic activity of the apostolic Church. It stands for blessings of all types, and for many and various expressions of contact and 'solidarity', as well as for commissionings of different kinds, with the gift of power to fulfil them, and for the communication of bodily and mental healing. Later in the Church's history it is employed in the reconciliation of penitents as a mark of restored fellowship with the Body of Christ. We may not unreasonably believe that the Church has been rightly guided in its use of this ceremony as the outward sign in Confirmation, a rite for whose administration we cannot find direct Scriptural instructions, for it is a singularly appropriate symbol, in our modern situation, of the incorporation of those baptized in infancy into the κοινωνία of conscious and active Church life. The confirmed person is not,

---

[1] Cf. Dix, *Confirmation or the Laying on of Hands?* p. 18.

it is true, associated in the apostolic mission of the Jerusalem disciples with its Spirit-manifestations of glossolalia, prophecy, and miracle; but through the prayer and blessing of the bishop as the representative leader of the Church he is brought within the sphere of its continuous apostolic mission to evangelize the world with the Gospel of the Kingdom. In the case of those baptized as adults, the ceremony, preferably administered as an integral part of the Baptism service, may be held to denote the 'solidarity' of the new members with the bishop (and through him with the whole Church) which has resulted from their Baptism into Christ. They too are made participants in the evangelistic activity of the apostolic Church, so that the ancient sign still retains something of its original significance, enough indeed to warrant the claim that it is 'after the example of the holy Apostles' that the bishop lays his hands upon the candidates in Confirmation. It is much to be regretted that this slight allusion to Acts viii. 14–17 in the 1662 Prayer Book should have received in the 1928 Book the addition of a Preface to the Confirmation Service which includes the reading of the entire passage describing the visit of Peter and John to Samaria, an episode which in all probability has no direct relevance to the Service at all.

On the question whether unction was employed in apostolic times as a supplementary rite to Baptism we need say little. The passages which expressly mention anointing in connection with the reception of the Holy Spirit[1] clearly refer, as we have seen, to the Messianic unction of Jesus[2] which His baptized followers are enabled to share through being made members of the Christ. An outward act of anointing would be a natural piece of symbolism by which to convey to the newly baptized the truth that they had become χριστοί in the Christ and had been made, in Him, a 'royal priesthood', and the ordinary use of oil in washing would lend itself readily to a symbolical interpretation in connection with the bath of Baptism; there is no evidence that this act was in fact carried out in New Testament times.[3] The contrary view can be supported only by the

[1] 2 Cor. i. 21–2; 1 John ii. 20, 27.
[2] Cf. Luke iv. 18; Acts iv. 27, x. 38; Heb. i. 9.
[3] As Basil recognized (*Spir.*, 27, 66).

supposition that the practice of much later times, as reflected in the *Apostolic Tradition* of Hippolytus, really represents a continuous liturgical tradition from the primitive Church; but such an assumption would be dangerous in the extreme. It is true, of course, that we know very little of how things were actually done in the apostolic Church. It is conceivable that liturgical practice was more fully developed than our documents, when they are taken as a whole, suggest; for example, it is possible that I Peter ii. 2 implies that an administration of milk to catechumens took place after Baptism at the time when this epistle was written. It seems, however, all the more remarkable that, if it were practised, no reference should be made to chrismation in documents which were accepted as canonical because they were recognized as embodying the authentic apostolic tradition. If our interpretation of the New Testament conception of Baptism be correct, no such rite would, in any case, be regarded in the primitive Church as conveying the bestowal of the Spirit, which is but one aspect of the Baptism into Christ whose outward sign was water and not oil.

It remains for us to consider rather more fully whether the theory that the 'seal of the Spirit' should be identified with a Confirmation rite can be justified from an analogy between Jewish and Christian methods of initiation. The view that Confirmation is the New Testament counterpart of circumcision under the Old Covenant was advanced by Seeberg,[1] Stromberg,[2] and others, and it has been strongly advocated by Dix who, following up the line of investigation laid down by F. Gavin,[3] finds a very close and detailed parallel between the initiatory rites of the two religions.

The rite by which the Jewish proselyte was admitted into membership of Israel consisted of the following principal ceremonies. Preliminary questions were addressed to the candidate, testing his motives; he then received a brief instruction on certain moral and ceremonial obligations of the Law. This part may be likened to a kind of rudimentary catechumenate. It was apparently followed by circumcision. Later the convert

---

[1] *Der Katechismus der Urchristenheit*, p. 232 f.
[2] *Studien zur Theorie u. Praxis der Taufe*, p. 158.
[3] *The Jewish Antecedents of the Christian Sacraments*, p. 26 f.

baptizes himself in the presence of witnesses, is greeted on his emergence from the water as a genuine Israelite, and utters his first benediction, a thanksgiving for baptism.[1] These two rites were, generally speaking, the indispensable elements in the initiation, and although the necessity of baptism was a matter of rabbinical argument, it was probably of great importance from a practical point of view, both because the number of women proselytes no doubt exceeded that of the men, and because, since baptism was the easier rite, it might be to the advantage of proselytising among the Gentiles if it received greater emphasis than circumcision—a point which is suggested by the fact that one of the earliest pieces of evidence for the practice of baptism comes from a Gentile source.[2]

A third element in the procedure was the offering of a sacrifice by the new convert, but this was not indispensable, and it was in any case probably a merely ideal or theoretical regulation, since there is no real evidence that this complex of ceremonies dates back to the days of the Temple.

Of these rites, circumcision was the vitally important ceremony of entry into the Covenant, and, as we have already remarked, it constituted the 'seal' upon the people of God, the mark of His ownership distinguishing them from the unclean heathen who stood without the Law; baptism was a lustration for the removal of the ceremonial uncleanness of heathenism; the sacrifice was an expiatory rite, itself also intended as a purification from uncleanness,[3] whose offering was necessary before the proselyte could take part in the festivals, and, in particular, join in the Passover celebration.

Considered individually, these rites are quite unlike Christian initiation. Both in their outward aspect and in their inner significance they lie poles apart from the Christian rite which springs from the Messianic Baptism of Jesus. Circumcision, other than the 'true circumcision of the spirit' such as the prophets foretold, is not likened to Baptism by the New Testament writers, but contrasted with it.[4] The view of Coppens, Umberg, and others, that circumcision is the equivalent of Confirmation,

[1] See *Gerim* (text and transl., G. Poster: *Angelos* 2 (1926), pp. 1–38), *Yeb.*, 47; *Pesach.*, 7b; cf. *Berach.*, 51a.
[2] Arrian, *Epict.*, 2, 9.   [3] Moore, *Judaism*, i, pp. 332–4.
[4] Col. ii. 11; cf. John vii. 22–3.

and that perhaps the 'council of Jerusalem' may have authorized the substitution of the latter rite for the circumcision which
it declared to be unnecessary for Gentiles, is entirely without
foundation, and represents a complete misunderstanding of the
point of the circumcision controversy; it was not to be solved by
the simple expedient of merely replacing one legalistic ceremony by another. To interpret Acts xv. 8 as an allusion to Confirmation and its adoption in place of circumcision is merely
perverse; circumcision had nothing to do with the Spirit, and
the reception of the Spirit by St. Peter's converts was not
mediated by any sort of 'Confirmation'.

Dix, in his anxiety to establish the equation, 'circumcision
in the Old Covenant=confirmation in the New', asserts that
the *Apostolic Tradition's* prohibition against participation by
catechumens in the Eucharistic worship of the faithful, 'is of
course the Jewish proscription of the uncircumcised Gentile'.[1]
Why this perfectly natural and commonsense regulation should
have to be assigned to a Jewish source it is hard to understand;
yet we are asked to accept this quite unwarranted assertion as
a valid piece of evidence for the arbitrary assumption that
Confirmation replaced circumcision, an assumption which has
ranged against it the general weight of early patristic opinion.
Ephrem, it is true, compares circumcision with the 'seal' of
chrismation,[2] but by his time consignation with chrism has become widely established as the particular part of the initiation
rite by which the Spirit is believed to be bestowed; it has
therefore been identified with the Pauline 'seal', and the analogy of the covenant sign of the Old Testament naturally
suggests itself. For the period nearer to the apostolic age the
evidence is clear that it was *Baptism* which was believed to
have been foreshadowed by the circumcision which it superseded.

'Barnabas' for example, explains the fulfilment by Baptism
of the type of circumcision,[3] and Justin asks, τίς οὖν ἔτι μοι
περιτομῆς λόγος ὑπὸ τοῦ θεοῦ μαρτυρηθέντι; τίς ἐκείνου τοῦ βαπτίσματος χρεία ἁγίῳ πνεύματι βεβαπτισμένῳ.[4] There is no reason to
suppose that Justin intends an allusion to any other rite of

---

[1] *Confirmation or the Laying on of Hands?* p. 7.
[2] *Hymn. Epiph.*, 3, 2–4.   [3] *Barn.*, 9, 6.   [4] *dial.*, 29, 1; cf. *ibid.*, 43.

Spirit-baptism than the Christian sacrament whose outward
sign is water, and whose inward effect is the bestowal of the
Spirit.[1] The *Odes of Solomon* contain the same comparison of
circumcision with Baptism;[2] Lactantius relates the superses-
sion of the old rite by Baptism to the Baptism of Jesus.[3]
Cyril of Jerusalem points out the parallel between these two
rites, and it is to be noticed that it is in the actual water-
baptism (λουτρόν) that the Holy Spirit 'circumcises' the convert[4]—a thought which resembles that of Aphraates when he
says that in the New Covenant, 'those who are circumcised in
their hearts have life, and are circumcised in the true Jordan,
the baptism of remission of sins'[5]—hence Baptism is the real
fulfilment of circumcision.[6] This equation of Baptism as New
Testament antitype with circumcision as Old Testament type
is very frequently met with in the Fathers, Augustine, for
example, remarking that under the old covenant circumcision
was reckoned for Baptism.[7]

Apart from the patristic commentators, the evidence of the
New Testament on this point is clear enough. In Col. ii. 11
St. Paul plainly contrasts circumcision with the spiritual circumcision in Christ effected through Baptism.[8] The argument
here is in any case *ad homines*, and the opposition of the two rites
is artificial; elsewhere, as in Rom. ii. 25 and Eph. ii. 11, circumcision is contrasted with the new dispensation of grace
without reference to any rite at all.

[1] See E. C. Ratcliff, *Theology*, April 1948, pp. 133-9.
[2] 11, 10.
[3] *inst.*, 4, 15 (*CSEL*. p. 329, 14) : 'Tinctus est ab Iohanne . . . ut lavacro spiritali
peccata non sua . . . sed carnis quam gerebat aboleret, ut quemadmodum Iudaeos
suscepta circumcisione, sic etiam gentes baptismo, id est purifici roris perfusione
salvaret.'
[4] *catech.*, 5, 6.   [5] *dem.*, 11, 10.
[6] *ibid.*, 12, 6; see Koch, *Taufe u. Askese in der alten ostsyrischen Kirche*, ZNTW.
1911, pp. 37 ff.
[7] 'Circumcisio antiquis sanctis pro baptismo fuisse creditur,' *ep.*, 187, 11, 34;
cf. *pecc. orig.*, 32, 37; *Julian*, 6, 7, 18; cf. also, 'Quia enim patri Abrahae carnaliter
nascentis filii signaculum circumcisionis corporale fuit, ita et eorum qui spiritaliter
nascuntur, spiritale signum est circumcisio cordis,' Ps. Aug. *Qu. V. et N.T.*, 48, 50
(i.e. the antitype of circumcision in the New Covenant is the spiritual circumcision
of the heart and not any external rite, though the inward circumcision is linked
with the spiritual birth of Baptism).
[8] In this text συνταφέντες, is clearly explanatory of the περιετμήθητε περιτομῇ
ἀχειροποιήτῳ of the previous verse. Yet Dix argues that the order in which
spiritual circumcision and Baptism are mentioned indicates that the former refers
to an actual rite (of Confirmation) which preceded Baptism! (*Op. cit.*, p. 9.)

Jewish baptism is so far removed from the Christian sacrament in its meaning (being a ceremonial washing away of ritual uncleanness, and only a part of the ceremonies by which a convert entered the covenant people) that it is unlikely to have exercised any great influence upon the latter. Christian practice in both the sacraments seems to have been derived mainly from the example of Jesus and the reading of the Old Testament, and not from the ceremonies of contemporary Judaism, though no doubt the latter were a contributory factor in the development of the Christian rites, and Dix has pointed out certain affinities between the sacramental procedure of the *Apostolic Tradition* and Jewish ritual.

Thus, there is very little warrant for the supposition that early Christian Baptism was self-administered like that of the Jews. B. S. Easton,[1] it is true, calls attention to the use of the middle voice of βαπτίζειν in Acts xxii. 16 and as a variant reading in 1 Cor. x. 2, and suggests that these passages represent an archaic form of the Christian rite, originating before the final break with Judaism. In the former passage, however, in which St. Paul describes the divine command to himself to be baptized, the use of the middle voice, βάπτισαι, is obviously due to its combination with the following words, ἀπόλουσαι τὰς ἁμαρτίας σου. If the precise meaning of the Greek is to be pressed, it is surely to be interpreted, 'have yourself baptized', a sense in which the middle voice of βαπτίζειν is frequently used in the Fathers, who certainly do not understand it in the reflexive sense.[2] It is, in any case, balanced by the use of the passive in Luke's account of the same incident in Acts ix. 18. In the second text mentioned above, the reference is not directly to Christian Baptism, and it is fairly evident that the meaning is not reflexive here either. The other instances of the middle voice (in variant readings), cited by Easton, do not refer to the Christian sacrament. It is true that the *Apostolic Tradition* does not specifically say that anyone actually baptizes the candidate, but the evidence of early Christian art is entirely against the theory of a primitive practice of self-baptism; the very frequent use of the *passive* of βαπτίζειν is to be taken into account; and

---

[1] *Self-Baptism, AJTh.*, 24, 1920, pp. 513–18.
[2] No Latin Father speaks of *se baptizare*, so far as I am aware.

the active verb is hardly to be explained away as meaning, 'to preside at a (self-administered) baptism'. If Baptism really was administered by the candidate, the language of St. Paul in 1 Cor. i. 13–16 would be difficult indeed to understand. On the face of it, it is unlikely that anyone could baptize himself into Christ; only Christ Himself, through the representative of His Church, can baptize a man in the Christian sense, as the early Christians must surely have been well aware.[1]

The suggested parallel between the proselyte's sacrifice and the neophyte's First Communion is far-fetched. Obviously the first action of the newcomer into the Church would be to take part in the common meal and Eucharist of the congregation he had just joined; but there is not the slightest reason to see any connection with the totally different Jewish practice. In the apostolic Church the Eucharist is not a sacrifice in any sense remotely comparable with Jewish sacrifices, and even though Hippolytus prescribes the bringing of a προσφορά by the convert for use at his first Eucharist, this action has no relationship to an expiatory sacrifice for the removal of ceremonial defilement.

It appears, then, that when we examine these supposed parallels between Jewish and early Christian ceremonies of initiation the argument that circumcision is the type or forerunner of Confirmation breaks down. There is, however, one further argument by which Dix tries to sustain it, an argument based upon the *order* of the three elements in the Jewish initiation rites. The sequence of circumcision, baptism, and sacrifice found its authority in Joshua v. 5 (where it is assumed that the

---

[1] The ordinary use of βαπτίζεται in the actual formula of administration clearly represents the passive and not the middle voice. The same tense, σφραγίζεται, is used in the later liturgies as the formula of chrismation, which no one is likely to suppose to have been self-administered (cf. Nestorian rite ap. Denziger, *Ritus Orientalium in administrandis Sacramentis*, vol. 1, p. 49, cited by Jugie, *Theol. Dogmatica Christianorum Orientalium Dissidentium*, vol. 5, p. 290). Theodore of Mopsuestia tells his catechumens that the passive formula is used in order to show that only the divine grace and not the human agent can bestow the grace of Baptism (*lib. ad Baptizandos*, Mingana, p. 59). It is true that he speaks elsewhere in this treatise of the candidate 'immersing' between the naming of each Person of the Trinity, so that, 'you immerse yourself in water three times' (*ibid.*, p. 63); but the procedure is very different from that of the Jews. The priest is the baptizer; his hand is retained on the candidate throughout, and it is of course he who pronounces the formula. In all cases where total immersion is used, the candidate must dip himself below the water at the appropriate moment; it would hardly be seemly for him to be pushed under water by main force.

Israelites were circumcised in Egypt), in the washing of the people's garments before the Sinai Covenant was made (Exod. xix. 10), and in Num. xv. 14: 'And if a stranger sojourn with you, or whosoever be among you throughout your generations, and will offer an offering made by fire, of a sweet savour unto the Lord; as ye do, so he shall do.' The emphasis laid on this last point in Num. xv. 14–16—'As ye are, so shall the stranger be before the Lord'—was evidently taken to imply the principle that the proselyte must, in a sense, enter Israel as the people had entered into the Covenant, by circumcision, washing, and sacrifice.

It is this sequence which Dix professes to see reproduced in a complex initiation rite in the primitive Church, and from this he argues that, since a sign of the gift of the Spirit preceded Baptism and stood in the same relation to it as circumcision stood to proselyte-immersion, it follows that this sign, i.e. Confirmation, can properly be regarded as the seal of the New Covenant, the seal of the Spirit.

The principal evidence adduced in support of this argument is, first, the passage in which St. Paul interprets the events of the Exodus in 1 Cor. x. 1–2: '. . . our fathers were all under the cloud, and all passed through the sea; and were all baptized unto Moses in the cloud and in the sea; and did all eat the same spiritual meat; and did all drink the same spiritual drink.' Here the 'cloud' plainly signifies the divine Presence, and Dix rightly points out that 'the Shekinah in Rabbinic teaching is closely identified with the Spirit of God';[1] but he draws a totally unwarranted inference from the text when he asserts that 'it seems that for St. Paul "Baptism in the Spirit" is something different from Baptism in water, and precedes it'.[2]

---

[1] *Op. cit.*, p. 9.

[2] On the theory that 1 Cor. x. 1–2 is evidence for an early initiatory rite, in which the 'seal', water-baptism, and the Eucharist were administered in that order, corresponding to the sequence of circumcision, baptism, and sacrifice, Dom B. Botte comments that such a rite, dating from the second century, would be a sensational discovery, for documents of the second century are rare. But the order . . . is attested by St. Paul, when he says that our fathers were baptized in the cloud and in the sea, the cloud designating the Holy Spirit; 'si l'existence de ce fameux rite ne repose que sur des indices de ce genre, j'aime autant dire d'avance que je n'y crois pas . . . S'il (Dom G. Dix) croit trouver dans S. Paul la preuve que l'on conférait le don de l'Esprit avant le baptême, je ne puis m'empêcher de croire qu'il est victime de l'esprit de système . . . On peut admirer la finesse chez autrui et préférer le bon sens pour soi-même' (*Bull. de Théol. Anc. et Med.* (Louvain) V,

As we have already observed,[1] Jeremias makes out a good case for supposing that the Pauline typology of the Exodus was suggested by the exegetical tradition of the Hillelite school; whether this be true or not, there is no reason to suppose that St. Paul is adapting the Exodus events to fit the pattern of Christian initiation, for the sequence which he is trying—not very successfully—to interpret typologically is that in which the events in question actually happened,[2] and he had to shape his exegesis accordingly.

There is no real evidence here to make us think that St. Paul actually thought of baptism in the Spirit as something independent of water-baptism and imparted to the convert under a different outward sign as a distinct moment in his experience. The whole tenor of his baptismal teaching runs counter to such a doctrine, for although he does not bind the action of the Spirit to the sacrament of Baptism, realizing as he does that the Spirit may seize, as it were, upon a man and lead him to justifying faith and so to Baptism, yet he certainly regards the gift of the Spirit as one aspect of the condition of being 'in' Christ, and this condition is always symbolized and effected in Baptism.

Another text cited as evidence for this theory of a correspondence between the order of the Jewish and Christian initiation rites is 1 Pet. i. 2: 'in sanctification of the Spirit, unto obedience and sprinkling of the blood of Jesus Christ'. Here the 'sanctification of the Spirit' is said to represent the bestowal of the Spirit upon the convert in 'Spirit-baptism' (which is certainly not what the text says), and the 'sprinkling of the blood' is arbitrarily equated with Baptism into Christ's death and resurrection. The exegesis is very strange. This preface to 1 Peter is part of the relatively small section of the book which appears to have no immediate relevance to Christian initiation, unless a rather obscure connection be discerned by way of tracing in it a reference to Isa. iv. 4 (ὅτι ἐκπλυνεῖ Κύριος τὸν ῥύπον τῶν υἱῶν . . . Σειών, καὶ τὸ αἷμα ἐκκαθαριεῖ ἐκ μέσου αὐτῶν ἐν πνεύματι κρίσεως καὶ πνεύματι καύσεως), in which case the thought would certainly be of Baptism, but it would still be hard to find

Jan.–Apr. 1949), No. 1279, reviewing Dix, 'The Seal in the Second Century, (*Theology*, 51, 1948).
[1] See above, p. 24.   [2] Exod. xiii. 21, xiv. 22, xvi. 15.

in the text any allusion to a distinct 'baptism of the Spirit'. The argument is not cogent. Stronger evidence might perhaps be adduced from 1 John v. 8, where it would be possible to claim that three successive sacramental rites were alluded to; we have, however, already endeavoured to show that this text can best be explained on other lines.[1]

More interest attaches to the suggestion that the Syrian practice of associating a chrismation (administered before Baptism) with the bestowal of the Spirit can be traced back into New Testament times. For this liturgical peculiarity Connolly[2] cites many instances from the Syriac *Acts of Thomas* where a 'seal' is given by chrismation before the actual water-baptism,[3] and from other sources which, together with certain other pieces of evidence bearing upon this characteristic feature of Syrian baptismal procedure, we must postpone for later discussion in connection with the various theories of the Fathers about the sacramental medium of the Spirit. It should be observed that the practice apparently takes its rise in Gnostic circles where, as we shall see later, chrismation was held to be highly important and was accorded a greater degree of emphasis than Baptism. The origin of this usage is therefore likely to lie in an heretical peculiarity. Dr. T. W. Manson, indeed, suggests that traces of a doctrine of the pre-baptismal bestowal of the Spirit may be discerned in the New Testament, and that the Syrian practice represents an archaic survival, the ancient idea being embodied in the liturgical practice. The principal passages adduced from the Pauline Epistles[4] do not, however, justify us in concluding anything more than that it may well have been the primitive belief that the Spirit's inspiration, under whose influence a man found himself able to cry 'Abba, Father', was independent of any external rite, and that in fact this inspiration may have been expected to come at a man's conversion and make it possible for him to offer himself for Baptism; it is also possible to argue that the primitive declaration of belief in Christ was

---

[1] See above, p. 40.
[2] *The Liturgical Homilies of Narsai* (T.S. 8, 1 (1909), pp. xlii ff.); see p. 188.
[3] Tr. Wright, pp. 166, 188, 258, 267, 289.
[4] Gal. iv. 6; Rom. viii. 15; 1 Cor. xii. 3.   See *JTS*. 48, 1947, pp. 25 ff.

made in the power of the Spirit before Baptism was administered. These texts may suggest, though the evidence is far from secure, that the bestowal of the Spirit in the primitive Church was not necessarily linked with Baptism, and that the Pauline doctrine of grace implied that an activity of the Spirit was operative upon the convert before his sacramental incorporation into Christ. They are not evidence for a pre-baptismal Confirmation in apostolic times, though the Syrian rite may possibly have been developed later on the basis of such a doctrine of the pre-baptismal activity of the Spirit; but the evidence of Theodore of Mopsuestia is against this (see p. 202 below). Dr. Manson's interpretation of 1 John v. 8 as signifying the three stages of initiation, the free 'descent' of the Spirit, Baptism, and the Eucharist, is rather more attractive, but, as we have remarked above, this text probably refers to the nature of Christ's own 'anointing' and its relationship to His death, rather than to any sacramental rites.[1]

We may conclude that the supposed analogy of circumcision does not help to establish that any rite signifying Spirit-baptism existed in New Testament times, other than the water-baptism of which Spirit-baptism was one aspect of the inward thing signified.

There is one genuine parallel between circumcision as a seal and Baptism as a seal, but it is of quite a different kind from the alleged parallels which we have been considering. Abraham's circumcision was a 'seal' in the sense that it was a ratification of the righteousness which he already possessed by faith.[2] Baptism may rightly be regarded as a seal or ratification set upon the convert's justification, and, as we shall see later, the Fathers often speak of it in this aspect. Circumcision, however, was a declaratory and not an effective sign (οὐχ ὡς δικαιοσύνης ποιητικὴ ἐδόθη, ἀλλὰ σφραγὶς καὶ σημεῖον τῆς ἐκ πίστεως δικαιοσύνης τοῦ ᾿Αβραάμ)[3] whereas the eschatological seal of the Spirit for the day of redemption, and the Baptism which is its outward part, are far more than a declaratory act of ratification; they are the great effective sign of union with Christ in His Body, the

---

[1] The reading of the Sinaitic Syriac version in John iii. 5, 'Spirit and water', reflects the Syrian practice.
[2] Rom. iv. 11.   [3] Sever. Gab., *Rom.* iv. 11 (Staab, p. 217, 11).

Church, through the 'Holy Spirit which has been given to us'.

We may conclude from the New Testament evidence that Baptism is an eschatological and Christocentric sacrament. It is centred upon the Baptism of Jesus, represented at the Baptism of every Christian. This truth is not lost sight of by later writers; Theodore of Mopsuestia, for example, instructs his converts on the matter at some length;[1] and the doctrine which is based . upon the conception of the application to every believer of the Baptism, and so of the death and resurrection, of Christ, teaches that it is in Baptism that men are made partakers of the Christ, sharers in the benefits of the Atonement, and, by virtue of belonging to Him, recipients of the Spirit. The Apostolic writers afford no adequate ground for the view that Spirit-baptism was ever regarded by them as something distinct from water-baptism, except in so far as the one represents the inward, the other the external part of the sacrament. The only exceptions to this direct connection of Spirit-baptism with the ceremony of baptizing in water occur in very exceptional circumstances, such as the conversion of Cornelius; certainly there is no evidence for the connection of Spirit-baptism with some other rite such as the imposition of hands or chrismation, of whose existence as either independent ceremonies of initiation, or regular parts of the baptismal rite, there is no proof at all.

On the other hand the New Testament affords plenty of instances of special gifts or endowments of the Spirit, or, as it would be truer to say, of the grant of fresh apprehension of the Holy Spirit, when particular individuals or groups are brought into the Christian body, or are commissioned by Christ in His Church for special work within it. This remains true; though a baptized person possesses the full endowment of the indwelling presence of the Spirit, his subsequent Ordination, for example, is a moment in his experience when he becomes conscious of a renewed understanding of the Spirit, and a fresh awareness of His grace in relation to a particular activity. This is, in itself, sufficient ground for the belief that a person baptized in infancy is 'strengthened' with the Holy Ghost, the Comforter, in the post-Scriptural, but most necessary, rite of Confirmation, that He will 'daily increase in them . . . manifold gifts of grace',

[1] Mingana, p. 66.

and that the confirmed Christian may 'daily increase in' the 'Holy Spirit more and more'; it even allows us to speak, if we will, of 'a special gift of the Holy Spirit' in Confirmation, so long as we do not suppose that the gift then bestowed for the first time is the Christian's initial possession of the Spirit which is one aspect of his membership of Christ. But this 'special gift' is not the seal, the 'stamp' set on God's property by which he will recognize His own, the Spirit which the Christian receives by becoming a member of the Christ, the Spirit-possessed Messiah, and by which he is marked as destined for 'a day of redemption'.

Additional Note: The question whether infant Baptism was ever practised in the primitive Church does not arise in this enquiry. The arguments of Leenhardt and Cullmann as against those by which Barth seeks to persuade the Church to abandon infant Baptism have demonstrated the plausibility of the argument that the children of Christian parents do not seem to have been baptized in later life, that the Church may have followed the Jewish practice of accepting as Israelites the children of proselytes (*Yeb.* 78a), and that the custom of circumcising on the eighth day may have suggested the desirability of baptizing in early infancy. Despite various possible indications of the existence of infant Baptism in the New Testament, the theology of Baptism therein presented to us is concerned with the Baptism of adults alone. The rise of infant Baptism as the regular and normal procedure changed the whole aspect of the question of the relationship of Confirmation to Baptism.

The reader will have observed that no mention has been made of the question whether New Testament baptismal doctrine and practice, and, in particular, the expressions παλιγγενεσία, ἀναγεννᾶν, were derived from, or influenced by, the pagan Mysteries. That mystery ideas infiltrated into the theology of Baptism is a possibility which we shall consider later, since I believe that there is no evidence that the process took place in New Testament times. J. Dey (*Παλιγγενεσία*) thinks that παλιγγενεσία in Titus iii. 5 may represent a borrowing from paganism, but the closest parallel to the idea of baptismal regeneration that is to be found in the pagan cults (until we reach

the late notion of the initiate who is 'renatus in aeternum') is
Tertullian's remark that 'certe ludis Apollinaribus et Pelusiis
tinguntur. Idque se in regenerationem et impunitatem periurio-
rum suorum agere praesumunt.' In all probability, however,
Tertullian is consciously or unconsciously exaggerating the
resemblance between pagan and Christian Baptism; he is
explaining in his own terms what may well have been only a
purificatory lustration.

A possible place where pagan notions have made an impact
upon St. Paul's teaching is the puzzling βαπτιζόμενοι ὑπὲρ τῶν
νεκρῶν in 1 Cor. xv. 29, which may represent a pagan practice
retained by converts to Christianity. This is, however, most
improbable, and the suggestion that St. Paul is drawing an
argumentum ad homines from pagan practice is equally unlikely.
The theory of H. Preisker (*ZNTW*. 1924, pp. 298–304) is
plausible, that the general resurrection could come only when
the fixed number of the elect had been made up; that some of
the Christians had died without Baptism, perhaps because at
first it was not regarded as vitally necessary to salvation; and
that when Baptism came to be regarded as essential, the practice arose of baptizing 'for the dead'. We might compare the
baptism of souls in Hades (Herm. *sim.* 9, 16, 5). It is, however,
hard to believe that Baptism was ever an 'optional extra'.
May τῶν νεκρῶν refer proleptically to the baptized themselves,
or rather, to their bodies? If Baptism is the means whereby the
earnest is given of the final redemption of the body, it would be
pointless to be baptized if there were to be no resurrection.
Those who were baptized without any firm belief or assurance
about the resurrection of the body were simply receiving a
'baptism undertaken on behalf of corpses'. Whether this be
correct or not, the passage affords no ground for imagining
that baptismal practice and theology were influenced by pagan
notions to any significant degree in the first century.

PART TWO

THE SEALING
OF THE FAITHFUL
IN THE
EARLY CHURCH

CHAPTER SIX

THE SECOND CENTURY

So far as the Church's history and the development of its doctrine are concerned, the second century, or rather the period which separates the Apostles from Irenaeus, Tertullian, Clement, and Hippolytus, is emphatically the 'Century of the Common Man'. Once the original 'pillars' of the Apostolic Church have been removed, and particularly when St. Paul has left the stage, no single character of really outstanding spiritual and intellectual power comes forward to take up their part.

Ignatius and Polycarp are heroes who die the death of martyrs, but the former is a strange and 'unapostolic' figure with his remarkable and peculiar psychological make-up and his sometimes very odd and strongly Hellenized doctrinal ideas, and the latter is a staunch and faithful pastor, but in no way a profound spiritual thinker or theologian. Nor can either the Apostolic Fathers or the early Apologists, considered as a whole, be fairly said to include any man of outstanding genius. Even Justin, despite the considerable contribution which he made to the Church's formulation of its belief, can scarcely be claimed as a really great teacher; and although the Church must have produced a number of interesting preachers and writers, such as Melito of Sardis, people of the stature of Tertullian, not to speak of St. Paul, are conspicuously lacking.

Meanwhile, the Church has expanded rapidly, and has been planted throughout the Greco-Roman world. Its congregations consist chiefly of humble people. It was indeed in some respects the glory of the Church that its membership comprised 'not many wise men after the flesh, not many mighty, not many noble', and the sneers of Celsus at the ignorant yokels who constituted the bulk of the Church's congregations and ministry merely reveal the ignorant prejudice of an educated pagan.[1] Nevertheless, the Church was left with second-class leaders at its head to face the critical period of consolidation with many urgent tasks to carry out in the development of its organization and the foundation of its doctrinal system.

Its congregations consisted in the main of small groups of urban people of the lower middle-class. They were set in the confused religious milieu of the Gentile world, side by side with the guilds and their hero-cults, and the devotees of the numerous mysteries; in places they were in close contact with the fringe of Judaism, particularly in those quarters where a syncretistic amalgam of Judaism and 'pan-Orientalism' had developed.[2] The Christians themselves must have often brought into their obscure assemblies in the back streets of Corinth, Antioch, and Rome, hardly distinguishable to the outside observer from the rest of the varied and ubiquitous religious fraternities and mutual-benefit societies of the poorer classes, many of the ideas which were current in the pagan environment in which they had been brought up, and in which they still lived and worked. The isolation of Ecclesiastical History as a special field of study has made it difficult for us today to gain a true perspective in these matters; we do not find it easy to envisage the early followers of Christ in their setting of the mixed Greco-Roman-Oriental civilization of the great cities of the pagan world, or to recognize how wide was the gulf which must have separated the intellectual and religious outlook of Paul, the ex-Pharisee, from that of the ordinary small shopkeeper of Ephesus or Alexandria. Yet an examination of a cross-section of the Christian congregations in a typical city of modern England, and still more of modern America, would soon make us realize the startling differences of outlook, belief, and practice which can still characterize the adherents of a common faith; not to speak of the distance which so often divides the trained theologian from the plain man, the difference between the outlook of various types of ordinary lay people would seem sufficiently striking. The ethos of an Anglican cathedral service, and that of a revivalist meeting in a mission

[1] ὁρῶμεν δὴ καὶ κατὰ τὰς ἰδίας οἰκίας ἐριουργοὺς καὶ σκυτοτόμους καὶ κναφεῖς καὶ τοὺς ἀπαιδευοτάτους τε καὶ ἀγροικοτάτους . . . θαυμάσι᾿ ἄττα διεξιόντας, Cels. ap. Or., Cels., 3, 55 (GCS. p. 250, 16; PG. 11, 993A).

[2] e.g. in the districts where the Sabazios-Sabaoth cult was popular.

hall in some back street of the cathedral city are so entirely
different that it is difficult at times to remember that the basic
principles of the faith proclaimed at each place are the same.

The common man's religion may at any one time exhibit
more genuine spiritual power than that of the educated layman
and the theologian; but it is the latter who in the nature of
things will ultimately bear the responsibility for guiding the
doctrinal formulation, and, to a lesser extent, for controlling the
liturgical development of that religion. Where the theological
leadership is lacking the plain man's religion, in the absence of
a closely-knit organization and a strong respect for tradition,
will almost inevitably develop a tendency towards fissiparous
sectarianism, and the doctrinal over-emphasis of certain
aspects of the Faith which in the last resort produces 'freak
religions'. In the sub-apostolic age and the second century
theological leadership of a really high quality was largely absent, and the Church had not as yet fully consolidated its
organization or crystallized its doctrinal tradition in the canon
of Scripture and the 'Rule of Faith'. The 'cathedral' as it
were, had not yet been finished, and Christianity was represented for a time, intellectually and spiritually, by the 'tin
tabernacle' of the ordinary man's religion—the religion of the
newly converted ex-pagan bourgeoisie. The consequences of
this situation are clear enough when we turn from the sublimity
of the Pauline Gospel to the relatively humdrum doctrinal and
ethical teaching of the Apostolic Fathers. What seems there at
first sight to be a startling 'slump' in the progress of Christian
doctrine actually begins to make its appearance within the
New Testament writings. We should be mistaken in supposing
that the abrupt transition from the soaring spirit of the Pauline
Epistles to the comparatively dull pedestrian level of the
'Pastorals' or 2 Peter represents a drop from a consistently high
level in the apostolic age to a less exalted type of Christianity
which had not previously made its appearance. On the contrary, it is more reasonable to suppose that the great intellectual and spiritual power of St. Paul was wholly exceptional in
his own day. The Apostle who most clearly grasped the essence
of Christ's revelation and understood its implications most
thoroughly and far-sightedly was quite certainly not typical of

the average Christian of his time. The syncretists of Colossae and the semi-heathen converts at Corinth must have been far more truly representative of the mass of ordinary people who claimed the title Christian. Far more typical than either of these extreme types, however, must have been the faithful and devoted presbyters and laity of the scattered churches, who received St. Paul's epistles, read them, and stored them away to be read to the faithful Sunday by Sunday, treasured them more and more as time went by, and reverenced them as the writings of *the* Apostle, yet, at the same time, found in them 'certain things hard to be understood'.[1] The primitive Church as a whole did not live continuously on the heights of St. Paul's Christ-mysticism. The remarkable change of atmosphere which we feel when we turn from the Pauline Epistles to the Pastorals, James, or even to the Lucan writings, represents not so much a change from the Christianity of the apostolic age to that of the sub-apostolic period, as a change from the unique quality of St. Paul to the general level of non-Pauline Christianity as it had existed during the Apostle's own lifetime and as it held the field after his death. Johannine Christianity represents another great spiritual peak rising far above the common level, and indeed, in some respects, above the height of Paulinism; but St. John's interpretation of the Gospel, at least in certain of its aspects, is more congenial to the popular type of religion than that of St. Paul.

Other factors, however, enter into the sub-apostolic development. In the primitive Church the new converts from Judaism or paganism were evidently always in some danger of swinging away from the Gospel towards one or the other of the two perversions of it; they tended either towards antinomian versions of Paulinism or towards a relapse into a Judaistic religion of moralism where salvation was once again to be won by human effort, the Kingdom of God was to be gained by merit,[2] and a simple untheological monotheism found it exceedingly difficult to accommodate within its narrow system of thought the experience of Christ as God. The growth of a 'Judaistic' piety was assisted, as Dr. Torrance has pointed out,[3] by a 'fundamentalist'

---

[1] 2 Pet. iii. 16.   [2] Cf. 2 *Clem.*, 11, 7.
[3] *The Doctrine of Grace in the Apostolic Fathers*, p. 133.

reading of the Septuagint, which seemed to necessitate the gradual incorporation into Christianity of the entire system, moral, sacrificial, and sacerdotal, of the Old Covenant; but for its saving use of allegorism, the Church might well have been compelled to choose between reimposing the full Law and submitting to the drastic surgery of Marcion. One result of this state of affairs is a weakening of the Church's understanding of the Pauline doctrines of justifying faith, and of the believer's incorporation into Christ through his apprehension by faith of Christ's saving work. The effect of this upon the theology of Baptism and participation in the Spirit was profound and far-reaching.

On the other side, the Christian congregations were exposed to the all-pervading influence of Hellenism in an environment where Christian and pagan ideas reacted upon one another. The effects of this interplay of ideas can be seen, so far as Baptism is concerned, in the deliberate efforts of Clement of Alexandria to interpret this sacrament in 'mystery' terms;[1] and it is plain that popular Christianity, even in circles which were not technically anything other than orthodox, was deeply influenced by the current religious ideas of the pagan world. The Epistle to the Colossians shows the pressure that was soon exerted upon Christianity to provide the sort of redemption and deliverance which the Greco-Roman world demanded. The various Gnostic heresies represent those elements in Christianity which were prepared to go farthest in surrendering to this demand, and in accommodating the Gospel to the needs of 'modern thought', so that in their systems the Gospel is changed into a syncretistic religion acceptable, and indeed most attractive, to the pagan or semi-pagan mind. Their contact with Hellenic religion is close and obvious; particularly is this the case with the Naassenes and their use of the myths of Attis and Eleusinian Demeter; and the great and really menacing danger to true Christianity arose from the fact that, until the Church's organization had been properly consolidated, its genuine doctrinal tradition safeguarded by the appeal to the witness of the apostolic churches (guaranteed by their episcopal successions), and the canon of the New Testament

---

[1] Cf. Clem., *prot.*, 12 (p. 84, 23; *PG.* 8, 241A).

approximately fixed, it was exceedingly difficult to tell which teachers were orthodox and which heretical. We are told that Cerdon, for example, was for a long time in and out, so to speak, of recognized membership of the Church of Rome,[1] and the same state of affairs is true to some extent of Valentinus and Marcion. In the large centres, and notably at Rome (whither not only the orthodox, but all kinds of heretics tended to gravitate), the situation in the second century must have presented an extraordinary spectacle of doctrinal confusion and liturgical chaos. Teachers of all descriptions seem to have set up their conventicles almost side by side, rather like the lecturers at a mediaeval university, and bishops were evidently hard put to it to decide which of them should or should not be received into communion.

Moreover, apart from the confusion caused by the different brands of Gnosticism, the religion of the common man, even if his orthodoxy were officially unimpeachable, was often deeply tinged with paganism. It was for him that the spate of apocryphal literature was produced; Infancy Gospels; narratives of the 'Harrowing of Hell' and the Resurrection, full of marvels more reminiscent of Apollonius of Tyana than of Jesus Christ; apocryphal Acts, naïve chronicles of marvellous adventures, at best Christianized versions of the Greek novel, at worst vehicles for debased and unorthodox teaching; and apocalypses of all sorts. The number of such works was very large, and the papyri afford striking proof of their wide popularity. The mental attitude of the ordinary believer evidently varied from the rather delightful simplicity reflected in the *Shepherd* to a syncretism not so very far removed from the crude superstition of the magical papyri.

It was in this age of confusion, while the Church was still evolving the means by which this confusion was soon to be reduced to order with astonishing success and surprising rapidity, that the liturgical tradition took shape, and it is in the context of this age that we have to examine the history of Baptism in relation to the 'seal of the Spirit'.

To attempt a full study of the subject in the patristic period would necessitate a full treatment of each Father's doctrine of

---

[1] Iren., *haer.*, 3, 4, 3.

the Spirit, and we cannot expect conclusive results from a cursory treatment of what the ancient authors have to say about the baptismal seal, considered in isolation from their thought as a whole. We must also bear in mind that the Apostolic Fathers and the Apologists have little to say about the doctrine of Baptism in relation to the Spirit; we have to wait until Tertullian for any dogmatic treatise on the subject; it is therefore dangerously easy to try to draw positive conclusions from the negative inference *ex silentio*. Nevertheless, the evidence of the scanty writings of the second century affords us certain clues or pointers to the doctrine and practice of the times, particularly when we set them against the background of the New Testament teaching which we have been discussing. The Epistle of Clement to the Corinthians throws little light on the subject, though we may notice that in his echo of Eph. iv. 4 (ἦ οὐχὶ ἕνα Θεὸν ἔχομεν καὶ ἕνα Χριστὸν καὶ ἕν Πνεῦμα τῆς χάριτος τὸ ἐκχυθὲν ἐφ᾽ ἡμᾶς),[1] he is in all probability thinking of the bestowal of the Spirit in Baptism, and that, though the conception is Trinitarian, the Spirit is thought of only in relation to activity in the Church; the Spirit is not fully personal, and we are still in the realm of the ideas which we have observed in Acts; the Spirit is a *gift* which is 'poured out' upon the believer.

That the Spirit is received in Baptism is made clearer by the writer of 2 *Clement*. In this homily Baptism is directly equated with the 'seal'.[2] In itself this thought is a not unnatural extension of St. Paul's conception of the seal of the Spirit bestowed sacramentally in Baptism. There is, however, one innovation in the thought of this writer, or rather preacher, for while he tells us that by 'preserving the seal' one may partake of the Spirit, and the Spirit is identified with Christ in the 'spiritual Church',[3] the seal has come to be regarded as something connected primarily with the flesh; Baptism imprints upon the mortal flesh a seal, which must be preserved intact by righteous living. The metaphor of the seal is still related to the idea of a mark set upon the believer to brand him as the property of God,[4] but it has also acquired something of the metaphorical

---

[1] 1 *Clem.*, 46.   [2] 2 *Clem.*, 6, 9; 7, 6; 8, 6.   [3] *Ibid.*, 14, 3–5.
[4] Cf. the eschatology of 2 *Clem.*, 16, 3–4.

sense of 'sealing up' a package to keep it inviolate. Ethical conduct (we are in a very un-Pauline atmosphere of 'works') enables the believer to preserve this seal unbroken—an idea which recurs many times in later authors[1]—so that the flesh, being joined to the Spirit, will ultimately be able to partake of life and immortality.[2] 'Barnabas', who relates Baptism to the Old Covenant seal of circumcision,[3] is closer to the thought of the New Testament. Looking back to the baptismal prophecy of Ezekiel xlvii. 1–12, he interprets the 'river' there described as the water of Baptism into which 'we go down laden with sins and filth'; we rise from it 'bearing fruit in the heart, having fear and hope in Jesus in the Spirit'.[4] Remission of sins and the gift of the Spirit are thus associated once more with Baptism into Christ; and the Spirit is God Himself dwelling in the believer, the sign and fruit of new life resulting from the 'new creation'.[5]

The thought of Christ's Baptism had already been prominently set out in the Ignatian epistles. Ignatius recalls His purpose, 'to fulfil all righteousness',[6] and it is possible that he is relating Christ's Baptism to the Atonement in the curious expression, ὃς ἐγεννήθη καὶ ἐβαπτίσθη ἵνα τῷ πάθει τὸ ὕδωρ καθαρίσῃ,[7] though the πάθος may perhaps mean no more than Christ's *experience* of Baptism. On the whole, however, the Pauline emphasis upon Baptism as the sacrament of the application of the Atonement to the believer is conspicuously lacking in these writers, whose thought is for the most part far from Christocentric.

Ignatius gives a new turn to the doctrine of Baptism when he describes it as affording us weapons for spiritual combat.[8] Here we have a hint of the idea, so prevalent in the popular mind, of the prophylactic character of Baptism and of the 'sealing' as a

---

[1] Though the use of σφραγίζειν is common to both Christian and pagan religious thought in the second and third centuries, its significance is not the same in its Christian and pagan use; in paganism it is employed of physical marking, or in the sense of 'fully initiate' into a mystery, its meaning being thus related to that of τελεῖν (cf. Tert., *apol.*, 8: 'Talia initiatus et consignatus vivis in aeternum,' and *Val.* 1 on Eleusinian 'sealing'). In the mysteries, τηρεῖν τὴν σφραγῖδα means 'preserve the seal' (of secrecy, from the uninitiate); in connection with the Christian conception of the seal as the inward marking with the Spirit conferred in Baptism, the expression has a purely ethical significance.
[2] *Ibid.*, 14, 5.　　[3] *Barn.*, 9, 6.　　[4] *Ibid.*, 11, 11.　　[5] *Ibid.*, 16, 8.
[6] *Smyrn.*, 1, 1.　　[7] *Eph.*, 18, 2.　　[8] *Polyc.*, 6, 2.

defence against the powers of evil. Ignatius also, it is interesting to observe, ascribes to Baptism that 'arming' of the believer for spiritual warfare which later comes to be regarded in Western theology as the special grace of Confirmation. He makes it clear, too, that Baptism is the rite of admission into the Church, and is therefore not to be administered 'without the bishop', the Church's local head and leader.[1]

The *Didache* has little to our purpose, beyond its description of the mode of Baptism and its indication that at a relatively very early date Baptism into the Lord's name (which is the necessary preliminary to participation in the Church's Eucharist) is, in fact, administered in the Threefold Name.[2]

Hermas offers us some more interesting material. The seal is conceived eschatologically; it is given to those who are admitted into the 'tower', and those who receive it are arrayed, like the sealed in the Apocalypse, in white robes,[3] the wearing of which is connected with the 'wearing of the name' of the Son of God.[4] A little later Hermas explains that the robe which is put on is the Holy Spirit,[5] which is given to the believer and must be preserved intact.[6] Those who have received the seal possess 'one thought and one mind' and they partake of one faith and one love, that is to say, they receive from their sealing the fruits of the Spirit.[7]

So far, then, Hermas has united several aspects of the seal which we shall find more fully thought out in later authors; it is the seal of the Spirit, the robe of the righteous, and the token of the Name of Christ. Its connection with Baptism is asserted in an eschatological context: 'Those . . . that had fallen asleep received the seal of the Son of God, and entered into God's kingdom. For before a man has borne the name of the Son of God, he is dead; but when he has received the seal he puts off his deadness, and receives life again; ἡ σφραγὶς οὖν τὸ ὕδωρ ἐστίν· εἰς τὸ ὕδωρ οὖν καταβαίνουσι νεκροί, καὶ ἀναβαίνουσι ζῶντες.[8] Here, though the believer's union with Christ in death and resurrection is not affirmed, and hence the whole conception is somewhat distorted, Baptism remains, as it was in St. Paul's

---

[1] *Smyrn.*, 8, 2. [2] 9, 5; 7, 1. [3] *sim.*, 8, 2, 2-3. [4] *Ibid.*, 9, 13, 2-3, 7.
[5] *Ibid.*, 9, 24, 2. [6] *Ibid.*, 9, 32, 4. [7] *Ibid.*, 9, 17, 4.
[8] *Ibid.*, 9, 16, 3-4. There is surely no need to follow Bousset (*Kyrios Christos*, p. 279) in supposing this phrase to be a marginal gloss.

theology, a means whereby the Christian 'rises' to newness of life. The seal is the gift of this new life through Baptism; hence it can be identified with the actual baptismal water, or perhaps more accurately with the rite of Baptism itself, for ὕδωρ is frequently used as a synonym for Baptism.[1]

Before we leave Hermas it is worth remarking that those who were converted and received the seal, but who subsequently 'broke' it, may receive a second sealing if they repent, so that they may be admitted into the company of the righteous.[2] We thus seem to find in Hermas that conception of Penance as a restoration of the seal of the Spirit, lost by post-baptismal sin, which is an important factor in the later history of the idea of 'sealing'.

Perhaps the most striking and dramatic illustration of the idea that Baptism is itself the seal which marks the believer for redemption is to be found in the famous story of Thecla's self-baptism in the arena. When the martyr is exposed to wild beasts in the amphitheatre, she throws herself into a pond full of water containing 'ferocious seals', with the cry: ἐν τῷ ὀνόματι Ἰησοῦ Χριστοῦ ὑστέρᾳ ἡμέρᾳ βαπτίζομαι.[3] As an example of the intensely eschatological significance which Baptism possessed for the early Church, Thecla's 'baptismal formula' is impressive; the baptized person is, as Ephesians expressed it, 'sealed for a day of redemption' (though the Pauline conception of sealing with the Spirit has to some extent yielded to a greater emphasis on the outward washing in water). For our present purpose the important point to notice is that when, according to the story, Thecla afterwards meets St. Paul she tells him, ἔλαβον τὸ λουτρόν, Παῦλε,[4] and the Apostle apparently regards her initiation as complete, requiring no further 'sealing'. Indeed, her self-baptism is evidently the fulfilment of the desire which she had expressed to St. Paul earlier in the story that she might 'receive the seal'. On that occasion, it should be observed, the reply to her request, 'Only give me the

---

[1] Cf. Tert., bapt., 1: 'felix sacramentum aquae nostrae; ibid., 15, 'felix aqua'. That the words ὕδωρ, aqua, can be so used is itself an argument against the view that water-baptism was generally regarded by the early Church as a mere preliminary lustration preceding a Spirit-baptism whose outward sign was a 'baptism in oil'. It also suggests that the word βάπτισμα is not to be taken as generally synonymous with a complex rite of 'Baptism plus unction'.

[2] sim., 8, 6, 3.   [3] A. Paul. et Thecl., 34.   [4] Ibid., 40.

seal in Christ, and trial (πειρασμός) shall not touch me', is, 'Thecla be patient, and you shall receive the *water*.'[1]

In the early *Acts of Paul*, Baptism is similarly described as a seal, or rather it would be truer to say that the term 'seal' is employed as a synonym for Baptism in water. In the story told in this popular Christian romance the doors of a prison at Ephesus were opened miraculously in order that Artemylla μνηθῇ τῆς ἐν κυρίῳ σφραγῖδος (the 'mystery' character of the language is striking), and we are told that the way in which the initiation takes place is that St. Paul and Artemylla are led by a supernatural guide to the sea (running water is evidently required for Baptism), where 'Paul having prayed laid his hand on Artemylla and [*desunt quaedam*] . . . the water in the name of Christ Jesus.'[2] The seal is evidently identical with the Baptism in water. The text is admittedly defective, but it does not appear that any further ceremony took place. The imposition of the hand is certainly not a 'confirmation'; it is the symbol of identification and 'solidarity' between the baptizer and the candidate which was employed during the actual baptism in Jewish practice and, to judge from early pictures of the rite, in the primitive Christian ceremony also.

A similar account of a sealing by baptism is given in the *Acts of Peter*, a Latin version of which is contained in the Vercelli MS. 108.[3] Here, again, the Baptism has to take place in running water, and since the candidate is the master of a ship in which St. Peter is travelling to Rome, and his conversion has happened at sea, we are presented with the somewhat comical picture of St. Peter sliding down a rope in order to baptize his convert in the Adriatic, while the rest of the ship's company 'omnes condormierant ebrii'. As in the *Acts of Paul*, the Baptism is accompanied by the apparition of a young man, whom St. Peter salutes as 'Deus Iesu Christe'; but this account differs from the former in that it is not entirely clear what the 'seal' represents. The shipmaster addresses St. Peter: 'Si vis me dignum habere quem intingas in signo Domini, habes occasionem.' He is subsequently baptized in the name of the Father, Son, and Holy Ghost. There is no other ceremony until the celebration

---

[1] *A. Paul. et Thecl.*, 32.   [2] *A. Paul*, 3, 24, 31 ff. (Schmidt, pp. 32 ff.).
[3] *A. Petr. cum Sim.*, 5 (Lipsius-Bonnet, pp. 50–51).

of the Eucharist, and in his thanksgiving after the baptism St. Peter says: 'Tu enim visus es, Deus Iesu Christe, in tuo nomine mox locutus et signatus est sancto tuo signo.' It is possible that the *signum* stands for the actual Baptism, but it is more probable that it denotes either the seal of the Cross, presumably administered at the close of the baptismal ceremony as in the *Apostolic Tradition* of Hippolytus (although we have been told nothing of any such consignation having taken place), or perhaps the threefold Name pronounced over the candidate. There is no suggestion that the sign or seal is to be identified with the seal of the Spirit.

The conception of the seal of Baptism as a safeguard against the powers of evil and a guarantee of salvation in the last day is to be found also in the *Acts of Xanthippe and Polyxena*, which are probably to be dated early in the next century. Here the seal is in the first place a mark by which God will recognize and acknowledge His people, and secondly a protection against the hostile powers of evil, affording to its recipient an assurance that he will obtain access to God after death.[1] As in the story of Thecla, so in this narrative, the seal is conferred in Baptism, and is virtually identified in a rather materialistic fashion with the outward washing. It is worth notice that here the seal is given in what Dr. Richards calls the 'bath-water of regeneration', and has no connection with any other baptism of 're-newal of Holy Spirit'.[2] A similar identification of the 'seal' with Baptism in water appears in the account given in the *Rest of the Words of Baruch* of the baptism which is said to have been imposed as a religious test after the revolt of Bar-cochba, when those Jews who were willing to be baptized as Christians were exempted from the general expulsion of their race from Jerusalem ordered by Hadrian: δοκιμάσεις δὲ αὐτοὺς ἐκ τοῦ ὕδατος τοῦ Ἰορδάνου· ὁ μὴ ἀκούων φανερὸς γενήσεται· τοῦτο τὸ σημεῖόν ἐστι τῆς μεγάλης σφραγῖδος.[3] These books which we have been considering represent the viewpoint of the 'common

---

[1] τάχυνον τοῦ σφραγίσαι με, ἵνα εἰ καὶ φθάσῃ ἐπ' ἐμὲ θάνατος ἀπέλθω πρὸς ἐκεῖνον τὸν εὐσπλαγχνον. A. Xant., 13 (*Texts and Studies* 2³, p. 67, 2) ; σφράγισόν με, καθάπερ Παῦλος σφραγίζει διὰ λουτροῦ παλιγγενεσίας ἵνα κἀγὼ λοιπὸν ἡ ταπεινὴ γνωρισθῶ ὑπὸ τοῦ Θεοῦ ἡμῶν, *ibid.*, 28 (p. 78, 33).

[2] This despite the fact that there is an unction before baptism, *ibid.* 2(p. 59, 6).

[3] 6, 23.

man'; they are essentially popular and untheological. We are on different ground when we turn to the writings of Justin. His familiar account of the meaning and practice of Baptism[1] need not be recounted here in detail; it is sufficient for us to remark that it is described as the means of regeneration, as a washing in water administered in the Threefold Name, that the authority for the practice rests on John iii. 5 and the prophecy of Isa. i. 16 ff., that by its means the believer obtains remission of sins, and that through it he receives illumination. In the *Dialogue* Justin explains that it is a 'washing' of repentance and of the knowledge of God, the 'water of life', to be contrasted as an inward and ethical cleansing with the Jewish baptism which cleanses the body alone.[2] It is a spiritual and effective circumcision,[3] and hence, although Justin does not explicitly say so, it is a sealing. Unlike the Jewish circumcision and baptism, it is a baptism with the Holy Spirit,[4] conferring on the believer God's testimony that he has been made one of His people. It is a spiritual circumcision effecting remission of sins through the mercy of God.[5] In all this the general view of the baptismal seal which we have followed through the post-apostolic writers remains the same. If our interpretation of Justin's language is correct, we cannot find in him any justification for the theory of a distinction between a water- and a Spirit-baptism, except in the sense that the one is the outward sign of the other, nor any indication that he knew of a second sacramental rite, or even a second part of a single ceremony, through which Spirit-baptism was conferred.[6]

Those who seek to maintain that such teaching is to be read out of Justin are compelled to rely upon two exceedingly fragile supports. They may suppose that his description of the Spirit coming upon Jesus ἀναδύντος ἀπὸ τοῦ ὕδατος [7] implies that, as His Baptism was typical of that of His followers, the gift of the Spirit follows, and does not accompany, Baptism in water; but, as Ratcliff observes, this expression may well mean no

---

[1] 1 apol., 61.   [2] dial., 14, 1.   [3] Ibid., 19, 2.

[4] τίς οὖν ἔτι μοι περιτομῆς λόγος, ὑπὸ τοῦ θεοῦ μαρτυρηθέντι; τίς ἐκείνου τοῦ βαπτίσματος χρεία ἁγίῳ Πνεύματι βεβαπτισμένῳ; ibid., 29, 1.

[5] Ibid., 43, 2.

[6] The question whether he did so has been argued by Oulton, Dix, and Ratcliff in *Theology* (March 1947, Jan. 1948, April 1948).

[7] dial., 88, 3.

more than that Jesus had *emerged* from the water,[1] i.e. that He was not actually under the water, when the Spirit descended; and, though no doubt Justin regarded the Baptism of Jesus as typical of the Christian sacrament, he does not actually say so, for when he tells us that Jesus went to the Jordan ὑπὲρ τοῦ γένους τῶν ἀνθρώπων, he does not mean that His Baptism was typical of that of Christians, but rather, as he clearly states, that, like the crucifixion and resurrection, His Baptism was undertaken for our salvation. It is therefore fairly clear that the order in which the Baptism and the descent of the Spirit took place is not to be pressed here as an analogy to Christian initiation. It has also been suggested that the mention of prayers being made by the congregation after the Baptism service for themselves and for the new converts[2] may indicate that a petition was offered for the gift to the latter of the Holy Spirit which they had not yet received; but this is pure speculation with no foundation in anything that Justin actually says.

Alternatively, the advocates of this view have to fall back upon the assumption that the reason why Justin makes no allusion to any ceremony other than Baptism in water as the means of conferring the seal of the Spirit is because in fact he means by βάπτισμα, not water-baptism alone, but a complex of rites in which water-baptism formed one element; because such a complex rite was traditional, Justin's readers would assume its existence as a matter of course, and there was no need for him to refer to it explicitly. It is, however, in that case very odd that, apart from the one obscure allusion to 'layings on of hands' in Heb. vi. 3, we should have so far found no evidence that any traditional ceremonies of initiation were regularly practised except Baptism in water. Of course, the presiding bishop may have received the converts into the fellowship with a sign of blessing; it would be rather surprising if he did not do so; but, in the absence of any information from Justin himself, we may not assume that this was the case. We may in any case reasonably conclude that had Justin known of any ceremony (of imposition of hands or of unction) which he believed to be the medium of the seal of which he speaks by implication in his language about Christian 'circumcision', he would at least

[1] See above, p. 43.   [2] I *apol.*, 65, 1–2.

have given it a passing mention. Certainly those writers who do attach a vital importance to unction or the laying on of hands rarely fail to tell us about it. It is quite likely that Justin may omit to mention ceremonial additions by which the rite of Baptism may have been already embellished—additions which were to make the complex rite of initiation as it was practised in the time of Tertullian or Hippolytus so impressive and awe-inspiring a ceremony. Some of these elements which we find in the fully developed rite of the late second century may already have been present in the service as known to the author of 1 Peter. The important point for us to notice is that there is no evidence that Justin, or any other writer up to his time, had begun to identify any ceremony, other than Baptism in water, either with the sacramental medium of the gift of the Spirit or with the means whereby the believer was given the 'seal for the last day'.

If J. H. Bernard is right in his interpretation of that extremely difficult book, the *Odes of Solomon*,[1] these poems afford good evidence that the complicated and splendid ritual of initiation had already been developed to its full extent in Syria before the end of the century and perhaps before its last quarter. Dr. Bernard holds that the key to the mysterious language of the Odes is to be found in the fact that they are permeated through and through by the imagery and symbolism of Baptism. Since he, alone among their editors, seems to find it possible to elucidate these extraordinary poems intelligibly and coherently, his interpretation may well be correct;[2] but we may not use the Odes as evidence for orthodox thought about the seal of Baptism without great caution. They have certain affinities with such Gnostic writings as the 'Hymn of the Soul' in the *Acts of*

[1] *Texts and Studies*, 8, 1912; *JTS*. 12 (1911), pp. 1 ff. The Odes are dated by Bernard to the period between 150 and 190; by Zwaan (*Quantulacumque*, 1937, pp. 285 ff.) to 190–200 at Edessa.

[2] Dr. Rendel Harris, however (*The Odes and Psalms of Solomon*, p. 11 f.), thought that the simile of 'drinking living water' could not be applied to Baptism, and that the conception of the seal in the Odes is derived from Ezek. ix. 6 without reference to Baptism. We have seen that the O.T. texts which speak of 'drinking' are frequently applied to the reception of the Spirit, and they are very commonly applied to Baptism by the Fathers; we shall also find that Ezek. ix. 6 is frequently regarded as a prophecy of the baptismal seal. Dr. J. Estlin Carpenter (*Phases of Early Christianity*, p. 48), also opposes Bernard's interpretation, and asserts that the Odes contain no reference to Church or sacraments. If this were true their exegesis would seem to be almost impossible.

Thomas, and the appearance of part of the work in *Pistis Sophia* is sufficient to arouse the suspicion that they emanate from Christian circles whose orthodoxy was by no means unimpeachable.

What they reveal is, however, of great interest. If Bernard is right in discerning the theme of Baptism in every Ode, we may infer that for this author Baptism unites the believer with Christ in a profound mystical union and bestows upon him the Spirit of the Lord;[1] it assures the convert of immortal life which is the 'Spirit within'.[2] The neophyte is apparently crowned with a garland, symbolizing the presence of Christ, like a crown on the head of the believer;[3] he was also apparently arrayed in a white baptismal robe, the symbol of the robe of the Spirit which replaces the 'coats of skin' (Gen. iii. 21) which represent the corruptible nature of the unredeemed posterity of Adam.[4] Alternatively, the putting on of the baptismal garment signifies the putting off of darkness and clothing with light,[5] or the forsaking of folly and the believer's renewal in the raiment of the Lord, His light, and immortality.[6] The thought is similar to that of St. Paul when he speaks of the 'putting on' of Christ in Baptism,[7] but the language of the Odes suggests that this sacramental clothing with Christ was now represented in an outward symbol; the idea expressed in this robing with the baptismal garment is similar to that which we find in the 'Hymn of the Soul',[8] where the soul leaves its robe behind in heaven and regains it when its mission is accomplished. We may compare the later conception of Christ as the garment of incorruptibility received in Baptism,[9] and Optatus' remarkable simile in which he speaks of Christ as: 'tunica natans in aqua, quae multos vestiat ... sed ne quis dicat temere a me filium Dei vestem esse dictum, legat apostolum dicentem: quotquot in nomine Christi baptizati estis, Christum induistis. O tunica semper una et immutabilis quae decenter vestiat et omnes aetates et formas nec in infantibus rugatur.'[10] The same notion, expressed in rather less picturesque

---

[1] Od. 3.   [2] 28, 7.
[3] 1, 1–3; 5, 9–10; 9, 11; 17, 1. Cf. Ephr., *Hymn. Epiph.*, 13, 11; Conybeare, *Rit. Arm.*, pp. 99, 101, 103.
[4] 25, 8.   [5] 21, 2.   [6] 11, 9–10.   [7] Gal. iii. 27.   [8] *A. Thom.*, 108.
[9] Gr. Naz., *or.*, 40, 31 (*PG.* 36, 404B).   [10] Opt., 5. 10 (*CSEL.* p. 140, 12 ff.).

terms, occurs frequently in the Fathers, and occasionally the inward vesture which is symbolized in the ceremony is explicitly said to be the Holy Spirit in which the baptized are 'clothed'. Aphraates, for example, explains that 'in the same hour that the priests invoke the Spirit, the heavens open and it cometh down and broodeth upon the waters, and they that are baptized are clothed with it. For from all that are born of the body the Spirit is far away until they come to the birth by water, and then they receive the Holy Spirit.'[1]

The robe of Christ or of the Spirit is apparently brought into close relationship with the 'seal' of Baptism in the curious and difficult verse: 'For thy seal is known: and thy creatures know it: and thy hosts possess it: and the elect angels are clad with it.'[2] Bernard, however, suggests[3] that some such expression as 'the archangels recognize it' underlies the Syriac text. If this be true, the thought of the verse is one which can be paralleled in many of the Fathers—the idea that the seal as the mark of God's ownership enables the faithful to be recognized by the angels in the hereafter.

A different conception of the baptismal seal is to be found in Od. 24, 5. Here the idea is that the abyss, the home of the demons, is 'sealed up' by the Baptism of Christ in the Jordan. In two instances[4] there appears to be a reference to the use of the sign of the Cross in the baptismal ritual, and this sign set upon the newly baptized is related to the conception which we have noticed in the Apocalypse of the elect being visibly marked with the stamp of the divine ownership on their foreheads. Here we have an early occurrence of the seal as the sign of the Cross, a conception which is later developed to such an extent that consignation sometimes comes to be regarded as the only 'sealing' in Baptism, so that the external seal of the Cross is either substituted for the inward seal of the Spirit's

---

[1] *hom.* 6, 14 (trans. Burkitt, *Early Eastern Christianity*, pp. 124–5). We may compare the equation made in *A. Phil.*, 38 between the φωτεινὴ σφραγίς and the ἔνδοξος στολή which is given by Christ to enable the soul to pass through the 'cosmocratores' and the 'opposing dragon' and meet Christ in the air. The concepts of Spirit and Light are, of course, very closely linked in the thought of the Greek Fathers. The Spirit is not infrequently thought of in Hellenistic terms as a garment of light, clothed in which the initiate is enabled to ascend through the heavenly spheres.

[2] 4, 8.   [3] *Op. cit.*, p. 52.   [4] 8, 16; 29, 6.

presence, or else is associated with it as its proper outward symbol.

Of this latter development, however, there is no trace in the *Odes*. Although, as we have seen, the ritual which they are apparently interpreting is complex and full of symbolical actions, there is no support, so far as these obscure poems can be deciphered, for the theory that a double Baptism of water and of the Spirit was generally recognized in the second century, and that the latter was symbolized by a second ceremony in the initiation rite, either of unction or of the laying on of hands. There is absolutely no indication here of the latter practice, and no clear reference to unction; it is unlikely that an allusion to an outward anointing is intended in the expression: 'According to His own newness has he renewed me; and He anointed me from His own perfection.'[1] Unction is not, in any case, associated with the seal in these poems, and it is more likely that the allusion is to the Spirit-anointing of Christ (in which the believer is enabled to share through his union with Christ) rather than to a literal anointing with oil.

The same difficulty arises in the interpretation of the explanation given by Theophilus of Antioch of the title 'Christian': ἡμεῖς τούτου εἵνεκεν καλούμεθα Χριστιανοί, ὅτι χριόμεθα ἔλαιον Θεοῦ.[2] In my opinion Theophilus is echoing the opinion of St. Paul and St. John, and is describing Christians as the 'Messianic people' who have been made members of the Anointed One whose unction of the Spirit is metaphorically the 'oil of God'.[3]

This interpretation does not, of course, rule out the possibility that the believer's participation in the Anointed may have been signified at some point in his initiation by a physical anointing. As we have seen, such an unction is by no means unlikely to have taken place; it would be an impressive piece of edifying ceremonial, and would have been suggested by biblical precedents and analogies. The important fact is that nowhere in the writers whom we have been considering is there any indication that such an anointing, if it did take place, was regarded as constituting or mediating the 'seal', or as conveying the gift of the Spirit.

---

[1] 36, 5.   [2] *Autol.*, i, 12 (*PG*. 6, 1041C).   [3] Cf. Ps. xlv. 8.

One possible exception to this general conclusion may be afforded by another somewhat obscure document, which may probably be dated early in the latter half of the second century, the *Epistula Apostolorum*. This may perhaps allow some rather better ground for postulating a distinction between Baptism and the seal, for here we read of a promise of Christ that 'Whosoever shall hear you and believe on me shall receive of you the light of the seal, and Baptism through me.'[1] At best, however, this passage is ambiguous, and the seal may be synonymous with Baptism; the expression, 'the light of the seal', suggests that the writer's intention is to draw attention to one aspect of the baptismal seal—its function of 'illuminating' the believer—rather than to distinguish Baptism from a sealing administered through some other piece of ritual such as a pre-baptismal unction.

If this latter interpretation be true, we may usefully compare this passage with the reference to the 'seal of the Lord' in the early story of St. John and the Robber contained in Clement's *Quis Dives Salvetur?* In this narrative the young man who afterwards 'went to the bad' is handed over by St. John to the local bishop who took him home, brought him up, τὸ τελευταῖον ἐφώτισε, καὶ μετὰ τοῦτο ὑφῆκε τῆς πλείονος ἐπιμελείας καὶ παραφυλακῆς, ὡς τέλεον αὐτῷ φυλακτήριον ἐπιστήσας τὴν σφραγῖδα τοῦ Κυρίου.[2] The seal which is here given to the young man as a prophylactic against evil is evidently identical with the Baptism with which he was 'enlightened', for a little earlier in the same book the 'seal' is equated with 'redemption' from sin[3] and remission of sins is one of the effects of Baptism which have never, in antiquity or modern times, been associated with the rite of Confirmation.

The surviving works of Melito of Sardis show a similar conception of the baptismal seal. He strongly emphasizes the theory of the Spirit's presence in the water, which, though quite unscriptural, becomes a commonplace in the Fathers and is developed by some ancient authors into a doctrine approximating to that of a 'Real Presence' of the Spirit in the font.[4]

---

[1] *Ep. App.*, 40 (James, *Apocryphal N.T.*, p. 500).
[2] Clem., *q. d. s.*, 42 (*GCS* p. 188, 18; *PG.* 9, 648C).
[3] *Ibid.*, 39. [4] *fr.*, ap Pitra, *AS.* 2, pp. 3 ff.

Baptism confers the seal of the Lord upon the believer, and in Melito's *Homily on the Passion* (which expounds the Passover in the context of an Easter address which is largely concerned with the baptism administered to converts at that season) we find the earliest example of another Patristic commonplace— the typology which saw the prophylactic seal of the Spirit in Baptism as an antitype of the blood of the Passover lamb sprinkled upon the doorposts of the Israelites.[1] His language is illuminating; it affords an interesting example of the highly eschatological sense which the concept of the seal continues to bear in the Fathers as in the New Testament: ὅποτε τὸ πρόβατον σφάζεται καὶ τὸ πάσχα βιβρώσκεται καὶ τὸ μυστήριον τελεῖται καὶ ὁ λαὸς εὐφραίνεται καὶ ὁ Ἰσραὴλ σφραγίζεται, τότε ἀφίκετο ὁ ἄγγελος πατάσσειν Αἴγυπτον τὴν ἀμύητον τοῦ μυστηρίου, τὴν ἄμοιρον τοῦ πασχᾶ, τὴν ἀσφράγιστον τοῦ αἵματος, τὴν ἀφρούρητον τοῦ Πνεύματος, τὴν ἐχθράν.[2] It also gives us a clear indication of the union in Baptism of the gifts of remission of sins, or rather, deliverance from the devil, and of 'stamping' with the sign of the Spirit, this 'sealing' being effected in the believer through the application to him of the 'Passover' sacrifice of Christ: ὡς ἀμνὸς ἀχθεὶς . . . ἐλυτρώσατο ἡμᾶς ἐκ τῆς τοῦ διαβόλου δουλείας ὡς ἐκ χειρὸς Φαραώ, καὶ ἐσφράγισεν ἡμῶν τὰς ψυχὰς τῷ ἰδίῳ πνεύματι καὶ τὰ μέλη τοῦ σώματος τῷ ἰδίῳ αἵματι.[3] Like the other second-century authors whom we have been considering, Melito affords us no evidence for supposing that at this period a distinction was drawn between a rite of water-baptism and another of Spirit-baptism by which the 'seal' was conferred.

The views of Irenaeus on this subject are less clearly defined. In the *Demonstration of the Apostolic Preaching*, however, he plainly teaches that the bestowal of the indwelling presence of the Holy Spirit is the inward counterpart of Baptism in water: 'The apostles', he tells us, '. . . wrought the conversion of the Gentiles . . . cleansing their souls and bodies by the baptism of

---

[1] Cf. Gr. Naz., *or.*, 1–3 (*PG.* 35, 397A); id., *carm.*, 1, 1, 9, 91 (*PG.* 37, 464A); Hil., *tract. myst.*, 2, 9 (*CSEL.* p. 35, 10); Aug., *catech. rud.*, 34; Const. Diac., *laud.*, 37 (*PG.* 88, 521C), this last instance affording an interesting example of the eschatological significance of the seal of the Spirit, as well as of the Passover typology: πάντων τὸ τέλος ἤγγικεν· εἴ τις οὐκ ἐνεσημάνθη τῇ σφραγῖδι τοῦ πνεύματος, σημειωθήτω φωτὶ τοῦ βαπτίσματος, καὶ τῷ ἀχράντῳ αἵματι τὰς νοερὰς ἐπιχρίσει φλιάς, καὶ τοὺς σταθμοὺς τῶν αἰσθήσεων· οὐ γὰρ ἄλλως τὸν ὀλοθρευτὴν διαφεύξεται.

[2] Bonner, p. 3, 4–14.   [3] *Ibid.*, p. 11, 4–9.

water and of the Holy Spirit.'[1] In the Christian believer there 'continually abides the Holy Spirit who was given by Him in Baptism. . . . For this soul has a resurrection in them that believe, the body receiving the soul again, and along with it, by the power of the Holy Spirit, being raised up and entering the kingdom of God.'[2] Here we are once again presented with a theory very similar to that of the Pauline doctrine of the Spirit as an earnest or first-fruits of the final redemption; indeed, a comparison of Irenaeus' work with the New Testament suggests that the title, 'Demonstration of the Apostolic Preaching', is by no means a misnomer. The same use of Old Testament proofs appears in his book as in the New Testament; thus, in a comment on Isa. xliii. 18 ff. he writes: 'A wilderness and a waterless place was at first the calling of the Gentiles; for the Word had not passed through them, nor given them the Holy Spirit *to drink*.'[3] It is not surprising to find that he regards Baptism as effecting both remission of sins and sealing for eternity: 'We have received Baptism', he reminds his readers, 'for the remission of sins, in the name of God the Father, and in the name of Jesus Christ the Son of God, who was incarnate and died and rose again, and in the Holy Spirit of God. And this Baptism is the seal of eternal life, and is the new birth unto God.'[4]

The only reference to unction to be found in this treatise relates to the Messianic anointing with the Spirit, both of Jesus and of His followers: 'The Son, as being God, receives from the Father, that is from God, the throne of the everlasting kingdom, and the oil of anointing above His fellows. The oil of anointing is the Spirit, wherewith He has been anointed; and His fellows are prophets and righteous men and apostles, and all who receive the fellowship of the Kingdom.'[5] A different use of the term 'seal' occurs once in this book, when it signifies the seal of faith which is constituted by the Trinitarian formula in Baptism.[6]

In the *Adversus Haereses* a similar theory of Baptism appears.

---

[1] *dem.*, 41.　　[2] *Ibid.*, 42.　　[3] *Ibid.*, 89.　　[4] *Ibid.*, 3.
[5] *Ibid.*, 47 (with ref. to Ps. xlv. 6).
[6] *Ibid.*, 100. By the 'Trinitarian formula' at this early date we should probably understand as a rule the baptismal interrogation and the candidate's response asserting his faith in the Three Persons.

Those who believe on the name of the Lord and are 'washed' (abluti), receive the Spirit and obtain the 'image of the heavenly'.[1] The gift of the Spirit to man is made possible by the Baptism of Christ when the Spirit descended, 'cum ipso assuescens habitare in genere humano, et requiescere in hominibus'.[2]

An important new development, however, occurs in one passage of Irenaeus. Unfortunately it comes in the form of a passing illustration, and Irenaeus does not pause to develop its implications. This important development consists in his peculiar exegesis of 1 Cor. iii. 2, which he takes to mean that St. Paul's Corinthian converts had not been strong enough in their 'spiritual senses' (an early instance of this idea) to receive the βρῶμα of the Spirit who is the βρῶμα ζωῆς, although the Apostle had the power to give them this βρῶμα, for those on whom they (i.e. the Apostles) laid their hands received the Holy Spirit.[3] Here we have the first clear instance of the impact of Acts viii. 17 on the Patristic theology of Baptism. As we have observed, Irenaeus merely makes a passing allusion to the passage of Acts; we cannot therefore expect from him any answer to the question whether he is really thinking here of the gift of the Spirit as regularly connected with the laying on of hands. If he did take this view, he could scarcely be acquitted of inconsistency, for the passages which we have considered above assert unequivocally that Christians are given the Holy Spirit in Baptism, which is of water and the Holy Spirit; he could scarcely suppose, therefore, that the Corinthians had to wait for an imposition of hands in order to receive the Spirit, and that if this did not happen to them their Baptism was deficient in its positive gift. It might be argued that Irenaeus is thinking here of the Spirit, not as the essential principle of Christian life, but as a special gift of grace—an 'augmentation' (to use the language of a later age) of the initial gift of the Spirit in Baptism. It seems much more likely, however, that Irenaeus is thinking of the text of Acts, and not of the current practice of his own day. He understands Acts to imply that the Holy Spirit was bestowed by the imposition of the apostolic hands, and he draws the conclusion that the Corinthians did

---

[1] haer., 5, 11, 2.   [2] Ibid., 3, 17, 1.   [3] Ibid., 4, 38, 2.

not receive the gift if St. Paul did not lay his hands upon them; he does not attempt to relate this supposed practice of the first century to what he has experienced himself in the baptismal rite of his own times. It cannot, of course, be demonstrated that the laying on of hands did not take place in the baptismal ceremony personally known to Irenaeus; but he gives no hint that it did in fact occur. He cannot be cited without great hesitation as a witness to such a practice in the second-century Church. Dix is probably right in his suggestion that 'it would hardly have been necessary to add this explanation (sc. 'for those on whom they laid their hands received the Holy Spirit') if the rite had been well known in his time, nor does he anywhere suggest that it was still practised'.[1] What we find in this passage is, in fact, the beginning of that confusion of thought which was to become so prominent in the third century, especially in the West, when Tertullian and Cyprian felt compelled to attempt to force the puzzling narrative of Acts viii. 1–17 into an uneasy synthesis with the received tradition that the gift of the Spirit was an essential aspect of the inward significance of water-baptism itself. These writers did not pause to enquire whether the conception of the Spirit in the mind of St. Luke was identical or not with that of St. Paul,[2] and whether his accounts of the laying on of hands are to be accepted as typical of the general practice of Christian initiation in the apostolic age; they assumed that this was so, and were left with the task of harmonizing Scriptural evidence which was, on the face of it, self-contradictory. Irenaeus may therefore have to bear the responsibility for having in his one passing illustration laid the foundation of a deep theological confusion which has persisted down the centuries and reappears in the Preface to the Order of Confirmation in the Prayer Book of 1928.

On the other hand, it is probably a mistake to press Irenaeus into service as a witness for the practice of unction in initiation, and for its significance as the outward rite of the seal of the Spirit. The passage cited for this purpose by Dix[3] is: 'Spiritus ergo Dei descendit in eum, eius qui per prophetas

---

[1] *Confirmation or the Laying on of Hands?* p. 19.
[2] Chrysostom did realize the difficulty (*hom.* 40. 1 *in Ac.*, 9, 303C).
[3] *Op. cit.*, p. 19.

promiserat uncturum se eum, ut de abundantia unctionis eius nos percipientes salvaremur.'[1] This is simply a repetition of the common New Testament thought that Christians have entered into the baptismal experience of Jesus and been made partakers of His Messianic anointing with the Spirit. There is no reason to suppose from this passage that Irenaeus has in mind any physical anointing, whether or not such a practice was known to him; and a similar reference to Christ's unction with the Spirit[2] strongly suggests the contrary. Here he describes the descent of the dove and applies to it the Isaianic prophecy of anointing with the Spirit;[3] he proceeds to remind his readers of the Apostles' reception of the 'potestas regenerationis in Deum' with the commission to baptize all nations,[4] of the Pentecostal outpouring, and the extension of the gift of the Spirit to all believers. This is illustrated by reference to water-baptism which is the external counterpart of baptism with the Spirit: 'Corpora enim nostra per lavacrum illam quae est ad incorruptionem unitatem acceperunt, animae autem per Spiritum.' The 'living water' of John iv. 7 is then explained as the gift which the Lord received from the Father and bestowed on those who became partakers of Himself, 'in universam terram mittens Spiritum sanctum'; the theme is illustrated by the citation of some regular Old Testament types and prophecies of Baptism, and the passage is concluded with an allusion to the seal of the Spirit, expressed in an allegorical interpretation of the Good Samaritan's 'duo denaria regalia' which represent the gift to man of the 'stamp' of the divine image: 'per Spiritum imaginem et inscriptionem Patris et Filii accipientes.'

Irenaeus is therefore not to be cited as an upholder of a theory of any 'sealing' administered with a rite of unction. Where such anointing was certainly practised in the second century, and held to be a means of sealing the believer for future redemption, is among the Gnostic sects.

At first sight the importance which many Gnostics attached to the ceremony of unction is surprising, for it might appear to be more in keeping with their depreciation of material things that they should avoid the use of material means of grace; and Irenaeus tells us that the Marcosian sect alleged that the mystery

haer., 3, 9, 3.   [2] haer., 3, 17, 1–3.   [3] Isa. lxi. 1.   [4] Matt. xxviii. 19.

of the ineffable and unseen power should not be celebrated
through visible and corruptible creatures, or the inconceivable
and bodiless through things which are corporeal and sensible.
Redemption must be 'spiritual'. The inward spiritual man must
be redeemed by knowledge.[1] Nevertheless, the great majority
of the Gnostic sects evidently practised unction in their initiations, and held it to be the means by which a believer is
'sealed'. We need not suppose that this was due to their having
inherited a good old Catholic tradition. As we have seen, the
orthodox writers of the second century afford us no good ground
for believing that there was any such custom to inherit. On the
other hand, the syncretistic outlook of the heretical sects would
naturally incline them to assimilate their initiations to the
pagan mysteries, and their dislike of a simpler and more elementary use of water as a sacramental means of grace would
dispose them to elaborate the ceremony of initiation and em-
bellish it with less ordinary and common symbols than that
of washing. Indeed, once the Christocentric theology of Baptism
had been abandoned—as the Gnostic denial of a true Incarnation and Atonement would logically necessitate—the retention
of water-baptism as the sacrament of 'sealing' would appear
otiose. Apart from the Baptism of Christ as represented in the
Christian rite and made available for believers to share, Baptism
in water would naturally seem an inappropriate symbol; they
therefore either replaced it or supplemented it with other rites
of which unction was the most important.

Moreover, in Gnostic circles the conception of the 'seal'
played a highly significant part, for the initiate, according to
their view, bears a seal which protects him against the evil
influence of the heavenly powers, affords him a passport to
carry him safely through the spheres of the 'Archontes', and
guarantees him redemption from the material world, and the
promise of future blessedness. The seal is the effective sign of the
Gnostic's transformation from his previous state of being χοικός
into a condition where he becomes πνευματικός. In its highest
and most Christian form this doctrine is recognizably connected
with traditional orthodox theories of the bestowal of the Spirit,
the power of the threefold Name in Baptism, or the believer's

[1] *haer.*, I, 21, 1–4.

recovery through the grace of Baptism of the stamp of the divine image.

This is notably the case in Clement's *Excerpta Theodoti*,[1] where we read: ὃν δὲ ἀναγεννᾷ Χριστὸς εἰς ζωὴν μετατίθεται, εἰς Ὀγδοάδα, καὶ ἀποθνήσκουσι μὲν τῷ κόσμῳ, ζῶσι δὲ τῷ Θεῷ, ἵνα θάνατος θανάτῳ λυθῇ, ἀναστάσει δὲ ἡ φθορά· διὰ γὰρ Πατρὸς καὶ Υἱοῦ καὶ ἁγίου Πνεύματος σφραγισθεὶς ἀνεπίληπτός ἐστι πάσῃ τῇ ἄλλῃ δυνάμει, καὶ διὰ τριῶν Ὀνομάτων πάσης τῆς ἐν φθορᾷ τριάδος ἀπηλλάγη· φορέσας τὴν εἰκόνα τοῦ χοικοῦ, τότε φορεῖ τὴν εἰκόνα τοῦ ἐπουρανίου . . . καὶ τὸ βάπτισμα οὖν διπλοῦν ἀναλόγως· τὸ μὲν αἰσθητὸν δἰ ὕδατος, τοῦ αἰσθητοῦ πυρὸς σβεστήριον· τὸ δὲ νοητὸν διὰ Πνεύματος, τοῦ νοητοῦ πυρὸς ἀλεξητήριον. In a short exposition of the 'Tribute to Caesar', the seal of the Spirit is compared with the 'image', and the divine Name with the 'inscription': οὕτως καὶ ὁ πιστός· ἐπιγραφὴν μὲν ἔχει διὰ Χριστοῦ τὸ ὄνομα τοῦ Θεοῦ, τὸ δὲ Πνεῦμα ὡς εἰκόνα· καὶ τὰ ἄλογα ζῷα διὰ σφραγῖδος δείκνυσι τίνος ἐστὶν ἕκαστον· καὶ ἐκ τῆς σφραγῖδος ἐκδικεῖται· οὕτως καὶ ἡ ψυχὴ ἡ πιστή, τὸ τῆς ἀληθείας λαβοῦσα σφράγισμα, τὰ στίγματα τοῦ Χριστοῦ περιφέρει. Here we are not far from orthodoxy. A more typical example of the Gnostic conception of a sealing which affords a safe conduct through the spheres of the aeons is to be found in the Naassene hymn preserved in Hippolytus.[2] Here Christ is represented as declaring to the Father His purpose of redeeming mankind, for the accomplishment of which he will descend through the heavenly spheres 'bearing seals': τούτου με χάριν πέμψον, πάτερ· σφραγῖδας ἔχων καταβήσομαι, αἰῶνας ὅλους διοδεύσω, μυστήρια πάντα διανοίξω, μορφὰς δὲ θεῶν ἐπιδείξω· καὶ τὰ κεκρυμμένα τῆς ἁγίας ὁδοῦ, γνῶσιν καλέσας, παραδώσω. It is possible that the 'seals' in this case are the potent names of heavenly powers, but whatever they may in fact be, the thought of the Gnostics is that just as the Redeemer possesses the seals which protect him from the hostile powers, so the initiate has the seal which gives him the key to mysteries and a safe conduct through the realms of the 'cosmocratores'.[3]

It is true that the conception of the seal as a prophylactic is to be found in the Bible, and we may notice it, in passing, in the

---

[1] *exc. Thdot.*, 80, 81, 86.
[2] *haer.*, 5, 10 (*GCS.* p. 102; *PG.* 16, 3159). [3] Cf. *A. Phil.*, 38.

Testament of Job's idea of a sealing, received from an angel, which protects its recipient from the attacks of the devil;[1] but in the Gnostic literature we are closer to the notions of Hellenistic religion than to the beliefs of Judaism, and very near the pagan mysteries with their 'sealings' of initiates as a token of their future attainment of a blessed immortality.[2] This type of thought is characteristic of the second century half-Christianized 'common man', and it persists; a typical instance of it occurs later in the *Acta Philippi*,[3] where the φωτεινὴ σφραγίς is identified with the ἔνδοξος στολὴ given by Christ to the soul to enable it to pass through the heavenly spheres unharmed and meet the Lord in the air. In an early liturgy[4] which represents the same sort of outlook there is an obscure allusion to the 'power of our first power' (perhaps the power of the Spirit in which we were baptized) by which, the worshipper prays, we may be sealed, given power, made strong, and raised on high.

When we turn to the more pagan forms of this mode of thought as we find them expressed in *Pistis Sophia* and the books of Jeû, we encounter the idea of the seal on almost every page.[5] It is a seal of protection against the Archontes;[6] it is marked on the forehead of the saved; it is given, according to *Pistis Sophia*, by the Light-Maiden; and seals, the form of each of which is described, follow in Jeû[7] the baptisms of water, fire, and Spirit. Here we are rapidly approaching the realm of magic, pure and simple; not dissimilar notions are to be found in the magical papyri.[8]

With so much insistence on the absolute necessity of the 'seal', it is not surprising that the Gnostic sects should have evolved quasi-sacramental means of conferring it, means which should be less 'psychic' and more obviously 'pneumatic' than water-baptism, and at the same time more esoteric. Hence we

[1] *Test. Job.*, 5 (Texts & Studies 5, p. 106, 20).
[2] Cf. Tert., *apol.*, 8; *CIL.* 3, 686.
[3] 38; cf. Anz, *Zur Frage nach dem Ursprung des Gnostizismus* (*TU.* 15⁴).
[4] Vienna Papyrus 19896ᵛᵒ· 16 (*PO.* 18, 446).
[5] Cf. *Pist. Soph.*, 86, 103, 108, 111; *Jeû*, 1, 33 (Schmidt, p. 290); 40 (Schmidt, p. 296, etc.).
[6] *Jeû*, 2, 43-7.   [7] 2, 46 ff.
[8] e.g. *P. mag. Berol.*, 1, 306 (Preisendanz, p. 16): ὁρκίζω κεφαλήν τε θεοῦ, ὅπερ ἐστὶν ᵓΟλυμπος, ὁρκίζω σφραγῖδα Θεοῦ, ὅπερ ἐστὶν ὅρασις, ὁρκίζω χέρα δεξιτέρην, ἣν κόσμῳ ἐπέσχες.

find in these heresies that a distinction tends to be drawn between water-baptism and Spirit-baptism (which has its own sacramental rite); here, in fact, is the first clear evidence of that separation of water-baptism and Spirit-baptism which so many writers have read into the New Testament and claimed to discover in the earliest orthodox Fathers, and which some would wish us to revive in our modern doctrine and practice.

Sometimes this distinction is made by referring the words of Jesus in John iii. 5 ff. to a 'spiritual birth' effected by a mysterious and spiritual 'great Jordan' which is a blend of the Red Sea of the Exodus and the Ocean of *Odyssey* 24, 11–12.[1] More frequently, as in the case of the Marcosians, the water-baptism for remission of sins is distinguished from the baptism of redemption or of perfection, which may take various forms (ὅσοι γάρ εἰσι ταύτης τῆς γνώμης μυσταγωγοί, τοσαῦται ἀπολυτρώσεις).[2] Hence the Baptism of Christ was divided into two separate acts, the baptism of the earthly (φαινόμενος) Jesus, and the ἀπολύτρωσις of the Christ who descended upon him εἰς τελείωσιν.[3] The former was 'psychic', the latter 'spiritual'. The texts in which Christ referred to the baptism which he had to be baptized with[4] were applied to the ἀπολύτρωσις which was to give His followers τελείωσις.

The second, pneumatic, baptism might be administered in several ways; by adding to the baptism in water quasi-magical formulae in which the Name played a prominent part, by baptizing by affusion with a mixture of oil and water; and by anointing with unguents. Some, however, regarded all such ceremonies as superfluous, and maintained that the true λύτρωσις was obtained purely through γνῶσις.[5] The Valentinians also employed an imposition of hands with the formula εἰς λύτρωσιν ἀγγελικήν.[6] Thus the Gnostic sects afford the first unambiguous evidence not only for the doctrinal separation of Spirit-baptism from the outward washing,[7] but also for the

---

[1] Naassene doctrine ap. Hipp., *haer.*, 5, 7 (*GCS.* p. 88, 12 ff.; *PG.* 16, 3138C ff.).
[2] Iren., *haer.*, 1, 21, 1; cf. Marcosian formula rendered by Irenaeus (1, 21, 3): ἐστήριγμαι, καὶ λελύτρωμαι, καὶ λουτροῦμαι τὴν ψυχήν μου ἀπὸ τοῦ αἰῶνος τούτου, καὶ πάντων τῶν παρ'αὐτοῦ ἐν τῷ ὀνόματι τοῦ Ἰααώ, ὃς ἐλυτρώσατο τὴν ψυχὴν αὐτοῦ εἰς ἀπολύτρωσιν ἐν τῷ Χριστῷ τῷ ζῶντι.
[3] *Ibid.*, 1, 22, 2; cf. Hipp., *haer.*, 8, 10 (p. 230, 17; *PG.* 16, 3365A).
[4] Mark x. 38; Luke xii. 50.   [5] Iren., *haer.*, 1, 21, 1–4.
[6] Clem., *exc. Thdot.*, 22, 5.   [7] Cf. the 'baptisms' of *Pist. Soph.*, 122, 143.

practice of unction with ointment at the ceremony of initiation. Anointing is in fact a regular feature of the Gnostic baptismal rite; it is true that the interesting reference by Theodotus to consecrated oil may perhaps allude, not to the use of it at Baptism (the mention of the oil is more closely associated with a reference to Eucharistic bread than to the allusion to the 'water of baptism' which follows a little later), but rather to its employment in the unction of the sick;[1] nevertheless, unction was certainly practised at Baptism by the Marcionites,[2] and by the Naassenes.[3] It is of some interest to observe that the latter sect, one of the most syncretistic of the Gnostic bodies, making great use of pagan mythology allegorized into mysteries of creation and redemption, introduced Attis into their system, and that it was the practice of unction in the mysteries of Attis which led Firmicus Maternus to contrast the 'christi' of the devil with Christians who were anointed with the spiritual unction of the Messiah.[4] At a slightly later date than Hippolytus' Naassenes (probably in the third century) we find the same emphasis on unction in an inscription from Rome whose language strongly suggests a Gnostic origin: λουτροῖς χρεισαμένη Χριστοῦ μύρον ἄφθιτον ἄγνον.[5]

The idea of anointing was frequently connected in these circles with the old notion of a saving unguent emanating from the Tree of Life. This strange conception (which may have its roots in the prominence given to the Tree of Life in the Apocalypse and perhaps also in the trees planted by the ὕδωρ ἀφέσεως in Ezek. xlvii) occurs in 4 Ezra ii. 12, and was evidently popular both in Jewish and Gnostic circles. A somewhat similar idea is to be found among the heretics described in the sixth book of Hippolytus' 'Refutatio',[6] and the belief itself is mentioned more fully by Origen as one of the 'unheard of things' adduced by Celsus as samples of what he supposed to be the tenets of orthodox Christianity.[7]

The sect with which Celsus had become acquainted was probably that of the Ophites. The initiate is here said to stand in a

[1] Clem., exc. Thdot., 82, 1.
[2] Tert., Marc., 1, 14.
[3] Hipp., haer., 5, 7 (GCS. p. 83, 7; PG. 16, 3131C).
[4] prof. rel. err., 22-3.
[5] CIG. 4, 9595a.
[6] haer., 6, 9 (p. 137, 11; PG. 16, 3210C).
[7] Cels., 6, 27 (GCS. p. 96 f.; PG. 11, 1332D ff.).

son-father relationship to the administrant of the 'sealing', an idea which is strongly reminiscent of the 'mystery' idea that the mystagogue is a 'father' to the neophyte.[1] The 'son's' liturgical response at the time of receiving the seal is: 'I have been anointed with white chrism from the Tree of Life.' A similar conception appears in *Pistis Sophia*, and in the *Gospel of Nicodemus* where there appears a story of how Seth was told to go to Paradise and seek oil from the tree of life for the benefit of Adam in his sickness. He was unable to obtain it then, but the promise was given to him that the Son of God would become incarnate, anoint Adam with oil, and raise him up. Then he would wash him in water and the Spirit and cure him from every disease.[2] Here, however, although the idea of the Tree of Life is essentially the same as that which we have seen in Origen's Ophite heresy, the thought is not primarily of any 'sealing' with the oil; the oil is evidently to be connected with healing, and with the symbolical representation of the new life granted to the convert in Christ, and the cleansing with the Spirit is not linked with the oil but with the water of Baptism. The thought of the Holy Spirit is, as a matter of fact, not really prominent in the Gnostic 'sealings', which are more closely related to the use of oil in pagan magic,[3] and to the practice of unction in the ceremonies of the mystery religions.[4] Their essential significance is the imprinting of a mark upon the soul of the initiate which the demons and the 'world-rulers' will recognize and fear, and which thus enables him to ascend through the planetary spheres and to be assured of salvation.

The outward signing is the medium of this quasi-magical sealing or marking of the soul. It is usually performed by means of unction, and the Marcosians appear to be the first to employ the unguent which was later used by all Christians in consignation and is to be distinguished from the ordinary oil which was employed for the catechumen's pre-baptismal unction. The Carpocratians, however, did not use unction, but a visible outward brand like the σφραγίς with which cattle were marked. They cauterized their disciples, says Irenaeus, behind the lobe

---

[1] Cf. the practice of the 'Archontici' in Thdt., *haer.*, I, 11.
[2] A. Pil., 14 (*Ev. Nic.*, 3), Tischendorf, pp. 325–6.
[3] P. mag., Par., 746, 772, 1338.
[4] e.g. Paus., 9, 39, 7; Firm. Mat., *prof. rel. err.*, 22, 1.

of the right ear.[1] On the authority of Heracleon, Clement remarks that ἔνιοι . . . πυρὶ τὰ ὦτα τῶν σφραγιζομένων κατεσημήναντο,[2] and adds that the practice was regarded by them as a fulfilment of the Baptist's prophecy of a baptism with fire. Epiphanius gives us a similar account, mentioning that the sign was either branded or tattooed.[3] But this is an eccentric development. In most of these heresies the sealing is connected with anointing, with which it is probable that there went consignation with the Cross.[4] The seal is also often connected with the power of the divine Name in initiation as well as with the external rite;[5] hence it is in these circles that we first find a reference to the exorcism of the baptismal water by the power of the Name of God.[6] On the whole, however, the Gnostic conceptions of the seal are crude in the extreme and represent the beliefs and superstitions of the popular or half-educated mind. They are very different from the orthodox idea of the seal of the Spirit; it must not be forgotten that Theodotus appears to regard the seal as something which perpetuated the spiritual state in which a man was at the moment of its reception, so that it is possible for unclean spirits to accompany a man to his baptism and receive the seal which will render them ἀνίατα τοῦ λοιποῦ.[7] It is in all probability, then, to these curious sects that we must go in order to find the source of the separation of Spirit-baptism from water-baptism which we meet from time to time in the third century, and it is to these circles that we probably ought also to look for the introduction of subsidiary ceremonies such as post-baptismal unction; even if these rites did not originate with the Gnostic or semi-Gnostic sects, they probably acquired a new and greatly enhanced significance at their hands.

It may well be asked how the Catholic Church could come to adopt the practices, and in some cases, the modes of thought, of those whom it condemned as heretics. Dix maintains that it is simply impossible that any such borrowing could take place.[8]

---

[1] haer., 1, 25, 6.   [2] ecl., 25, 1.
[3] hoer., 27, 5 (GCS. p. 308, 3; PG. 41, 372A).
[4] For the efficacy of the sign of the Cross as a prophylactic see A. Jo., 115 (Lipsius-Bonnet, p. 215).
[5] Iren., haer., 1, 21, 3.   [6] Clem., exc. Thdot., 82, 2; cf. Iren., fr., 35 (33).
[7] Clem., exc. Thdot., 83.   [8] The Apostolic Tradition, p. xxxix.

In respect of the *Apostolic Tradition* of Hippolytus, an early witness to the Catholic practice of a post-baptismal unction and 'sealing', and possibly (though I believe that this is not the case) the earliest orthodox witness to a separation of the gift of the Spirit from Baptism in water, Dix writes as follows: 'It is noticeable that the outlines of the same baptismal rite are clearly represented also in the Valentinian Gnostic writers excerpted by Clement of Alexandria. This evidence is older by a generation at least, than the Apostolic Tradition. . . . No one who has read the trouncing which Hippolytus accords the Valentinians in the *Philosophoumena*, including the statement that Valentinus was a Pythagorean and not a Christian at all, will suspect Hippolytus himself of being the borrower; and before him we are actually back in the very generation of Popes and presbyters at Rome who had witnessed the excommunication of Valentinus. We have to remember that Valentinus had been for years a venerated "teacher" of the Roman Church, and is even said to have been the narrowly defeated second candidate at a Papal election (Tert., *Valent.*, 4). It is far more likely that Valentinus carefully retained in use for his own followers the rites already ancient at which he had so often assisted as a loyal son of the Roman Church, than that there was once a direct borrowing of Gnostic rites by the most conservative and traditionalist Church in Christendom. . . . We may safely take it that in outline and essentials the rites and customs to which the Apostolic Tradition bears witness were those practised in the Roman Church in his own day, and in his own youth, c. A.D. 180.'

To this it may be replied that there is no question of Hippolytus himself being an innovator or composing this liturgical work out of his own imagination. It is not a new use, introduced for the first time by its author. It certainly represents, if the generally accepted view of its provenance and date be correct, the custom of the Roman Church at the beginning of the third century. Hippolytus is an exponent, and in some degree an embellisher, of material which he, and presumably his congregation, regarded as traditional. This is particularly the case so far as ritual actions are concerned; prayer-forms were not stereotyped, and in fact the prayers in the *Tradition* show traces of the distinctive outlook of the author. We need not therefore suppose that Hippolytus was in any way a conscious borrower from Gnostic sources.

It does not follow that the tradition was really 'apostolic' or even very old. On the contrary, we must bear in mind the general tendency in the ancient world to ascribe a hoary antiquity to anything which was known to have existed for as long as living people could remember—a tendency which the relative shortness of the average human life must greatly have facilitated, and which was most marked in the sphere of laws, customs, and constitutions. On the analogy of the many examples which could be cited of the ease with which Greco-Roman institutions could acquire an aura of immemorial antiquity, we need not feel compelled to ascribe anything like genuine apostolicity to the *Apostolic Tradition*; and there is certainly no reason to treat its claim to 'apostolicity', such as it is, with more respect than that of the 'Teaching of the Twelve Apostles'. The state of affairs which it illustrates may well have grown up at no earlier a period than the third quarter of the second century, and perhaps even later.

When we have made all due allowance for the unreliability of the *argumentum ex silentio* drawn from a scanty literature containing no major theological work, it remains true that the absence of any clear allusions to the practices of unction or consignation, or to any connection of the baptismal 'seal' with these ceremonies, in the orthodox writers of the period from the New Testament to Irenaeus is a fact to which we must attach considerable weight. In the absence of any evidence for these practices in the apostolic writings themselves, we may reasonably conclude that the initiation rite of Hippolytus represents a development of the early form of Baptism with the addition of impressive and edifying ceremonies in the building up of which a good deal of borrowing took place from Gnostic and semi-Gnostic sources.

If this was the case, it need cause us no surprise. Orthodox Christians, whether in Rome or elsewhere, did not consciously and deliberately borrow directly from the known leaders of heresy, nor did they import wholesale the semi-pagan fancies about unction and sealing which we have just considered; nor, in all probability, did teachers such as Tertullian and Hippolytus know the ultimate sources of the practices which were adopted. Liturgy, especially in ancient times, was in a measure shaped by the people. It was not directly controlled by theologians, bishops, or outstanding Churchmen. It 'grew', and its growth, particularly in the early days of the Church, might involve much borrowing and assimilation which would not infrequently take place almost subconsciously. In the case of baptismal procedure the borrowing is in any case not from the extreme Gnostics; an orthodox congregation would not deliberately imitate the Ophites or the Carpocratians, any more than Hippolytus himself (of whom Dix remarks[1] that he 'had nothing but contempt for "the People" and their dumb observances') would have consciously and deliberately borrowed from Judaism those elements in his rites of Baptism and Eucharist which, as Dix has shown, have affinities with Jewish practice.

The situation appears rather to have been that certain elements of belief and practice which the Gnostics developed to extreme lengths made a strong appeal to the mental and spiritual outlook of the man in the street; they were suited to the atmosphere of the time, and orthodox congregations would adopt such of them as they found most congenial, at the same time rejecting the fantasies which were sometimes associated with them in some forms of Gnostic speculation.

In fact the practices which had been assimilated by the Roman Church's liturgical tradition by the time of Hippolytus were subsidiary rites which would very naturally be added to the baptismal ceremony. Unction and signing with the Cross represent a translation into visible action of Scriptural metaphors, and their development would probably have taken place sooner or later even without the stimulus of the insistence laid upon them in Gnosticism. The former might signify participation in Christ's Messianic anointing, or, on the analogy of Old Testament unctions, membership of the royal and priestly community; it might also,.on Old Testament analogies, denote the gift of the Spirit. The latter signified the 'sealing' of the believer with an outward sign of his possession by Christ; the

---

[1] *Apostolic Tradition*, p. xlii.

general use of the sign of the Cross by Christians is of early origin.[1] The laying on of hands, probably signifying originally the believer's incorporation in the apostolic or missionary work of the Church, had, as we have seen, come to denote the gift of the Spirit, so far as the exegesis of Scripture was concerned. The development of these ceremonies, or at least of the first two, is symptomatic of a falling away from the New Testament conception of Baptism as a re-presentation of the Baptism of Christ in relation to the Atonement, and of a failure to realize the significance of Baptism into the death and resurrection of Christ as itself effecting and symbolizing all those things which were portrayed in unction and consignation. It represents a process which was carried to its furthest lengths by the Gnostics, among whom this falling away was most complete; but certain of their practices and, to a lesser extent, some of their ideas, could become the common property of Christians as a whole without any further detriment than that which was already involved in the general change in the theological climate between St. Paul and the end of the second century. The process of assimilation would be rendered easy and natural, perhaps even almost inevitable, by the relatively fluid state of doctrine and practice in the second century, and the difficulty of distinguishing the orthodox from the heretic. Congregations could readily adopt each other's practices without realizing that fundamental differences of doctrine were really beginning to divide them. Even in the highly organized and, by comparison with the Church of the second century, 'standardized' life and practice of the modern Church, it is by no means unknown for a church in an English city to adopt such rites and ceremonies as it deems edifying from a 'place next door' with whose fundamental beliefs and doctrines its own official formularies are wholly at variance. In the second century the process was easier and more complete, the differences of belief and basic doctrine were as yet hard to define, and the customs which found their way into the baptismal rite were relatively harmless and such as would exercise a strong appeal to the average Christian. It is only in the light of later developments that we can understand the theological dangers which lay in the

[1] Cf. A. Jo., 115; Tert., cor., 3.

adoption of ideas and practices which tended to encourage the making of a dichotomy between Baptism and the gift of the Spirit, and between outward 'sealing' with the Cross and the seal of the Spirit of which St. Paul had spoken as the inward earnest of redemption.

Our main problem is to decide whether the *Apostolic Tradition*, which certainly describes the ceremonies of episcopal unction and consignation, also inculcates the theory that the Spirit is given in the post-baptismal anointing and signing, or whether it connects the initial gift of the Spirit rather with 'water' than with these closing acts of the initiatory rite.

We will consider the document on the assumption that it represents in its basic outline a liturgical form older than the time of its author's exposition of that form (probably about 215). It is for this reason that we take it into consideration now, and postpone the evidence of Tertullian and Clement on Baptism and the 'seal' for later treatment. The *Apostolic Tradition* presents us with a description of a fully developed rite of Baptism, a prototype of those which appear in the later liturgies. It comprises an account of the selection of fit catechumens, their three-year period under instruction, exorcism, anointing after the renunciation of Satan, baptism, profession of faith, unction by a presbyter, and anointing and signing by the bishop in the presence of the congregation. The whole rite, which is immediately followed by Communion, is solemn and impressive in the highest degree; but its details do not now concern us. For our present purpose we must concentrate our attention on the last part of the baptism rite, the bishop's unction and 'sealing', for we have to enquire what is the significance of this 'Confirmation' and what relation it was believed to bear to the bestowal on the converts of the gift of the Holy Spirit.

First, however, a word must be said about the historical value of the treatise. Obviously, its importance as our earliest full liturgical text of the baptismal rite is very great. It supplements the information provided by Tertullian's *De Baptismo*, and enables us to carry our acquaintance with the liturgical tradition of the Church back to the beginning of the third century. Dix, as we have seen, is almost ready to accept it at its face value as 'apostolic tradition',[1] and as illustrating the actual practice of the age of the Apostles, but this, as we have remarked, is a rash judgment.

It is easy, too, to exaggerate its links with Judaism and their importance. Since both religions practised a baptism of converts, their methods of procedure would be almost bound to resemble each other to some extent; the Church, having sprung from Judaism, would naturally retain some features of Jewish liturgical forms in its ritual, just as it retained some elements of Jewish institutions in its organization and ministry. In their Christian setting, however, these Jewish features were radically transformed, and in a spirit of remarkable independence of the Jewish past, Christianity sought its inspiration and its models for liturgy and organization directly from the Old Testament rather than from the practice of the contemporary synagogue. In this baptismal rite there are many striking differences from the method of proselyte-baptism; the immersion, for instance, is not self-administered;[2] the emphasis on exorcism is peculiar to the Christian ceremony; and the credal interrogations put to the candidate during his baptism differ very widely from the recitation of certain precepts of the Law during a Jewish baptism. The candidate is being baptized into Christ in His Church, and he naturally makes his profession of faith during the baptismal act. As we have already suggested, it seems otiose to try to demonstrate any real connection between, on the one hand, Baptism, unction and signing with the Cross, and the bringing by catechumens of their προσφορά for the Eucharist (which, no doubt, the full members of the congregation also brought for themselves), and, on the other, proselyte-baptism, the seal of circumcision, and the expiatory sacrifice offered by the proselyte after his reception.

Further, it may be dangerous to argue from what we know of the author of the *Philosophoumena* that the writer of the *Apostolic Tradition* was anxious to prove against Callistus the traditional and primitive character of the doctrine and liturgical practice of his own community. Though Nautin has not

---

[1] Cf. *The Theology of Confirmation in Relation to Baptism*, p. 19.
[2] Cf. *Ap. Trad.*, 21, 14: 'manum habens in caput eius impositam, baptizet semel.'

6

established his theory which ascribes the former work to one 'Josippus',[1] he has at least shown that its Hippolytean authorship is not fully assured, and that we should be on unsafe ground in applying inferences drawn from it to the *Apostolic Tradition*. We may remember that L. Lorenz[2] ascribed the *Egyptian Church Order*, one of the forms in which the *Tradition* has come down to us, to some other author than Hippolytus, though he believed that it annexed Hippolytus' work περὶ χαρισμάτων. We may properly use this treatise as a piece of early and highly important evidence for an early form of Baptism and the doctrine to which that form gave expression, but must not assumé that the origin of the work and the circumstances in which it was written are adequately known to us. The title is in all probability a piece of propaganda, claiming a special antiquity for this rite as distinct from the practices of other people. No doubt Hippolytus believed that he was describing an ancient rite, but in the ancient world, as we have already remarked, 'time immemorial' often denoted no very high antiquity.

The important points for us to notice in this rite of initiation are as follows. The catechumens undergo a three-year course of preparation. During this time they join together in prayer after each instruction, but this worship takes place in isolation from the congregation of the baptized. After every such period of prayer the teacher lays his hands upon them, prays, and dismisses them. This laying on of hands is clearly a blessing; it is given by the teacher, whether he be a fully ordained cleric or a layman, and it is evidently the outward sign or counterpart of the catechist's prayer for his converts.[3] On the Easter Eve, preceding the Baptism service, which takes place at cockcrow on Easter Day, the bishop lays his hand upon the catechumens and exorcizes the evil spirits 'to flee away from them and never return to them henceforward';[4] an 'insufflation' follows, after which the bishop seals their foreheads, ears, and noses.[5] This

---

[1] *Hippolyte et Josipe*, 1947.
[2] *De Egyptische Kerkordening en Hippolytus van Rome*, 1929; cf. also Engberding in *Miscellanea Liturgica in honorem L. K. Mohlberg*, 1948, pp. 47–71; but the authenticity of the *Apostolic Tradition* has been ably defended again by Botte (*R. Théol. anc. et méd.*, 16 (1949), pp. 177–85).
[3] 19, 1.   [4] 20, 8.   [5] *Ibid.*

sealing consists in signing with the Cross, which, as is so often
the case, is regarded as a prophylactic sign, marking the catechumen for God and, by its inherent potency, causing the
powers of evil to flee in disorder. It is also thought of as a seal
which shuts up and protects against marauders. In this sense of
the term 'seal', the sign of the Cross closes, as it were, the body
of the convert and fortifies it against any attempt by demonic
powers to regain the possession from which the formula of
exorcism has driven them. An unction with 'oil of exorcism'
follows the candidate's renunciation of Satan and all his works.[1]
They are then baptized, professing their faith in answer to
interrogations before each of three immersions. Then they are
anointed with the 'oil of thanksgiving' by a presbyter, and led
into the congregation, where the bishop lays his hand upon
them with prayer, anoints them with 'holy oil in God the
Father Almighty, and Christ Jesus and the Holy Ghost',[2] seals
them on the forehead, and gives them the kiss of peace. This
concludes the ceremony of their initiation, and they may thenceforth pray with the congregation, 'non primum orantes cum
fidelibus, nisi omnia haec fuerint consecuti'.[3] Their initiation
has made them full members of the Church; it is the entire
rite, and within that rite, which was certainly thought of as a
unity, it is particularly their baptism, which has admitted them
into the brotherhood. The bishop's part is to complete the
ceremony with the laying on of his hand, prayer that they may
receive grace to serve God according to His will,[4] and signing
with the mark of Christ.

It is an unwarrantable assumption that 'it is Confirmation,
not Baptism, which here admits a man into the Church',[5] and
that the quite natural and indeed inevitable distinction which
had to be drawn between a catechumen and a baptized Churchman really represents 'the Jewish proscription of the uncircumcised Gentile'.

'Confirmation', if we are so to designate the final stage of the
initiatory rite, appears to be, at least according to the Latin
text of the Apostolic Tradition, a complex of subsidiary ceremonies expressive of the bishop's blessing, given by him as head

---

[1] 21, 10.   [2] 22, 1–2.   [5] 22, 5.   [4] 22, 1.
[5] Confirmation or the Laying on of Hands? p. 7.

of the congregation to its newly baptized members and corresponding to his former blessing and reception of them at the beginning of their initiation, of his prayer that they may receive grace for positive and active service for God, of the candidates' participation in the Messianic unction whereby they obtain a share in the royal, priestly, and prophetic character of Christ,[1] and of the signing with the Cross which Hippolytus later compares with the Passover blood as a sign of faith, and an outward token of the power of the Spirit which puts to flight the Adversary.[2] All these signs are highly edifying and significant, but of relatively small importance as compared with the Baptism itself which gives them meaning and of which they are, so to speak, an explanatory extension.

In the Latin text contained in the Verona MS. LV (53),[3] the gift of the indwelling Spirit appears to be linked with the actual Baptism, the function of the bishop's 'Confirmation' being rather to add a special endowment of grace for the service of God, and not to confer the eschatological seal of the Spirit 'for a day of redemption'.

The Bishop, laying his hand on the neophytes, prays: 'Domine Deus, qui dignos fecisti eos remissionem mereri peccatorum per lavacrum regenerationis Spiritus sancti, inmitte in eos tuam gratiam ut tibi serviant secundum voluntatem tuam.' On the face of it, this appears to refer the gift of the Spirit to what has already taken place in the water-baptism rather than to what is going to happen in the 'confirmation'. The theory of this treatise is then in full accord with the New Testament doctrine as we have seen it in the Pauline Epistles and the Fourth Gospel; the only difference between this rite and the Baptism of apostolic times lies in the multiplication of subsidiary ceremonies which has taken place. There is, indeed, an obvious echo here of Titus iii. 5—'the washing of regeneration and renewal of Holy Spirit.' B. S. Easton remarks in a rather confused note: 'Hippolytus contributes little to clarifying the difficult subject of Confirmation. In Acts viii. 17, xix. 6, the

---

[1] Cf. 5, 2. [2] 37, 1-4.
[3] On this version see A. Wilmart, RSR. 9 (1929), p. 66, and G. Bardy, La Question des Langues dans l'église ancienne, pp. 283–4. The MS. dates from the late fifth or early sixth century; the translations contained in it may well have been made before the end of the fourth century.

rite conveys the gift of the Spirit, but Hippolytus' prayer, which cites Titus iii. 5, follows the Pauline-Johannine doctrine (1 Cor. xii. 13; John iii. 5) in attributing this gift to baptism in accordance with the Spirit, that is, immersion after confessing the Spirit. So only grace for service is besought. But, as in Acts, the essential ceremony is the imposition of hands, so that the anointing and the sign of the Cross are only supplementary rites.'[1] Dr. Easton's meaning is far from clear, and his conclusion appears to be quite arbitrary, but he evidently regards the episcopal prayer quoted above as following the main line of New Testament thought—namely, that Baptism in water confers the gift of the Spirit, together with regeneration, as the two inseparable aspects of its sacramental grace.

It should be observed that it is hardly possible to hold with Easton that in this rite 'the essential ceremony is the imposition of hands'. There is no suggestion that the laying on of the bishop's hand is symbolical of the gift of the Spirit. The anointing which he performs after the conclusion of the prayer is evidently more important than the 'imposition of hands' (the Latin text reads *manu*, and may be restored as either *manus* or *manum*, the latter being supported by the other versions of the treatise and intrinsically more probable).

The text proceeds: 'Postea oleum sanctificatum infundens de manu et imponens in capite dicat: "Unguo te sancto oleo in Domino Patre omnipotente et Christo Jesu et Spiritu sancto."' Exactly what this pouring of oil on the head is intended to signify is not clear. In one aspect it appears to be a visible demonstration that Baptism has made the convert a Christian. The Trinitarian formula looks back to the Trinitarian profession of faith which he made in the water; the oil would naturally signify the fact that he has thereby been made a partaker of the 'Anointed', the Christ, and, to judge from an earlier section of the treatise, it also symbolized the royal and priestly character with which the baptized believer had been endowed.[2] All this is in accordance with what we have already seen to be the thought of the *Odes of Solomon* and other works of this period, and it is easily deducible from Scripture. But the prayer which precedes the unction suggests that it is also

[1] *The Apostolic Tradition of Hippolytus*, p. 93.   [2] *Ap. Trad.*, 5, 2.

intended as a means of grace, the grace of God bestowed upon the newly baptized convert to fit him for active Christian service. In this respect the *Apostolic Tradition* seems, rather curiously, to hold a theory of 'Confirmation' which anticipates the later 'mediaeval' doctrine of the 'augmentum gratiae' or 'robur'; perhaps after all Hippolytus may be claimed as a forerunner of Aquinas and of Cranmer.

The consignation which follows is the 'sealing', the marking with the Christian sign which indicates to the baptized that he has become one of Christ's people bearing the stamp of the Christian covenant. Here the 'seal' is the imprint of the Cross, as the mark of Christ's ownership; it has, according to the Latin text, no such association with the gift of the Spirit as might cause it to be confused with the inward seal of the possession of the indwelling Spirit.

It is a natural conclusion of the rite when the bishop gives the convert the kiss and the salutation 'Dominus tecum' which assures him that he has been received into the Christian family of Christ's people.

So far, as we follow the Latin text, the meaning of the rite is fairly clear; in the derived versions, however (the *Testament of Our Lord*, and the Sahidic, Arabic, and Ethiopic texts of the *Egyptian Church Order*), the sense of the bishop's 'Confirmation Prayer' is widely different. The echo of Titus iii. 5 gives place to a dichotomy between the regeneration effected in water-baptism and the gift of the Spirit which is still to follow, and is presumably bestowed in the anointing by the bishop: '. . . who didst count them worthy of deserving the forgiveness of sins by the laver of regeneration, make them to be filled with thy Holy Spirit, and send upon them thy grace . . . etc.'

If this were the authentic text of the *Apostolic Tradition*, we should have to conclude that the treatise, so far from supporting the biblical conception of the gift of the Spirit in Baptism, and foreshadowing the later doctrine of the grace of Confirmation, actually affords early evidence of a divorce in orthodox circles of Spirit-baptism from water-baptism, and that the bad theology which we meet later had already come to be accepted as traditional—the theology which postulates a separation of the gift of the Spirit from regeneration, and dissociates the negative grace of remission of sins from the positive gift of the Spirit which ought to accompany it as being only another aspect of the benefits which result from acceptance by Christ and incorporation into His Church.

Dix maintains that this is in fact the conclusion which we ought to draw from the *Apostolic Tradition*—though he would not agree that its theology is bad. He asserts that the version of the text reproduced in the *Testament of our Lord* and in the Coptic, Arabic, and Ethiopic versions represents Hippolytus' original, and it is to a large extent upon this textual judgment (taken in conjunction with his belief that the *Apostolic Tradition* is in essence representative of the practice of the very early days of the Church) that he bases his theory that the ancient 'Baptism' consisted of a complex rite in which water-baptism was a ceremony of purification preparatory to a Spirit-baptism administered by the bishop with the external sign of 'sealing' with chrism.

In *The Theology of Confirmation in Relation to Baptism*[1] Dix simply quotes as an English version of what Hippolytus wrote the form of the text given in the *Testament* and the other Oriental versions. He offers no hint that the Latin text bears an entirely different sense. In his edition of the *Apostolic Tradition*[2] his critical note on this passage reads: 'make them (worthy to be filled) with: *so* T(est.). Ar. E. Boh. K (i.e. *Canons of Hippolytus*); *om.* L which is corrupt here.'

But is the Verona text really corrupt here? The question is worth investigation, for upon the answer we give to it will depend whether or not we admit the *Apostolic Tradition* as a witness for a separation of water- from Spirit-baptism. We must not overlook two important facts about the textual materials available for the reconstruction of this treatise. First, that 'it is possible to show that E. together with Ar. S. Boh. all descend from the same slightly adapted version of the *Apostolic Tradition*, and that this adaptation can scarcely be earlier than the fifth century. They therefore all rest ultimately on a single MS. of the *Apostolic Tradition*, and that unfortunately not of the best. Ar. E. S. Boh. are therefore ultimately *one* witness to the text of the *Apostolic Tradition*, not four.'[3] Secondly, as Dom B. Botte

---

[1] p. 11.   [2] p. 38 n.   [3] Dix, *Apostolic Tradition*, p. lii.

remarks: 'To add to, or subtract from, the Latin on the authority of the other witnesses is always a risky adventure. This kind of correction can only be assigned the value of conjecture.'[1]

Bearing in mind these principles, let us re-examine the text of the Verona palimpsest. We notice first that the manuscript, though admittedly difficult to read, affords no sign of any major dislocation at this point, nor of any lacuna. Hauler's apparatus[2] informs us only that the letters l and c of *lavacrum*, and the letters e s t of *eos tuam* are illegible, and also that *spiritus* is restored from *spu*. The question is therefore simply whether or not a reasonably clear Latin text is to be judged corrupt by reference to the other versions.

If the latter are to be accorded priority over the Latin, we must suppose that the latter's text has suffered alteration, either accidentally or deliberately. The alteration in question would consist in an omission of the words represented in Dix's English translation by 'make them to be filled with', that is, of some such words as *dignos fac eos repletionis* (cf. *repletionem sps sci* which occurs again in the same Latin text in a passage dealing with the Eucharist.[3]) This would represent a Greek text on the lines of ποίησον αὐτοὺς ἀξίους πληρώσεως (πνεύματος ἁγίου). It is just conceivable that these words may have been accidentally omitted; we might suppose that two consecutive lines of text began with -*tionis*, and the first dropped out accidentally, thus:

> 'qui dignos fecisti eos remissionem mere-
> ri peccatorum per lavacrum regenera-
> tionis *dignos fac eos reple-*
> *tionis* spiritus sancti; inmitte in eos tuam grati-
> am . . .'

A contributory factor might be the repetition within three lines of *dignos fecisti eos*, *dignos fac eos*. Against this conjecture, however, there stand two considerations which make it appear exceedingly improbable; first, that the accidental omission of the *dignos fac eos* clause ought to have left the *et* standing before

---

[1] *Hippolyte de Rome 'La Tradition Apostolique'* (Sources chrétiennes), p. 13.
[2] *Didasc. Apost. Fragmenta Veronensia Latina*, p. 111.
[3] 4, 12 (Dix, p. 9).

inmitte; secondly, that the line, tionis *dignos fac eos reple-*, is unnaturally short in comparison with the lines of the rest of the manuscript.

The only alternative hypothesis which would justify us in preferring the reading implied in the Eastern versions is that the Latin text has been intentionally altered. This is highly unlikely. All the probability of the matter suggests that the reference to Titus iii. 5 stood in the original, and that the Eastern versions represent an adaptation to the common theory of later times which frequently associates the gift of the Spirit with unction and the seal of the Cross rather than with 'the laver of regeneration'. Further, the reading of the Verona text yields a perfectly clear and natural sense which is in general accord with the early Latin liturgical tradition.[1]

The significance which we attach to the *Apostolic Tradition* for the purpose of this study is therefore, not that it throws light on very early, still less upon authentic apostolic, procedure, nor yet that it testifies to a complex baptismal rite in which the bishop's 'sealing' conveys the gift of the Spirit while water-baptism represents a preparatory, 'Johannine', washing of repentance. It is rather that this interesting treatise is an early witness for a distinction between 'regeneration by the Holy Spirit' as the inward thing signified by water-baptism, and 'grace to serve God according to His will' as the blessing particularly associated with the bishop's post-baptismal prayer and with the subsidiary ceremonies in which the neophyte is anointed and marked with the seal of the Cross—ceremonies which have now become attached to Baptism and will in due

---

[1] Dom. B. Botte, whose opinion on this passage I have consulted while preparing articles on σφραγίς and related words for the forthcoming *Lexicon of Patristic Greek*, reinforces my preference for the Latin text. He kindly calls my attention to the fact that its sense, though not its exact text, has been preserved by the *De Sacramentis* (2.24): 'Deus . . . qui te regeneravit ex aqua et spiritu sancto concessitque tibi peccata tua ipse te unguet. . . .' Similarly, the 'Verona' prayer, with the addition of the later petition for the sevenfold gifts, recurs in the Gregorian and Gelasian rites: 'Omnipotens sempiterne Deus, qui regenerare dignatus es hos famulos . . . ex aqua et spiritu sancto quique dedisti eis remissionem omnium peccatorum, emitte (Gel. inmitte) in eos septiformem Spiritum . . .' (Wilson, pp. 57–8; 86). He also points out that *Test.* offers a much amplified text, and that it is likely to be the source of the insertion of the words 'Fac eos dignos ut impleantur'. At the same time, Botte mentions the difficulty presented to this view by the agreement of S, Ar, E with *Test.*, but conjectures that the Egyptian tradition has been influenced by the latter.

course come to be regarded in the Western Church as the quite distinct and separate rite of Confirmation, wherein grace is still likewise bestowed to enable the baptized Christian to serve God in a life of spiritual activity.

The *Apostolic Tradition*, unlike certain contemporary and later writers on Baptism, has not been compelled by a misleading interpretation of Acts viii. 17, xix. 6, to attempt an artificial dichotomy between the Spirit's activity in the process of regeneration, and His indwelling presence in the believer. Its doctrine is still Scriptural, and the accretion of supplementary ceremonies which it attests is in itself a harmless and edifying development, free from the dangerous implications which these ceremonies tended to bear in the Gnostic circles where perhaps they originated.

The Latin text of the treatise has supplied the Church of later centuries, including the Church of England, not only with its 'Confirmation Prayer', but with a liturgical expression of the doctrine of Baptism and Confirmation which, allowing for the difference caused by the separation of the single rite of initiation into two parts, would have been approved in its essentials by Aquinas, and, granted the transference of the sealing with the sign of the Cross to the earlier part of the service—the water-baptism, by Cranmer and the classical Anglican theologians.

The text of *Test.*, Ar. E. Boh., represents a perversion of the biblical doctrine. Its form of the 'Confirmation Prayer' implies logically either that Baptism itself is something less than an effective symbol of our union with Christ in His death and resurrection, or that such a union can be effected without the Holy Spirit's indwelling presence being bestowed on the believer[1]—a very unsatisfactory doctrine from the standpoint of Trinitarian theology. Either Baptism is depreciated into a Jewish purification or a Johannine preparation, or the essential unity of the Holy Spirit with Christ, Whom He mediates to mankind, is broken so that the 'gift of the Spirit' comes to be thought of primarily in terms of outward ceremonies like the 'spiritual regenerations' of the Gnostics.

The so-called *Canons of Hippolytus* seem to occupy a doctrinal position intermediate between that of the Latin text of

[1] Cf. Botte, *Bull. de théol. anc. et méd.*, 5 (Jan. 1949), p. 424.

the *Apostolic Tradition* and the Eastern versions: 'Ibi episcopus manum imponens omnibus qui baptizati sunt, haec orat, dicens: Benedictus tibi, omnipotens Domine Deus, quia hos dignos reddidisti qui iterum nascerentur, et super quos Spiritum tuum Sanctum effundis, ut iam uniti sint corpori ecclesiae numquam separandi operibus alienis. Da potius quibus iam dedisti remissionem peccatorum etiam ἀρραβῶνα regni tui per Dominum nostrum Jesum Christum . . . Deinde insignat frontes eorum signo caritatis, osculaturque eos dicens, Dominus vobiscum.'[1]

Here it is not clear what element in the rite is regarded as the sign of the bestowal of the Spirit; the writer is, in fact, probably being intentionally obscure on this point and unwilling to commit himself beyond the general statement that in their initiation as a whole the converts are incorporated into the body of the Church and that this incorporation is inseparable from their reception of the Holy Spirit. It is remarkable that there is no mention of any unction by the bishop in the sense of a pouring of oil, but the consignation, which appears to be associated with the promise of inheritance of Christ's kingdom, would certainly have been performed with chrism or oil.

How far are we to suppose that the *Apostolic Tradition* represents Hippolytus' personal views on the baptismal gift of the Holy Spirit and its relation to the 'seal'? To answer this question is no easy matter, for the teaching of Hippolytus on this subject is exceedingly obscure and by no means free from confusion. He speaks of Christ having given a 'seal' to His followers, and declares that Antichrist will do the same.[2] Since Hippolytus probably has Apoc. xiii. 16 in mind at this point in his argument, it is reasonable to suppose that he is thinking of the Christian seal as an outward physical marking—presumably the sign of the Cross made on the foreheads of the newly baptized. Elsewhere, however, in the same treatise he shows plainly that he regards the indwelling of the Holy Spirit as the seal which inwardly stamps the believer as God's property; for in his ingenious, if somewhat laboured, comparison of the Church to a ship he likens the sail to the Church's motive power, which is

[1] Ps.-Hipp., *can.*, 136–7 (Achelis, *TU*. 6¹, pp. 98–9).
[2] *antichr.*, 6 (*GCS*. p. 8, 10; *PG*. 10, 733B).

the 'Spirit from heaven through which the believers are sealed'.[1] It is not clear in this elaborate simile whether he conceives this sealing as something independent of the 'laver of regeneration' by which the faithful are renewed (which, incidentally, corresponds to the ship's bilge), and when we turn to the other works of Hippolytus we find a certain confusion of thought on the matter.

The last chapters of the *Homily on the Theophania* suggest that the Spirit and the baptismal water are indissolubly connected. As a result of Christ's institution of Baptism with water and Spirit, we are told, man is capable of deification. The water of Baptism is τὸ ὕδωρ τὸ πνεύματι κοινωνοῦν in which Christ was baptized, which regenerates man and gives him life. Hippolytus recalls the primal brooding of the Spirit upon the waters, and invites his hearers to become 'born anew to sonship of God'; the proof of this sonship is the bestowal of the Spirit, the Paraclete; and sonship is put on in exchange for the condition of a slave when a man descends into the 'laver' of Baptism, to emerge λαμπρὸς ὡς ὁ ἥλιος.[2] At the same time we are told that man's 'deification' takes place δι' ὕδατος καὶ πνεύματος ἁγίου μετὰ τὴν τῆς κολυμβήθρας ἀναγέννησιν.

Again, on the other hand, the doctrine of a sort of 'Real Presence' of the Spirit in the water of Baptism is clearly expressed in the *Homily on the Blessing of Jacob*,[3] and the Arabic fragment commenting on Gen. xxxviii. 19 apparently interprets the signet ring given by Judah to Tamar as a type either of Baptism or of the baptismal confession of faith;[4] yet, on the other hand, in another of the elaborate allegories of which Hippolytus is so fond, Susannah's bath represents the Church's Baptism, but the oil with which she anointed herself is the power of the Spirit, and this, in turn, is associated with the chrism with which the faithful are anointed after Baptism.[5]

---

[1] *antichr.*, 59 (*GCS*. p. 40, 1; *PG*. 10, 780A).

[2] *theoph.*, 8–10 (*GCS*. pp. 262–3; *PG*. 10, 860–61). The language suggests that Dölger is right in interpreting the λαὸν δ'εἶδον ἐκεῖ λαμπρὰν σφραγεῖδαν ἔχοντα of the Epitaph of Abercius as referring to Baptism, or rather to the Christian 'character' bestowed therein. This view is on the whole more likely to be correct than that which sees here a reference to the sign of the Cross. The *Theophania* is at best a dubious work of Hippolytus.

[3] *Ben. Jac.* (*TU.* 11, 1 (1904), p. 30, 9).

[4] *fr. in Pent.* 12 (*GCS*. p. 96, 10 ff.).

[5] *Dan.*, 1, 16, 3 (*GCS*. p. 26, 24; *PG*. 10, 693A).

The *Homilies on the Pascha* included in the spuria of Chrysostom, but attributed by some to Hippolytus in whole or in part,[1] do not throw much light on the question; they do, however, indicate that Hippolytus, if they are indeed his work, has a clearer and more Scriptural doctrine than would appear from these artificial allegories, and that he is fully conscious of the interrelation of the gift of the Spirit with the application to the believer of the atoning sacrifice of Christ. In these homilies we find a typological application of the anointing of the doors at the Passover to Christ's sacrifice; Christ effected the salvation of the firstborn because, having been offered as a sacrifice on our behalf, He expunged the record of our old life and gave us a new beginning of life through the 'laver of regeneration' in which we share in the likeness of His death and resurrection.[2] We receive regeneration in Baptism because Christ was offered for us, ἐφ' ᾧ ἀνέστη, καὶ τὸ Πνεῦμα τὸ ἅγιον εἰς ἀνακαίνισιν ἡμῶν ἐνεφύσησεν.[3] The sonship of the believer is due to his possession of the Spirit.[4] It is, however, particularly by the ceremony of unction that the application of the saving work of Christ to the believer is symbolized. God preserves (the Passover typology is still being worked out here) those who have been anointed for Him through faith with the life of Christ which has destroyed death.[5] Unction signifies the appropriation of the blood of Christ, and through His blood shed for us we receive the Holy Spirit ἵνα διὰ τοῦ ὁμογενοῦς ἡμῖν αἵματος· τὸ μὴ ὁμογονὲς ἡμῖν Πνεῦμα τὸ ἅγιον λαβεῖν δυνηθῶμεν. The 'seal' of Christ's blood is twofold, being applied to the reason, which corresponds to the lintel of the Passover door, and to the παθῆ which are typified by the doorposts. This unction is a putting on of Christ's holiness by those who are conformed to His suffering. All this, says the writer to the newly baptized, is the mystery of the unction they have received in the course of their initiation.[6] On the other hand, the true Christian circumcision is typified, not by the unction, but by the Baptism itself; this

---

[1] Martin, *RHE*. 33 (1937), pp. 255 ff.; but see Connolly, *JTS*. 46 (1945), pp. 192–200, who makes out a convincing case against the theory of Hippolytean authorship. They are mentioned here chiefly because Dix apparently assumes that the whole series is the work of Hippolytus (e.g. in *The Apostolic Tradition*, pp. 74–5).
[2] *pasch.*, 1 (Ben. i, 251D).   [3] *Ibid.* (252C); cf. Just., *dial.*, 40, 1.
[4] *Ibid.* (253C).   [5] *Ibid.* (254B, C).   [6] *Ibid.* (8, 254E–255B).

circumcision is performed by the Spirit and is perfected in Christian living.[1] The author interprets the blood and water from the side of Christ as symbols of the Baptism with the Holy Ghost and fire, and it is worth noticing that it is the *water* which represents the Spirit, while the blood corresponds to the baptism of fire.

Taken as a whole the teaching of Hippolytus on Baptism is fundamentally true to the biblical doctrine, for it links together the essential elements of remission of sins, regeneration, incorporation into the Body of Christ, and the gift of the indwelling Spirit; he is, however, inclined to associate the last of these aspects of Baptism with the unction administered by the bishop after the water-baptism. On this point, it must be admitted, he is not clear in his views, and he has not faced the question whether the gift of the Spirit is mediated by Baptism in water or by some other rite. At times he suggests that water-baptism is itself the sacrament of the reception of the indwelling Spirit; at times he connects the Spirit's bestowal with the anointing.

This does not of course imply that Hippolytus ever connects the gift of the Spirit with a rite of 'Confirmation' distinct from the complex ceremony of Baptism. All that he does is to associate it at times with a ceremony of anointing which had come to form an integral part of the Baptism service. The tendency to link the gift of the Spirit with the anointing no doubt had its roots, as we have remarked, in the Old Testament. The unction, whose primary significance in the baptismal ceremony was to denote the royal and priestly character which the believer possesses by virtue of his membership of Christ and of His Church, was closely connected as a symbol with the descent of the Spirit upon chosen men of God; particularly is this the case in relation to the anointing of the Messiah.

Nevertheless, though this development of thought is quite natural and readily explicable, the effect of the tendency to regard the bishop's unction as the special moment of the Spirit's approach to the baptized was singularly unfortunate. The essential connection, and indeed identity, between regeneration, remission of sins, incorporation into Christ, membership of His

[1] *pasch.*, 3 (8, 258A).

Church, adoptive sonship of God, and possession of the Holy Spirit which mediates Christ to man, began to be broken,[1] and the Spirit came to be thought of as a gift bestowed independently of the believer's regeneration through Christ. Not infrequently it is identified for all practical purposes with $\phi \hat{\omega} s$, a gift of illumination, or even a garment of light, put on by the initiate to enable him to ascend to heaven. Even where these semi-pagan notions are excluded, any separation of the reception of the Spirit from the dying and rising with Christ which are symbolized in the water-baptism indicates a loss of the Church's hold on the New Testament doctrine of justification. Though Hippolytus does not formally or explicitly make this separation, his thought is evidently moving in that direction.

The 'seal of the Spirit', too, is becoming identified, or at least associated, with the outward and visible sealing administered by the bishop as the head of the Christian family to mark its new member as one of Christ's men. This association in turn has far-reaching consequences. *Consignatio* will be able in due course to stand on its own feet as an independent rite in the Western Church; the way has been opened to the exaltation of this latter rite at the expense of Baptism itself; and the terms σφραγίς, *signaculum*, originally used in this connection to denote the sign of the Cross, come to signify the entire baptismal 'character'.

Hippolytus himself is groping his way towards these dangerous notions amid considerable confusion of thought. On the whole, it is probably fair to say that his own conception of the matter stands not far distant from that of the oriental versions of the *Apostolic Tradition*. If we are right in preferring the Latin text and its less ambiguous doctrine of the work of the Spirit in water-baptism, the fact that the views of Hippolytus as presented to us in his other works show some disagreement with the *Tradition* may be an argument for the belief that the latter, although far from 'apostolic', may have been of some relative antiquity, at least in the main outlines of its liturgical information, when Hippolytus began to set it out in order.

It may properly be argued that by the time that we reach the

---

[1] Hippolytus himself, nevertheless, asserts the indissoluble connection between the grace of adoption and possession of the Spirit (*theoph.* 3, if this is his).

writings of Hippolytus (excepting the *Tradition*) the primitive pattern of thought and practice, so far as Christian initiation is concerned, is beginning to break up and give place to a period of great confusion of thought on the matter. Such a process, discernible in Hippolytus, had already been advanced by Tertullian. We must accordingly turn back for a moment to examine its effects.

CHAPTER SEVEN

THE DISINTEGRATION OF THE NEW TESTAMENT DOCTRINE OF THE SEAL OF THE SPIRIT

DURING the century and a half which separates the age of the Apostles from the turn of the third century the biblical conception of the seal of the Spirit and its relationship to the union with Christ effected and symbolized in Baptism came to be deprived to a considerable extent both of its simple clarity and its theological depth. The Pauline doctrine treated Baptism as the efficacious sign of a dying with Christ and a rising and ascending with Him to a new quality of life, an earnest of the eschatological hope of the total redemption which is to be expected at the Parousia. Of this hope the guarantee is the inward seal set upon the believer's soul by that possession of the Holy Spirit which is the necessary concomitant of the union with Christ which has been brought about through the response of faith to grace. Baptism is a sacramental rite which looks back to the Messiah-Servant Baptism of Jesus and to the saving and atoning death and resurrection of which His Baptism was a foreshadowing and prefiguring. It re-presented that Baptism and it was the external symbol through which the atoning work of Christ was applied to the believer and made available for him to share; the convert was figuratively buried and raised with Christ in the baptismal water; and in the union with Christ effected by faith in response to the divine act (whose visible expression was the sacrament itself) he found the realization of the promise of remission of sins. At the same time it was a rite which looked forward to the future hope and guaranteed its fulfilment. It pointed not only to the victory of Christ incarnate but to the culmination of that victory at the Parousia. Through being made a partaker of Christ and sharing in His Messianic-Servant character, entering with Him into newness of life, the believer received the assurance of the Holy Spirit, the seal of the covenant of promise, the stamp which marked him as God's own possession awaiting the day of redemption.

The fading of the eschatological expectation in the sub-apostolic age, and the failure of the second century writers to appreciate and develop the Pauline doctrine of justification led to a certain dimming of the significance of both sacraments, and especially of Baptism. The outline of the early Church's teaching on Baptism became blurred and confused as a result of a failure to maintain a hold on the full meaning of the central idea of ἐν Χριστῷ; for in the conception of being 'in Christ' there is summed up the thought of all the gifts of grace which the justified sinner receives—remission of sins, the status of sonship, assurance of inheritance of the kingdom of heaven and of the consummation of the 'adoption' in the 'redemption of the body', and the indwelling presence of the Holy Ghost.

Consequently, in the post-apostolic writers there is a tendency for the grandeur of the New Testament theory of Baptism to begin to fade; it ceases in some degree to find its focus and centre in the saving work of Christ, and the spiritual gifts bestowed in it begin to be thought of in isolation from the focal point of the Atonement in which they ought to co-inhere. In particular, the seal of the Spirit, received in Baptism, begins to be conceived in quasi-magical terms as a mark impressed upon the soul by the due performance of the baptismal ceremonial, a stamp whose purpose is to safeguard the recipient from the hostile powers of the Devil, and preserve him in soul and body unharmed for the enjoyment of immortality.

The development of subsidiary ceremonies as part of the general rite of initiation, however impressive and edifying they may have been in themselves, certainly afforded an opportunity for a wrong distribution of emphasis on the various parts of the whole rite and began to prepare the way for Baptism itself to be evacuated of much of its meaning and treated as a preparatory ceremony, a prelude to the true 'baptism of the Spirit', whose outward ceremony was either chrismation or the imposition of hands. The Gnostic aspirations towards 'spiritual redemptions', mediated through more refined and esoteric means than the apparently commonplace lustration which

Baptism seemed to be when their theology had emptied it of all fuller significance, naturally encouraged, if they did not originate, the development of this theory of a Spirit-baptism independent of the washing in water; and when Spirit-baptism begins, as it were, to look for an external symbol to which it can attach itself, there is ready to hand the outward marking or sealing with the sign of the Cross, performed with the chrism of anointing which both the Old Testament and the language used in the primitive Church about the 'anointing' of the Messiah connected with the bestowal of the Holy Spirit. It was only natural that the ideas of Spirit-baptism, the seal of the Spirit, and the external marking with the Christian sign, should converge upon the ceremony of the chrismation and signing by the bishop of the newly baptized.

Yet the seal of initiation could not simply and exclusively be identified with the consignation; the conception of Baptism itself as the seal persisted; there was the frequent and widespread extension of the sense of the 'seal' to mean the 'character' impressed upon the convert at Baptism; in many quarters the seal given in Baptism was connected particularly with the invocation over the candidate of the Threefold Name, or with the branding, as it were, of the convert with the name of his divine owner in his assent to the Trinitarian interrogations; there was the more profound notion of the believer's reception of the renewed impress of the divine image, defaced since the Fall, renovated through the work of the Son who is the Father's perfect image, and mediated to man through the Holy Spirit; and, by way of a further complication, we are presented with the tendency (which sets in towards the end of the second century) to identify Spirit-baptism with the rite of the imposition of hands described in the Acts of the Apostles.

So long as all the various baptismal ceremonies were held together as part of one single rite of initiation, the full consequences of these developments were to some extent mitigated or disguised.. It is when the liturgical rite begins in the West to show a tendency to break up into Baptism and Confirmation as independent sacramental rites that the disintegration of the primitive Church's doctrine of the seal of the Spirit becomes immediately apparent. So long as the various ceremonies of the initiation rite together formed but one complex whole, it did not matter that Christians should have found it difficult to say at what point in the whole rite they received the Holy Spirit. What was serious was that the essential truth should so often have been forgotten that the Holy Spirit is received through and because of the believer's union with Christ in the fellowship of His mystical Body, with the consequence that the gift of the Spirit came to be associated with particular ceremonies which were in fact wholly secondary to the central act of Baptism in which the convert 'put on Christ'.

It is in the third century that there begins to set in a disintegration both of the New Testament doctrine of the seal and of the primitive liturgical pattern. It was then that to the effects of the general adoption of the rites of unction and consignation, the influence of the supposed teaching of Acts about the laying on of hands, and the tendency to associate the ancient conception of the covenant-seal with a visible signing with the Cross instead of with the state of belonging to Christ and so of possessing His Spirit, there were added the growth of the Church (making it impossible, especially in Rome, for the bishop to remain the sole regular minister of Baptism), and some unfortunate consequences of the controversy on rebaptism. These last factors contributed heavily to the development of a separation between Baptism and the secondary rites which came to be regarded as the independent sacrament of Confirmation, with a corresponding divorce between Baptism as the sacrament of remission of sins and regeneration and Confirmation as the outward sign of the bestowal of the Spirit. In the East the unfortunate results of this disintegration are to some extent disguised by the continuing survival of the united liturgical action, but even there the difficulties and inconsistencies to which the doctrinal changes give rise are revealed after the rise of infant Baptism as the normal practice has added a further grave complication to a difficult theological situation, and revealed the Fathers' lack of understanding of some of the essential features of the teaching of 'the Apostle'.

The more serious developments in the West produced a sad crop of theological problems and unsatisfactory solutions. Confirmation came to be regarded as the sacrament of the Spirit.

Yet to deny that the Spirit was given in Baptism would evacuate the essential sacrament of the Gospel of much of its positive content and reduce it to a 'baptism of John'. To assert, on the other hand, that the Spirit is given in different modes, or for different purposes, in both rites easily leads to the making of false distinctions of a quantitative kind in respect of the Spirit's presence, or to artificial attempts to discriminate between His 'external' and 'internal' operations. It is these difficulties and dilemmas which we are asked to solve today by assigning to Baptism the effects of remission of sins, and perhaps also re-generation and membership of the Church, while we reserve the gift of the Spirit to Confirmation, thereby leaving un-answered the question how we can become members of Christ and of His Body without being animated by His Spirit, whether or not we have received Confirmation. They are difficulties and dilemmas which begin to make themselves felt in some degree as early as the time of Clement and Tertullian. It may be con-venient to glance first at the teaching of the former on the sub-ject of the baptismal seal, since it is not confused, as it is in the case of Tertullian, by the question of the importance to be assigned to the ceremony of the imposition of hands.

Clement, for the most part, in using the terms σφραγίς, σφραγίζειν, is thinking of Baptism, not of a gift of the Spirit conferred subsequently to the actual 'laver'. The argument is sometimes adduced against this interpretation that in one in-stance he appears to differentiate 'baptism' from the 'blessed seal',[1] and that the latter is accordingly to be understood as Confirmation. This exegesis, however, is almost certainly as incorrect as that which seeks to establish a reference to 'Con-firmation' in q. d. s. 42;[2] in both cases the terms 'seal' and 'baptism' appear to be synonymous. To Clement, however, it is not the actual rite of Baptism so much as the baptismal 'character' which constitutes the seal with which the flock of Christ is marked, although there is a clear equation of the 'seal' with Baptism itself in his remark that εἶεν δ'ἄν αἱ τρεῖς ἡμέραι (the reference is to the Resurrection) τῆς σφραγῖδος μυστήριον, δι' ἧς ὁ τῷ ὄντι πιστεύεται θεός.[3] The Spirit is the 'character'

---

[1] str., 2, 3 (GCS. p. 118, 32; PG. 8, 941C). [2] See above, p. 115.
[3] str., 5, 11 (GCS. p. 375, 17; PG. 9, 112A).

or 'seal' stamped upon the believer's soul, the mark of Christ's ownership. The soul of the Christian carries upon itself the marks of Christ, which are the Spirit, the image of God: ὁ πιστὸς ἐπιγραφὴν . . . ἔχει διὰ Χριστοῦ, τὸ ὄνομα τοῦ θεοῦ, τὸ δὲ πνεῦμα ὡς εἰκόνα· καὶ τὰ ἄλογα ζῷα διὰ σφραγῖδος δείκνυσι τίνος ἐστὶν ἕκαστον· καὶ ἐκ τῆς σφραγῖδος ἐκδικεῖται· οὕτως καὶ ἡ ψυχὴ ἡ πιστή, τὸ τῆς ἀληθείας λαβοῦσα σφράγισμα, τὰ στίγματα τοῦ Χριστοῦ περιφέρει.[1] The same idea of a divine stamp set upon the believer which enables him to be recognized in the hereafter is to be found in the curious notion that the engraving of the high-priestly *petalon* with the divine Name typifies the stamping of the body with the Name which enables it to pass 'the second veil' and enter the κόσμος νοητός. Here the body, even the 'light', 'pure', body is laid aside and the soul 'passes over into the spiritual sphere, being made truly rational and high-priestly'.[2]

Clement's doctrine of the 'sealing' of the Christian for future redemption often savours of the superstitious and the magical, especially when he is laying stress upon the prophylactic aspect of the seal; but his teaching is to some extent redeemed from this tendency by its insistence upon the conception of the stamp of the *imago Dei* impressed upon the soul of the true 'gnostic'. The righteous man becomes 'the Lord's coin' and receives the stamp of the 'royal χάραγμα';[3] the spiritual seal is stamped upon the soul by Christ who is Himself the 'express image of the glory of the Almighty',[4] and Christians bear about with them the image of God, 'in the living and moving image, man.'[5]

This 'character' or impress of the divine image is in fact the seal of the Spirit; the 'shining χαρακτήρ' of righteousness is a χρῖσμα εὐαρεστήσεως indicating the quality of a life which participates in the Holy Spirit; it is a 'holy symbol' which the 'gnostic' displays to the angels as his soul ascends into the heavenly spheres.[6] The indwelling Spirit, in fact, is a 'shining χαρακτήρ', a token of the believer's membership of Christ.

Clement is at pains to emphasize the ethical significance of this seal. The perfection of the true 'gnostic' consists in assimila-

[1] *exc. Thdt.*, 86, 2 (generally ascribed to Clement himself).
[2] *Ibid.*, 27. [3] *str.*, 6, 7 (p. 462, 2; *PG.* 9, 281B).
[4] *str.*, 7, 3 (p. 12, 20; *PG.* 9, 421A). [5] *prot.*, 4 (p. 46, 16; *PG.* 8, 157C).
[6] *str.*, 4, 18 (p. 299, 18; *PG.* 8, 1325A).

tion to God;[1] its source lies in his possession of ἡ δικαιοσύνης σφραγῖδα ἐπιφανῆ, φῶς ἡνωμένον ψυχῇ δι' ἀγάπης ἀδιαστάτου θεοφορούσης καὶ θεοφορουμένης.[2] Elsewhere Clement speaks of the 'seal of knowledge',[3] and it is probably to this seal (though it is possible that it may be rather the invocation of the Trinity at Baptism) that he refers in an obscure allusion to the 'house, empty, swept, and garnished', which symbolizes the soul that has been purged of evil; when what was empty has been filled by the goodness of God, 'then the seal follows, in order that it may be preserved in holiness for God.'[4]

The conferring of the seal in Baptism is associated especially with the moment of the invocation of the Trinity. The clearest exposition of this theory is contained in one of the *Excerpta* which is authentically Theodotean,[5] but the thought of the passage is paralleled in Clement's *Eclogae propheticae*[6] where in a baptismal context he explains that 'when we were χοικοί, we were Caesar's. Caesar is the ruler of this age, whose earthly image is the "old man". . . . Now the Lord has stamped another χάραγμα on us, and other names and letters. . . . Thus we are translated from the material sphere to the spiritual, bearing the image of the heavenly.' At Baptism the believer passes from his 'hylic' or 'choic' state into a heavenly or spiritual condition, because he is transferred from the power or 'name' of the ruler of this world into the 'name' of the Trinity, and receives the seal in Baptism whereby the Trinitarian name is stamped upon him. The seal is thought of especially as a safeguard against the hostile activities of evil spirits.[7] We may well believe that it was this aspect of the baptismal seal, the notion of the soul's liberation from the demonic powers and its protective sealing against their attacks, which appealed most strongly to the popular mind, outweighing in the opinion of the semi-pagan multitude the more ethical conception of baptismal remission of sins; and this theory of the soul's reception of a defensive seal against the Devil must have placed yet another difficulty in the way of finding a solution to the problem of post-baptismal sin.[8]

[1] Cf. review by Daniélou of A. Mayer, *Das Bild Gottes im Menschen nach Clemens v. Alexandrien* (*RSR.* 35, 4 (1948), p. 603).
[2] *str.*, 6, 12 (p. 484, 18; *PG.* 9, 325B).
[3] *str.*, 1, 5 (p. 20, 17; *PG.* 8, 725A).
[4] *ecl.*, 12, 9.
[5] *exc. Thdot.*, 80, 3.   [6] *ecl.*, 24.   [7] *ecl.*, 12.   [8] Cf. *q. d. s.*, 39.

Clement delights in expressing his doctrine of Baptism in terms which deliberately echo the phraseology of the pagan mysteries: δᾳδουχοῦμαι τοὺς οὐρανοὺς καὶ τὸν θεὸν ἐποπτεύσας ἅγιος γίνομαι μυούμενος, ἱεροφαντεῖ δὲ ὁ κύριος καὶ τὸν μύστην σφραγί- ζεται φωταγωγῶν, καὶ παρατίθεται τῷ πατρὶ τὸν πεπιστευκότα αἰῶσι τηρούμενον.[1] Yet this language, although it is so ex- tremely pagan in sound as to seem almost like a caricature of the terminology of the mysteries, is really only an expression of a regular early Christian conception of the seal as the character bestowed in Baptism.

It is with Baptism itself, and not with any other ceremony, that Clement appears to associate the reception of this charac- ter. The divine gifts which lead to Christian perfection, remis- sion of sins, immortality,[2] divine sonship, illumination are all received through Baptism,[3] and there is no reason to suppose that Clement would separate the gift of the Spirit from these other blessings by postulating a Spirit-baptism distinct from baptism in water and associating it with some other moment in the rite of initiation; indeed, he explicitly connects the son- ship which is granted in Baptism with regeneration through the Spirit.[4] His statement that: μοι δοκεῖ αὐτὸς οὗτος πλάσαι μὲν τὸν ἄνθρωπον ἐκ χοός, ἀναγεννῆσαι δὲ ὕδατι, αὐξῆσαι δὲ πνεύματι, παιδαγωγῆσαι δὲ ῥήματι εἰς υἱοθεσίαν καὶ σωτηρίαν ἁγίαις ἐντολαῖς κατευθύνων,[5] should not be taken to indicate that Clement really thinks of an incrementum Spiritus following regeneration (given through Baptism) in a time-sequence. Nor does Clement seem to have in mind any post-baptismal gift of the Spirit, or any consummation of Christian initiation by a rite of Confirmation, when he speaks of the baptized convert as being not yet in possession of the 'perfect gift'.[6] He is fairly certainly alluding to the final state of perfection which is foreshadowed in Baptism, but which is to be attained only in the life to come.

Clement's references to unction appear to be metaphorical, but it would be surprising if he knew of no ceremony of chrisma-

[1] prot., 12 (p. 84, 25; PG. 8, 241A).
[2] paed., 1, 6 (p. 119, 24; PG. 8, 308C); cf. ibid., 1, 6 (p. 105, 21; PG. 8, 281A).
[3] Ibid., 1, 6 (p. 105, 23; PG. 8, 281A).
[4] Ibid., 1, 5 (p. 102, 20; PG. 8, 276A).
[5] Ibid., 1, 12 (p. 148, 18; PG. 8, 368A).
[6] Ibid., 1, 6 (p. 106, 30; PG. 8, 284B); ἀλλ' οὐδέπω, φασίν, εἴληφε τὴν τελείαν δωρεάν· σύμφημι κἀγώ· πλὴν ἐν φωτί ἐστι, καὶ τὸ σκότος αὐτὸν οὐ καταλαμβάνει .

tion after Baptism. Certainly he nowhere suggests that any form of unction is the outward symbol of the gift and seal of the Spirit, despite the fact that he speaks metaphorically of the 'unction of the Holy Spirit' and of the Christian as a sharer in the anointing of the Christ which symbolized His death.[1]

As for a rite of laying on of hands, there is no hint in Clement's writings of any use of such a practice in connection with Baptism, unless we assume that his obscurely worded objection to artificial coiffures[2] contains an allusion to Confirmation; in all probability, however (as indeed his use of ὁ πρεσβύτερος suggests), the reference is to the reconciliation of a penitent, or perhaps to an ordinary act of blessing performed in the normal course of Church life.

When we turn to Tertullian, on the other hand, we are faced with a very different situation so far as the imposition of hands is concerned. In his teaching the influence of the reading of Acts, and perhaps of fairly old African custom based upon the texts relating to the practice, has caused a good deal of confusion of thought, for which we must make full allowance in interpreting Tertullian's doctrine of Baptism and the gift of the Spirit.

Dix tells us that Tertullian in his *Liber de Baptismo*, 'written perhaps ten years before the *Apostolic Tradition* . . . explicitly affirms that "the giving of Baptism is the right of the High Priest who is the Bishop" and others have it only as his delegates.[3] And for Tertullian *baptismum* does not mean only the Baptism in water, but other things as well. "Not that in the water we obtain the Holy Spirit, but that, cleansed in the water, we are prepared for the Spirit. . . . Leaving the laver we are forthwith anointed in the blessed oil . . . which lent its name to the Lord. The oil flows upon our flesh, but profits our spirit. . . . Then a hand is laid upon us, by its blessing calling down and inviting the Holy Ghost."[4] For Tertullian *all this together is baptismum*, and it is not the water but the "seal" which imparts the Spirit. But the whole rite is one and its minister is

---

[1] *paed.*, 2, 8 (p. 197, 1; *PG.* 8, 472B).
[2] *Ibid.*, 3, 11 (p. 271, 20; *PG.* 8, 637B): τίνι γὰρ ὁ πρεσβύτερος ἐπιτίθησι χεῖρα; τίνα δὲ εὐλογήσει; οὐ τὴν γυναῖκα, τὴν κεκοσμημένην, ἀλλὰ τὰς ἀλλοτρίας τρίχας, καὶ δι᾽ αὐτῶν ἄλλην κεφαλήν.
[3] *bapt.*, 17.   [4] *Ibid.*, 6.

the Bishop. I will venture to assert that this is the general pre-Nicene understanding of the rite. There are differences to be found in pre-Nicene writers about details. . . . The majority regard the Bishop's unction with chrism as the actual "seal". A few—chiefly in Africa—lay more emphasis on the simultaneous imposition of one hand.'[1] Mason interpreted Tertullian as affording valuable evidence for his theory that Baptism conveys remission of sins and regeneration, but 'distinctly not the gift of the Holy Ghost'.[2]

These statements need careful examination. Tertullian says little about the 'seal of the Spirit' in the New Testament sense of that phrase. He does, however, speak frequently of Baptism setting a seal upon faith; that is to say, the believer's response of faith to the grace of God is sacramentally sealed in Baptism, and his actual profession of Christian belief is sealed in his Baptism in the Threefold Name. The baptismal remission of sins is gained by 'fides obsignata in Patre et Filio et Spiritu Sancto'.[3] 'Ubi fides aucta est credendi in nativitatem, passionem, resurrectionemque eius, addita est ampliatio sacramenti, obsignatio baptismi, vestimentum quodammodo fidei quae retro est nuda.'[4] 'Lavacrum illud obsignatio est fidei.'[5] It is perhaps not without significance, in view of Dix's contention that for Tertullian *baptismus* means more than water-baptism, that he can use the terms *aqua* and *baptismus* synonymously, and, further, that he can speak of *aqua* as the seal set upon the faith of the Church.[6] Elsewhere we find the renunciation of the devil mentioned as something which the believer performs '*in signaculo fidei*', that is, in the rite of Baptism.[7]

For Tertullian, then, the 'seal' usually means the sacrament of Baptism regarded as a 'sealing' of the faith of the convert, and this sealing is particularly associated with the convert's profession of faith in the Trinity and with the baptismal formula of the Threefold Name.[8] He can, however, also speak of the laver of Baptism as the 'seal' which is typified by the ring given to the prodigal son.[9] The ring at the same time signifies the 'vestem priorem, indumentum Spiritus sancti' which was

---

[1] *The Theology of Confirmation in Relation to Baptism*, pp. 14–15.
[2] *The Relation of Confirmation to Baptism*, p. 63.   [3] *bapt.*, 6.
[4] *Ibid.*, 13.   [5] *poenit.*, 6 (*PL.* 1, 1349B).   [6] *praescr.*, 36.
[7] *spect.*, 24.   [8] Cf. *Prax.*, 26.   [9] *pudicit.*, 9.

lost at the Fall, but has been restored to man by the gift of the Spirit in Baptism. The clear implication of this passage is that the seal of the Spirit is given in the 'laver', that is, water-baptism.

Occasionally, on the other hand, it is the baptismal 'character' itself,[1] and more often it is the post-baptismal signing with the Cross which is described as the 'seal', in the sense of the mark set upon the Christian.[2] Signing with the Cross is compared by Tertullian with a devilish imitation of it to be found in the mysteries of Mithras, who 'signat illic in frontibus milites suos'.[3] The sign of the Cross is the *signaculum frontium* foretold in the vision of Ezekiel,[4] and the sign or seal given to the newly baptized is the same as that with which in every action of daily life 'frontem terimus'.[5]

The 'seal' in this sense of the term is thus, according to Tertullian, a mark of Christian service, a sign of the Christian *militia*, a seal set upon the elect of God, and a defence against the power of the devil; it is not the sacramental sign of the bestowal upon the baptized of the Holy Spirit.

Tertullian's references to unction are not very numerous, nor are they very clear in their meaning. He certainly regards the post-baptismal anointing (which probably corresponds to the unction administered by a presbyter immediately after Baptism in the *Apostolic Tradition*) as an important part of the ceremonies of initiation; it is an anointing with *benedicta unctio* performed on the authority of the unction of priests in the Old Testament, but connected with the Messianic character of Christ, and it confers a spiritual benefit upon its recipient.[6] This benefit is explained as consisting in a consecration;[7] that is to say, unction signifies the priestly character which through Christ has been imparted to the baptized; but despite the connection between *oleum divinae unctionis* and *vinum Spiritus* in an allusion to Old Testament symbolism,[8] there is no evidence that Tertullian thinks of the post-baptismal chrismation as a sacramental sign of the gift of the Spirit, nor indeed as conferring *grace* at all; it is in his view a consecration to the universal

[1] *Marc.*, 1, 28.   [2] *res. carn.*, 8.   [3] *praescr.*, 40.
[4] *Marc.*, 3, 22.   [5] *cor.*, 3.   [6] *bapt.*, 7.
[7] *res. carn.*, 8.   [8] *Ibid.*, 26.

priesthood which Christians possess in virtue of their membership of Christ, the true Priest.

What, then, does Tertullian consider to be the outward sign
of what he calls the 'clothing with the Holy Spirit'?[1] The
answer is by no means obvious. Occasionally Tertullian follows
the general line of thought pursued by his predecessors in the
first and second centuries, and ascribes this function to Baptism. Thus we find remission of sins, liberation from death,
regeneration, *consecutio Spiritus sancti*, 'sealing', and washing,
all brought together as the spiritual effects of Baptism.[2]

It would be dangerous to cut the argument short by asserting,
as Dix does, that when Tertullian speaks of Baptism he regularly means something wider in its scope than water-baptism.
In the title of his treatise *De Baptismo*, he does of course extend
the meaning of *baptismus* to cover the entire ceremony of initiation; but there is little evidence to show that in his normal use
of the word he means anything more than Baptism in the strict
sense of the term, and there are positive indications to the
contrary; thus he writes: 'sic in nobis carnaliter currit unctio,
sed spiritaliter proficit; quomodo et ipsius baptismi carnalis
actus, quod in aqua mergimur, spiritalis effectus, quod delictis
liberamur.'[3] On this passage Lupton justly comments: '*ipsius
baptismi*, i.e. baptism as distinguished from its accompanying
rites.' Tertullian's reservation of the administration of Baptism
to the bishop and his delegates has no bearing upon this question. The bishop was the original minister of Baptism as of the
Eucharist,[4] and the administration of *baptismus* would be his,
even if the term comprised water-baptism alone.

The same conception of Baptism as the means whereby the
Spirit is received would seem, on the face of it, to be suggested
by the opening chapters of the *De Baptismo*. Here there is a
strongly expressed theory of the Spirit's activity in the Baptism
proper. The interaction of Spirit and water is in fact emphasized
so extravagantly that Tertullian was not without some excuse
for his fear 'ne laudes aquae potius quam baptismi rationes
videar congregasse'.[5] We are reminded of the eulogy of water-
baptism in the Clementine Homilies.[6] It is this conception

---

[1] *praescr.*, 36. [2] *Marc.*, 1, 28. [3] *bapt.*, 7. [4] Cf. Ign., *Smyrn.*, 8.
[5] *bapt.*, 3. [6] 2, 24: τὰ πάντα τὸ ὕδωρ ποιεῖ.

which underlies the famous simile of the hydraulic organ, with its theory of a *concorporatio* of water and Spirit.[1]

At this point, however, in the argument of the *De Baptismo* Tertullian seems to pull himself up short. The analogy of the pool of Bethesda to the water of Baptism suddenly gives way to the reflection, 'Non quod in aquis Spiritum sanctum consequamur, sed in aqua emundati sub angelo Spiritui sancto praeparamur',[2] and in the simile of the organ it is through the *hands* of the player that the Spirit has to be brought into union with the water, for 'manus imponitur per benedictionem advocans et invitans Spiritum sanctum'.[3] For this theory Tertullian can offer support only from the far-fetched typology of Gen. xlviii. 14, but that his mind has been influenced by Acts is strongly suggested a little later in the treatise by a reference to the episode of the 'Ephesian disciples'.[4] The same doctrine that the medium of the gift of the Spirit is not the 'seal' but the laying on of hands is to be found elsewhere in his writings: 'caro manus impositione', he remarks, 'adumbratur, ut et anima spiritu illuminetur'.[5] It is of course conceivable that Tertullian is following ancient tradition (possibly reflected in Heb. vi. 2) in ascribing the gift of the Spirit to the post-baptismal imposition of hands; but it is more probable that his theory either reflects the introduction into the African Church of a practice directly modelled upon the episodes recorded in Acts, or represents a reinterpretation, in the light of the supposed teaching of Acts on the gift of the Spirit, of an old custom whereby the bishop as the local head of the Christian community laid his hand in blessing on the head of the new member. We shall observe the effect of the reading, or misreading, of Acts again in the thought of Cyprian.

There is thus a real confusion in Tertullian's theology: the soul's *secunda nativitas* is 'ex aqua et superna virtute';[6] yet Tertullian feels himself bound to deny that the Spirit is actually bestowed upon the believer at the moment of his regeneration. We can only suppose either that he distinguishes between the regenerating activity of the Holy Spirit and His personal indwelling (a distinction which Mason held to be true but which

---

[1] *bapt.*, 8. [2] *Ibid.*, 6. [3] *Ibid.*, 8..
[4] *Ibid.*, 10. [5] *res. carn.*, 8. [6] *anim.*, 41.

seems to differentiate unwarrantably and unintelligibly between these modes of the Spirit's activity), or that he thinks of the gift bestowed by the laying on of the hand as a charisma different from, and additional to, the Spirit's indwelling in the soul—something corresponding to the 'grace for service' of the *Apostolic Tradition* (though Tertullian does not say anything of the kind)—or we must admit that he is confused and misled by his interpretation of Acts and by the Old Testament allusion with which he seeks to support his theory. The wording of *bapt.*, 6 suggests that there were those who held a contrary view, or at least that Tertullian was conscious of being an innovator in respect of the doctrine there expressed.

The unfortunate fact appears to be that Tertullian's theory of the Holy Spirit in relation to Baptism can be defended only at the cost of his consistency; and we must hold his confused thought on Baptism and the laying on of hands responsible in no small measure for the difficulties and ambiguities which have continued from his days to our own to hamper the working out of a reasoned theology of the operation of the Holy Spirit in Baptism and Confirmation.

These difficulties and ambiguities increased as a result of the perplexities which arose out of the baptismal controversy between Cyprian and his opponents; but before we consider these developments it may be well to glance briefly at Origen's conception of the relation of the Spirit to Baptism, for it is to a large extent representative of the subsequent Eastern tradition on this matter, a tradition in which, although there was much confusion in theory, the liturgical practice remained unaltered and no actual separation was made between the parts of what had been a single rite of Baptism and its associated ceremonies.

So far as the idea of the 'seal' is concerned, most writers of the third and the following centuries use the term in a variety of senses, and it does not always denote either the bestowal of the Spirit or the means by which that bestowal is believed to be effected. Origen differs from most of his successors only in so far as he makes rather less use of the term than they. We can best understand his conception of the 'seal' if we set it against the background of his general view of Baptism.

In his baptismal theology Origen is a conservative thinker. Apart from the peculiar conception of a kind of 'purgatorial' baptism of fire administered before the entrance to Paradise— an interesting notion, by which he seeks a way of escape from the theological difficulties of post-baptismal sin, but a part of his doctrine which we need not now examine[1]—Origen follows the ecclesiastical tradition of his day and makes no startling innovations in the received ideas about the sacrament.

His particular emphasis lies upon the inward significance of the rite and its spiritual effects; he is less interested in its outward forms, and he may be thought to afford something of a contrast with the general patristic tendency to attach immense weight to particular liturgical actions. He is anxious to lay great stress on the ethical requirements of Baptism, and, unlike Clement, to draw a sharp distinction between the quasi-magical redemptions and deifications offered to their initiates by the mysteries and the profound ethical and spiritual conversion expressed by and mediated through Christian Baptism. Origen is therefore at pains to insist upon a proper disposition on the part of the catechumens who are being prepared for the sacrament, and to recommend to them the duty of penitence and sincere faith and humility as the necessary preparation for the reception of the remission of their sins and the gift of the Spirit, which they will, apparently, receive in their actual Baptism.[2] He is also quite clear that the effect of Baptism is neither sudden nor momentary; it is something which is, in a sense, 'given' at a particular moment of time, but which has yet to be worked out over the whole period of the baptized person's earthly life. The entire course of the Christian's progress in the spiritual life is an unfolding or a realization of what he already possesses and what in a sense he has already attained by virtue of being baptized. This conception, so strongly developed by Gregory of Nyssa and other Greek Fathers, is one of Origen's important contributions to the theology of

---

[1] *hom.* 2. 3. *in Jer.* (p. 19, 15; *PG.* 13, 1281A); *Lc.*, 24 (p. 158, 20 ff.; *PG.* 13, 1864C ff.); *ibid.*, 26 (p. 165, 11; *PG.* 13, 1868C).
[2] *hom.* 6. 2. *in Lev.* (p. 361, 7 ff.; *PG.* 12, 468B): 'Sed et vos, qui sacrum baptisma desideratis accipere et gratiam Spiritus promereri, prius debetis ex lege purgari, prius debetis audito verbo Dei vitia genuina resecare . . . ut mansuetudine et humilitate suscepta possitis etiam gratiam sancti Spiritus capere'; cf. *Lc.*, 21–2).

Baptism which is of profound value in relation to the relatively modern problems of infant Baptism and Confirmation.

Origen has a firm hold upon the New Testament doctrine that in Baptism the believer is united to Christ in His death and resurrection.[1] It is therefore the sole means of obtaining remission of sins,[2] through it we gain release from the power of the devil,[3] regeneration,[4] and membership of the Church as Christ's Body,[5] and in it the Church as the Bride is united to Christ.[6] Origen is anxious to leave his reader in no doubt that salvation is not automatically guaranteed by Baptism, and that some are 'baptized to condemnation';[7] he is even reluctant to seem to tie down the operation of the Holy Spirit too rigidly to the external sacramental rite. It is, indeed, this insistence on the inward and ethical which at times leads Origen to employ some rather confused language when he is speaking of the bestowal of the Spirit.

Not infrequently Origen speaks of the gift of the Spirit being received in Baptism itself,[8] although when he is expounding the Pauline teaching on the ἀρραβών of the Spirit he does not directly connect the gift of that 'earnest' of our final redemption with Baptism; it is to be obtained by making the response of faith to the preaching of the Gospel of salvation.[9]

Normally, however, Origen appears to think that the reception of the Holy Spirit takes place in the actual rite of Baptism; the convert is 'baptized in Christ, in the water and the Holy Spirit'.[10] Nevertheless he is prevented from maintaining this position unequivocally by his reading of the passages in Acts which suggested a post-baptismal gift of the Spirit, and at times he is induced, on the ground of these passages alone, to distinguish between a water-baptism and a Spirit-baptism. He

---

[1] hom. 19. 14 in Jer. (p. 172, 24; PG. 13, 493C): ἔστι γὰρ ταφῆναι μετὰ Χριστοῦ . . . διὰ τοῦ βαπτίσματος.
[2] mart., 30 (p. 26, 21; PG. 11, 600C): οὐκ ἔστιν ἄφεσιν ἁμαρτημάτων χωρὶς βαπτίσματος λαβεῖν.
[3] hom. 5. 5 in Ex. (p. 190: PG. 12, 330D ff.).
[4] Jo., 6, 33 (p. 143, 12; PG. 14, 257B).
[5] Rom., 8, 5 (PG. 14, 1168).
[6] hom. 10. 5 in Gen. (p. 100, PG. 12, 220C).
[7] hom. 6. 5 in Ezek. (PG. 13, 713D).
[8] Cf. princ., 2, 10, 7 (p. 181, 7; PG. 11, 239B).
[9] Eph., 8 (JTS. 3, p. 243).
[10] hom. 5. 5 in Ex. (p. 190, 13; PG. 12, 330D).

speaks, for example, of Philip baptizing with water, but of Peter baptizing with the Spirit,[1] and in the same passage he explains that the Spirit was given to Philip's converts only through the laying on of Peter's hands.[2] It is, however, quite plain that he is not really thinking of two independent rites of Baptism and Confirmation, except in so far as that idea is forced upon him by his interpretation of Acts. What he is trying to emphasize is rather the distinction between the outward sign and the inward grace. Not all who are baptized receive the Spirit, for some, like Simon Magus, are not sincerely converted. On the other hand, there may be a Cornelius among those who have not yet received the baptism for which they are preparing. This is the real heart of his thought; but since the illustrations which he draws are taken from Acts, they are complicated by the fact that they seem to point to a double distinction, between the outward sign and the divine blessing, on the one hand, and, on the other, between Baptism itself and the laying on of hands by which, according to Acts, the supreme divine blessing is conferred.[3] His only remedy is to try to hold together the rites of Baptism, laying on of hands, and chrismation as essentially one and the same ceremony of initiation, and to use any one of them indiscriminately as equivalent to 'Baptism' for the purposes of his exegesis. In emphasizing the inward effects of Baptism, he lays stress upon the unity of the initiatory rite and treats the laying on of hands (the mention of which in Acts is clearly an embarrassment to his own thought on Baptism)[4] and chrismation as purely subordinate elements in the single rite of 'baptism'. It is owing to this desire to emphasize the centrality of Baptism and the subsidiary character of the other elements in initiation that Origen occasionally uses such curious and loose expressions as 'baptizati simus in aquis istis visibilibus

---

[1] 1 Cor. 1. 17 (JTS. 9, p. 234).   [2] Ibid.
[3] hom. 3. 1 in Num. (p. 14, 4; PG. 12, 594A ff.) : 'Non enim omnes qui ex Israhel, hi sunt Israhelitae, neque omnes qui loti sunt aqua, continuo etiam sancto Spiritu loti sunt; sicut e contrario non omnes qui in catechumenis numerantur, alieni et expertes sunt Spiritu sancti . . . Cornelius catechumenus erat, et antequam ad aquas veniret, meruit accipere Spiritum sanctum. Simon baptismum acceperat, sed quoniam cum hypocrisi accessit ad gratiam, repudiatur a dono Spiritus sancti.' This passage is typical of Origen's interest in the spiritual preparation for Baptism as contrasted with the external ceremony; he is not concerned with a rite of 'Confirmation' as distinct from 'Baptism'.
[4] Cf. Dix, Confirmation or the Laying on of Hands? p. 20.

et in chrismate visibili'[1] (in a passage in which he is contrasting the inward and outward aspects of Baptism). Similarly, with special reference to the narrative of Acts viii. 17, Origen remarks that 'in Actibus apostolorum per impositionem manuum apostolicarum Spiritus sanctus dabatur *in baptismo*'.[2] It must not, however, be argued from these examples of his right and proper concern to emphasize the fundamental importance of Baptism as against the secondary ceremonies associated with it that Origen really uses the terms βάπτισμα and βαπτίζειν to signify the administration of a complex rite of which water-baptism is only one constituent element. Certainly we must not infer from his reference to 'Baptism in visible waters and visible chrism' that he really thinks of Baptism as a sacrament administered in oil as well as water. He is simply trying, for the purposes of his argument, to bring the gift of the Spirit into as close a relationship with water-baptism as his reading of Acts and his own experience of the ceremony of chrismation and the ideas associated therewith will permit. That βάπτισμα indicates water-baptism alone is clearly shown by the fact that his interpretation of Acts compels him to differentiate sharply the grace of Baptism (βάπτισμα) from the gift of the Spirit in the laying on of hands.[3] Simon Magus received βάπτισμα although he did not obtain the gift of the Spirit which is normally expected to result from Baptism provided that the recipient comes to the sacrament with faith and penitence.[4] Origen's thought is here again concentrated on the distinction between the outward sign and the inward reality signified and effected by it, rather than on the question of the temporal relationship of the gift of the Spirit to the water-baptism with which it is associated. Elsewhere, when discussing the same case of Simon Magus, Origen uses language which suggests that

---

[1] *Rom.*, 5, 8 (*PG.* 14, 1038C).   [2] *princ.*, 1, 3, 2 (p. 50, 4; *PG.* 11, 147B).
[3] *Ibid.*, 1, 3, 7 (p. 58, 20; *PG.* 11, 153A) : 'Per impositionem manuum apostolorum post baptismi gratiam et renovationem, sanctus Spiritus tradebatur'—an interpretation which does violence to Titus iii. 5.
[4] *Jo.*, 6, 33 (17; p. 143, 4 ff.; *PG.* 14, 257A): μαρτυρεῖ . . . ἡ ἐν ταῖς τῶν ἀποστόλων Πραξέσιν ἀναγεγραμμένη ἱστορία περὶ τοῦ οὕτως ἐναργῶς τότε τὸ Πνεῦμα τοῖς βαπτιζομένοις ἐπιδεδημηκέναι, προευτρεπίσαντος αὐτῷ τοῦ ὕδατος τοῖς γνησίως προσίουσιν ὁδόν, ὡς καὶ τὸν μάγον Σίμωνα . . . θελεῖν μὲν τὴν χάριν ταύτην ἀπὸ τοῦ Πέτρου λαβεῖν . . . παλιγγενεσίας ὀνομαζόμενον λουτρὸν μετὰ ἀνακαινώσεως γινόμενον πνεύματος, τοῦ καὶ νῦν ἐπιφερομένου, ἐπειδὴ παρὰ Θεοῦ ἐστιν, ἐπάνω τοῦ ὕδατος, ἀλλ'οὐ πᾶσιν μετὰ τὸ ὕδωρ ἐγγινομένου.

his real understanding that reception of the Spirit accompanies
Baptism in water as the spiritual reality signified by the sacramental sign has proved stronger than the theory of the communication of the Spirit by the imposition of hands—the theory
apparently necessitated by the narrative of Acts, and which in
deference to the implications of that narrative he has generally
felt compelled to adopt. 'Simon', he comments, 'lotus est et
baptisma consecutus perseverabat in Philippi societate. . . .
Qui lavatur in salutem et aquam accipit et Spiritum sanctum.
Quia non fuit Simon lotus in salutem, accipit aquam, et non
accipit Spiritum sanctum, putans quia possit donum Spiritus
pecunia comparari, in qua non est lotus in salutem.'[1] It is to
be observed that Origen treats the question of the function of
the imposition of hands primarily in relation to the narrative of
Acts and not to current ecclesiastical practice.

We have already remarked that Origen was familiar with the
use of chrism in initiation. He does not, however, appear at any
time to attach the bestowal of the Spirit to this rite as its outward sign. He is inclined rather to regard it as a ceremony
which denotes either faith in the Anointed,[2] or the inward
unction of the Spirit which is conferred in Baptism,[3] and may be
figuratively represented by unction with oil, though it is not in
fact bestowed by its means. It is not connected by Origen with
the 'seal'. In fact, as we have already noticed, his references to
the conception of the seal are few, and he is certainly not an
author who can be pressed into service to support a general
identification of the seal with Confirmation.

It is not improbable that Origen would agree that the
Christian convert is marked with a seal of God's ownership
through the invocation over him of the Threefold Name, for
Origen brings out very clearly the high importance of the Name
in Baptism.[4] Nevertheless, his actual use of the term 'seal' is

---

[1] hom. 6, in Ezek. (PG. 12, 713C).

[2] In a reference to the Passover (sel. in. Ex. 12, 7) (PG. 12, 284C): χρίομεν
τοὺς οἴκους ἡμῶν τῷ αἵματι. λέγω δὲ τὸ σῶμα, εἴπερ χρίσις πίστις ἐστὶν ἡ εἰς αὐτόν,
δι' ἧς πιστεύω τὴν τοῦ ὀλοθρευτοῦ δύναμιν καταργουμένην· μετὰ δὲ τὸ χρισθῆναι ἡμᾶς,
τουτέστι πιστεῦσαι εἰς τὸν Χριστόν, τότε καὶ ἐπὶ τὴν βρῶσιν ἔρχεσθαι κελευόμεθα.

[3] καὶ ἔλουσά σε ἐν ὕδατι· τῷ λουτρῷ καὶ τῇ χάριτι τοῦ ἁγίου πνεύματος, καὶ τῷ
ἁγιοποιῷ λόγῳ, καὶ ἔχρισά σε ἐν ἐλαίῳ· χρῖσμα ἐστὶν ἐνοίκησις τοῦ ἁγίου πνεύματος ἐν
γνώσει τῆς ἀληθείας (sel. in Ezek. 16) (PG. 13, 812A).

[4] princ., 1, 3, 2 (p. 50, 6; PG. 11, 147C); Jo., 6, 33 (17; p. 142, 27; PG. 14, 257A);
cf. Cels. 1, 6 (p. 59, 21 ff.; PG. 11, 665B); ibid., 1, 25 (p. 77, 3; PG. 11, 708A).

usually metaphorical or quasi-metaphorical. So, for example, the mind is given form by the impression on it of the seal of θεολογία and it is therefore to the mind thus shaped or stamped that the πηγὴ ἐσφραγισμένη of Canticles iv. 12 can be referred:[1] His nearest approach to any kind of association of the seal with unction occurs in his typology of the oil of Lev. xiv. 26. This signifies the believer's anointing with the Holy Spirit, and, together with the gift of the Spirit, there is given to him the prodigal son's robe and ring which symbolize the restoration to fallen man of the image of God.[2] The 'ring' of this parable is very frequently interpreted by the Fathers as an illustration of the seal or stamp of the divine image restored to the soul in Baptism.[3]

If this conception of the seal had been fully worked out by Origen he would have come near to making a distinction between water-baptism as a negative symbol of purification and remission of sins, and chrismation as the means whereby the positive gift of the Spirit, or of the seal of the divine image, is conferred. He would thus have been anticipating the theories of certain later patristic authors and of the modern theologians of the Puller-Mason-Dix schools of thought. Indeed, he would have been carrying their views to extreme lengths, for he would be suggesting that reconciliation and regeneration, which are summed up in the reception of the status of sonship to God, are bestowed through chrismation and not through Baptism, for Origen never attempts to separate the activities of the Spirit in regeneration and in the gift of His indwelling presence and of the stamp of the divine image. Origen does not, however, work out the implications of his exegesis of this passage, nor does he follow them up elsewhere in his writings.

The most explicit treatment of the idea of the seal in Origen is concerned with the notion of Baptism as the seal of faith, and he lays particular emphasis on the catechumen's renunciation

---

[1] schol. in Cant. iv. 12 (PG. 17, 273A); cf. viii. 6 (285B).
[2] hom. 8. 11 in Lev. (p. 417, 15; PG. 12, 508A).
[3] The passage runs: 'Sic ergo conversis a peccato purificatio quidem per illa omnia datur, quae superius diximus, donum autem gratiae Spiritus per olei imaginem designatur, ut non solum purgationem consequi possit is qui convertitur a peccato, sed ut Spiritu sancto repleri, quo et recipere priorem stolam et anulum possit et per omnia reconciliatus patri in locum filii reparari' (hom. 8. 11 in Lev. (pp. 417–18; PG. 12, 507).

of the devil, and his acceptance of Christ, as the seal set upon his Christian profession.[1] In this sense, as a token or proof of a covenant relationship to God, circumcision played a similar part in the Old Testament to that of Baptism in the New.[2]

In the baptismal theology of Origen the idea that the seal is connected with a particular point in the initiation ceremony evidently played no considerable part. His thought is too firmly fixed upon the inward significance of Baptism as a whole to permit this notion to assume much importance for him. The Gnostic sects, who emphasized the necessity for such initiatory rites as unction to supplement Baptism or even to replace it, based their doctrine of Christian initiation upon a theory of 'natural' redemption. For the Scriptural doctrine of justification by faith responding to the free grace of God in Christ they substituted a doctrine of 'justification' (if such it can be called) by the sacramental reception of a new, spiritual, nature. By the due performance of certain rites and by the attainment of 'gnosis', the believer is transformed into a 'pneumatic' person. In total contrast with this type of quasi-pagan thought,[3] Origen is concerned to emphasize the ethical character of redemption.[4] Baptism, the sacrament of union with Christ, brings with it both freedom from sin and the dominion of evil, and also the positive gifts of a new status and the possession of the Holy Spirit.

In a remarkable passage Origen explains that Baptism is the proleptic summing up of the spiritual life which, in its turn, is the working out in practice of that which Baptism symbolizes; in and through the sacrament the believer is united to Christ, but the Logos comes to the soul as a child, and as it were grows within it.[5] The union which is effected in Baptism is a union with Christ in His death,[6] and as in Christ's own Baptism the dove descended, so at our incorporation into Christ and His

---

[1] *hom.* 12. 4 *in Num.* (p. 105, 25; *PG.* 12, 665C).
[2] *hom.* 3. 3 *in Gen.* (p. 42, 2; *PG.* 12, 177A).
[3] Cf. Menander's idea that Baptism confers immortality and eternal youth (Iren., *haer.*, 1, 23, 5; cf. Tert., *anim.*, 50).
[4] Cf. Rahner, H., *Taufe u. geistliches Leben bei Origenes* (*Zeitschr. für Askese u. Mystik*, 1932, pp. 205–23).
[5] *hom.* 10. 4 *in Ex.* (p. 250, 22; *PG.* 12, 373B).
[6] *hom.* 4. 2 *in Jos.* (p. 309, 26; *PG.* 12, 843D).

saving work, the Spirit comes upon us,[1] so that we possess the gift of the Spirit and become 'pneumatic'.[2]

It is therefore a logical consequence of his fundamentally Scriptural doctrine of Baptism that Origen should do his utmost to lay stress on the unity of the baptismal rite, and in spite of the conclusions which he draws from Acts, and despite his acquaintance with 'chrisma visibile', to avoid making any suggestion that Christian initiation consists of two parts, a negative cleansing and a positive sealing, capable, at least in theory, of being separated from each other and treated as the distinct sacramental rites of Baptism and Confirmation.

A not dissimilar theological emphasis is to be discerned in Cyprian's rather muddled thought on this subject. He, like Origen, fully understands that, since Baptism is the sacrament of union with Christ, it must bring the believer into the sphere of all the gifts which Christ bestows upon His Church through the Spirit; the gift of the indwelling Spirit cannot rightly be isolated from incorporation into Christ and His mystical Body, and water-baptism must not be treated as though it were merely a necessary preliminary to some other sacramental rite which conveys a higher positive gift of grace. The situation in which Cyprian was placed, however, rendered it much more difficult for him than for Origen to maintain this point of view.

He is hard pressed by the apparent implications of Acts. A great influence was exerted upon his thought by those passages in which the bestowal of the Spirit appeared to be confined to the rite of laying on of hands, and in this respect, as in so many others, Cyprian proved himself a faithful pupil of his 'magister', Tertullian. Among some, at any rate, of his opponents in the baptismal controversy—those represented for us by the *De Rebaptismate*—water-baptism was being isolated from the 'Confirmation' part of the early initiation ceremony, and its depreciation was already being carried to extreme lengths. In the Church of Rome there was already a widespread tendency to connect the gift of the Spirit exclusively with 'Confirmation' rather than with Baptism, and, in the reconciliation of heretics and schismatics, to emphasize the laying on of hands as the means by which they received the Spirit—the positive gift con-

[1] *Lc.*, 27 (p. 171, 6).   [2] *Lc.*, 22 (p. 145, 13).

ferred in this ceremony being all that was needed in order to supply the deficiency of the Baptism which they had received outside the Church. No doubt there were several factors which contributed to the notion of a separation of Baptism and Confirmation: the growth of the Church, especially in Rome, the retention of the administration of the 'Confirmation' part of the initiatory rite as the prerogative of the bishop, and, to some extent also, the growth of the regular practice of infant Baptism which was bound sooner or later to cause a modification of the full New Testament significance of Baptism, and to necessitate the development of Confirmation, in the proper sense, in order to render the change theologically justifiable. All these factors must have made it easy to create a distinction between the negative effects of water-baptism and the positive graces conferred in Confirmation, and to hasten the distintegration of the pattern of Christian initiation as it existed at the beginning of the third century.

Cyprian does his best to halt this process, to maintain the unity of the whole rite, including its subsidiary elements, and to emphasize the central importance in the initiation ceremonies of the actual Baptism. It is through washing in water that the convert is reborn to new life,[1] and Cyprian naturally and properly connects baptismal regeneration with the reception of the Spirit.[2] It is by means of Baptism that the Holy Spirit is bestowed,[3] and there can be no doubt that the word *baptisma* in this context means 'Baptism' in the ordinary sense of the word, and not a complex rite. Cyprian clarifies this point when in the same context he remarks that in the 'water' of John iv. 13–14, 'baptisma salutaris aquae significatur',[4] and enunciates the general principle that 'Quotiescumque aqua sola in scripturis sanctis nominatur, baptisma praedicatur'[5]—an exegetical theory which would have relatively less point if *baptisma* meant more than baptism in water. Similarly, Cyprian identifies *baptisma* explicitly with *lavacrum*.[6] The Holy Spirit is granted in

---

[1] *Donat.*, 3: Ut quis renasci denuo possit utque in novam vitam lavacro aquae salutaris animatus, quod prius fuerat, exponeret.

[2] *Ibid.*, 4: Postquam caelitus Spiritu hausto in novum me hominem nativitas secunda reparavit.

[3] *ep.*, 63, 8: Per baptisma autem Spiritus accipitur, et sic baptizatis et Spiritum sanctum consecutis ad bibendum calicem Domini pervenitur.

[4] *Ibid.* (*CSEL.* p. 707, 16).   [5] *Ibid.* (p. 706, 3).   [6] *ep.*, 74, 6.

Baptism even to infants, according to their capacity,[1] and it is perhaps worth noting that Jewish circumcision is said by Cyprian to have received its fulfilment or antitype not in the 'seal' administered by the bishop, but in the *spiritalis circumcisio* of infant Baptism.[2]

Thus Cyprian seems naturally inclined to see in Baptism in water the effectual sign of the coming of the Spirit upon the believer. He is not, however, able to follow out the logic of this tendency. Nevertheless, he is determined so far as possible to maintain the unity of Baptism with its subsidiary rites, and not to allow the 'Confirmation' part of the ceremony to be detached from Baptism and exalted into a separate rite for the gift of the Spirit. For instance, he takes strong exception to the depreciation by Stephen's party of 'clinical baptism' and its effects. In contrast with Cornelius of Rome,[3] Cyprian pours scorn on the very word 'clinici', and refuses to admit that they are not Christians in the full sense.[4] It is true that his concern is mainly to show that those who are baptized in sickness have lost no spiritual gift through having been *perfusi* instead of *loti*, but he goes on to assert that such persons have received the gift of the Spirit no less than their fellow-Christians who were immersed at their Baptism.[5] Cyprian evidently does not hold that the essential gift of the Spirit was conferred in any Confirmation or 'sealing' administered subsequently by the bishop to those who had been clinically baptized.

In the baptismal controversy one of Cyprian's primary concerns is to prevent the gifts of Baptism from being isolated from one another and assigned to different outward rites instead of being held in conjunction as aspects, inseparable except in theory, of the 'putting on' of Christ. Thus he refuses to distinguish remission of sins from the gift of the Spirit. Stephen's party admits the reality of schismatic baptism. It therefore confers remission of sins. Yet the schismatics are said not to possess the Holy Spirit, and accordingly hands (or rather the hand) is laid upon them when they are reconciled to the Church in order to supply their defect. Cyprian will have none of this. Either schismatics possess the Spirit or they do not. If they do,

[1] *ep.*, 64, 3.   [2] *Ibid.*, 4.   [3] See below, p. 178.
[4] *ep.*, 69, 12, 13.   [5] *ep.*, 69, 13–14.

then why should they be reconciled with the laying on of the hand 'ad accipiendum Spiritum'?[1] If they do not, then it follows that they do not receive remission of sins either, since this can only be conferred where the Spirit is present. There can be no Baptism without the Spirit.[2]

The same insistence on the essential unity of the baptismal gifts of grace is expressed by Firmilian of Caesarea. He will not allow that the baptism of schismatics can confer Christ's presence and sanctification; whoever is baptized in Christ puts on Christ, 'si autem induit Christum, accipere potuit et Spiritum sanctum qui a Christo missus est, et frustra illi venienti ad accipiendum Spiritum manus imponitur: nisi si a Christo Spiritum dividunt ut apud haereticos sit quidem Christus, non sit autem illic Spiritus sanctus.'[3]

However misguided may have been the views of Cyprian and Firmilian upon the nature and character of the Church, they are right, when judged by New Testament standards, in their refusal to countenance any disintegration of the fundamental unity of Baptism and the spiritual gifts bestowed through it. Firmilian, like Cyprian, seems inclined to associate the gift of the Spirit with Baptism; but his reading of the Scriptures appears to forbid him to disregard what he holds to be the teaching of Acts xix. 6, that the Spirit was bestowed upon the Ephesian disciples by the laying on of St. Paul's hands, and that this episode represents the regular practice of the apostolic age. Even so, this text serves to encourage him in his insistence that the imposition of the hand must not be divorced from Baptism, nor remission of sins and 'second birth' from the gift of the Spirit.[4] The laying on of the hand is insufficient to confer the Spirit upon a person baptized in schism; his Baptism was void and therefore he must be baptized de novo.

Cyprian acknowledges that the contemporary practice of bringing the baptized to the bishop for the imposition of the hand is identical with the action of the Apostolic Church in sending Peter and John to pray for, and lay their hands upon, the Samaritans in order that they might receive the Holy Spirit. By prayer and the laying on of the bishop's hand the Christians of the Church of Carthage are enabled to receive the Holy

[1] ep., 69, 11.   [2] ep., 74, 5.   [3] ep., 75, 12.   [4] Ibid., 8.

Spirit and it is by this means that 'signaculo dominico consummentur'.[1] It is possible that the *signaculum* is to be identified with the grace of the Holy Spirit given by the laying on of hands, that is, that it denotes the 'seal of the Spirit'. If so, Cyprian is the first writer by whom the seal, in the full New Testament sense of the term, is directly associated with the ceremony of the imposition of hands;[2] but it is more probable that it signifies the *consignatio*, the signing with the Cross which completes the convert's initiation, as in the *Apostolic Tradition*. In any case, Cyprian here yields to the pressure of the accepted, and in Africa, at any rate, traditional, interpretation of Acts viii. 17, and ascribes the gift of the Spirit to the laying on of hands.

Cyprian is not entirely happy in this view. As we have seen, his own theological presuppositions tend to lead him to a different conclusion. He is therefore constrained to try to resolve this difficulty by finding a type of Baptism in the original creation of man, and of the bestowal of the Spirit through the laying on of hands in the breathing into him of the breath of life. Baptism is thus the new birth, and the imposition of the hand confers the quickening power of the Spirit.[3] Cyprian's object in devising this typology, as the context makes clear, is not to emphasize a distinction between water-baptism and the sacrament of the Spirit; on the contrary, it is designed to bring what he regards as the teaching of Acts on the laying on of hands into harmony with his conception of the prior importance of Baptism. Against his opponents, who are evidently attaching undue weight to the ceremony of laying on of hands, he is insisting on the fundamental and central character of the gift received in Baptism. The imposition of hands can be no substitute for the Church's Baptism, for it is in the latter that the believer is spiritually born. Cyprian is manifestly somewhat hard pressed in his endeavours to reconcile the function which

---

[1] *ep.*, 73, 9.

[2] Cf. 'manum imponi ut Spiritum sanctum consequatur et signetur', *ep.*, 73, 6, which again may refer to signing with the Cross.

[3] *ep.*, 74, 7: 'Porro autem non per manus impositionem quis nascitur quando accipit Spiritum sanctum, sed in baptismo, ut Spiritum iam natus accipiat, sicut in primo homine Adam factum est. Ante eum Deus plasmavit, tunc insufflavit in faciem eius flatum vitae. Nec enim potest accipi Spiritus, nisi prius fuerit qui accipiat.'

he feels bound to assign to the imposition of the hand with his own more Pauline conception of the significance of Baptism. His typology of the Creation story is a rather desperate expedient which is not taken up by his successors. He has in fact already tried to make his point, without using this analogy from Genesis, when he declares that those who have been 'tincti' outside the Church in heresy or schism, 'baptizari oportere, eo quod parum sit eis manum imponere ad accipiendum Spiritum nisi accipiant et ecclesiae baptismum. Tunc enim demum plene sanctificari et esse filii Dei possunt, si sacramento utroque nascantur.'[1]

To support his view that Baptism and the laying on of hands must go together he adduces John iii. 5 and the birth 'of water and Spirit'. The disintegration of the ancient and Scriptural conception of Baptism has evidently proceeded so far that even Cyprian interprets the 'water' and 'Spirit' as indicating two *sacramenta* of Baptism and the laying on of the hand, instead of as denoting the inward and outward aspects of the single sacrament of Baptism; but, at the same time, he is fighting hard, against the views of Stephen's party, to retain the closest association of the two rites and to treat them theologically as virtually constituting one sacrament. He will allow no separation of the two, and he cites the baptism of Cornelius as evidence for his insistence on the necessary connection between Baptism in water and Baptism with the Spirit.[2]

As we have already noticed in connection with another passage from his writings, Cyprian refuses to dissociate one aspect of baptismal grace from another. He cannot conceive that remission of sins can be granted in circles where the gift of the Spirit is not available.[3] He will not separate the effects of Baptism and assign some to Baptism proper and some to Confirmation. The *Sententiae Episcoporum* reinforce Cyprian's views on the unity and centrality of Baptism. Nemesianus of Thubunae insists, like Cyprian, on the necessity for maintaining the essential unity of the laying on of hands and Baptism, and even implies that the former should occupy a subordinate place in the ritual of initiation. After quoting John iii. 5, he declares that 'Hic est Spiritus qui ab initio ferebatur super aquam.

[1] *ep.*, 72, 1.   [2] *Ibid.*, 53.   [3] *ep.*, 73, 6.

Neque enim Spiritus sine aqua separatim operari potest, nec aqua sine Spiritu. Male ergo sibi quidam interpretantur ut dicant, quod per manus impositionem Spiritum sanctum accipiant et sic recipiantur, cum manifestum sit utroque sacramento debere eos renasci in ecclesia catholica.'[1] There can be no bestowal of the Spirit by means of the laying on of hands where there is no true Baptism.[2]

The extent to which the opponents of Cyprian were ready to separate Baptism from Confirmation, and to ascribe the essential Christian possession of the Spirit to the effect of the latter, is singularly difficult to determine. We have to infer the views of Stephen and his party from the angry comments of Cyprian and Firmilian and to derive what light we can from that highly confused and obscure work, the *De Rebaptismate*. The question is further clouded by the difficulty of deciding what Stephen intended to signify by the practice of the laying on of hands in the reconciliation of schismatics. It seems to have been generally agreed on both sides of the controversy that in the laying on of hands there was bestowed a gift of the Spirit;[3] but Stephen explicitly declares that it is a form of the practice of the imposition of hands in penance,[4] whereas Cyprian clearly thinks it is a part of the ritual of initiation. The complicated question of the relation between the ceremonies of post-baptismal benediction and of penance, and the further question how far the laying on of hands was believed to confer a renewal of the baptismal gift of the Spirit, forfeited through sin, are not problems which need detain us at present. The important point for us to notice is Cyprian's vigorous attempt to prevent any further disintegration of the ancient pattern of initiation. His theories about heretical baptism were in due course rejected by the Church as a whole; but in his conception of the relationship of the Holy Spirit to Baptism he stood on firmer ground than that on which his opponents took up their position.

It is with the laying on of hands that Cyprian, following the

---

[1] *Sent. Episc.*, 5.   [2] *Ibid.*, 24.

[3] It is, however, significant that Vincentius of Thibari regards the imposition of the hand in reconciliation as a kind of exorcism, and quotes as an authority for the practice a Dominical command: 'Ite in nomine meo, manum imponite, daemonia expellite.' It is to be *followed* by the 'regeneration of Baptism' (*ibid.*, 37).

[4] 'traditum est ut manus illis imponatur in paenitentiam,' Cypr., *ep.*, 74, 1.

African tradition of Tertullian and finding Scriptural authority in the Acts of the Apostles, has to associate the gift of the Spirit. About unction with chrism he says comparatively little. Like his second-century predecessors, he regards it as a subsidiary ceremony which follows Baptism with the object of demonstrating to the newly baptized that he has become a member of Christ, a sharer in the Messianic character of the Lord, and a partaker of the grace of Christ.[1]

The marking of the newly baptized with the sign of the Cross is the 'sealing' which denotes that the convert belongs to Christ; hence, like the soldier of the Empire, the Christian has received the seal which marks him out as one of those who serve in the Christian *militia*.[2] It is most closely connected with Baptism,[3] and though in itself it is the outward sign of the Cross, it symbolizes and represents the whole inward 'character' which Baptism has bestowed on the convert. It is therefore an eschatological pledge of salvation from the wrath of God in the last day;[4] in it there is fulfilled the prophecy of Ezek. ix. 4 ff., and the type of the Passover blood.[5] It is the *signum Christi*, the proof of rebirth which will enable the sealed to escape the fiery destruction of the Day of Judgment.[6] Here is the ancient conception of the eschatological seal; but, though no doubt Cyprian does not think of the seal as constituted simply by the outward mark of the Cross on the newly baptized, but regards this signing as a symbol of the baptismal character, yet he does not specifically connect it with the gift of the Holy Spirit. In Cyprian's teaching the idea of the seal has really very little to do with his conception of Baptism and its relationship to the reception of the indwelling Spirit. His thought on the seal represents an extension of that of Tertullian. Generally, Tertullian thinks of Baptism as the rite of sealing, even though he is compelled by his exegesis of Acts to ascribe the bestowal of the

[1] *ep.*, 70, 2 : 'ungi quoque necesse est eum qui baptizatus est, ut accepto chrismate id est unctione esse unctus Dei et habere in se gratiam Christi possit.'
[2] *Donat.*, 15.   [3] *ep.*, 69, 2.
[4] *testimon.*, 2, 22 : 'Quod in hoc signo crucis salus sit omnibus qui in frontibus notentur.'
[5] *Ibid.*
[6] *Demetr.*, 22. 'Succendi et cremari alienigenos praeconavit Dominus, id est alienos a divino genere et profanos, spiritaliter non renatos nec Dei filios factos. Evadere enim solos posse qui renati et signo Christi signati fuerint alio in loco (sc. Ezek. ix. 4) Deus loquitur.'

Spirit to the laying on of hands. In his military metaphor of *signing* he has come very close to an equation of the sign of the Cross with the seal; but Cyprian has followed this thought considerably further and made a positive identification of the seal with the mark of the Cross and the Christian 'character' which the Cross symbolizes. Yet Cyprian nowhere suggests that it is in the *consignatio* that the believer receives the Holy Spirit, by which, in a deeper and more indelible fashion than by the outward sign of the Cross, the Christian is sealed for a day of redemption.

Cyprian's opponents in the baptismal controversy take up a very different position as regards the sealing of the baptized with the Holy Spirit. We know less of their doctrine and practice than of Cyprian's, but it is fairly clear that whereas the latter tried to hold together Baptism and its attendant ceremonies together in one rite and to give a single theological significance to the whole, with the chief emphasis upon Baptism itself, the tendency of Rome was to separate Baptism from the subsidiary rites which followed it, and to lay the greatest stress upon the importance of consignation as the medium of the bestowal of the Spirit.

This is the standpoint from which Cornelius viewed the question. As Cyprian's correspondence tells us, the Roman party took the very low view of clinical Baptism which the logic of their position demanded. The language of Cornelius in his letter to Fabius of Antioch relating the history of Novatian reinforces the information which we may gain from Cyprian. Novatian, says Cornelius, received Baptism by affusion on what was thought to be his death-bed, and it was then his duty to receive the rest of the sacramental graces which his initiation should confer upon him, but which clinical Baptism could not bestow. He ought, in particular, to have had himself sealed by a bishop, according to the 'canon' of the Church: τούτου δὲ μὴ τυχών, πῶς ἂν τοῦ ἁγίου Πνεύματος ἔτυχε.[1]

It is not entirely clear to what outward ceremony of conferring the seal Cornelius is alluding, but Rufinus is probably correct in his interpretation of the passage when he introduces into it an explicit reference to consignation with chrism. A more

[1] Cornel., ap. Eus., *h.e.*, 6, 43, 15.

important point to notice in the letter of Cornelius (an exaggerated and grossly unfair piece of rhetorical denunciation) is the clear and unmistakable distinction which its writer draws between Baptism proper and the 'seal' as the external sign of baptism with the Holy Spirit. It seems that the tendency to apply the word 'seal' to the signing of the newly baptized with the Cross in the bishop's chrismation has now led to the making of an identification of that sealing with a sacrament of sealing with the Spirit. In any case, the Spirit is explicitly said to be bestowed, not in Baptism, but in a rite of 'sealing', which in certain cases, such as clinical Baptism, may be separated from Baptism by a considerable interval of time.

This view of Baptism and Confirmation was by no means a novelty at Rome in the time of Cornelius; we have seen a strong tendency towards a similar doctrine in Hippolytus, though not, if the Latin text be accepted, in the *Apostolic Tradition*. Its history, however, is extremely hard to determine, and we can only guess at some of the causes which may have brought about this tendency to divide the baptismal rite, and assign the positive gift of the Spirit to Confirmation. One cause, as we have suggested, may have been the effect of Gnostic sacramental rites of 'Spirit-baptism' on the thought and practice of the orthodox; but more than this factor is required to account for the striking development which appears to have taken place in the teaching and practice of the Church at Rome between about the end of the second century and the middle of the third. In the course of this development Baptism comes to be regarded in some quarters as a mere preparation for a rite of Confirmation in which the Holy Spirit was believed to be conferred on the believer. This rite probably consisted in the laying on of hands and unction with chrism. Cornelius may have emphasized the importance of the latter, and Stephen's party certainly laid stress on the former. The chief reason for this change was probably, as we have already suggested, the growth of the Roman Church during the long period of peace in the first part of the third century. The rapid increase in the number of Christians precluded the possibility of the bishop continuing to act as the regular minister of all baptisms, and this fact probably led to a greater degree of importance being attached to those parts of the initiatory service (the 'Confirmation') which the bishop had always performed in his own person, and which were naturally retained as his prerogative after he had ceased to be regularly present to preside at the actual Baptism.

It is also possible that the increasingly widespread acceptance of infant baptism as a normal practice may have raised the question what gifts and graces the baptized infant might properly be said to have received. The asking of this question would be sufficient in itself to take off the edge, as it were, of the New Testament doctrine of the positive significance of the putting on of Christ in Baptism.

The possibility must also be borne in mind that even before any separation of Confirmation from Baptism had taken place in the West, the full significance of Baptism as an eschatological sacrament may have become blurred to some extent owing to a change on the part of many Christians in their attitude to the present world. It is during the early part of the third century that the first real signs begin to appear of the possibility that the Church and the secular order may be able in due course to come to terms. In a 'world-accepting', somewhat secularized Church, Baptism may well have lost some of the meaning which it possessed for Christians of a 'Puritan' or world-renouncing type. For the latter it represented a drastic severance from this world, a violent break with the past, and it was so fully charged with significance for the world to come that it would be unlikely that any Christian of this sort would depreciate the importance and significance of the 'washing' and 'dying' which Baptism signified, and seek to lay emphasis on a separate rite of Confirmation as the means whereby the gift of the Spirit was received. It is perhaps for this reason that Novatian, as we infer from Cornelius' scathing attack on his failure to complete his initiation and from the explicit statement of Theodoret about his followers,[1] rejected the 'seal' of Confirmation altogether.

In striking contrast to those who wished to retain the ancient emphasis on water-baptism itself as the sacrament of the Spirit, or, at least, to insist that any other rite for the Spirit's bestowal must be united to water-baptism as part of one form of initiation, there stands the anonymous author of the *De Rebaptismate*.

[1] *haer.*, 3, 5.

The bearing of this treatise upon the controversy with which it deals is not within the scope of our present enquiry, and in fact it is no easy matter to investigate, for the writer's thought is thoroughly confused, and his arguments and their illustrations are by no means easy to follow.

The important points for us to notice are that this writer's work is the first in which an explicit distinction is made in so many words between 'baptisma aquae' and 'baptisma Spiritus' or 'spiritale',[1] and that in this book Baptism is practically reduced to the status of an outward lustration, not unlike the Jewish purificatory washings, since the inward Baptism with the Spirit is no longer regarded as the counterpart of the external washing which symbolizes and conveys it, but has become detached from it and associated instead with the imposition of hands. Baptism has therefore become a mere ceremony of preparation for the subsequent 'washings' of the soul.[2] The rite has reverted tô little more than the baptism administered by John in preparation for the coming Spirit-baptism of the Messiah; in itself it is but a 'dimidiatum et non consummatum mysterium fidei';[3] the Baptism with water is 'minus'; baptism with the Spirit (represented by another outward sign) is 'maius';[4] and our salvation is actually said to reside in the Spirit-baptism, which may be linked with baptism in water as part of the same rite of initiation (when a bishop administers it and can complete the ceremony immediately with the laying on of hands), but which may, on the other hand, be separated from it by an indefinite interval of time.[5] The writer of this treatise evidently has in mind the changing situation of the middle of the third century, with the rapid growth of the Church and the emergence of separate 'parishes' within the sphere of one bishop's activity. Many people are accordingly baptized by presbyters and subsequently die before they have received the laying on of the bishop's hand,[6] for Baptism is being increasingly delegated to priests while 'Confirmation' is reserved as a separate rite to be performed by the bishop. The early Church was convinced that, except for the martyr, no unbaptized person could be saved. Baptism therefore could not be postponed (especially in

---

[1] 11 (*CSEL*. p. 82, 5, 17). [2] 18 (p. 91, 19). [3] 5 (p. 74, 29).
[4] 6 (p. 78, 2). [5] 10 (p. 82, 5 ff.). [6] 4 (p. 74, 3).

the numerous cases where its reception had been put off until a serious illness forced the candidate to apply for it) until a bishop could be available to administer it. On the other hand, it was natural and fitting that the laying on of the hand, by which the new member was given a token of his reception into the Church and his share in its apostolic character, and the consignation, by which his participation in the Church's royal priesthood was symbolized, should be kept for the bishop as the Church's recognized local head.

The effect of this development was to make it increasingly difficult to hold the various ceremonies together in one rite of initiation, and to maintain the full biblical doctrine of Baptism. The pattern of initiation is disintegrating, and in the *De Rebaptismate* the process is already far advanced. Spirit-baptism, administered through the imposition of hands by the bishop,[1] may be separated from baptism in water by a longer interval, as it was in the case of Philip's converts, and of the Apostles themselves, whom this writer supposes to have been baptized by Christ, but whose Baptism was not consummated by the gift of the Holy Spirit until Pentecost.[2]

This baptism of the Spirit is identified with the grace conferred upon reconciled heretics and schismatics by the laying on of hands: 'Haeretici vero iam baptizati aqua in nomine Iesu Christi, tantum in Spiritu sancto baptizandi sunt.'[3]

It is highly significant that this author depends for his most important Scriptural proof-texts upon the Acts of the Apostles. Like Tertullian and Cyprian (from whom, of course, he is poles distant on the question of rebaptism), he owes his conception of the meaning of the laying on of hands to the famous passages, Acts viii. 17, ix. 17, xix. 6. He shows no sign of having assimilated St. Paul's teaching on Baptism, despite his one or two scattered Pauline quotations. The text which he finds it hardest to accommodate to this theory is John iii. 5. He knows that his opponents will adduce it to confute him,[4] and he seeks to forestall their arguments by distinguishing between 'water' and 'Spirit' as between two separate baptisms. Against his opponent, who maintains that 'Baptisma solum prodesse cui

[1] 4 (p. 74, 15).
[3] 12 (p. 84, 15); cf. 1 (p. 69, 20).
[2] 3 (p. 73, 14); 4 (p. 73, 25).
[4] 3 (p. 72, 31).

possit etiam Spiritus sanctus inesse', he declares that those things which are united in this passage are elsewhere in the New Testament found in isolation from each other, and may sometimes occur by themselves without loss.[1] Thus, were the baptized to die before receiving the imposition of hands, the baptism would avail for salvation; similarly, the laying on of hands can be efficacious even if the water-baptism has not been received—as occurred in the case of Cornelius, who received the gift of the Spirit and remission of sins immediately, and whose subsequent baptism was necessary only in order that 'invocationem quoque nominis Iesu Christi acciperent, ne quid eis deesse videretur ad integritatem ministerii et fidei'.[2] It may be observed that in this passage the anonymous writer is apparently suggesting that remission of sins, no less than the gift of the Spirit, is a grace of Confirmation rather than Baptism; he is adopting a more extreme position even than that of those modern writers, such as Mason, who otherwise so closely follow him.

The process of depreciating the significance of the sacrament of Baptism could scarcely be taken further. On the basis of the usual proof-texts from Acts the ceremony of the laying on of hands has to all intents and purposes superseded Baptism as the effective sign of the believer's reception of the Spirit, and even the forgiveness of sins is implicitly associated with it. When we have made all due allowance for the fact that this writer is pleading a case, that his theology is being shaped by the needs of a controversy, that he is faced with a novel and perplexing problem created by the schism of Novatian, and that he is determined to find an alternative to Cyprian's unsatisfactory solution to that problem, it remains true that in this work the conception of Baptism which we find in the New Testament and the second century writers has broken down and been replaced by something very different, which can scarcely claim to be the Gospel sacrament as the New Testament speaks of it.

Yet this writer has not really thought out his views. His doctrine of Baptism and the laying on of hands is an *ad hoc* device whose full consequences he has not entirely realized. Hence he falls into inconsistency. He attempts to show that a

---

[1] 3 (p. 73).   [2] 5 (p. 75, 22 ff.).

person baptized in heresy may receive the necessary 'correction' to his baptism not only through the imposition of the bishop's hands but also through martyrdom. Yet martyrdom is said to be the equivalent, not of Confirmation, but of baptism in water. Like Tertullian, and so many other patristic writers, this author knows of a double baptism, of water and blood, prefigured in the blood and water from the side of Christ. The martyr has therefore received a true Baptism, equivalent to Baptism in water; and this writer would no doubt be no more prepared than his contemporaries to deny that the martyr has received both the remission of sins and the full possession of the Spirit through his 'baptism'. It should logically follow that the same gifts can both be received in water-baptism. In developing this theory of the martyr's 'baptism', the author even goes so far as to assert that Baptism is threefold: there is Baptism of water, of blood, and of the Spirit. Sometimes the Spirit may be associated with water, sometimes with martyrdom, and sometimes the gift of the Spirit may precede the water, follow it, or fall on believers without any baptism in the ordinary sense being employed at all.

The *De Rebaptismate* is thus neither consistent nor sound in its exegesis of the New Testament, and its confusion is typical of the unsatisfactory state into which the doctrine of the Holy Spirit in relation to Baptism falls during the third century. The most serious result of this confusion is that while Baptism is regarded as the sacramental means by which a man becomes incorporated into Christ and His Church, it becomes an open question, to which no satisfactory answer is given, whether the same sacramental rite is the means by which the Spirit is received. Many writers, from the time of the *De Rebaptismate* onwards, maintain, like Mason, Dix, and Thornton in modern times, that it is not until Confirmation has been received that the believer can possess the gift of the Spirit; unlike Dix, however, the *De Rebaptismate*, and much subsequent Western thought, is willing to contemplate the separation of Confirmation from Baptism and its treatment as an independent sacrament; and, unlike Thornton, the *De Rebaptismate* makes no use of the idea of the 'seal' in the sense either of the inward presence of the Spirit as the token of future redemption or of the external rite of Confirmation. The nearest approach to the language of 'sealing' in this book is the statement that the laying of hands on reconciled heretics is a *signum fidei iteratum atque consummatum*.[1] This, however, refers only to the idea of the imposition of hands as a seal or pledge of faith, and not to the eschatological seal which marks the Christian for redemption.

In fact, the notion of sealing is employed in so many different ways by the Fathers, especially after the Pauline conception of Baptism into Christ and sealing with His Spirit has begun to be abandoned, that it throws little light upon their theory of Baptism and its relation to the gift of the Spirit. What that theory was differs greatly from one author to another, and even in the thought of a single theologian we can often discern inconsistencies on this subject and much confusion of ideas. The chief lesson that the study of the Fathers has to teach us on the subject of Baptism and Confirmation is that, from the time when the Pauline teaching had given way to a conception which associated the gift of the indwelling Spirit with external rites rather than with the believer's faith-union with Christ, the thought of the early Church was at least as muddled as our own is today.

On one side there stands such a writer as Novatian, who was apparently clear-sighted enough to recognize that the endowments of the Spirit are strictly speaking not 'gifts' at all, but aspects of the personal activity of one and the same Holy Ghost. They cannot be thought of separately and in isolation, as being, so to speak, parcelled out between different sacraments, nor can they be thought of quantitatively as though the Spirit were given 'by measure'. The Spirit's activity is experienced in the believer's union with Christ through faith. Through Baptism the activity of the Spirit regenerates us, confers upon us all the other blessings, promises, and privileges of the Christian's status, and indwells the soul with His personal presence. Novatian makes no mention of Confirmation in any form, nor directly of the seal, although the New Testament idea of the seal of the Spirit is implicitly contained in what he says of the agency of the Spirit as the 'earnest' of eternal salvation.[2] It is perhaps

[1] 1 (p. 69, 22).
[2] *Trin.* 29: 'Hinc est qui operatur ex aquis secundam nativitatem, semen quoddam divini generis, et consecrator caelestis nativitatis, pignus promissae hereditatis, et quasi chirographum quoddam aeternae salutis; qui nos Dei faciat templum, et

unfortunate for the history of the doctrine of the Holy Spirit and Christian initiation that few subsequent writers were as lucid as Novatian in their exposition of the Spirit's activity towards the believer; much confusion would otherwise have been avoided, at least so far as concerns the theory of Confirmation and believers' Baptism.

Occupying a somewhat different position there stand Cyprian and his fellow-bishops at the Council of 256. They, as we have seen, are led by certain Scriptural texts to conclude that the proper outward sign of the bestowal of the Spirit is the imposition of hands, but at the same time they are ready to speak of Baptism itself as the medium of the reception of His indwelling presence, they do not seek, like the author of the *De Rebaptismate*, to twist the sense of John iii. 5 in order to accommodate it to their interpretation of Acts, and they do their utmost to emphasize the unity of Baptism and Confirmation as parts of a single whole, of which Baptism is the more important.

In direct opposition to this view there stands the theory, so far as it is consistent, of the *De Rebaptismate*, and on the same side we find in the East the not dissimilar teaching of the *Didascalia*. From what we can gather from the latter's incidental and somewhat disjointed comments on the rules which it prescribes for Baptism and for the reconciliation of penitents, it appears to recognize that remission of sins is conferred in Baptism,[1] and that at Baptism the evil spirit which would otherwise hold possession of the soul is driven out and replaced by the indwelling presence of the Holy Ghost.[2] This thought has close affinities with the common idea of the seal of Baptism as a prophylactic sign sealing the soul against the inroads of the hostile powers of Satan.[3] There can, however, be no doubt that in the mind of the compiler of the *Didascalia* it is the pre-Baptismal exorcisms and renunciation of the devil which in this sense constitute the seal, rather than Baptism or any rite of

nos eius efficiat domum: qui interpellat divinas aures pro nobis gemitibus ineloquacibus, advocationis implens officia, et defensionis exhibens munera; inhabitator corporibus nostris datus, et sanctitatis effector: qui id agens in nobis ad aeternitatem et ad resurrectionem immortalitatis corpora nostra producat, dum illa in se assuefacit cum caelesti virtute misceri, et cum Spiritus sancti divina aeternitate sociari.'

[1] 6, 12, 2; 6, 14, 6.   [2] 6, 21, 4-5.   [3] Cf. A. *Paul. et Thecl.*, 32.

Confirmation. The baptismal 'character' is itself a seal which must be preserved intact,[1] and Baptism confers the seal of the New Covenant, the 'circumcisio cordis spiritalis'.[2] On the other hand, the effectual sign of the reception of the Spirit in the case of a restored penitent is the laying on of the hand, this sign is said to be equivalent to Baptism, and it is implied that it is through the imposition of the hand (which, with chrismation, precedes Baptism in this as in most early Syrian rites) that the new convert, no less than the penitent, receives the Holy Spirit.[3] The assertion in this treatise of an equivalence between Baptism and the laying on of hands as the outward sign of the gift of the Spirit is strongly reminiscent of the thought of the *De Rebaptismate*. On the other hand, where we might expect again to see some emphasis on the seal and some connection suggested between it and the imposition of hands, we find in fact that very little attention is paid to the idea, and where it does appear it is, so far as can be judged from an obscure passage, connected simply with Baptism.[4]

This example may serve us as a warning against too ready an identification of the 'seal' in the writings of the Fathers with any ceremony of Confirmation. It does not follow that when an author expresses a belief that the gift of the Spirit is conferred through a particular rite—baptism, chrismation, laying on of hands—he will necessarily use the term 'seal' to denote that rite. From the early third century onwards the words σφραγίς, *signaculum*, may mean any of the following things: the inward stamp of the Spirit on the soul, the kindred conception of the impress of the *imago Dei*, Baptism by which the inward stamp is received, unction by which, according to some writers, one receives the Spirit's presence, or, most commonly of all, the *consignatio* with the sign of the Cross, whereby one is marked as Christ's soldier or branded as one of His flock. The particular sense which any author may assign to the term will not necessarily be directly related to his theory of the means whereby the Spirit's indwelling presence is bestowed. Anointing and sealing with the Cross, about which so little is said in the works we have just considered, are far more prominent in the *Acts of Thomas*, which probably date from the third century. Though the

[1] 3, 12, 3.   [2] 6, 12, 2.   [3] 2, 41, 2.   [4] 2, 39, 6.

language of the baptismal prayers and formulae in these Acts is extraordinarily obscure and hard to interpret, it would seem that they present us with another example of the common Syrian idea that the bestowal of the Spirit is to be associated with a pre-baptismal unction, such as we have already encountered in the *Didascalia*.

This practice and the theory which it expressed persisted until a late date in eastern Syria. Dr. Manson believes that the practice is very ancient,[1] and the theory of the relationship between the coming of the Spirit and Baptism which underlies the practice may perhaps have some New Testament warrant; but, as we have already suggested, it is highly improbable that an actual rite embodying that theory can be assigned to the apostolic age. It is, however, widespread in the third and fourth centuries. Dom Connolly[2] adduces as examples of it five instances in the Syriac *Acts of Thomas*,[3] and passages in the *Acts of John the son of Zebedee*,[4] the *Vita Rabbulae*,[5] Ephrem,[6] the homily on Constantine's baptism falsely ascribed to Ephrem,[7] Aphraates,[8] Narsai,[9] and the *Apostolic Constitutions*,[10] based on the *Didascalia*. To these there should perhaps be added an instance from the *Clementine Recognitions*,[11] and another from Theodoret.[12]

Despite this strong Syrian tradition of emphasis upon the pre-baptismal unction as the medium of the Spirit's reception, the use of the term 'seal' in the above mentioned writers is by no means uniform. The usage in the *Acts of Thomas* is not easy to grasp. As is so often the case in the more popular literature, the idea of the seal retains to the full its original eschatological content. The seal is the brand by which God recognizes His own sheep.[13] Yet the manner in which this seal is impressed upon the sheep is not clearly explained. The candidates for initiation first receive a sealing with oil; this appears to consist of a signing with the Cross. They are anointed and a prayer is offered

---

[1] *JTS.* 48, 1947, pp. 25 ff.   [2] *Texts and Studies*, 8, 1 (1909), pp. xlii ff.
[3] Tr. Wright, pp. 166, 188, 258, 267, 289.
[4] Tr. Wright, pp. 38–42, 53–5.   [5] Overbeck, *Ephrem*, p. 165.
[6] *hymn. Epiph.*, 3, 4 (Lamy, 1, 30).   [7] Overbeck, p. 355 f.
[8] *hom.* 12, 13.   [9] *hom.* 22, 21 (*Texts and Studies* 8, p. 48).
[10] 3, 16, 4; 7, 22, 2.   [11] 3, 67.   [12] *Cant.*, 1, 2.
[13] *A. Thom.*, 26: δὸς ἡμῖν τὴν σφραγῖδα· ἠκούσαμεν γάρ σου λέγοντος ὅτι ὁ θεὸς ὃν κηρύσσεις διὰ τῆς αὐτοῦ σφραγῖδος ἐπιγινώσκει τὰ ἴδια πρόβατα.

in which the Spirit is asked to give them an added or completed seal (ἐπισφράγισον αὐτούς) in the name of the Trinity. They are then sealed, and this second sealing is described as the ἐπισφρά-γισμα[1] τῆς σφραγῖδος, without which they cannot hope to see the Lord. The Syriac text explicitly informs us that this sealing consists in Baptism.[2] In another description of a baptism we find that the apostle lays his hand upon the candidate before the Baptism, but that the term 'seal' is fairly certainly applied not to this ceremony but to the actual Baptism; the Syriac again makes the point clear, for it tells us that the apostle 'went to the river that was close by there' in order to administer the seal.[3] Mygdonia is described elsewhere as having received the seal when she has been both anointed and subsequently baptized in the Threefold Name.[4] There is a similar instance a little later in the book, when Thomas delivers an address on Baptism in which he explains that by its efficacy men are both regenerated and made partakers of the Holy Spirit.[5]

There can be little doubt that in the *Acts of Thomas* the principal meaning conveyed by the term 'seal' is that of a mark, given in Baptism, by which God recognizes His own; but it is also closely connected with the idea that the Threefold Name in which Baptism is administered is itself the brand which the believer carries for recognition by his divine owner. This point is brought out in a passage where the oil of unction is connected with the virtue of the Cross (as the tree of life), and the 'seal' is fairly certainly linked, not with this unction, but with the use of the Name in Baptism.[6]

In the *Acts of Philip* the seal is generally identified with Baptism;[7] we have already noticed the passage in which the seal, representing the character given to the Christian in his Baptism, is a protective symbol safeguarding its 'wearer' against the hostile power of the 'cosmocratores'.[8] This notion recalls the intentionally mysterious language of the *Epitaph of Abercius*, which probably also refers to Baptism.[9] A similar use of the term occurs in other apocryphal Acts.[10]

---

[1] Cf. Eus., *h.e.*, 10, 1: δέκατον . . . τόμον . . . τοῦτον ἐπιγράψομεν, ὥσπερ ἐπισφρά-γισμα τῆς . . . ὑποθέσεως.
[2] 26–7. [3] 49. [4] 121. [5] 131–2.
[6] 152, 157. [7] 29, 44, 134, etc. [8] 144. [9] *Epit. Aberc.*, 9.
[10] e.g. *Mart. Mt.*, 8; *ibid.*, 27; *A. Petr. et. Andr.*, 21.

The break-down of the early conception of the relation between Baptism, the gift of the Spirit, and the inward 'seal' for a day of redemption has thus left the idea of the seal ill-defined, unattached to any firm doctrine of the gift of the Spirit, and expressed in no single or uniform rite of initiation. The long period of confusion and obscurity has begun, in which we still find ourselves groping today. In that confusion the idea of the seal plays many parts, but before we consider what those parts signify we must briefly examine the various conclusions at which the Fathers arrived on the thorny question of the relation of the rites of Baptism, consignation, and the imposition of hands to the reception by the Christian of the indwelling presence of the Holy Spirit.

PART THREE

THE
SACRAMENTAL
RECEPTION OF THE
HOLY SPIRIT

CHAPTER EIGHT

THE SPIRIT IN BAPTISM

THE teaching of the Fathers on the question by what sacramental medium the Christian believer receives the gift of the Holy Spirit is a subject which requires a full and fresh examination. If our analysis of the New Testament and early patristic doctrine on this topic is at all correct, it appears that the teaching of the Church in the first two centuries was in the main that the gift of the indwelling Spirit (the use of 'gift' language, though misleading, is so frequently employed by the writers we are considering that we cannot well avoid it) is an aspect of the spiritual condition in which the sinner who responds in faith to the grace of God in Christ is placed as a result of the personal union with Christ which is granted to him by the love of God within the fellowship of the Church as the Body of Christ. It is therefore mediated through the sacrament of Baptism which signifies union with Christ in His Church, and by Baptism is meant the actual rite of dipping in water in which the believer shares the Messianic Baptism of Jesus.

After this early pattern of teaching and practice has broken down in the late second and early third centuries, it is extremely difficult for any of the Fathers to define by what means the Christian enters into the possession of the Spirit. The problem was not in fact attacked seriously until a relatively late period; for a long time the Fathers were content to ascribe the endowment of the Spirit indiscriminately and without any full consideration of the matter to Baptism itself, or to the laying on of hands, or to post-baptismal unction and consignation, regarded either as a separate rite from the imposition of hands or as virtually identical with it.

We have already considered some of the probable causes of the growth of this confusion. Perhaps the most important of all was the influence of a number of Scriptural texts which were applied to Baptism or to its ancillary ceremonies. It is not easy for us to realize to how great an extent the Fathers were at the mercy of their 'fundamentalist' exegesis of Scripture, notwithstanding (or rather, at times, because of) their adoption of an allegorical or typological method. It is largely due to this factor that so many writers in the period from the third to the sixth century (and in many cases, especially in the East, until much later) are content to ascribe the gift of the Spirit in Christian initiation either to Baptism in water or to consignation, or to the laying on of hands, with scant regard for consistency, simply in order to suit their exegesis of the particular text which may happen at any moment to be engaging their attention.

As we have remarked, the problem of resolving this confusion was not an urgent one so long as the rite of initiation continued to comprise both Baptism and its subsequent ceremonies in one complex whole; but when, as we have seen, the liturgical pattern began to disintegrate in the West, it became a matter of pressing importance to work out an intelligible and consistent doctrine of Baptism and Confirmation. The task of producing such a doctrine has, however, proved extraordinarily difficult, and, complicated as it is by the special difficulties raised by infant Baptism, it still awaits its fulfilment.

It is particularly unfortunate that the investigations which have been made into the patristic doctrine on this subject have generally failed to make due allowance for the confusion and inconsistency which evidently reigned in the minds of most of the ancient writers who raised the question of the relation of the Spirit to initiation—at least from the early third century onwards—and that they have omitted to take full account of the degree to which the Fathers were the slaves of their exegesis of Scripture. To many of them the most fanciful interpretation of a text from Canticles was as valuable as a direct utterance of St. Paul or a saying from the Gospels.

Many modern writers have adopted the unhappy course of trying to pick out from the vast mass of patristic literature on Baptism such texts as favour their own theories. Such methods ignore the confusion to which we have just referred. The Fathers did not try to resolve this confusion as long as the rite of initiation remained one whole, comprising both Baptism and Confirmation, for so long as that state of affairs was maintained the theological difficulties remained latent. It is not therefore surprising to find that, for example, Mason and Umberg were able to discover plenty of authority for the view that the gift of the indwelling Spirit is bestowed by means of the laying on of hands, and not by water-baptism, Wirgman was no less easily able to show that the Fathers taught that the indwelling presence of the Spirit was conferred by water-baptism and that an increase of grace was given for spiritual progress by the laying on of hands, while Thornton finds it equally possible to demonstrate that in the teaching of the Fathers the indwelling of the Spirit is regarded as being withheld until Confirmation, which he associates particularly with anointing.

It is also unfortunate that some important books were written on this subject before the date and authorship of some of the relevant documents had been fairly established, and that, as a result, the picture which they present of the historical development of the doctrine of Baptism and Confirmation is distorted. Thus, F. J. Dölger[1] and J. Behm[2] cited as evidence for the doctrine of the gift of the Spirit in the imposition of hands 'pseudo-Ambrosiaster' on Heb. vi. 2 as though this were a fourth or fifth century work, whereas it is probably to be ascribed to Alcuin and represents the developed theory of Confirmation and its relation to Baptism as it was held in the Carolingian age. J. B. Umberg[3] similarly cites 'pseudo-Primasius' on the same text, a commentary which is generally ascribed to Haymo of Auxerre;[4] and even the admirable short study of the subject by J. C. Sladden[5] appears to cite as authentic the 'Carolingian' view of Confirmation assigned to Urban I in the forged Decretals.

There is an urgent need for a full and impartial investigation of the real teaching of the Fathers on Baptism and the gift of the Spirit, taking into account their Scriptural proof-texts, and refraining from making yet another journey round the

[1] *Das Sakrament der Firmung historisch dargestellt.*
[2] *Die Handauflegung im Urchristentum.*
[3] *Die Schriftlehre vom Sakrament der Firmung.*
[4] Riggenbach, 'Die ältesten lateinischen Kommentare zum Hebräerbrief' (Zahn's *Forschungen*, 8, 1 (1907)); Souter, *Earliest Latin Commentaries on the Epistles of St. Paul*, 1927, p. 210.
[5] *Church Quarterly Review*, 146, 1948.

well-worn course in order to collect those particular passages which can be fitted into one or other of the modern theories of Baptism.

Such a task is far beyond the limits of the present study. We are concerned only to show that the idea of the 'seal' is not in itself a clue capable of guiding us to a clear patristic doctrine of Confirmation. At the same time, if we are to understand the very varied patristic conceptions of the 'seal' correctly, we must set them against the background of the ideas of the Fathers about the gift of the Spirit in Christian initiation. We must therefore attempt, if only in a summary and incomplete fashion, a survey of these ideas; and we may take as our starting point the assertion of Dix[1] that the statement of Rabanus Maurus[2] that it is through the unction with chrism that the baptized receive the gift of the Spirit represents 'the last time at which the teaching of the New Testament that Baptism in the Spirit is *not* baptism in water, but something else which follows closely upon it, finds a clear echo in the West'. Apart from the question whether this definition of New Testament teaching is correct (and we affirm emphatically that it is not), this sentence suggests that the early Fathers ascribed the gift of the Spirit to Confirmation and that it was only gradually that this view gave way to the 'mediaeval' doctrine of Confirmation. It might lead the reader to suppose that until a relatively late period the patristic teaching is both uniform and definite.

We believe, on the contrary, that there is a clear doctrine in the New Testament that the indwelling presence is one aspect of the gift sacramentally bestowed on the believer in water-baptism, that this was the teaching of the early Fathers, but that by the first quarter of the third century the clarity and relative simplicity of the primitive doctrine had become obscured and gradually replaced by great confusion of thought on the subject, a confusion reproduced to some extent, especially in the West, in liturgical practice. In this period of confusion, the gift of the Spirit is ascribed to water-baptism, pre- or post-baptismal anointing with chrism, and the laying on of hands,

---

[1] *The Theology of Confirmation in Relation to Baptism*, p. 22.
[2] *inst. cleric.*, 1, 28 (*PL.* 107, 313C): 'necessarium est ut . . . succurratur baptizato cum chrismatis unctione, ut Spiritus sancti participationem accipiens, alienus a Christo non existat.'

each of which is from time to time regarded as its sacramental medium.

In the brief compass of this study we must consider these various opinions under the heading of Baptism, Unction and Consignation, and the Imposition of Hands. It will not be possible to embark on a detailed treatment of the doctrine of each of the Fathers, considered individually, on this subject.

The Spirit and Baptism

Patristic texts which connect the gift of the Holy Spirit's indwelling presence with Baptism are very numerous. Some refer simply to 'Baptism' as the sacramental medium, others more explicitly to the 'water' or the 'laver'.

Thus the *Gospel of Nicodemus*[1] tells how Seth, seeking oil from the Tree of Mercy to heal Adam in his sickness, is given the promise that the Son of God will become incarnate, anoint him with oil, and raise him up. Then he will wash him in water and Spirit. It is the water which is connected with the gift of the Spirit, not the oil which is linked with healing.

Athanasius maintains that the Holy Spirit is granted to those who believe and are born again through the laver of regeneration.[2] It is perhaps an instance of the confusion of so much patristic thought on this subject that when, later in the same treatise, his mind is directed to the texts of Acts about the imposition of hands, Athanasius says that it is through the laying on of the Apostles' hands that the Holy Spirit was given to the regenerate.[3] It should, however, be noticed that this is an historical comment and not a reflection on contemporary practice. He never ascribes the gift to chrismation.

The confusion is still more marked in Cyril of Jerusalem, who bids his catechumens give heed, τῇ μετὰ τοῦ ὕδατος διδομένῃ πνευματικῇ χάριτι,[4] whereas elsewhere he connects the gift of the Spirit with chrismation;[5] but it may be urged that the grace given by the Spirit's operation in Baptism is to be distinguished from the full gift of the Spirit in chrismation. On the other hand, Hilary is quite clear in his implication that the

---

[1] 3 (Tischendorf, pp. 325–6). See p. 126, above.
[3] *Ibid.*, 1, 6 (544B).
[5] *Ibid.*, 21, 1 (1089A).

[2] *Serap.*, 1, 4 (*PG.* 26, 537B).
[4] *catech.*, 3, 3 (*PG.* 33, 429A).

8

Spirit is given in Baptism; for he applies to the Holy Spirit a simile of a river and of living water to show that the presence of the Spirit within the soul begins when the convert is regenerated in Baptism.[1] The same teaching is implied in the homily on Ps. 28 ascribed to Basil,[2] and is developed at length by Jerome.

Jerome is certainly influenced by his desire to magnify the office of presbyter and to represent the bishop merely as a presbyter exercising special functions; but he is too hardly treated by some apologists of a supposedly primitive theory that the seal of the Spirit in initiation consists simply in episcopal Confirmation. Thus Dix alleges that in Jerome for the first time in extant Christian literature all the effects of Confirmation by a bishop are attributed to Baptism in water by a presbyter,[3] and Thornton attributes to Jerome's 'unfortunate theories about the Christian Ministry which bore their Dead Sea fruit in Presbyterian systems', the 'lowering of belief about Confirmation' by which Baptism became 'the sufficient sacrament of salvation apart from the episcopal act which should be its culmination'.[4]

Now it is true that Jerome has his 'presbyterian' axe to grind; it is also true that he finds it impossible to treat any controversial topic without bringing to bear upon it the typical rhetorician's full armoury of sneers, abuse, and the most unpleasant Juvenalian sarcasm; there is the further fact to be considered that it was only when the bishop had ceased to administer Baptism regularly that the question arose who was the proper minister of Baptism, chrismation, and the imposition of hands, and that it received different answers in different parts of the Church;[5] it remains true, nevertheless, that in his

[1] *tract. in Ps.*, 64, 15 (*PL*. 9, 421D).   [2] (1, 361; (*PG*. 30, 81B).
[3] *Op. cit.*, p. 20.   [4] *Confirmation Today*, p. 11.
[5] Cf. Innoc., *ep.*, 25, 3, reserving the administration of consignation to the bishop (though Gregory subsequently allows presbyteral Confirmation where no bishop is available—*ep.*, 4, 26); *Qu. V. et N.T.* 101, allowing it to presbyters; *Const. App.*, 7, 22, 2, assigning sealing with chrism to the bishop or the presbyter; *C. Tolet.* (400), *can.*, 20, permitting presbyters to administer chrismation in the bishop's absence or, with his permission, in his presence, but restricting the confection of the chrism to the bishop; Jo. Diac., *ep. Senar.*, 7 (*PL*. 59, 403D ff.), restricting chrismation to the bishop, but mentioning that in Africa it is performed in case of necessity by presbyters (cf. *cod. Afr. can.*, 6); the Gallican practice of a presbyteral chrismation, and that alone, directly following Baptism (*Miss. Bobb.* (*PL*. 72, 502), etc.).

defence of the sufficiency of Baptism in water for the mediation of both remission of sins and the gift of the Spirit Jerome is simply following the solid and consistent tradition of the New Testament and the early Fathers, and echoing the teaching implicit in many utterances of later writers whose doctrine on the matter was admittedly neither fully thought out nor self-consistent.

Where Jerome failed was in his inability to realize that, although Baptism in water, representative of Christ's own Baptism, is the sacrament of the initial gift of the Spirit, and although he was right in his objection to the notion that 'ad episcopi tantum imprecationem Spiritus sanctus defluit' (a theory no less false and irreligious in its modern expressions than it was in Jerome's day), yet the action of the bishop in 'running around' (excurrat) to lay hands on the baptized was something very much more significant and important than a mere piece of prelatical pretentiousness ('ad honorem potius sacerdotii quam ad legem necessitatis'). In other words, correct as he was in his doctrine of Baptism, he had failed to develop a theory of Confirmation; he had not discerned in it a necessary completion of Baptism administered in infancy (a making explicit and real, in response to the awakening of personal and conscious faith, of what had been implicitly granted and unconsciously received in Baptism), nor had it occurred to him that it could signify the equipping of Christ's soldier and servant for active service in the Church militant, or the association of a new member in the Church's apostolic task, with a solemn blessing of the Holy Spirit acting through the representative leader of the community of the Spirit. Jerome, however, need hardly be attacked for failing to think ahead of his times, and he ought not to be blamed for holding a more Scriptural and less confused doctrine of the gift of the Holy Spirit in Baptism than we find in many of his predecessors and contemporaries.[1]

---

[1] The relevant passages of Jerome are chiefly the following from the *Dialogus c. Luciferanos*:

(a) The 'water and Spirit' of Gen. i. 2 are mentioned, 'ex quo apparet baptisma non esse sine Spiritu sancto. . . . Igitur si Arianus Spiritum sanctum non potest dare, ne baptizare quidem potest quia Ecclesiae baptisma sine Spiritu sancto nullum est. Tu vero, cum baptizatum ab eo recipias, et postea invoces Spiritum sanctum, aut baptizare eum debes, quia sine Spiritu sancto non potuit baptizari,

Didymus of Alexandria evidently understood that man's renewal, the restoration of the *imago Dei*, and the reception of the new status of adoptive sonship to God were inseparably connected, or rather, that they were different aspects of the same act of divine grace, and that it is in Baptism that this single divine activity is sacramentally mediated.[1] It is to be observed that in these passages it is explicitly the water, the λουτρόν, which is the sacramental medium; it is not the more comprehensive and sometimes ambiguous term βάπτισμα.

Similarly, Epiphanius[2] connects the gift of remission of sins with the bestowal of the Spirit, assigning both alike to the λουτρόν. There is a striking contrast between this teaching and the common assertion that remission of sins is signified by the baptismal washing but that the bestowal of the Spirit is to be sharply distinguished from this 'negative' aspect of Christian initiation and is to be assigned to Confirmation. There is also a notable difference between the views of these writers and those of certain earlier authors at whom we have already glanced;[3]

aut si est baptizatus in Spiritu, desine ei invocare Spiritum, quem tunc cum baptizaretur accepit' (6; *PL.* 23, 169B, C).

(*b*) The Luciferian makes much of the imposition of hands as the rite for the invocation of the Spirit, and, citing Acts as his authority, ventures to assert that 'etiam si Scripturae auctoritas non subesset, totius orbis in hanc partem consensus instar praecepti obtineret'. His orthodox opponent replies: 'Non quidem abnuo hanc esse Ecclesiarum consuetudinem ut ad eos qui longe a maioribus urbibus per presbyteros et diaconos baptizati sunt, episcopus ad invocationem sancti Spiritus manum impositurus excurrat. . . . Quod si hoc loco quaeris quare in ecclesia baptizatus, nisi per manus episcopi, non accipiat Spiritum sanctum, quem nos asserimus in vero baptismate tribui, disce hanc observationem ex ea auctoritate descendere quod post ascensum Domini Spiritus sanctus ad apostolos descendit. Et multis in locis idem factitatum reperimus, ad honorem potius sacerdotii quam ad legem necessitatis. Alioqui, si ad episcopi tantum imprecationem Spiritus sanctus defluit, legendi sunt qui in villulis, aut in castellis, aut in remotioribus locis per presbyteros et diaconos baptizati ante dormierunt quam ab episcopis inviscrentur. Ecclesiae salus in summi sacerdotis dignitate pendet cui si non exsors quaedam et ab omnibus eminens detur potestas, tot in ecclesiis efficiantur schismata quot sacerdotes. Inde evenit ut sine chrismate et episcopi iussione, neque presbyter neque diaconus ius habeant baptizandi. Quod frequenter, si tamen necessitas cogit, scimus etiam licere laicis' (9; *PL.* 23, 172B–173B).

[1] Cf. ἡμᾶς ἀνακαινοῖ, καὶ πάλιν εἰκόνας ἀναδείκνυσι Θεοῦ διὰ λουτροῦ παλιγγενεσίας, Didym. (Ps. Bas.) *Eun.* 5 (1, 303A; *PG.* 29, 725D); σκέψαι πῶς υἱοὺς ἀπεργάζεται τοὺς ἁγιαζομένους· εἰ δὲ σὺ διὰ τοῦ Πνεύματος υἱὸς Θεοῦ, πῶς τὸ πνεῦμα ξένον υἱότητος, ibid. (1, 305B; *PG.* 29, 732C); cf. *Trin.*, 2, 12 (*PG.* 39, 680B).

[2] καταξιωθήσονται τῆς Πνεύματος ἁγίου ἐν τῷ λουτρῷ τῆς δωρεᾶς,καὶ ἀφέσεως ἁμαρτιῶν διὰ τῆς χάριτος τῆς ὑπ᾽ αὐτοῦ δοθείσης, haer., 51, 20 (p. 278, 19; *PG.* 41, 925B).

[3] e.g. Hipp., *Dan.*, 1, 16 (p. 26, 24; *PG.* 10, 693A).

there can be little doubt that the former are truer to the teaching of the New Testament. It is instructive to notice a curious passage where Chrysostom feels himself called upon to explain how it could happen that even the Apostles at Pentecost could receive 'Spirit-baptism' without at the same time undergoing water-baptism. The absence of water in the upper room is something for which the commentator has to account. The answer which he suggests is that, since it is only through the Spirit that the water of Baptism can effect anything, the power of the Spirit is such that it may work independently of the water, just as in Christ's Messianic unction the Spirit operated even without the outward element of oil. Alternatively, the necessary water-baptism had taken place when the Apostles were baptized by John, and in their case the inward reality followed the external sign after a long interval.[1] This passage is important. It serves as an example to show how far the Patristic writers are from presenting us with what Thornton[2] calls the 'solid weight of Church teaching' that Baptism in water is a mere rite of preparation for the positive gift of the Spirit which is independent of the former and is connected with chrismation.

Chrysostom elsewhere explains more fully the essential link between water-baptism and the gift of the Spirit,[3] and in another important commentary on a crucial passage of Acts he maintains that the Spirit is bestowed in Baptism along with remission of sins and the status of sonship; the imposition of hands on the Ephesian disciples was for the purpose of conferring on them certain special charismata manifested in the working of 'signs'. Now that the age of 'signs' is over, remarks Chrysostom, these charismata are expressed in the believer's possession of faith, hope, and charity.[4]

In a discussion of the relation of Confirmation to Baptism as a type of the Christian 'seal', Chrysostom maintains that in the λουτρόν the Christian becomes a king, a priest, and a prophet. He is a king by virtue of having overthrown his evil deeds and slain his sins; a priest as having consecrated himself and offered

---

[1] ἄλλως δὲ καὶ ὕδατι βαπτιζομένους αὐτοὺς ἔστιν εὑρεῖν, καὶ ἐν διαφόροις καιροῖς· ἐφ' ἡμῶν γὰρ ἀμφότερα γίνεται ὑφ'ἕν, τότε δὲ διεσπασμένως· παρὰ γὰρ τὴν ἀρχὴν ὑπὸ Ἰωάννου ἐβαπτίσθησαν, hom. 1. 5 in Ac. (9, 9D).

[2] Confirmation Today, p. 7.   [3] hom. 24. 2 in Jo. (8, 140C).

[4] hom. 40. 2 in Ac. (9, 305A).

the sacrifice of his own self; and a prophet in that he has received the 'earnest' of the Spirit.[1] Thus remission of sins, self-offering, and the gift of the Spirit are all combined as the inward effect of water-baptism, and the reason why the sacrament produces this effect is, so it is clearly implied, because it enables the believer to become a member of Christ and to share in His threefold character of priest, king, and prophet. Similar teaching is to be found elsewhere in Chrysostom, though he cannot be claimed as an entirely consistent upholder of this theologically true conception of Baptism; Scriptural types suggestive of other theories sometimes prove too attractive for him to resist.

Theodore of Mopsuestia similarly asserts that at the same time as we receive Baptism, which typifies the death and resurrection of Christ, we obtain the gift of the Holy Spirit, who is bestowed in Baptism; the Spirit is the first-fruits of our future perfection, and, since the Spirit regenerates us as though we were given a second life, we speak of the Spirit of regeneration.[2] Here, although the word βάπτισμα is used, and not λουτρόν (cf. Ambrosiaster's, 'Spiritus . . . qui datur in baptismo', 1 Cor. xiv. 14, PL. 17, 255B), it is quite clear that water-baptism is indicated; no other Baptism 'formam habet mortis et resurrectionis Christi'. Theodore, we may infer, would not countenance that separation which Mason postulated between the regenerative activity of the Holy Spirit and His indwelling presence; both are simultaneously made available to the believer in Baptism.[3] Nor can remission of sins be separated from the gift of the Spirit, since the former consists in the renewal of the latter; the Spirit's presence, forfeited by sin, is restored to sinful men in Baptism.[4]

---

[1] hom. 3. 7 in 2 Cor. (10, 454A, B).

[2] Gal. ii. 16 (Swete, p. 30, 11); cf. also Ps. xliv. 16 (Devréesse, p. 298).

[3] Rom. vi. 17; cf. Col. ii. 13, 1 Tim. iii. 6 (Swete, p. 112, 8); Jo. xv. 1–6 (Devréesse, p. 395, 28; PG. 66, 780A); cf. ibid., xvii. 22–3 (Devréesse, p. 407, 24) where there is a very clear exposition of Theodore's doctrine of the gift of the Spirit in Baptism.

[4] See Theodore's catecheses (Mingana, p. 114), and the comments thereon of W. de Fries, 'Der "Nestorianismus" Theodors von Mopsuestia in seiner Sakramentlehre' (Orientalia Christiana Periodica 7 (1941), p. 110), who demonstrates, against Jugie (Echos d'Orient 34 (1935), p. 263), that Theodore does not ascribe the gift of the Spirit to a post-baptismal unction. His language about anointing (Mingana, p. 68) is not to be taken literally but as a reference to the unction of the Spirit that is received in Baptism (de Fries, pp. 132 ff.).

Cyril suggests the same doctrine, as, for example, when he explains that ἔνθα γὰρ ἂν εἰσέλθοι τὸ ὕδωρ (δῆλον δὲ ὅτι τοῦ ἁγίου βαπτίσματος) ἐκεῖ καταλύσει Χριστός· παντὸς γὰρ ἡμᾶς ἀπαλλάττει ῥύπου, ὥστε καὶ ναὸν ἡμᾶς ἅγιον γενέσθαι Θεοῦ, καὶ τῆς θείας αὐτοῦ φύσεως κοινωνοὺς διὰ μετοχῆς τοῦ ἁγίου Πνεύματος.[1] The interpretation of this passage is not entirely clear, but it seems more probable that Cyril means that we participate in the Holy Spirit at the time when the water of Baptism cleanses us than that he thinks of the baptismal cleansing as a mere preparation for a subsequent entry of the Spirit into a temple made ready for Him. Other passages in the works of Cyril express the same conception, but a certain ambiguity attaches to them on account of their use of βάπτισμα instead of either λουτρόν or ὕδωρ.[2]

Cyril, however, has never felt any need to think out the question of the relation of the gift of the Spirit to particular elements in the initiation sacrament, and such views as he expresses on the matter are by no means consistent.

Nilus appears to share the general view which we have seen expressed in the passages of Cyril which we have considered. According to him, the convert who approaches the sacrament of Baptism with faith receives the gift of the Spirit through the sign of water; the person who receives it without sincerity, however, like Simon Magus, obtains no gift of the Spirit but is baptized ψιλῷ ὕδατι.[3]

A similar view is expressed by Zeno of Verona, when he refers to the candidates for Baptism as 'omnes . . . Spiritus sancti munere mox divites processuri (i.e. from the actual font, not from their initiation as a whole)'.[4]

Less clear of interpretation are the very numerous passages in which the Fathers speak of the gift of the Spirit in 'Baptism' as distinct from 'the water', or 'the laver'. In these cases (of

[1] Lc., 22, 8 (PG. 72, 904C).
[2] e.g. ἡ διὰ τοῦ βαπτίσματος χάρις δι᾽οὗ πάντα ῥύπον ἀποτριβόμενοι, κοινωνοὶ τῆς θείας ἀναδεικνύμεθα φύσεως, ἐνοικοῦντος ἡμῖν διὰ τοῦ πνεύματος τοῦ Χριστοῦ, glaph. in Num. (1,400C) ; τὴν διὰ τοῦ ἁγίου βαπτίσματος εὐκλεᾶ χάριν καὶ τὴν ἐν αὐτῷ ζωοποίησιν καὶ τὴν θεοῦ μέθεξιν δι᾽ ἁγιασμοῦ ἐν Πνεύματι διὰ Ἰησοῦ Χριστοῦ πεπράχθαι, inc. unigen. (5[1], 705D) = Thds. 36 (33). The Paraclete received by faith and Baptism renews the imago Dei in the soul (Jo. 12, 1 (4, 1097B)) ; cf. hom. pasch. 10 (5[2], 128D). The newly-baptized has ἐνοικοῦν ἐν αὐτῷ τὸ ἅγιον Πνεῦμα, Jo. 5, 2 (4, 475C).
[3] epp., 2, 223 (PG. 79, 316D). [4] tractat., 2, 31.

which we have already noticed some examples, and of which Hieronymus of Jerusalem provides a typical instance when he says of the newly baptized that 'the Spirit of God dwells in them, whom they obtained in Baptism'),[1] it is not always easy to determine whether 'Baptism' could be used in a wider sense to denote more than actual Baptism in water; but in the great majority of such instances it is likely that the term primarily denotes the actual water-baptism. Sometimes this is made explicit in the text; thus Gaudentius of Marseilles speaks of the Gentiles 'quibus . . . per aquam baptismatis poculum sancti Spiritus propinaret'.[2] Sometimes it may be properly inferred from the context. Augustine, for example, is in all probability thinking of Baptism in the font when he says, 'Dicimus ergo in baptizatis parvulis, quamvis id nesciant, habitare Spiritum sanctum',[3] and, 'Deus ergo dat etiam baptizante (sc. an unworthy minister) Spiritum sanctum'.[4] It is, according to Faustus of Riez, because Baptism itself bestows on the faithful regeneration and the 'putting on' of Christ that a heretic who is converted needs only a 'benedictio chrismatis' on rejoining the Church.[5] Although Faustus does not actually refer at this point to the gift of the Spirit, he wisely makes no attempt to distinguish the reception of the indwelling Spirit from the 'putting on' of Christ. It is difficult to think that in his mind the two were not identical.

Marcus Eremita connects the gift of the Spirit primarily with the baptismal invocation of the Trinity.[6] It has been alleged that this author elsewhere postulates a distinction between Baptism proper and the bestowal of the Spirit, and that he assigns the latter to Confirmation; but when he speaks of the Spirit being given εὐθέως ἀπὸ τοῦ βαπτίσματος,[7] he does not mean that it is given *after* Baptism, but that it proceeds immediately from the outward act of Baptism.[8] The same phrase is used by

---

[1] *Christ.* (*PG.* 40, 861B).   [2] *serm.* 9 (*PL.* 20, 903B).   [3] *ep.*, 187, 8, 26.
[4] *bapt.*, 5, 20, 28.   [5] *grat.* 1, 14 (*CSEL.* p. 47, 14; *PL.* 58, 807D).
[6] *opusc.* 4 (*PG.* 65, 1008D).
[7] The passage runs, ἐπείσθης ἄρα κἂν νῦν, ὅτι, εὐθέως ἀπὸ τοῦ βαπτίσματος δίδοται τὸ πνεῦμα . . . τοῖς βεβαιοπίστοις . . . τίς οὖν καθόλου τούτων τῶν ἐνεργημάτων ἀμύητος μετὰ τὸ βάπτισμα τυγχάνει, ἵνα ἀρνήσεται, λέγων τὴν τοῦ πνεύματος χάριν μὴ εἰληφέναι ἀπὸ τοῦ βαπτίσματος, *opusc.* 4 (*PG.* 1004A, 1005A).
[8] Cf. διὰ τοῦ βαπτίσματος χάρις δίδοται μυστικῶς, καὶ ἐνοικεῖ κρυπτῶς (*ibid.*, 1001B).

Chrysostom.[1] In both instances the preposition ἀπό is used in the same sense in which Cyril speaks of the Holy Spirit ἀπὸ τῆς τοῦ Σωτῆρος ὑπάρχον οὐσίας, καὶ τῆς μιᾶς θεότητος οὐκ ἀλλότριον.[2] Both authors are asserting that the gift of the Spirit is an immediate consequence of the outward administration of the sacrament of Baptism, not that it follows Baptism in a temporal sequence of ceremonies. The ἀπὸ τοῦ βαπτίσματος of Marcus Eremita and Chrysostom is, in fact, practically equivalent to the διὰ τοῦ βαπτίσματος which the former uses a little earlier in the same treatise.

While many writers, including Leo[3] and Oecumenius,[4] continue to teach that it is in 'baptisma' that the Spirit is received, others, such as Diadochus Photicensis,[5] assert less ambiguously that the indwelling presence of the Spirit, as well as His regenerating activity, is mediated through 'water'; others again, like the author of Barlaam and Joasaph, who connects the baptismal gift of the Spirit with the restoration of the divine image,[6] and the writer of the late treatise De mystica contemplatione, assign the bestowal of the Spirit to the λουτρόν.[7]

Many of the writers whom we have noticed are inconsistent, as we have already observed, in their views of the relation between the sacramental efficacy of the water of Baptism to the gift of the Spirit. In their comments on Scripture they often maintain that the Spirit is conferred by the laying on of hands if they are trying to expound the relevant passages of Acts,[8] whereas familiar and accepted liturgical practice, as well as many supposed proof-texts from the Old Testament, induce them with equal readiness to ascribe it to the rite of unction with chrism.[9]

We are dealing with a period of theological confusion when the New Testament teaching on Baptism and the indwelling of the Spirit is rarely fully understood (owing in large measure, to a failure to maintain in its completeness the New Testament doctrine of justification), and at the same time the various

---

[1] hom. 30. 2 in 1 Cor. (10, 271A). [2] thes., 33 (5¹, 334D).
[3] 'Per baptismatis sacramentum Spiritus sancti factus es templum,' serm., 21, 3.
[4] Apoc. i. 16.   [5] perf., 78.   [6] 8 (PG. 96, 920A).
[7] PG. 98, 385D.
[8] e.g. Ath., Serap., 1, 6 contrasted with 1, 4 (PG. 26, 544B, 537B).
[9] e.g. Cyr. H., catech., 3, 3 contrasted with 21, 1 (PG. 33, 429A, 1089A), if we accept Cyril as the author in each case.

8*

theories which were later advanced to explain the respective functions and efficacy of Baptism and Confirmation have scarcely begun to be worked out. Thus, we sometimes observe a tendency to distinguish between Baptism as the sacrament of regeneration and Confirmation as the medium of the gift of the Spirit. In Serapion's blessing of chrism, for example, prayer is made that those who have been regenerated and renewed through the laver of regeneration may also become (as a result of chrismation) partakers of the gift of the Holy Spirit.[1] A similar theory is expressed by Jobius Monachus,[2] and, as we have already noticed, is introduced into the Eastern versions of the *Apostolic Tradition* of Hippolytus.[3] On the other hand the Scriptural doctrine that regeneration takes place by water and Spirit as external and inward aspects of one sacrament, and not as two 'baptisms', is also strongly maintained. Aphraates, for example, declares that 'from Baptism we receive the Spirit of the Messiah. For in the same hour that the priests invoke the Spirit the heavens open and it cometh down and broodeth upon the waters, and they that are baptized are clothed with it. For from all that are born of the body the Spirit is far away until they come to the birth by water, and then they receive the Holy Spirit.'[4] Ambrose asks, 'Quis est autem qui baptizatur Spiritu sancto, nisi qui renascitur per aquam et Spiritum sanctum? . . . Spiritus enim nos per adoptionem filios Dei fecit, sacri fontis unda nos abluit, sanguis Domini nos redemit. Alterum igitur invisibile, alterum visibile testimonium sacramento consequimur spiritali; quia Spiritus testimonium reddit spiritui nostro.'[5] That baptismal regeneration cannot be isolated from the believer's reception of the Holy Spirit is thus explained by Augustine: water and Spirit are the outward and inward parts of the sacrament, for 'aqua . . . exhibens forinsecus sacramentum gratiae, solvens vincula culpae . . . regenerat hominem in uno Christo'.[6] Leo follows the same line of thought; the difference between the Johannine and Christian baptisms lies, according to him, in the fact that in the latter the

---

[1] 25, 2.   [2] *inc.*, 2 (*PG*. 86², 3316B, C).   [3] See above, p. 142.
[4] Theodore of Mopsuestia declares that we receive the Spirit in Baptism because the Baptism of Jesus was in all respects the prototype of our own, *fr. inc.* 8 (Swete, 2, p. 298, 27); *hom.* 6, 14 (transl. Burkitt, *Early Eastern Christianity*, pp. 124–5).
[5] *Spir.*, 3, 10, 64.   [6] *ep.*, 98, 2.

Spirit regenerates the convert,[1] and, though he distinguishes between regeneration by water and the Spirit, conferred in Baptism, and, on the other hand, the 'chrisma salutis et signaculum vitae aeternae',[2] yet he does not interpose any interval or separation between the regeneration effected in Baptism and the gift of the Spirit. It is interesting to observe that John of Damascus selects the two media of baptismal regeneration, water and the Spirit, as an illustration of the sacramental principle; the former is related to the latter as the external sign to the internal reality.[3] There is evidently no question in his mind about the significance of the Johannine text, and no trace of any idea that two baptisms, of water and of Spirit, are indicated by it.

Many of the Fathers also point out that the sonship bestowed in Baptism is inseparable from the gift of the Spirit. Athanasius makes this point clear,[4] as also does Didymus;[5] Ambrose in this connection compares the operation of the Spirit in the birth of Christ with His activity in baptismal regeneration.[6] The same doctrine is implied in Cyril's exposition of the connection of the Spirit's operation with the regeneration of the Christian in Baptism,[7] perhaps also in the comment of Augustine which has been already mentioned, 'Dicimus ergo in baptizatis parvulis, quamvis id nesciant, habitare Spiritum sanctum',[8] and certainly in the assertion of Maximus of Turin that for regeneration and for entry into the Kingdom of God, 'Spiritus sanctus in illa aqua operatur'.[9]

Gradually signs begin to appear in the patristic teaching of a synthesis between the desire on the one hand to assign regeneration to Baptism and the gift of the Spirit to Confirmation, and on the other to maintain the traditional doctrine of the Spirit's operation in baptismal regeneration and the essential connection between the gift of adoptive sonship and the bestowal of the Holy Spirit's indwelling presence. An example

[1] ep., 16, 6 (PL. 54, 701A–702A).   [2] serm., 24, 6 (PL. 54, 207B).
[3] imag., 3, 12 (PG. 94, 1336B).   [4] Ar., 1, 37 (PG. 26, 89A).
[5] (Ps. Bas.) Eun., 5 (1, 305B; PG. 29, 732C); Trin., 2, 14 (PG. 39, 700B).
[6] myst., 9, 59: 'Si ergo superveniens Spiritus sanctus in Virginem conceptionem operatus est, et generationis munus implevit: non utique dubitandum est quod superveniens in fontem, vel super eos qui baptismum consequuntur, veritatem regenerationis operetur.'
[7] Is., 4, 2 (2, 609B).   [8] ep., 187, 8, 26.   [9] bapt., 2 (PL. 57, 775C).

of this tendency is to be seen in the *De Sacramentis*,[1] where, after the ancient prayer (which we have already discussed in connection with the *Apostolic Tradition*), 'Deus Pater omnipotens, qui te regeneravit ex aqua et Spiritu sancto . . . ipse te ungat in vitam aeternam', we are told that the 'spiritale signaculum' of consignation 'superest ut perfectio fiat, quando ad invocationem sacerdotis Spiritus sanctus infunditur, spiritus sapientiae et intellectus . . . septem quasi virtutes Spiritus . . . Istae sunt septem virtutes quando consignaris'. Here two distinct operations of the Spirit are envisaged; He is active in regenerating the believer through water-baptism, but the seven-fold gifts are bestowed later through the grace given in the consignation.[2] This is explicitly asserted in such liturgical texts as the Gelasian Sacramentary, in which, after the 'qui te regeneravit ex aqua et Spiritu sancto, quique dedit tibi remissionem omnium peccatorum', there follows the rubric, 'Deinde ab episcopo datur eis Spiritus septiformis. Ad consignandum imponit eis manum in his verbis: 'Deus omnipotens . . . qui regenerasti famulos tuos ex aqua et Spiritu sancto, quique dedisti eis remissionem omnium peccatorum . . . inmitte in eos Spiritum sanctum paraclctum, et da eis Spiritum sapientiae et intellectus . . . etc.' The idea is being developed that an initial union of the believer with the presence of the Spirit may be followed by further endowments of the same Spirit, with their own sacramental sign— a most valuable conception so far as infant Baptism is concerned, and the only satisfactory doctrine of Confirmation, but less easy to apply to those baptized as believers, for in their case to distinguish between the Spirit's presence in regeneration and His gift of the seven-fold endowment is artificial and hard to sustain. In these passages we see the beginnings of the rationale of Confirmation which had been long demanded by the development of the ancillary ceremonies in Baptism and the subsequent disintegration of the rite in the West. A doctrine of Confirmation in relation to Baptism is being established after the period of confusion, and some of the features of the doctrine

---

[1] 2, 7, 24; 3, 2, 8; 3, 2, 10. The treatise is by Ambrose.
[2] On the other hand, *serm.* 44 of the spurious sermons of Augustine (Ben. 5, 2431D) appears to attribute the seven-fold gifts to water-baptism: Naaman dipped seven times in Jordan to signify the coming of the seven-fold gifts to Jesus in the same river.

of the mediaeval and Reforming theologians are becoming discernible.

Like the relation of the gift of the Spirit to regeneration and sonship, the relation between remission of sins in Baptism and the reception of the Spirit is the subject of very diverse comments from the Fathers. On one side there are passages which make a sharp distinction between the two gifts, as between the negative and positive aspects of the grace bestowed on the Christian initiate, the former being assigned to Baptism and the latter to Confirmation. The doctrine of Pacian of Barcelona, who ascribes the gift of the Spirit to chrismation,[1] is thus described by Mason:[2] 'The Spirit is not given by the laver, of which the function is to wash away sins; it is given by the chrism, together with the hand and mouth of the bishop. When that has been received Baptism is complete, and the man regenerate.'[3] The *Apostolic Constitutions*[4] appear to suggest at one point that water-baptism in itself is equivalent only to a physical purification, though elsewhere this is contradicted.[5] Maximus Confessor describes the function of Baptism in water to be the cleansing of the conscience, and that of the Spirit (apparently separated from Baptism) as the inward working of perfection in the soul.[6] Isidore of Seville maintains that, 'sicut in baptismo peccatorum remissio datur, ita per unctionem sanctificatio Spiritus adhibetur . . . in ipsa baptismi gratia visibilis actus, quod in aqua mergimur, sed spiritalis effectus, quod delictis mundamur . . . manus impositio ideo fit, ut per benedictionem advocatus invitetur Spiritus sanctus'.[7] The thought of this passage is confused, like that of Tertullian upon which it is based. The imposition of the hand is regarded as exactly equivalent to chrismation, and, in the passage which follows the above citation, the Scriptural analogy chosen to illustrate the bestowal of the Spirit after Baptism is the description of the Spirit brooding on the Creation waters, a text more often employed to prove that the Spirit is conferred in the font itself. The Gelasian Sacramentary, as we have seen, makes a similar separation of the remission of sins from the full gift of the Spirit.

[1] *ep. Sempron.*, 1, 6 (*PL*. 13, 1057C); *bapt.*, 6 (1093B).
[2] *The Relation of Confirmation to Baptism*, p. 143.
[3] Cf. Pacian., *bapt.*, 6.   [4] 7, 44, 3.   [5] Cf. 7, 22, 3.
[6] ap. Cram., *cat. in* 1 *Jo.* 3, 9 (p. 126, 9).   [7] *etym.*, 6, 19, 51–4.

On the other side Didymus emphasizes that the activity of the Spirit in the remission of sins is inseparable from His operation in regeneration, sanctification, renewal of the divine image, and sealing.[1] Ambrose[2] implies a similar doctrine, which is also involved in Jerome's insistence upon the manifold activities of the Spirit in Baptism[3] and appears, as we have seen, in the catechetical instruction of Theodore of Mopsuestia.

Once again we can begin to see traces of the shape which was to be taken by the later theories of Baptism, Confirmation, and the gift of the Spirit. Augustine, for instance, suggests a conception of partial and fuller bestowals of the Spirit—a dangerous idea, which tends to encourage the notion of quantitatively measured 'portions' of an impersonal Spirit. There is a partial gift in Baptism for remission of sins, while the perfect bestowal in the form of charity is reserved until later.[4] An alternative, and more valuable, solution to the problem is hinted at in the conception of a multiplicity of 'moments' in the believer's reception of the Spirit, which is given anew, perhaps many times, for fresh purposes. Thus in the Bobbio Missal the rite of insufflation contains the words (said to an as yet unbaptized catechumen), 'Accipe Spiritum sanctum et in corde teneas'— a gift which in no way prevents the same candidate from receiving the gift of the Spirit later.

It may be briefly noticed in passing that many Biblical texts continue to suggest to patristic commentators that the Spirit is received in Baptism in water. The Scriptural identification of the Holy Spirit with the 'water of life' receives much attention from Didymus[5] in connection with Baptism, and Cyril observes that water is the Scriptural symbol for the Spirit because both alike are life-giving and supply growth and renewed existence. to all things.[6] Such interpretations of Scripture exercised a profound influence upon baptismal theology. This is especially true of the picture given in Genesis of the Spirit brooding on the water; Gregory of Nyssa, for example, believes that Baptism in water is overshadowed by the Holy Spirit when faith is present and that He gives life to the soul,[7] and Jerome comments:

---

[1] Trin., 2, 12 (PG. 39, 680, 681).
[3] Lucif., 6 (PL. 23, 169B, C).
[5] Trin., 2, 6 (PG. 39, 553B, C).
[7] v. Moys. (PG. 44, 361D).

[2] Spir., 1, 6, 69–73.
[4] serm., 71, 18, 30–19, 32.
[6] Is., 4, 2 (2, 581).

'Super aquas ferebatur Spiritus. Iam eo tempore baptismum significabatur. Non enim poterat esse baptismum sine Spiritu.'[1] There are, in conclusion, two important features in the thought of the early Church which helped to maintain the essential link between the sacrament of Baptism and the gift of the Spirit, despite the fact that one was a theory which, especially in popular piety, tended to gross superstition. This was the belief in a kind of 'Real Presence' of the Holy Spirit in the water of Baptism. We are not now concerned with such abuses as the reservation by the faithful of the consecrated water. We have only to glance at those passages in the Fathers which express a more rational doctrine of the presence of the Spirit in Baptism. Tertullian and Hippolytus had already spoken of the presence of the Spirit *in* the element of water.[2] Firmicus Maternus says that, 'alia est aqua qua renovati homines renascuntur . . . Illam quam despicis ignitam, venerandi Spiritus maiestate decoratur'.[3] τῷ πνεύματι, says Basil, τὸ ὕδωρ συμπαρελήφθη.[4] The sanctified water is compared by Gregory of Nyssa, among others, with the bitter waters of Marah; it is sanctified and sweetened by the ἐπιφοίτησις of the Spirit.[5] So Chrysostom can speak fancifully of the 'serpent' who, seeing the river (into which the martyrs Domnina, Bernice, and Prosdice, had thrown themselves) thereby turned into a baptismal font and θείῳ πνεύματι τὸ ῥεῖθρον ἀνακιρνώμενον τοῖς πυρὶ πνευματικῷ κερασθεῖσιν ὕδασιν, ἀνεκρούετο.[6]

Zeno of Verona describes the baptismal water as 'aqua viva Spiritu sancto et igne dulcissimo temperata',[7] and Gaudentius connects the miracle of Cana with the presence of the Spirit in the water and its reception by the baptized.[8] These are, no doubt, expressions of pious rhetoric, but Cyril has a genuine doctrine of the Spirit's 'real presence' in the water, a theory amounting almost to a conception of the transubstantiation of water into Spirit,[9] John of Damascus explains that the Spirit

---

[1] tractat. de Ps. 76 (Anecd. Mareds. 3, p. 54).
[2] bapt., 4; theoph., 8 (p. 262, 17; PG. 10, 860B).
[3] prof. rel. error., 2, 5.   [4] Spir., 15, 35 (PG. 32, 129C).
[5] bapt. (PG. 46, 420D).   [6] quatrid. Laz. (Ben. 2, 649B, C).   [7] tractat., 2, 35.
[8] serm., 9 (PL. 20, 907C): 'Jesus invisibili virtute hanc aquam convertit in vinum ita ut baptizati . . . confestim divini Spiritus in se operantis saporem . . . testarentur.'
[9] Jo., 2, 1 (4, 147D); cf. Qu. V. et. N.T., 59, 1 (CSEL. p. 105).

comes upon the water through *epiclesis*,[1] and we must not ignore the significance of the common practice of dipping torches into the font to signify the ἐπιφοίτησις of the Holy Ghost.[2] Such ideas do not, admittedly, necessitate a belief that the operation of the Spirit in the font effects the bestowal on the baptized person of His indwelling presence. It is possible to hold a 'real presence' doctrine of this kind and yet maintain that the full gift of the Spirit is granted in Confirmation, though the language of the above-quoted passage of Gaudentius at least suggests the contrary. Nevertheless, the strength of these beliefs about the operation of the Spirit in the water did much to prevent Baptism in water from being totally divorced from 'Spirit-baptism' and relegated to the status of Levitical washing, a ceremony of purification in preparation for Confirmation as the sacrament of the gift of the Spirit.

The second traditional belief which affected the theology of initiation is the ancient conception of martydom as a baptism. The martyr was indeed baptized, for he shared literally, and not in a figure, in the death of Christ and His resurrection; and it is simply with water-baptism that the 'baptism of blood' is equated. Yet there is no suggestion that the martyr's baptism was incomplete, and, so far from there being any notion that the martyr received the remission of sins alone and not the gift of the Spirit, the unanimous belief of the Church was always that the martyr is pre-eminently πνευματικός. Indeed, until the rise of the monk, the martyr shares with the inspired prophet the highest possible title to Spirit-possession. In some quarters the number of martyrs which a Christian sect could claim was regarded as the criterion of that sect's possession of the Spirit.[3] Yet it is water-baptism alone whose effects the martyr claims to possess, and which would, by implication, give him the same full privileges which he has obtained through martyrdom. Chrysostom expresses the general teaching of the Fathers on this point when he tells his congregation, μὴ θαυμάσητε, εἰ βάπτισμα τὸ μαρτύριον ἐκάλεσα· καὶ γὰρ καὶ ἐνταῦθα τὸ Πνεῦμα μετὰ πολλῆς ἐφίπταται τῆς δαψιλείας, καὶ ἁμαρτημάτων ἀναίρεσις

---

[1] *f.o.*, 4, 9 (*PG*. 94, 1121A).
[2] Amalarius of Metz, *eccl. off.*, 1, 26 (*PL*. 105, 1046A).
[3] Eus., *h.e.*, 5, 16, 20.

καὶ ψυχῆς γίνεται καθαρμὸς θαυμαστός τις καὶ παράδοξος· καὶ ὥσπερ
οἱ βαπτιζόμενοι τοῖς ὕδασιν, οὕτως οἱ μαρτυροῦντες τῷ ἰδίῳ λούονται
αἵματι.[1] The doctrine of 'baptism in blood' must inevitably
have contributed towards the maintenance of the essential
connection of Baptism with participation in the death and
resurrection of Christ, and served to enhance the importance
of the actual rite of Baptism in water as the sacrament
whereby the believer received all the benefits of union with
Christ, of which the possession of the indwelling presence of the
Holy Spirit is the greatest.

Note: We have more than once had occasion to refer to a certain
ambiguity inherent in the use of the word 'baptism' when it is
spoken of as the medium of the reception of the Spirit, and it
has been pointed out that occasionally the terms *baptisma,
baptismus, baptizare,* etc., are loosely employed to denote the
whole rite of initiation including the ancillary ceremonies such
as chrismation. Normally, however, these words indicate, as
their etymology suggests, 'water-dipping'; and the extension of
their meaning to cover the whole process of initiation, is a lax
usage which can be paralleled in the case of the word λουτρόν.
This, it will be agreed, means 'water-baptism'; yet John of
Damascus can say that *oil* and water become by the grace of the
Spirit λουτρὸν ἀναγεννήσεως.[2] It would not on this account be
suggested that the real meaning of λουτρόν is 'initiation by
baptism and unction together'. The reverse process also occurs:
the word χρῖσμα can be employed to denote the entire complex
rite comprising Baptism as well as chrismation.[3]

We have seen instances of the extended use of the words for
'baptism' in Origen. The Didascalia, similarly, speaks of
'Dominus in baptismo, impositione manus episcoporum, testimonium praebens',[4] and the same usage may be present in the
curious remark of Optatus that Christ was baptized, 'quia . . .
superventurum oleum aqua debuit antecedere ad mysteria
initianda et ordinanda et implenda baptismatis';[5] this statement is followed by a description of a rite consisting in washings

---

[1] *pan. Luc.,* 2 (Ben. 2, 526A). For earlier instances of this teaching see above,
p. 184.
[2] *f.o.,* 4, 13 (*PG.* 94, 1141).
[3] Eus., *d.e.,* 4, 16 (p. 190, 27; *PG.* 22, 317C).
[4] 2, 32, 3.   [5] 4, 7 (on Ps. cxl. 5).

unction, and imposition of hands. Cyril speaks of chrismation taking place at the time of Holy Baptism[1]—a natural expression, since chrismation took place at the same service as Baptism proper.

This wide use of the terms is not confined to the earlier centuries; there is no justification for the belief that it represents an early usage which was gradually discarded in favour of the narrower significance. It persists as an occasional inaccuracy, and it is found as late as the time of Haymo of Auxerre (pseudo-Primasius).[2] While it is true, therefore, that we must beware of resting too great a weight of argument on passages where the gift of the Spirit is assigned to 'baptism' without further definition, and that we should be careful not to assume that in every such case water-baptism alone is indicated, it would be far more rash to suppose that in their strict use the words for 'baptism' when employed by orthodox writers ever denoted anything more than Baptism in water. We must not assume that when Tertullian asserts that Baptism gives remission of sins, regeneration, and the gift of the Spirit[3] he means that these benefits result from Baptism and Confirmation together, or that when Ephrem likens the unbaptized man to an empty palace awaiting its king[4] he has in mind the man who has not been both baptized and confirmed, or that Chrysostom's statement, ἐπὶ σὲ βαπτιζόμενον τὸ Πνεῦμα ἔρχεται,[5] really presents no difficulty to those who wish to distinguish separate rites of water- and Spirit-baptism.

[1] *Is.* 3, 1 (2, 353E).
[3] *Marc.*, 1, 28 (*CSEL.* p. 330, 7).
[5] *hom.* 12. 2 *in Mt.* (Ben. 7, 163D).

[2] *Heb.*, 6 (*PL.* 68, 794B).
[4] 2, 244F.

CHAPTER NINE

CHRISMATION AND THE SPIRIT

FROM the latter part of the second century, as we have seen, chrismation and signing with the Cross, generally performed after Baptism by the bishop—except in Syria where it long continued to take place before the candidate came to the font— acquired a steadily growing importance in the rite of initiation. From the middle of the third century onwards this ceremony comes to be associated more and more frequently with the bestowal of the indwelling presence of the Spirit, although, as we have seen in the first chapter of this part, this fact does not prevent many writers from continuing to connect the gift of the Spirit with Baptism itself. The relation between these rites, or these elements in the rite of initiation had not been thought out, and we need not dwell at any length on the many passages from the Fathers in which chrismation is treated as the vehicle of the Spirit. They add little to what has already been said, and their importance for our present purpose is that, taken in conjunction with the passages on Baptism which we have just considered, and with those which deal with the imposition of hands, they serve to illustrate the confusion which existed on this subject during the first five centuries.

Nor need we stay to examine the very numerous Scriptural texts which appeared to warrant this theory of the gift of the Spirit. We need only remark that the Fathers assumed that there was excellent biblical authority for the view that the ancient ceremony associated with the ritual of coronation and with the conception of the anointing of the Spirit-possessed Messiah had been divinely appointed for all Christians as the means whereby they were to receive the bestowal of the Holy Spirit. Not that the practice depended upon such Scriptural authority. On the contrary, Basil expressly denies that it rests upon any direct warrant of Scripture; it is part of the tradition of 'our fathers'.[1] Yet the custom was in all probability suggested originally by supposed Old Testament types and by New Testament metaphors interpreted literally, together with the common Gnostic and semi-pagan emphasis upon ritual unction, and it was certainly supported by a very large and varied collection of proof-texts.

For the present we must be satisfied with a brief glance at some of the patristic teaching that chrismation confers the Spirit, then at some other meanings which the Fathers attach to the rite, and thirdly, since they often by implication or explicitly ascribe the gift of the Spirit to both Baptism and chrismation, at such indications as their works afford of a possible synthesis in the form of a reasoned doctrine of the relation of the latter ceremony to Baptism.

Cyril of Jerusalem, who, as we have observed, sometimes ascribes the bestowal of the Spirit to Baptism, tells the newly baptized that an external unction is the sacramental symbol of sanctification by the Spirit.[2] The chrism is the antitype of the Holy Spirit with which Christ was anointed.[3] Here the representation of Christ's anointing as Messiah has been transferred from its original symbol, Baptism, to the physical unction which follows the Baptism in water. It is possible that Hilary is thinking on the same lines when, if this reading is authentic, he speaks of the *sacramenta* of Baptism and the Spirit.[4] This is a surprisingly strong statement of the theory that the sacrament of the Spirit is 'not Baptism but something else', and in fact there is fairly good evidence for the variant reading *sacramento* in this passage. It is, however, true that he implies a theory of this sort elsewhere in the same treatise,[5] when he remarks on the subject of Christ's Baptism that 'baptizato eo ... Spiritus sanctus emittitur. ... Post aquae lavacrum ... in nos Spiritum involare.' Similar teaching is involved in the wording of Serapion's prayer for the consecration of chrism[6] and the Apostolic Constitutions ascribe the gift of the Spirit to the anointing and not to Baptism, though in this case it is the pre-baptismal unction with oil which signifies its

---

[1] *Spir.*, 27, 66 (*PG.* 32, 188B).
[3] *Ibid.*, 21, 1, 3.
[5] *Ibid.*, 2, 6.

[2] *catech.*, 21, 3.
[4] *comm. in Mt.*, 4, 27.
[6] *euch.*, 25, 2.

bestowal whereas the post-baptismal consignation furnishes the 'seal'.[1]

A very extreme statement of the necessity of chrismation, considered as the medium of the reception of the Spirit, is given by Gregory of Nyssa. His insistence on it may perhaps be due in some measure to his desire to vindicate what he believes to be a rite with important doctrinal implications in relation to the question of the divinity of the Holy Spirit against attacks on that doctrine by the Macedonians. He says: τῷ μέλλοντι αὐτοῦ (Χριστοῦ) διὰ τῆς πίστεως ἅπτεσθαι, ἀναγκαῖον εἶναι προεντυγχάνειν διὰ τῆς ἁφῆς τῷ μύρῳ· οὐ γὰρ ἐστί τι μέρος ὅ γυμνόν ἐστι τοῦ ἁγίου Πνεύματος.[2] There could be no more striking indication of the confusion into which the liturgical and theological developments of the age of the Fathers had reduced the doctrine of the reception of the Spirit in relation to conversion and Baptism. The New Testament teaching is almost the reverse of what Gregory of Nyssa here offers us, for it tells us that it is through the apprehension of Christ by faith, or rather, that it is as one aspect of our apprehension of Christ by faith, that we come to possess the 'anointing' of the Holy Spirit which came upon Christ Himself. Here, on the other hand, it is through an external anointing which symbolizes and effects the reception of the Spirit that we come to lay hold on Christ.

The theory which was held by Cyril of Jerusalem, namely that the oil of anointing typifies Christ's reception of the Spirit, occurs again in Didymus,[3] who identifies the outward unction also with the 'anointing' of 2 Cor. i. 22 and 1 John ii. 20. In the West, however, we find other Scriptural authority cited for the belief that chrismation, or rather consignation, is the effective sign of the gift of the Spirit. This is the passages of Acts which refer to the imposition of hands, for the ceremony there described is identified with the action of the bishop when he signs the newly baptized with the Cross in the consecrated chrism. This supposed warrant for what is almost certainly, as Basil realized, an unscriptural practice is adduced by Innocent I in the famous letter to Decentius of Gubbio, in which consignation, as distinct from the unction administered by the presbyter

---

[1] 3, 17, 1; 7, 22, 2.   [2] *Maced.*, 16 (*PG.* 45, 1321A).
[3] *Trin.*, 2, 6 (*PG.* 39, 557C, 560A).

immediately after Baptism, is reserved for the bishop and is declared emphatically to be the medium by which 'bishops confer the Spirit, the Paraclete'.[1] The valuable effect of this letter was that it maintained the episcopal administration of Confirmation at Rome against the normal practice of the East and for long periods of most of the West as well.[2] It thus enabled a rationale of Confirmation to be developed in later times in which the element of blessing and commissioning by the representative leader of the Church should have its proper place and importance. Apart from this unwitting contribution to later, and perhaps particularly Anglican, doctrine the letter did little to resolve the confusion into which the doctrine of the relation of the gift of the Spirit to Christian initiation had fallen, or to elucidate the problems of the proper matter of its sacramental sign and the Scriptural authority which that sign could claim.

To Augustine chrismation is a *sacramentum* distinct from Baptism;[3] Cyril of Alexandria explains that it is a symbol of our participation in the Holy Spirit;[4] and Theodoret speaks of the anointed receiving the unseen grace of the Spirit in the 'type' of the chrism.[5] It is probably with the same conception in mind that Theodoret describes the 'oil whose significance is known to the initiates' as 'pneumatic',[6] and the same idea probably underlies the thought of Hesychius of Jerusalem that the patriarchs were 'christoi', even though they had not been anointed with oil, because they partook of the Spirit.[7] That chrism bestows 'the gift of the Holy Spirit' is explicitly asserted in the spurious 'seventh canon of Constantinople (381)',[8] and in the sixth century the teaching of the 'Areopagite' emphasizes that it is in the rite of unction that the ἐπιφοίτησις of the Spirit is mediated to the initiate.[9] Gregory the Great[10] interprets the

---

[1] ep., 25, 3 (PL. 56, 515B, C).
[2] The provisions of the First Council of Orange are particularly difficult to understand. In case of urgency, 'si desit episcopus', a presbyter may 'consign' converted heretics (can. 1); 'De eo autem qui in baptismate quacumque necessitate faciente non chrismatus fuerit, in confirmatione sacerdos commonebitur' (can. 2). Episcopal administration of chrismation was at any rate not regarded by this council as essential.
[3] Petil., 2, 104, 239.   [4] Is., 3, 1 (2, 353E).   [5] Cant. i. 2 (1, 30).
[6] Ps. xxii. 5 (1, 749).   [7] Ps. civ. 15 (PG. 93, 1293C).
[8] Addressed by the church of Constantinople to Antioch about 465.
[9] e.h., 4, 3, 11 (PG. 3, 484C).   [10] exp. in Cant. 1 (PL. 79, 478D).

'unguents' of Cant. i. 1 as signifying the Spirit with which Christ was anointed, and, in an author of this date, it is fairly safe to assume that he would infer that they therefore foreshadowed the actual chrism used in the Church. Such writers as John of Damascus[1] continue to teach that it is in unction that the Spirit is bestowed.

The gift of the Spirit was not, however, the only spiritual reality which was believed to be typified by the rite of chrismation. Other meanings continue to be assigned to it which we have already met in earlier authors. Thus it is often regarded as a symbol of the believer's participation in Christ, so that the positive significance of Baptism as the sacrament which makes a man a member of Christ is transferred to the outward anointing as a type of the anointing of the Messiah. It is probably with the ceremony of initiation in mind that Basil expounds Matt. vi. 17 with the comment, 'Wash thy soul from sins; anoint thine head with holy chrism that thou mayest become a partaker of Christ'.[2] Jerome explains this at rather greater length: 'Quando descenditis in vitalem fontem cum Salvatore, tunc habetis discere quomodo unguentum veniat in caput Salvatoris. Si enim caput viri Christus est, vestrum caput autem unguendum est, post baptisma ungimur.'[3] 'Pseudo-Justin' maintains that unction after Baptism is a symbol of the Christian's participation in the sufferings and the glory of his Lord,[4] and Augustine declares that it signifies that we are indeed the Body of Christ.[5]

In all these passages there is no reference to any gift of the Holy Spirit in the unction, which is treated rather as an edifying symbol of our membership of Christ and our fellowship in His death and resurrection than as a sacrament by which the Spirit is conferred. It may, however, rightly be argued that if chrismation typifies our union with Christ it must necessarily also be a symbol of our reception of the Spirit.

Cyril of Jerusalem sees in chrismation the act which confers upon us the status of 'Christians',[6] and John of Damascus[7] repeats the ancient doctrine that it makes us literally 'christs' and therefore signifies our identification with the Christ.

---

[1] f.o., 4, 9 (PG. 94, 1125B).   [2] hom. 1, 2 (PG. 31, 165A).
[3] tractat. in Mc. xiii. 32–3, xiv. 3–6 (Anecd. Mareds. 3, p. 368).
[4] qu. orth. 137 (PG. 6, 1389C, D).   [5] enarr., 2, 2 in Ps. xxvi.
[6] catech., 21, 5.   [7] f.o., 4, 9 (PG. 94, 1125B).

According to the 48th canon of Laodicea, it is unction with chrism which makes us sharers in Christ's kingdom, and it is a commonplace of patristic teaching that it signifies the baptized convert's admission into the status and privileges of the kingship and priesthood of the Messiah. The idea that it denotes consecration to the Christian 'royal priesthood' is already prominent in Tertullian's doctrine of initiation;[1] it is to be found in the *Apostolic Constitutions*,[2] and it is explained in some detail by Chrysostom,[3] who adds that it signifies not only kingship and priesthood, but also the charismata of a prophet. Prudentius describes the *unguentum* as *regale*,[4] and Augustine remarks that the royal priesthood of the Church is prefigured by David's anointing.[5] It is because it symbolizes the royal and priestly status of Christians that chrismation signifies entry into membership of Christ's Body.[6] Similar ideas are expressed by Prosper[7] and by Salvian.[8] The holy chrism is to be kept safe from possible desecration, according to the Council of Tours of 461,[9] because it is 'illud unde Christo incorporamur, et unde omnes fideles sanctificantur, unde reges et sacerdotes inunguntur'. This thought is developed by Maximus of Turin, who adds an eschatological colour to the conception of the royal priesthood,[10] and by Isidore of Seville who says that our unction is administered after Baptism because we are a priestly and royal race; the whole Church is now consecrated by chrismation in virtue of its membership of the eternal Priest and King, whereas before the Incarnation it was only the king and the high priest who were so anointed.[11] The same explanation of the symbolism is given at a later date by the *De Mystica Contemplatione* falsely ascribed to Germanus of Constantinople.[12]

In the Fathers of this period there are a few indications of the possible direction of a line of theological advance beyond the confused situation in which the gift of the Spirit is assigned to

[1] *bapt.*, 7.
[3] *hom.* 3. 5 *in* 2 *Cor.* (10, 448B ff.).
[5] *serm.*, 351, 5, 12.
[7] *sent. Aug.*, 344.
[9] Mansi 7, 949D.
[10] *tractat.* 3 (*PL.* 57, 777D–779A): 'chrismate . . . per quod ostenditur baptizatis regalem et sacerdotalem conferri a Domino dignitatem . . . Mirum . . . vos illo chrismate regnum futurae gloriae et sacerdotium esse consecutos.
[11] *eccl. off.*, 2, 26, 2 (*PL.* 83, 823B).

[2] 3, 16, 4.
[4] *psychomach.*, 361.
[6] *enarr.*, 2, 2 *in Ps.* xxvi.
[8] *gub. Dei.*, 3 2 (*PL.* 53, 58B, C).

[12] *PG.* 98, 385C.

Baptism at one moment and to chrismation at another. The great number of passages in which chrismation is explained as a symbol for the newly baptized of their membership of Christ and participation in His Body's priestly and kingly character suggests that, granted a greater measure of fidelity to the teaching of the New Testament, the rite could fall into place as an edifying, although wholly secondary, ceremony, expressing in visible and dramatic form one aspect of the gift and status which the Christian has received in Baptism. Further, Serapion[1] suggests that one effect of the gift of the Spirit in chrismation is the 'strengthening' of the candidate, a conception which is taken up in later doctrines of Confirmation. Cyril contributes the valuable thought that it signifies the *perfecting* of those who were justified in Christ through Baptism,[2] and this idea is taken up and developed by Dionysius in the teaching which centres round his famous phrase χρῖσις τελειω-τική.[3] This conception is given an eschatological application by Augustine when he says that 'Unctio ista perficiet nos spiritaliter in illa vita quae nobis promittitur'.[4]

As a symbol of the completion and perfecting of the baptismal gift, a token of the progress of sanctification, and a sign of a process whose end will not be realized on this side of 'illa vita quae nobis promittitur', chrismation could properly become the visible sign in Confirmation, associated, and confused with, the laying on of hands in Western practice. As a symbol of priesthood and kingship it could appropriately follow the Baptism of believers as an edifying ceremony; but it is unsuitable as the external sign in the Confirmation of those baptized in infancy, once an interval of time has been interposed between the two rites, for membership of Christ and of His royal and priestly Body is not a thing which can be separated from Baptism itself.

As the sacramental sign of the gift of the Spirit it is wholly out of place, since this depends upon the membership of Christ which has been effected in Baptism. If, however, we substitute 'a gift' for 'the gift', and chrismation be regarded as the matter of a Confirmation—a renewal of the Spirit's activity strengthening and equipping the baptized for his spiritual warfare, the

---

[1] *euch.*, 25, 2.
[3] *e.h.*, 4, 3, 11 (*PG.* 3, 484C).

[2] *Joel*, 2, 32 (3, 224E).
[4] *enarr.*, 2, 2 *in Ps.* xxvi.

conception is less objectionable, but for this purpose the symbolism of chrismation is clearly less suitable than that of the
laying on of hands. The latter is the ancient sign of blessing and
of the imparting of spiritual power and authority; the former
has no such obvious connotations, for its Old Testament asso-
ciations with the spiritual 'fitting out' of kings, priests, and prophets have been largely exhausted, so far as Christian thought
is concerned, in their fulfilment in the Messianic anointing of
Christ. It is this unction of the Messiah which is the natural
antitype of the Hebrew anointings, and it is in Baptism, and not
in any subsequent moment of his experience, that the believer
is both brought into union with the Christ and also made a
partaker of His anointing with the Holy Spirit.

CHAPTER TEN

THE LAYING ON OF HANDS

THE view that the presence of the Holy Spirit is conferred upon
the believer by the laying on of hands after Baptism is largely
absent from the writings of the second-century Fathers. That
the practice existed, however, at any rate in some circles, from
an early date is indicated by the Epistle to the Hebrews, and,
as we have observed, the narratives of the visit of Peter and
John to Samaria and the baptism with an imposition of hands
of the Ephesian 'disciples' exercised a strong influence upon
baptismal theology which is already apparent in the teaching
of Tertullian; it was generally supposed that the ceremony
described in Acts was a universal practice of the Apostolic
Church and that it was the normal means by which the indwelling of the Spirit was sacramentally conveyed to the baptized. Consequently, when they are commenting on Acts, or
have the relevant texts in mind, Christian writers frequently
ascribe the gift of the Spirit to the imposition of hands with
which, in certain parts of the Church, the rite of initiation
closed. Where no ceremony existed exactly parallel to that
recorded in Acts, these texts were commonly applied to the
practice of consignation by the bishop. It was frequently inferred from the Scriptural texts concerning the laying on of
hands that the authority to confer the gift of the Spirit through
that sign belonged exclusively to the Apostles, and that from
them the prerogative had descended to the bishops.

Many of the references in the Fathers to the laying on of
hands are, as we have seen in the case of third-century writers,
directly connected with the interpretation of Acts. As an actual
practice in the Church of the early centuries the rite is by no
means prominent, and can claim no such universal observance
or high importance as consignation with chrism. In the East
it disappears at a relatively early date, the matter of

223

Confirmation being generally held to consist in consignation; in the West the laying on of hands becomes to a large extent fused with the ceremony of consignation. Many of the allusions which the Fathers make to the practice seem to refer to the historical facts recorded in Acts rather than to contemporary practice. Thus Athanasius, alluding to the incidents described in Acts, says that through the imposition of the Apostles' hands the Holy Spirit was given to the regenerate,[1] but he does not indicate that a similar custom was followed in the Church of his own day. Similarly, Cyril of Jerusalem asserts that Christ gave the Apostles power to impart the Spirit through the imposition of hands,[2] and that both Moses and Peter did in fact confer the gift in this way,[3] yet, although he tells the catechumens that they will receive the same grace when they are baptized, when he comes to describe the bestowal of the Spirit in the baptismal rite as it was actually carried out at Jerusalem he speaks only of chrismation, and the imposition of hands receives no mention.[4] The reference made by Serapion to a laying on of the hand[5] concerns an ordinary blessing only.

It is probably with the text of Acts in mind that Hilary describes as one of the chief features of the New Covenant the fact that the gift of the Holy Spirit was available, to be bestowed on the Gentiles by the imposition of the hand with prayer.[6] It is certainly on the strength of his interpretation of Acts that Chrysostom maintains that the gift of the Spirit took place in the primitive Church through the laying on of hands, and that it was an Apostolic prerogative to administer it.[7] When he comes to comment on Heb. vi. 2 it is with an explicit allusion to Acts xix. 6 that he says of the laying on of hands, 'Thus they used to receive the Holy Spirit'.[8] Chrysostom makes no reference to any contemporary practice of laying hands on the baptized, and in his commentary on Acts viii. 17 he is plainly at a loss to explain how it was that the Samaritans had not received the gift of the Spirit in their Baptism and to account for the necessity for them to wait for the visit of Peter and John before they could obtain it. His explanation is that the Spirit was given

---

[1] *Serap.*, 1, 6 (*PG.* 26, 544B).   [2] *catech.*, 14, 25.   [3] *Ibid.*, 16, 26.
[4] *Ibid.*, 21, 1.   [5] *euch.*, 6.
[6] *comm. in Mt.* 19, 3 (on Matt. xix. 13).
[7] *hom.* 18, 3 *in Ac.* (Ben. 9, 146E ff.).   [8] *hom.* 9, 2 *in Heb.* (12, 95C).

in varying measure. The Samaritans received the Spirit of remission; they had not yet obtained the Spirit of 'signs'.[1] This
exegesis represents an interesting attempt to distinguish between
different modes of the Spirit's activity, to recognize that the
Spirit is bestowed in various ways for different purposes, and
to combat the view that the Spirit was bestowed by the imposition of hands or chrismation alone and not at all in Baptism.
It shows, too, that Chrysostom realizes that for St. Luke it was
the signs and marvels accompanying the progress of the
Church's mission which were the primary tokens of the presence of the Holy Spirit who directs that mission's course. It is
the text of Acts again rather than any contemporary liturgical
practice which inspires Chrysostom's somewhat similar comments elsewhere.[2]

The view that the Apostles alone were entitled to confer the
gift of the Spirit is strongly expressed by Epiphanius[3] and
Isidore of Pelusium.[4] These writers derive their belief primarily from their reading of Acts, but part of their purpose may
have been to restrain the growth of the practice of presbyteral
consignation, the precedent of the Apostolic imposition of
hands being adduced, as it was in the West by Innocent, to
support the doctrine that a different rite must be performed by
bishops alone. That the power to administer the gift of the
Spirit by the laying on of hands was restricted to the Apostles
is implied by the *Quaestiones in Vetus et Novum Testamentum*[5] in a
free rendering of Acts viii. 14 ff.: 'Miserunt ad Petrum et
Iohannem ut venirent, et his qui crediderint, darent Spiritum
sanctum per manus impositionem.' Isidore of Seville is keenly
anxious to maintain that the Holy Spirit is conferred by bishops
alone in the imposition of hands;[6] he cites Acts viii. 14–17 and
xix. 6 to establish his argument, and quotes Innocent's letter to
Decentius as evidence for the episcopal prerogative, oblivious
of the fact that Innocent quotes the texts of Acts which deal
with the imposition of hands and yet speaks only of consignation. Obviously the two rites have been virtually identified with
each other.

[1] *hom.* 18. 2 *in Ac.* (9, 146A).
[2] *hom.* 40. 2 *in Ac.* (9, 304D ff.).
[3] *haer.*, 21, 1 (p. 239, 4; *PG.* 41, 285C).
[4] *epp.*, 1, 451 (*PG.* 78, 429C).
[5] 101, 6 (*CSEL.* p. 196, 17).
[6] *eccl. off.*, 2, 27 (*PL.* 83, 824–6).

Many other instances could be adduced of cases where the Fathers ascribe the gift of the Spirit to the imposition of hands because of the influence upon their thought of the supposed Scriptural warrant in Acts.[1] The story of the Ethiopian eunuch, on the other hand, causes much difficulty. We may pass over the exegesis followed by Jerome, who read the Western version of Acts viii. 39 and used the text as a proof of his theory that the conception of the bishop's hands as the medium of the bestowal of the Spirit was a piece of prelatical presumption. It is more important for our purposes to notice the assertion of Chrysostom that although the Ethiopian received no imposition of hands, he yet obtained the gift of the Spirit in Baptism.[2] Nevertheless, despite the difficulty of this episode, most writers assert in their comments on Acts that the laying on of hands is the medium by which the Christian receives the Spirit. Plenty of Old Testament texts were ready to hand to support this exegesis, especially the incident of the conferment of the Spirit upon Joshua by the imposition of the hands of Moses.

The influence of these passages of Scripture is immensely important in the history of the Christian use of the laying on of hands in initiation. We shall not, of course, suppose that the practice was artificially invented as a result of the reading of these texts; the fact that when they are speaking of the ecclesiastical ceremony the Latin authors generally use the singular *manus* instead of the plural is itself an indication that the practice represents a tradition independent of the New Testament text. Yet the importance attached to it as the sign of the bestowal of the Spirit probably owes its origin to Scriptural exegesis.

We have already seen that the practice receives special emphasis in the African Church of Tertullian and Cyprian; it was established in Firmilian's church of Caesarea; and the Council of Elvira[3] lays it down that an imposition of the bishop's hand must complete any baptism which may have been administered in case of necessity by a layman. In the last instance there is no mention of the gift of the Spirit. The emphasis seems to lie

---

[1] e.g. Anast. Sin., *qu.*, 86 (*PG.* 89, 712C); Oecum., *Heb.* vi. 1-3 (*PG.* 119, 333C).
[2] *hom.* 19. 2 *in Ac.* (9, 155B).   [3] can. 38.

rather upon the importance of enabling the candidate to receive the completion[1] of his initiation at the hands of the bishop with whom otherwise he would not be brought into contact on his entry into the Church.

Optatus[2] regards the laying on of hands as a normal and regular element in Christian initiation; accordingly he looks for its equivalent or prototype in the pattern of all Christian Baptism, the Baptism of Christ. He finds it in the voice of God speaking from heaven. It is remarkable that he does not see its prototype in the descent of the Spirit; that is typified by the 'spiritale oleum' of chrism. The laying on of hands is the equivalent in the Church's Baptism of the Father's blessing which was conferred upon Jesus. This is a point of considerable importance, for it seems that Optatus is perpetuating something of what was probably the original meaning of the laying on of hands—its significance as a benediction and a sign of fellowship and unity in the apostolic body of the Church of Christ. The passage also illustrates once again the manner in which the idea that the Spirit is imparted to the believer by the imposition of hands—always a rather artificial conception, based on a confused interpretation of Acts—is absorbed and replaced by the theory that consignation with chrism is the sacramental sign of the initial gift of the indwelling Spirit.

In the East the imposition of hands retains some degree of importance in the Apostolic Constitutions,[3] although it is fused with the episcopal consignation; the latter is the 'type of spiritual baptism', but it takes place ἐν τῇ χειροθεσίᾳ. A possible reference to the practice occurs in Cyril's statement that Aaron's benediction of the people with his hands upraised σημεῖον ἂν γένοιτο σαφές, ἡ χειρὸς ἐπίθεσις, τῆς τοῦ παναγίου Πνεύματος εἰς ἡμᾶς καταβολῆς.[4] Theodoret in his commentary on Heb. vi. 2 is more explicit. He mentions the imposition of hands before proceeding to discuss Baptism, and says that converts receive the grace of the Spirit through the ἱερατικῆς χειρός.[5] The same author has an interesting notion that John the Baptist laid his hand on the head of Christ, an action which he connects

[1] 'ad episcopum eum perducat ut per manus impositionem proficere (v. l. perfici) possit.'
[2] 4, 7.
[3] 3, 16, 3-4.
[4] ador. 11 (1, 404A, B).
[5] Heb. vi. 2 (3, 577).

with the reception of the Spirit.[1] Possibly Theodoret may have derived this conception from his observation of an imposition of the hand in Confirmation, but it is more probable that he had seen pictures of the Baptism in which John was represented as placing his hand on the head of Jesus in accordance with the Jewish, and, to judge from archaeological evidence, early Christian, practice of Baptism. The 'laying on of hands' in all these cases probably means no more than the bishop's action in the consignation. As a distinct ceremony the imposition of hands does not long retain a place in the East,[2] and consignation with chrism becomes the 'seal of the gift of the Holy Spirit.'

In the West, on the other hand, the laying on of hands continues and is regarded as an important element in initiation. Jerome's strictures on it are not generally shared by other writers. Thus the Latin treatise *De Trinitate et Spiritu* included in the *spuria* of Athanasius explains that 'omnes sancti in nomine Patris et Filii et Spiritus sancti per impositionem manuum sacerdotis Dei Spiritum sanctum consecuti, ad antiquum restituuntur in quo erant ante praevaricationem Adam'.[3] In this case, however, the use of the plural, *manuum*, perhaps indicates a direct dependence upon Acts rather than a reflection on the general custom of the Church.

It was greatly to the advantage of Western theology that the ancient sign of blessing, fellowship, and commissioning, with its long history from the days of the Patriarchs, its connection with endowments of the Spirit, and its employment by the Apostles in the furtherance of the Church's mission, should have been retained to be employed, particularly in those parts of the Church where chrismation was discarded at the Reformation, as the appropriate symbol of the blessing and commissioning at Confirmation of those who had been baptized in infancy. It was

[1] *Qu. in Num.* 47 (1, 253); cf. Syriac liturgy of Severus: 'Accessit Iohannes tamquam sacerdos benedictus, et imposuit dexteram suam capiti Domini sui. Et Spiritus sanctitatis in similitudinem columbae volans descendit, mansitque super caput filii' (transl. Resch, *TU.* 5 (1889), p. 363).
[2] A curious passage is, however, worth notice in Theodore Lector: a certain Persian, Xenaias, appointed bishop of Hierapolis, is reported to be unbaptized; it is decided that ἀρκεῖν αὐτῷ τὴν τοῦ ἐπισκόπου χειροτονίαν πρὸς ἀναπλήρωσιν τῆς θείας μνήσεως, *fr. h. e.* (*PG.* 86, 216C). Does this mean that the imposition of hands which he would receive at his consecration would convey the effects of Baptism?
[3] 21 (*PG.* 26, 1217A).

also of great importance that its administration should be reserved to the bishop, for none but the leader of the local community and the representative of the whole Church Catholic could so properly convey such a symbol.

If the laying on of hands were held merely to duplicate the function of chrismation, there would be little reason for its independent survival, and in fact it was for many centuries often virtually identified with the latter ceremony. Augustine, however, shows signs of attaching a somewhat fresh meaning to it. According to him, its purpose is to convey the particular gift of charity which the Spirit bestows only within the fold of the true Church. This is the 'proprium donum catholicae unitatis et pacis',[1] which has replaced the 'miracles and tongues' in which the operation of the Spirit was formerly manifested. Augustine is of course thinking primarily of the imposition of hands upon Donatists who come over to the Catholic side, and much of his argument is shaped by that consideration. The laying on of hands takes place 'propter caritatis . . . copulationem, quod est maximum donum Spiritus sancti, sine quo non valent ad salutem quaecumque alia sancta in homine fuerint'.[2]

It is true that Augustine speaks as though the gift of the Spirit were usually conveyed by the laying on of hands; the miracles of Pentecost and of Cornelius' conversion consisted partly in the fact that the Spirit was received 'nullo homine in terra manum imponente . . . ante ipsum baptisma, ante impositionem manus'.[3] The Apostolic precedent is followed in the Church by the bishops,[4] and the imposition of hands bestows the Spirit even upon infants.[5] It is, however, particularly in the bond of charity that this gift is expressed, so that the laying on of hands can be regarded primarily as the sign of incorporation into a fellowship. Unlike Baptism, it is repeatable; 'Quid est enim aliud nisi oratio super hominem?'[6] These developments contain valuable material for the construction of a theory of Baptism and Confirmation in relation to the gift of the Spirit.

[1] *bapt.*, 3, 17, 22; cf. 3, 16, 21.
[3] *Parmen.*, 2, 15, 34.
[5] *tractat.*, 6, 10 *in* 1 *Jo.*

[2] *Ibid.*, 5, 23, 33.
[4] *Trin.*, 15, 26, 46.
[6] *bapt.*, 3, 17, 22.

9

Later writers continue to assert that the Spirit is bestowed by the imposition of the bishop's hands,[1] but the confusion between the respective functions of Baptism, chrismation, and this rite is well illustrated by Isidore's explanation of the matter: the remission of sins is given in Baptism; the sanctification of the Spirit is bestowed in unction; the imposition of hands takes place in order that the Spirit may be called down through the benediction (Tertullian's phrase); the Paraclete descends and rests upon the water of Baptism as He brooded at the Creation.[2] In the Gelasian sacramentary the laying on of hands has become amalgamated with consignation,[3] and the Carolingian theologians seem to attach no separate importance to it.[4] This is perhaps surprising in view of the ancient identification of the Hand of God with His Spirit.[5] There are, however, hints of a distinction between the conferring of particular endowments of the Spirit through the laying on of hands and the initial gift of possession of the Spirit in Baptism. These are already present in Chrysostom's distinction between the indwelling Spirit and the Spirit's gift of 'signs' to which we alluded above; it is perhaps implied in Augustine's emphasis on the special gift of *caritas* bestowed in the laying on of hands, and in Leo's statement that the gift of the Spirit 'confirms' those returned heretics who receive it through this rite.[6] Haymo of Auxerre (pseudo-Primasius) carries this thought further in his assertion that by the laying on of hands '*plenissime* creditur accipi donum Spiritus sancti; quod post baptismum ad confirmationem veritatis in ecclesiae a pontificibus fieri solet.'[7]

We are not, however, at present concerned with the doctrine of the grace of Confirmation as a special 'strengthening' by the Spirit for service to Christ in the fellowship of the Church.[8] It has been our object to trace in rough outline the tangled and

---

[1] e.g. Ps.-Gennadius, *eccl. dogm.*, 41: 'manus impositione pontificis accipit Spiritum sanctum.'
[2] *etym.*, 6, 19, 51–4.
[3] 'Ad consignandum imponit eis manum.'
[4] Cf. Theodulph of Orleans, *ord. bapt.*, 17 (*PL.* 105, 236); Raban. Maur., *cler. inst.*, 1, 28 (*PL.* 107, 313).
[5] Cf. Cyr., *Jul.*, 2 (6, 55A); Aug., *Gen. ad Lit.*, 6, 12, 20.
[6] *ep.*, 159, 7.   [7] *Heb.*, 6 (*PL.* 68, 720B).
[8] It must not be forgotten that the imposition of hands is important only in so far as it accompanies prayer; cf. Euthal. Diac., *Ac.*, 28 (*PG.* 85, 660A): τῆς τοῦ ἁγίου Πνεύματος δωρεᾶς δοθείσης διὰ προσευχῆς τοῖς ἐν Ἐφέσῳ πιστεύσασιν.

confused history of the doctrine of the baptismal gift of the Spirit during the age of the Fathers. We now have to enquire what part was played in these theories of Christian initiation by the ancient conception of the eschatological 'seal' with which the Christian is marked out as Christ's soldier and servant and given a pledge of his redemption hereafter.

PART FOUR

PATRISTIC THEORIES
OF SEALING

CHAPTER ELEVEN

SEALING IN BAPTISM

IF our interpretation of the teaching of the New Testament is correct, every spiritual blessing which the Christian convert receives (his justification, remission of sins, new life in Christ, and the indwelling presence of the Holy Spirit through Whom the resurrection life in Christ is mediated to him), is simply one particular aspect of a single and indivisible experience; he has been brought into a new relationship with the Father as an adopted son, and, through the application to him of the saving work of God in Christ, he has been enabled to share in his own degree in the filial relationship of the Son to the Father. He has been made a member of Christ, and all the various aspects of that new status which we confusingly tend to treat as separate spiritual endowments are different modes in which that membership of Christ is realized. It is by the inward presence of the Spirit, which is one of these aspects, that the believer receives the seal of his membership of the people of the New Covenant and the earnest of his salvation.

We have traced the development of early patristic thought on the subject of the 'seal' as far as the point at which it can be said that the pattern of the New Testament doctrine about it has broken up and the conception of the seal has been resolved into many different forms, varying from the profound idea of the stamping of the *imago Dei* upon the soul of the believer by the indwelling of the Spirit to semi-magical notions of the eschatological importance of the invocation of the sacred Name and the outward marking of the faithful with the sign of the Cross. We have examined in outline the confusion of much patristic teaching on the sacramental bestowal of the gift of the Spirit, and we shall expect to find that the Fathers express widely divergent views about the manner in which the believer receives the seal; but the divergence does not follow the same lines as those pursued by their doctrine of the reception of the Spirit. In many cases the Pauline doctrine is maintained that the seal consists in the indwelling of the Spirit; in these instances the question how the seal is received will naturally depend upon the particular author's view on the sacramental medium of the gift of that indwelling, so that for some writers Baptism will be the means by which the seal is received, and may even be regarded as itself constituting the seal; for others chrismation will be the medium of the seal. In other cases, however, the inward stamp of the divine image is considered to be the seal by which the believer is recognized as one of the elect, and, where this conception prevails, the medium of sealing is most naturally held to be Baptism itself. We shall, however, gravely misunderstand the patristic idea of the seal if we fail to realize that it is fundamentally a simple notion : the seal is the 'recognition-signal' by which the faithful are known to belong to Christ. We must also remember that by far the commonest meaning of the term is simply 'the sign of the Cross', and that in very many instances—perhaps the great majority—in which σφραγίζειν and *consignare* are used by the Fathers they denote the marking of people or things with the Cross as the symbol of Christ's ownership. Thus, when we find the term 'seal' used of the consignation which follows Baptism, we must not jump to the conclusion that the seal is believed to consist in 'episcopal Confirmation'. In these very numerous cases the seal means the mark of the Cross which is 'signed' on the candidate at that point in the ceremony. Its equivalent in the baptismal rite of the Book of Common Prayer is the 'signing with the sign of the Cross' administered by the priest immediately after Baptism.

With these considerations in mind we shall look at some samples of the various patristic conceptions of the seal, noticing first a few examples of the view that the seal is the presence of the Spirit conferred in Baptism, or Baptism itself, then some instances of the idea of the seal as the divine image restored to man through Christ and made available sacramentally in Baptism; thirdly, the much more common notion that the seal is the sign of the Cross; and finally the theory that the believer is stamped as one of the elect through the mysterious potency of the invocation of the Name. With this last view there is to be associated the rather different conception of Baptism in the threefold Name of God as the seal or confirmation of conversion to orthodox faith.

The Seal and Baptism

The eschatological idea of the sealing of the believer in its relation to Baptism is perhaps best illustrated by three passages from the Greek Fathers which date from fairly widely separated periods.

Severian of Gabala asks his congregation: 'How will you enter Paradise without having been sealed by Baptism? The flaming sword turns its back upon the faithful, but presents its edge to the unsealed.'[1] Through Baptism the believer receives the seal of the light of the Lord's countenance which the angels will recognize and acknowledge hereafter. Without the seal he will not be distinguishable as a friend and may be taken for an enemy; he will be like an unbranded sheep, a prey for any robber.[2] A very similar and extremely interesting passage occurs in the imaginary speech which Constantine the Deacon puts into the mouth of the martyrs. It well illustrates the prophylactic aspect of the seal of the Spirit as a defence against the destroying forces of the devil; it repeats the old analogy between the sealing of the elect with the blood of Christ and the anointing of the Passover doorposts, and it equates the seal with the illumination received in Baptism, 'Little children, it is the last hour; the end of all things is at hand. Whoever has not been stamped with the seal of the Spirit let him be stamped with the light of Baptism, and let him anoint with the undefiled blood the pillars of the understanding and the doorposts of the senses. For in no other way shall he escape the destroyer.'[3] More briefly, John of Damascus explains that 'through Baptism we receive the Holy Spirit dwelling in us, which is a royal seal with which the Lord brands his own sheep'.[4]

All these passages are typical of the general thought of the

---

[1] Sever. (ps.-Bas.), *bapt.*, 2 (2, 115; *PG.* 31, 428C).
[2] *Ibid.*, 4 (2, 117B; *PG.* 31, 432C).
[3] *laud.*, 37 (*PG.* 88, 521C).   [4] *confess.*, 3 (*PG.* 95, 285B).

9*

Fathers on the nature of the seal. There is, however, the ambiguity which we have already considered in their use of the word βάπτισμα. We cannot say with certainty that these writers attach the reception of the seal to the actual Baptism in water as distinct from other elements in the rite of initiation. They are perhaps thinking of the entire complex ceremony as they knew it in the East, and in any case their attention is concentrated not on the means by which the seal is received but upon what it is and what its effects will be in the next world.

On the other hand, there are many instances of the connection of the seal, not with 'baptism' but with 'the laver' or 'the font' (κολυμβήθρα), and in some cases the use of these terms by a particular writer will serve to indicate that when he elsewhere uses 'baptism' in this connection he means the actual rite of Baptism in water and not the complex initiation ceremony as a whole. Didymus, for example, says that we are conformed to the primal image as a result of our reception of the seal of the Spirit in Baptism,[1] and elsewhere he associates sealing with regeneration as part of the activity of the Holy Spirit which we experience when we descend into the font.[2] We may therefore assume that in the former passage Didymus is thinking of Baptism in water, as he undoubtedly is in the latter.

Cyril of Jerusalem, whose apparent inconsistencies on this subject might well lend support to the view that the Catechetical Lectures are a composite work,[3] is emphatic that the Spirit's bestowal takes place in the post-baptismal chrismation; yet even he is on one occasion apparently prepared to assign the believer's reception of the seal to the 'laver'.[4] It is in connection with the λουτρόν of Baptism that Chrysostom gives us one of the clearest descriptions of what the early Church understood to be the significance of the 'earnest of the Spirit which the believer receives in Baptism'. In the 'laver', he declares, the Christian has become a king, a priest, and a prophet; he has been made ἔνθους and sealed; for, just as a σφραγίς is laid upon soldiers, so is the Spirit upon the faithful. If you desert Christ's

---

[1] *Trin.*, 2, 15 (*PG.* 39, 717A).   [2] *Ibid.*, 12 (680A).
[3] See W. J. Swaans, 'A propos des Catéchèses Mystagogiques attribuées à S. Cyrille de Jérusalem' (*Le Muséon* 55 (1942), pp. 1–43), who would ascribe the *Catecheses Mysticae* to John of Jerusalem.
[4] *catech.*, 5, 6.

service, you will be detected as a deserter by all men; for the Jews had circumcision as a seal, but we have the earnest of the Spirit.[1] There could be no better illustration of the fundamental meaning which underlies the entire conception of the seal of the Spirit. It is a sign which stamps the Christian as the tattoo-mark distinguished the soldier, signifying the obligation of his calling, and proclaiming him to all the world as a deserter should he break those obligations. The sign is the inward ἀρραβών of the Spirit, and it is given to the faithful through the 'washing' of Baptism.

We have had occasion more than once to notice the common typological comparison between the Christian seal and the blood of the Passover. It is interesting to observe that Gregory Nazianzen makes the comparison between the blood of Christ and the blood of the Passover victim in the context of teaching about the baptismal 'laver'; the effect of the laver is said to be analogous to that of the Passover seal; it preserves the faithful from destruction and stamps them as the elect people of God. The seal which is received in the baptismal laver is applied to infants as a seal to safeguard them from hostile powers and as a sign that they belong to God; for adults, who have sinned, it is more in the nature of a 'cure' (ἄκος).[2]

Many other instances might be cited of passages in which patristic authors speak of Baptism in water (the 'laver', or the 'font') as the medium of the sealing of the faithful with the Holy Spirit. It is therefore not surprising to find that Baptism is itself described as the seal, and, in the light of the passages we have just considered, it is probably fair to assume that this generally means Baptism in water; in some cases, however, it is fairly clear that the whole rite of initiation is indicated, including the final consignation. Constantine, for example, spoke of his baptism as a sealing; no doubt he has in mind the whole of his initiation and is not distinguishing any specific part of it as the medium by which he was sealed, but it remains true that it is primarily the Baptism in water with which he associates the seal, and that in his view it is this which overshadows all the other elements in the complex rite and gives to the whole its meaning and title. Hence he says that he had contemplated the

[1] *hom.* 3. 7 *in* 2 *Cor.* (4, 454A, B). [2] *carm.*, 1, 1, 9, 90 ff.

possibility of receiving the seal at the Jordan.[1] Cyril of Jerusalem, too, speaks of Baptism as comprising remission of sins,
regeneration, the 'shining robe', the unbreakable seal, the
grace of sonship, and other blessings, all of which are brought
together as various aspects of the gift of Baptism; but in this
case we know from other parts of his work that the author
regards the bishop's consignation of the baptized as the moment
of their sealing, and we may conclude that he has in mind the
whole series of baptismal ceremonies and is holding them together under the general heading of 'Baptism'.[2]

The mention of the 'robe' in the last passage to which we
have referred recalls a remarkable development of that conception of baptismal grace which is to be found in the same
author.[3] Here the idea of the robe is brought into close association with that of the seal. Both alike are signs by which the soul
is recognized at the Day of Judgment; both are aspects of the
grace conferred on the believer at his Baptism. The robe must
be preserved unspotted, just as the seal must be kept unbroken,
for if the robe is soiled by sin it will give away the character of
its wearer on the Last Day; he will be revealed as 'hairy', like
Esau, and numbered among the goats.

Baptism, according to Ephrem,[4] is the seal of life, that is to
say, the sign which admits its bearer to eternal life; and it is
Baptism which is compared by Gregory Nazianzen with the
Passover blood by which the elect are marked out for salvation.[5]
It does not, of course, afford an automatic guarantee that the
sealed will be saved, for the seal can be broken by sin, since sin
means the withdrawal of the indwelling presence of the Spirit;
it is only those who can, as it were, point to their unbroken seal,
or to a seal broken, but repaired by penitence, who are numbered among the elect at the Judgment. Nevertheless, the seal
is a 'character' which, as conferring a certain status, is indelible whether the final issue be salvation or damnation.
Basil suggests that the Holy Spirit is specially present with
those who have once received the seal, even though they may

---

[1] ap. Eus., *v. Const.*, 4, 62 (p. 143, 8; *PG.* 20, 1216A) : ὥρα καὶ ἡμᾶς ἀπολαῦσαι τῆς
ἀθανατοποιοῦ σφραγῖδος, ὥρα τοῦ σωτηρίου σφραγίσματος μετασχεῖν· ἐπὶ ῥείθρων
Ἰορδάνου ποταμοῦ τουτ' ἐνενόουν ποτὲ ποιῆσαι.
[2] *procatech.*, 16.   [3] *catech.*, 15, 25.   [4] 2, 6C.
[5] *or.*, 1, 3 (*PG.* 35, 397A).

have lapsed from holiness, and awaits their conversion and salvation.[1]

Of the very numerous cases in which the seal is equated with Baptism, or at least is regarded as conferred by Baptism, we can give only a few more instances. The *Apostolic Constitutions* make the somewhat remarkable assertion that Simon Magus received the seal;[2] this must presumably mean that he was baptized by Philip, not that he was 'confirmed' by Peter and John. Didymus also indicates that the process of sealing is identical with Baptism in water when he declares that we are both 'sealed and baptized' in the Name of the Trinity.[3] There can be little doubt that Didymus is alluding to one and the same moment in the convert's experience, considering it in its external and inward aspects; Baptism is the outward ceremony and 'sealing' is its spiritual effect. There is no reference to two distinct stages in the process of initiation.

The case is not so clear when Ambrose, discussing the general significance of Baptism, reminds his hearer: 'Repete quia accepisti signaculum spiritale, spiritum sapientiae et intellectus, spiritum consilii atque virtutis, spiritum cognitionis atque pietatis, spiritum sancti timoris: et serva quod accepisti. Signavit te Deus Pater, confirmavit te Christus Dominus, et dedit pignus Spiritus in cordibus tuis.'[4] We cannot be certain that Ambrose is concerned to ascribe this 'confirmation' and endowment with the seven-fold gifts of the Holy Spirit to the 'laver' of Baptism. Nevertheless, the context shows that, even though he may well have the entire rite of initiation in mind, it is the actual Baptism which dominates the whole and gives it its general character. A plainer identification of Baptism with the seal is to be found in a striking passage of Chrysostom where he bewails the lot of those who depart this life without 'illumination' and without the 'seal'.[5] Illumination is the special *charisma* of Baptism, so that φωτισμός is one of the commonest synonyms for βάπτισμα. Here it is apparently identical with the 'seal'; at any rate, the seal and the illumination are coupled together so closely that they are clearly regarded as parallel

---

[1] *Spir.*, 16, 40 (*PG.* 32, 141C).
[2] 2, 14, 7.
[3] *Trin.*, 2, 15 (*PG.* 39, 720A).
[4] *myst.*, 7, 42.
[5] *hom.* 3. 4 *in Phil.* (11, 217C).

modes in which the grace of Baptism is made effective. Chrysostom's implication that where illumination is received there also
the believer is sealed—that is, at the font—is brought out with
great clarity in the course of a discussion of the common practice of postponing Baptism until the approach of death. The
recipient of Baptism on his death-bed is said to receive the seal,
which is thus equated absolutely with water-baptism, even
when that Baptism is clinically administered.[1] There is a striking contrast between this view and that which was expressed
in the third century by Cornelius of Rome.

'Eusebius of Alexandria,' in a sermon included among the
spurious works of Chrysostom, expresses a similar opinion to
that of the above passage. He implicitly identifies Baptism with
sealing, for in an appeal to parents not to defer the Baptism of
their children, he explains that: πρόβατον ἀσφράγιστον μερὶς
λύκου; 'for the seal of Christ protects him who possesses the
seal'.[2] This is a typical example of the patristic teaching on the
eschatological significance of the seal as a safeguard against
evil and a defence for those who are marked out by it as people
who belong to Christ's flock. It is important to observe that the
seal is believed to be given in Baptism; 'unbaptized' and 'unsealed' are interchangeable terms. Severian of Gabala similarly
warns the neophytes to whom his baptismal homily is addressed
that Baptism constitutes a seal which must not be broken,[3] and
Theodoret calls Baptism the seal of the Lord's ownership;[4] in
the latter case, however, it would seem that the term 'baptism'
is being used in a wide sense, for Theodoret elsewhere connects
the reception of the seal with chrismation.[5]

The use made by Augustine of the conception of 'sealing'
is especially interesting. For the purpose of his anti-Donatist
argument he identifies Baptism with a seal by means of which
the baptized has been stamped with an indelible character.
Baptism is one and unrepeatable; it must be recognized as
Christ's Baptism by whomsoever it may be administered. It is
true that it cannot be received profitably outside the Christian
Church; a Baptism administered in schism has therefore to be

[1] hom. 7. 4 in Heb. (12, 135C).
[2] serm., 5 (PG. 86, 349A)=ps.-Chrys. scient. (10, 842E).
[3] (ps.-Bas.) bapt., 5 (PG. 31, 433).   [4] h.e., 4, 18, 11 : ἡ δεσποτικὴ σφραγίς.
[5] Cant. i. 2 (2, 30).

made effective through the imposition of hands upon the person schismatically baptized who is thus incorporated into the fellowship of the Spirit, whose distinctive characteristic is possession of the supreme gift of charity. Yet it is Baptism, not the laying on of hands or consignation, which constitutes the *signaculum* by which a man is characterized once and for all. This idea is worked out in a well-known passage in which the metaphor of the military 'sealing' is fully developed.[1] Of course, this sealing is not the bestowal of the seal of the Spirit, for the Spirit is *ex hypothesi* absent from a schismatical sacrament. Nevertheless, it is the permanent impress of the baptismal 'character'. Augustine does not seem to have been pressed to explain how a schismatic could receive the baptismal stamp and yet possess, or at least possess effectively, none of the gifts of grace in which that stamp properly consists. He might have found it a hard doctrine to defend. Nevertheless, he maintains that those who have been baptized in schism have, as it were, been branded with the royal mark, but have still to be brought into possession of the faith which they lacked, in the charity of the Spirit, within the Body of Christ.[2] This conception of the seal is an unusual one, though the military metaphor is to be found in Chrysostom[3] and elsewhere, and in the more fully developed thought of the homily on Baptism falsely ascribed to Eusebius of Emesa the metaphor is so extended as to make it perfectly clear that it is Baptism which constitutes the sealing of the Christian soldier, whereas Confirmation represents his equipment with weapons for the fight.[4] More usual examples of the identification of the seal with Baptism are to be seen in Basil of

[1] ' Si quisque sive desertor, sive qui numquam omnino militavit, nota militari privatum signet, nonne ubi fuerit deprehensus ille signatus pro desertore punitur et eo gravius quo probare potuerit numquam se omnino militasse, simul secum punito, si eum prodiderit, audacissimo signatore? At si forte illum militiae characterem in corpore suo non militans pavidus exhorruerit et ad clementiam imperatoris confugerit ac . . . impetrata venia militare iam coeperit, numquid homine liberato atque correcto character ille repetitur ac non potius agnitus adprobatur?' *Parmen.*, 2, 13, 29.

[2] *ep.*, 88, 9: '. . . non baptismo quem sicut regalem characterem desertores acceperant, sed fidei quae illis defuit, et Spiritus sancti charitati et Christi corpori sociamus.' Cf. *enarr. in Ps.* 39, 1 (*PL*. 36, 433) : 'Baptismus ille tamquam character infixus est : ornabat militem, convincit desertorem.'

[3] *catech.*, 2, 5 (2, 244C).

[4] *hom. Pent.* (Paris, 1547, p. 77) : '. . . ut cum imperator quemcumque in militum receperit numerum, non solum signet receptum sed etiam armis competentibus instruat pugnaturum.'

Seleucia's *Life of Thecla*, in which Thecla is described as 'sealing' many converts in Asia Minor,[1] and Gregentius' account of converted Jews coming to Holy Baptism, and, having received the seal, being enrolled among the Christians.[2] The same equation of the seal and Baptism is to be seen in *Barlaam and Joasaph*.[3]

In a somewhat different sense John Moschus describes Baptism as a sealing. In this case the seal is not a mark of identification but a seal placed on a money-bag to keep it safe.[4] It is worth noticing that the bag is already full before the seal is applied to it; the baptized person is possessed of the Spirit, and has not merely been cleansed of sin to await a further spiritual endowment. The idea here expressed is closely akin to that of Clement's *Excerpta Theodoti*, in which, as we have seen, the suggestion is made that if an impenitent person receives the sacrament devils are sealed up inside his soul.

Another variation from the more normal conceptions of the seal of Baptism is afforded by Gaudentius of Brescia in his comparison of it with a betrothal ring given by Christ to His bride, the Church.[5]

These citations are sufficient to show that Baptism is not only regarded by many of the Fathers in every century as the medium of the Christian's reception of the seal, but is also itself referred to as the seal which marks him as Christ's, and that 'Baptism' generally means baptism in water and nothing else is shown by the many cases in which the seal is identified specifically with the 'laver'. Gregory Nazianzen, for instance, in a remarkable eschatological passage, declares that τὸ λουτρόν ἐστι δευτέρου βίου σφραγίς.[6] In his story of Joseph, the converted Jew, Epiphanius makes the patriarch Ellel ask for the seal in Christ, and in answer to his request water is made ready and he is given the 'laver'.[7] With this equation of sealing with Baptism in water we may compare the notion contained in a late poem that the water from the side of Christ seals the faithful with the Holy Spirit.[8]

---

[1] 1 (*PG.* 85, 557C).   [2] *disp.* (*PG.* 86, 780C).
[3] 18 (*PG.* 96, 1021B): λελυτρωμένος τῆς τοῦ κόσμου ἀπάτης, τὴν σφραγῖδα τηνικαῦτα δέξωμαι τοῦ σωτηρίου βαπτίσματος.
[4] *prat.*, 198 (*PG.* 87, 3085D).   [5] *tract. pasch.*, 8, 23 (*CSEL.* p. 66).
[6] *carm.*, 1, 2, 34, 237.   [7] *haer.*, 30, 4 (p. 339, 10; *PG.* 41, 412B).
[8] ps.-Jo. D., *carm. pent.* (*PG.* 96, 833C).

Another form of this equation of Baptism with the seal is to be seen in the analogy which the Fathers so often draw between circumcision under the Old Covenant and Baptism under the New. For this they had New Testament precedent, and the fourth-century writers could draw on a long exegetical tradition. It is clear from many of the instances of this analogy that the antitype of circumcision is Baptism in water. Lactantius, for example, holds that Christ was baptized 'ut quemadmodum Iudaeos suscepta circumcisione, sic etiam gentes baptismo, id est purifici roris perfusione, salvaret'.[1] Cyril of Jerusalem asserts that we, like Abraham, receive the spiritual seal, being circumcised by the Holy Spirit through the laver with the true circumcision of the heart.[2] The parallel between water-baptism and circumcision is more fully worked out by Aphraates: 'those who are circumcised in their hearts have life and are circumcised in the true Jordan, the Baptism of remission of sins';[3] Baptism is the true fulfilment of the type of circumcision.[4] According to Chrysostom, the seal of the Spirit corresponds to circumcision and it is made available in the 'laver'.[5] Elsewhere he shows that, whereas circumcision consisted in a fleshly 'putting off', the Christian has put off his sins. This has happened in Baptism, when he was symbolically buried—that is, in the font.[6] Epiphanius sees the fulfilment of circumcision in 'Baptism which circumcises us in the name of God'.[7] Here again the seal denotes no form of Confirmation, but simply Baptism in the threefold Name. As a sign by which the faithful are recognized, says Severian, and as a passport with which they may enter Paradise, Baptism corresponds to the ancient distinguishing token of circumcision.[8] The analogy of the two rites receives much attention from Augustine, who sees in the administration of circumcision on the eighth day a type of Christ's resurrection for our justification; the type prefigured our regeneration through the risen Christ.[9] Circumcision was reckoned under the old Covenant for Baptism,[10]

---

[1] *inst. div.*, 4, 15 (*CSEL.* p. 329, 14).
[2] *catech.*, 5, 6.
[3] *dem.*, 11, 10.
[4] *Ibid.*, 12, 6.
[5] *hom.* 2. 2 *in Eph.* (11, 11A–12B).
[6] *hom.* 6. 2 *in Col.* (11, 367C).
[7] *haer.*, 8, 6 (p. 192, 19; *PG.* 41, 213C); cf. id.,*fid.*, 24 (p. 525, 5; *PG.* 42, 829q).
[8] (ps.-Bas.) *bapt.*, 2 (*PG.* 31, 428C).
[9] *Julian*, 6, 18; cf. *pecc. orig.*, 32, 37.
[10] *ep.*, 187, 11, 34.

and Baptism is now as necessary for Christians as circumcision was for the ancient Hebrews.[1] Zeno of Verona makes it clear that in his view the seal of the New Covenant which has replaced circumcision is Baptism, either in water or in the blood of the martyr.[2]

That Baptism itself is considered by many writers to be the medium by which Christians are sealed for a day of redemption is indicated also by their use of the term 'unsealed' to describe the condition, not of the baptized but unconfirmed, but of the unbaptized.[3] It was not the absence of consignation or of the laying on of hands which was held to deprive the soul of its hope of the day of salvation. The Greek Fathers, it is true, sought to hold Baptism and Confirmation together in the unity of a single rite—hence their practice of presbyteral consignation —but their equation of the seal of Baptism with the martyr's blood as a guarantee of redemption is in itself sufficient to show that it was the actual Baptism of water 'informed' by the Spirit which was regarded as the seal without which the soul was doomed to lose its hope of blessedness.

The theory of the baptismal seal is not, however, merely formal and mechanical. Though Baptism is so often called the seal, it is never forgotten that the seal is spiritual, an impress on the soul stamped by the Spirit of God, restoring man to the primal 'likeness' in which he was created. A more profound conception of the seal was thereby developed, an idea of the seal as the imprint on man of the *imago Dei*.

---

[1] *ep.*, 265, 4.   [2] *tractat.*, 1, 13, 11.
[3] Eus. Al., *serm.*, 5 (*PG.* 86, 349A) cf. Or.,*fr. in Pr.* i. 6 (*PG.* 17, 156B); Chrys. in *ibid.* (*PG.* 64, 661D). Gr. Nyss., *bapt. diff.* (*PG.* 46, 424B). Ast. Am., *hom.*, 20 (*PG.* 40, 455C).

CHAPTER TWELVE

THE SEAL OF THE DIVINE IMAGE

THE profound religious idea of the indwelling Spirit of God as a mark set upon the believer in Jesus Christ so as to stamp him as a member of the chosen people of the New Covenant and assure him of his hope of future salvation has little in common with the crude and naïve notions of 'sealing' in popular eschatology except the basic conception of a stamp of divine ownership from which every idea of sealing in the religious sense ultimately springs. In the early centuries of the Christian era, however, popular piety and, to a lesser extent, the teaching of many theologians show dangerous signs of losing their grasp of the deep spiritual significance which the idea of the seal possessed in the New Testament and of reverting to less ethical and less genuinely religious conceptions of it as a semi-magical sign, visible or invisible, by which the sealed could be guaranteed a sure passport to the Kingdom of Heaven. As we shall see, the 'seals' of the Name of the Trinity and of the sign of the Cross, regarded as they so often were in popular Christianity as charms against demons, and tokens of election and future blessedness, lent themselves all too readily to debased theology and cheap superstition. Yet the history of the conception of the seal in the early centuries of the Church is by no means all a story of decadence—of a lapse into materialistic and semi-Gnostic ideas. There is one extremely important aspect of the notion of sealing which, already present in the writings of Philo, became more fully worked out and appreciated as patristic thought developed. This is the idea that the seal consists in the renewal and 're-stamping' of that divine image which man bore at his creation but which was defaced and broken by the Fall.

In the development of this conception the Greek Fathers, together with certain of the Latin theologians, made one of their most important contributions to Christian thought. As applied to baptismal theology, their doctrine of the divine image is of high importance and can yield valuable results for modern thought. We must, however, remember that relatively little of the vast amount of patristic teaching on the subject of the image of God is directly concerned with Baptism. In any case it is far beyond our present scope to try to sketch the outlines of so huge and complicated a subject as the doctrine of the *imago Dei* in the ancient Fathers. What we are concerned to show is that one of the commonest uses of the term 'seal' is to express the thought that by virtue of his divine creation there was impressed upon man the image of God; that this 'seal' was set upon him by the Logos, who is the exact and exhaustive likeness of God, the perfect and complete image of the Father; that when this image had become defaced and obliterated through the Fall (we are not here concerned with the problem whether the image was defaced or totally destroyed, nor need we deal with the relationship of the 'image' to the 'likeness') the archetypal Logos restamped it on man by His Incarnation and the raising of man to participate in the divine nature; and that by incorporation into Christ men receive the renewal of the image through the indwelling of the Spirit. As we might expect, although this conception of the seal has no immediate connection with Baptism, the idea of the indwelling Spirit is so closely related to that of the seal of the image that the thought of Baptism as the medium by which the Spirit is received is never very far from the minds of those who employ the conception of the seal of the image in their theology.

It is sometimes dangerously easy to become so fully preoccupied with detailed problems of the manner of the seal's bestowal—Baptism, consignation, the imposition of hands—and to become so far confused by the patristic tendency to apply the term 'seal' to external rites, that one forgets that orthodox doctrine does not really lose sight of the essential truth that the seal which is impressed upon the faithful is in the last resort no outward sign but the activity and presence of the Holy Spirit. Thus Origen, commenting upon the crucial text, Eph. i. 13, explains that the seal is ἀληθῶς ἐκτύπωσις καὶ τράνωσις τούτων ἃ πρέπει ἐκτυποῦσθαι καὶ τρανοῦσθαι ὑπὸ τοῦ τῆς ἐπαγγελίας πνεύματος,[1] and Didymus remarks that it is the Spirit Himself who is the σφραγίς and the χρῖσμα.[2] Proclus expresses the same truth more obscurely in relation to the Atonement as the antitype of the Passover.[3]

This truth that the Spirit is the seal has an obvious bearing upon the thought that the faithful are sealed with the divine image, a thought which, as we have pointed out, is prominent in the teaching of Philo.[4] The idea that the image of God is impressed as a seal upon man at his creation is briefly and simply explained by the *Clementine Homilies* as: τῇ γὰρ αὐτοῦ μορφῇ ὡς ἐν μεγίστῃ σφραγῖδι τὸν ἄνθρωπον διετυπώσατο.[5] The context of this statement is a discussion of the question why the human body dies in spite of the fact that it bears the stamp of the Creator's image; but elsewhere in these homilies we find that the image impressed upon man is virtually identified with the Spirit of God.[6] A similar equation of the image and the indwelling Spirit had been made by Tatian when he remarked that man, although made in the image of God, became mortal when the Holy Spirit departed from him.[7] This very important conception was developed by Cyril, who interprets the in-breathing of the breath of life to mean that man was 'sealed in the divine image through the Spirit'.[8] The breathing into man of the Spirit of God is also the engraving upon him, through the Spirit, of the image of the divine nature.[9]

It is, of course, as a creature that man bears the impress of the image of God. The Fathers who lay such stress on the idea of man's sealing with the stamp of the divine nature are no pantheists, and they emphasize the truth that the quality of being in the image of God is not a natural endowment of mankind but an ethical and spiritual character bestowed by the grace of God.[10]

---

[1] *Eph.* i. 3 (*JTS.* 3, p. 243, 22).   [2] *Trin.*, 2, 1 (*PG.* 39, 452C).
[3] *or.*, 13, 1 (*PG.* 65, 792B).
[4] Cf. *leg. alleg.*, 1, 12, 13 on the image in Adam.   [5] 17, 7; cf. 16, 19.
[6] 3, 17; 3, 20.   [7] *orat.*, 7 (*PG.* 6, 821A).   [8] *Jo.*, 2 (4, 122B).
[9] *ador.*, 1 (1, 9D); cf. *dial. Trin.*, 7 (5, 638B): τὸ τὴν θείαν ἡμῖν ἐγχάραττον εἰκόνα καὶ σημάντρου δίκην ἐμποιοῦν τὸ ὑπερκόσμιον κάλλος, οὐχί τὸ πνεῦμα ἐστίν; cf. *Jo.*, 9, 1 (4, 822D, E): καθάπερ τινὰ σφραγῖδα τῆς ἑαυτοῦ φύσεως ἐνέπηξεν ὁ Δημιουργὸς τὸ Πνεῦμα ἅγιον, τουτέστιν τὴν πνοὴν τῆς ζωῆς, δι᾽ ἧς πρὸς τὸ ἀρχέτυπον διεπλάττετο κάλλος, ἀπετελεῖτο δὲ κατ᾽ εἰκόνα τοῦ κτίσαντος . . . δυνάμει τοῦ ἐνοικισθέντος αὐτῷ . . . πνεύματος.
[10] Cyr. *dial. Trin.*, 1 (5¹, 393E).

As the result of the Fall the image was lost, or defaced and obscured. Macarius asserts that fallen man bears the image of Cain[1] and Origen goes so far as to maintain that by sinning man comes to be in the image of the devil.[2] It was the object of the divine economy of the Incarnation to restore the image to its original condition. Both in man's creation in the image, and in his restoration to his primitive state, the same agent is active, the Logos who is the 'express image of his person'. The doctrine of redemption which the Greek Fathers worked out in terms of the restoration of the image by the Incarnation of its archetype is well illustrated by a familiar passage of Athanasius;[3] it need not here detain us, but before we go on to examine the relevance of the doctrine of the image to the sealing of the initiates we ought to glance at some expositions of the ancient conception of the Logos as the seal—the stamp which bears the exact likeness of God and reproduces it in the human persons upon whom, like wax, the seal is impressed, so that by His gracious action in redemption the divine image is restored in fallen man.

Christ, says Basil, was sealed (John vi. 27), because the image of the Father was in Him—that is to say, because the impression of the seal of God's image was perfectly displayed in Him.[4] He is sealed and He is the seal which stamps others because He is the Father's image. This is, of course, an idea which had its counterpart in philosophy. The metaphor of a seal is not uncommonly applied to the Platonic ideas, each of which is unique in itself, but capable, like a seal, of reproducing itself in an indefinite number of impressions.[5] It is very often employed by Philo, for whom the seal is the archetypal idea and divine Logos[6] which imprints the stamp of the divine image in the soul.[7] Among the Christian writers it is Cyril who develops most fully the conception of the Second Person of the Trinity as the seal of the divine image. The proof-text, John vi. 27, is adduced by him often. Thus he explains that: ὥσπερ ... ἐν κηρῷ

[1] hom. spir., 5, 2, 3.
[2] Jo., 20, 22 (20) (p. 355, 3; PG. 14, 621A).
[3] inc. 14, 1–2 (PG. 25, 120C).   [4] Spir., 6, 15 (PG. 32, 92A).
[5] Arius Didymus ap. Eus., p.e., 11, 23 (PG. 21, 908); cf. Proclus, def., 1 (Friedlein, p. 90, 14 ff.). See p. 17.
[6] opif. mund., 6, 25, 1.   [7] plant., 5, 18, 1.

τις ἐμπήξει σφραγῖδα χρυσῆν ἤγουν ἐξ ἑτέρας ὕλης πεποιημένην, ὅλην ἐξ ὅλης τὴν αὐτῆς ἐμφέρειαν ἐνσημαίνεται· οὕτω καὶ ὁ Θεὸς καὶ Πατὴρ τοὺς τῆς ἑαυτοῦ φύσεως χαρακτῆρας οὐσιωδῶς ἐμπρέποντας ἔχει τῷ Υἱῷ καὶ τοῦτό ἐστι τὸ ἐσφράγισθαι λέγειν αὐτὸν παρὰ τοῦ Πατρός.[1] Cyril develops this idea further and indicates its bearing upon man's possession of the image of God when he says: σφραγὶς γὰρ τοῦ Θεοῦ ... ὁ Υἱὸς ὅλην αὐτοῦ ... ὁμοίωσιν ἔχων, καὶ ἐν ἰδίῳ κάλλει τὴν τοῦ γεννήσαντος ἀναστράπτων φύσιν· ἐν αὐτῷ δὲ καὶ ἡμᾶς εἰς ὁμοίωσιν ἰδίαν κατασφραγίζει Θεος· εἴπερ εἰς Χριστὸν μορφούμενοι, τὴν ὡς πρὸς Θεὸν εἰκόνα κερδαίνομεν.[2] The theological significance of John vi. 27 is a point of dispute between Cyril, who holds that the Son is naturally the image of the Father, and Nestorius, who maintains that the text signifies the unction of the Son of Man and his 'sealing' after the image of the Father.[3] In the late hymnographer, John Monachus, we find the same thought that the Second Person of the Trinity is both sealed and sealer. In this case the conception is applied to Wisdom.[4]

The stamp of the Logos is naturally connected with the activity of the Holy Spirit. Basil, for example, connects the thought of the illumination of the Spirit by which we are enabled to see Christ, the effulgence of God's glory, with the idea of the impression which is the exact replica of the seal.[5] Tatian had already expressed the connection of the indwelling Spirit with the image and similitude of God,[6] and the connection of the gift of the Spirit with the renewal of the image of God in man is made very clear by Athanasius, when he describes the Holy Spirit as the seal whereby Christ stamps us with the divine image.[7] It is in the writings of Cyril that we find the most explicit teaching on the identity between the restored image in man and the indwelling of the Spirit which man possessed at the first but which he lost through the primal sin. God seals the saints with the Spirit, says Cyril in the context of a discussion of the divine image;[8] and elsewhere he speaks of human nature

[1] regin. (5, 97A).   [2] Ag., 20 (3, 650E).
[3] Jo., 3, 5 (4, 300C ff.).
[4] hymn. Chrys., 8 (PG. 96, 1384B) : σοφία ... ἡ ἀπαράλλακτος τοῦ πατρὸς εἰκών, ἡ ζῶσα σφραγίς ... ὁ ἀκριβὴς χαρακτήρ.
[5] Spir., 26, 64 (PG. 32, 185C).   [6] orat., 15, 1, 2 (PG. 6, 837A, B).
[7] Serap., 1, 23 (PG. 26, 585A).   [8] Jo., 3, 5 (4, 302E).

being refashioned in accordance with the image through participation in the Spirit.[1] He explains that the sealing of the faithful means that Christ is formed in their hearts through their possession of the Spirit.[2] By being sealed with the Spirit we are transformed into the likeness of God.[3]

The ancient idea of the seal has thus acquired a new and deeper significance. It had originally meant, in the main, an external physical marking which served to distinguish the people of the Covenant from those who stood outside the promises of God. This conception, which played so large a part in the apocalyptic literature, was transformed in the New Testament into the idea of the inward 'brand' of the Spirit of God; but this conception of the seal of the Spirit sometimes lacked content and definition. In some of the writings of the Fathers, however, particularly in Cyril and other Greek authors, it is combined with the other Pauline teaching that Christ is formed in the soul of the believer,[4] and that the faithful, 'with unveiled face reflecting as a mirror the glory of the Lord, are transformed into the same image from glory to glory, even as from the Lord the Spirit'.[5]

The idea of the seal of the divine image is very closely related to that of the robe of light, the shining garment of incorruptibility and immortality which the redeemed assume in exchange for the 'coats of skin', the mortal and corruptible nature of sinful humanity which fallen man had worn since his Fall and expulsion from Paradise.[6] The robe of light is sometimes expressly identified with the gift of the Holy Spirit.[7]

The indwelling presence of the Spirit is made available to the believer only as a result of the finished work of Christ. Origen, echoing the Philonic notion that the Holy Spirit did not rest upon the human soul, but only touched it, points out that the Spirit did not rest upon Moses, Joshua, and the prophets, but upon Christ the Spirit of wisdom and understanding did rest,

---

[1] *Jo.*, 11, 10 (4, 988B).   [2] *Is.*, 5, 6 (2, 917E).
[3] *thes.*, 34 (5, 360A).   [4] Gal. iv. 19.   [5] 2 Cor. iii. 18.
[6] Gr. Nyss., *or. catech.*, 8 (*PG.* 45, 33C); Jer., *ep.*, 64, 20: 'Praeceptis Dei lavandi sumus, et cum parati ad indumentum Christi, tunicas pelliceas deposuerimus, tunc induemur veste linea, nihil in se mortis habente, sed tota candida: ut de baptismo consurgentes, cingamus lumbos in veritate, et tota pristinorum peccatorum turpitudo celetur'; cf. the description of Christ as 'tunica natans in aqua', Opt., 5, 10.
[7] e.g. *Hom. Clem.*, 9, 19.

and through Him may in turn rest upon His people.[1] According to Cyril the Spirit did not rest upon man when it was bestowed on him at the Creation, for its presence was temporary, being lost at the Fall; but the Spirit rested upon the Word Incarnate as on the first-fruits of the new creation, and through Him it can now rest upon His people.[2] A few illustrations must suffice of the various modes in which the idea of this 'clothing' with the Spirit, or of the Spirit's 'resting' upon the faithful, finds expression in the Fathers in connection with the notion of 'sealing'.

There is, for example, the curious idea expressed in the *Martyrdom of Matthew*[3] that the heathen are by nature amorphous, but that they receive form through having the image of God stamped upon them by conversion and participation in Christ. Origen links the conception of the image with the 'seal' of Cant. viii. 6.[4] Macarius asserts that to recover the heavenly image man must be born of God. Christ as his father, and the Holy Spirit as his mother, imprint their likeness upon the soul, as human parents stamp their image upon a child.[5] This image in the soul is identified with the seal of the Spirit and with the 'wedding garment';[6] and because the image is impressed upon the soul as by a seal, the believer may perceive within his own soul the image of Christ.[7] Ambrose compares the seal of the image with the tattoo mark worn by slaves and soldiers: Valentinian II had within himself the image of Christ; he was marked with it as with a seal, in the same manner in which 'charactere domini inscribuntur et servuli, et nomine imperatoris signantur milites'.[8] The image thus plays the part of the ancient seal of the covenant, which identifies the faithful and allows them to be numbered among the elect at the Parousia. 'He will set them in two divisions,' says Macarius, 'and those who possess His own sign, that is the seal of the Spirit, He will place on His right hand and address as His own.'[9] It is the 'brand' by which the Shepherd will know His flock: 'Let us seek to possess in ourselves the brand and seal of the Lord;

[1] *hom.* 3. 1 *in Is.* (*PG.* 13, 230C).
[2] *Is.*, 2, 1 (2, 193E); cf. *Joel.*, 2, 35 (3, 228B).
[3] 6.
[4] *schol. in Cant.* viii. 6 (*PG.* 17, 285B).
[5] *hom. spir.*, 28, 4.
[6] *Ibid.*, 30, 5; cf. 15, 35.   [7] *Ibid.*, 25, 3.
[8] *obit. Valent.*, 58.
[9] *hom. spir.*, 5, 12.

because in the time of the Judgment . . . when the Shepherd calls His own flock, as many as have the brand recognize their own Shepherd and the Shepherd makes known those who have his own "seal" and gathers them from all the nations.'[1] The seal which the soul receives during this life will shine forth and clothe the body in glory hereafter.[2] The seal, which he identifies with wisdom, is, according to Synesius, a spiritual sign which constitutes the password for the heavenward journey and is feared by the powers of evil.[3]

A very frequent illustration of the idea of the seal of the image is the simile of a coin stamped with the emperor's portrait. As a coin bears the image of Caesar, so does the believer bear engraved upon himself the seal or stamp of the Spirit and the inscription of the Name of God.[4] The righteous man becomes the Lord's coin and receives the royal $\chi\acute{\alpha}\rho\alpha\gamma\mu\alpha$.[5] Gregory of Nyssa makes much use of this simile, which the Fathers could find in Philo[6] as well as in the story of the tribute-money (where a reference to the divine image in man may have been originally intended by Jesus). Macarius elaborates the illustration. The soul which does not bear the image of the Spirit is like a coin unstamped with the royal portrait; it cannot be put into the royal treasuries of the Kingdom of Heaven, and it is rejected by the Apostles, the merchants of that Kingdom, 'for this is the sign and token of the Lord engraved on the souls, the Spirit of ineffable light'.[7]

The seal of the image is to be discerned in the moral character of the soul. Righteousness, says Clement, is a shining symbol which shows forth the quality of a life which participates in the Holy Spirit; this inward seal in turn expresses itself in an outward token; the light in the face of the believer is the seal or proof of his righteousness.[8] The soul's moral character is the seal by which God recognizes His own; the 'inscription' which the soul bears consists of good works, and the essential character of the seal is the avoidance of wrong-doing, for no one can claim

---

[1] *hom. spir.*, 12, 13.   [2] *Ibid.*
[3] *hymn.*, 1 (3) 530 ff.; 620 ff.   [4] Clem., *exc. Thdot.*, 86. See p. 154.
[5] *str.*, 6, 8 (p. 462, 2; *PG*. 9, 281B).
[6] *plant.*, 5, ap. Eus., *p.e.*, 7, 18 (*PG*. 21, 560B).
[7] *hom. spir.*, 30, 5.
[8] *str.*, 4, 18 (p. 299, 18; *PG*. 8, 1325A); 6, 12 (p. 484, 18; *PG*. 9, 325B).

to be the property of the righteous God who himself acts unrighteously.[1]

It is these conceptions of the seal of the divine image which at a relatively early date begin to make their influence felt upon the theology of Baptism. Tertullian maintains that remission of sins and the restoration of man to the divine likeness are inseparably connected aspects of the grace of Baptism. It should follow that the gift of the Spirit is mediated in the same manner as remission of sins, for the divine likeness is identical with the Spirit's presence in the soul; but, as we have already seen, Tertullian is forced at this point in his argument to correct himself by reference to his interpretation of Acts and to deny that the Spirit is actually communicated in water-baptism[2]— a correction which accords ill with the emphasis which he lays in this passage upon the essential unity of the inward grace of Baptism and the consequent impossibility of separating the negative grace of remission of sins from the positive benefit of the recovery of the image of God and the reception of the Spirit. Methodius says that the seal of the Word of truth is stamped upon the souls of the regenerate—that is, the baptized.[3] The same author draws an elaborate picture of the Church which bears children in the likeness of Christ through the laver of regeneration.[4] The application to baptismal doctrine of the Pauline teaching that Christ is formed within the believer is well illustrated by the phrase of Philo of Carpathus, ὁπόταν μορφωθῇ εἰς τοὺς νεοφωτίστους ὁ Χριστός.[5]

That the recovery of the image is connected with Baptism is implied in Serapion's prayer for the consecration of the baptismal water,[6] and it appears again in the simile used by Gregory Nazianzen as an argument against those who attach decisive importance to the worthiness of the minister of the sacrament; the same image of a king, he maintains, can be engraved either upon an iron or a gold signet: in either case it makes the same impression on the wax.[7] In Didymus this teaching becomes more explicit. The seal which is received in Baptism is the divine image,[8] and the divine image and likeness,

[1] Chrys., hom. 5. 3 in 2 Tim. (11, 688E).
[2] bapt., 5.
[3] symp., 8, 8 (p. 91, 2; PG. 18, 152A).
[4] Ibid., 8, 6 (p. 88, 12; PG. 18, 148B).
[5] Cant., 223 (PG. 40, 141A).
[6] euch., 19, 3.   [7] or., 40, 26 (PG. 36, 396C).   [8] Trin., 2, 15 (PG. 39, 717A).

which Didymus interprets as signifying sinlessness and the freedom of the will, are equated with the baptismal gift of the
Spirit, which in turn is identified with that 'putting on' of
Christ to which he likens the neophyte's assumption of his
baptismal robe.[1] The same doctrine is asserted by Ambrose,
who expounds Eph. i. 13 to the effect that we are sealed with the
Holy Spirit not by nature but by the grace of God. As we die
and are reborn in Christ, so also we are sealed with the Spirit
in order that we may possess the spiritual seal of His brightness
and image. Although we are visibly sealed on the body (it is not
clear whether Ambrose is here thinking of the consignation
with the sign of the Cross or of the actual Baptism which he
has just been discussing), in reality we are sealed in our hearts
so that the Holy Spirit may imprint in us the stamp of the
heavenly image; it is the work of the Spirit to produce in us the
image and similitude of God.

Ambrose elsewhere makes use of the familiar analogy of the
prodigal son's robe and ring: 'Qui autem anulum habet, et
Patrem habet et Filium et Spiritum sanctum; quia signavit nos
Deus, cuius imago Christus, et dedit pignus Spiritum in cordibus nostris, ut sciamus hoc anuli istius qui in manum datur
esse signaculum, quo cordis interiora, factorumque nostrorum
ministeria signantur. Ergo signati sumus, sicut legimus: cre-
dentes inquit, signati estis Spiritu sancto.'[2]

The gift of the Spirit in Baptism is equated with the recovery
of the image (or the likeness, according to each writer's doctrine of the *imago Dei*) because both alike are the consequence
of union with Christ in His death and resurrection, and it is
this union which Baptism symbolizes and effects. This truth is
well expressed in the *De Sacramentis*, where the seal of the Cross
as the sign of the convert's participation in Christ's death is
brought into the closest connection with the seal of the image:
'Quemadmodum Spiritus sanctus in corde, ita etiam Christus

---

[1] *Trin.*, 2, 12 (*PG*. 39, 680) : καταδύοντες μὲν γὰρ ἐν τῇ κολυμβήθρᾳ, εὐδοκίᾳ τοῦ Θεοῦ
καὶ Πατρὸς γυμνούμεθα, τῇ χάριτι τοῦ Πνεύματος αὐτοῦ, τῶν ἁμαρτιῶν, ἀποτιθέμενοι
τὸν παλαιὸν ἄνθρωπον, καὶ τῇ βασιλικῇ αὐτοῦ δυνάμει ἀναγεννώμεθα καὶ σφραγιζόμεθα·
ἀνιόντες δὲ ἐνδυόμεθά τε τὸν Σωτῆρα Χριστόν, στολὴν ἄφθαρτον καὶ ἰσότιμον τοῦ ἀναγεν-
νήσαντος καὶ σφραγίσαντος ἡμᾶς ἁγίου Πνεύματος . . . καὶ αὖθις εὑρισκόμεθα οἷοί περ
ἐπὶ τοῦ πρωτοπλάστου ἐγενήθημεν, ἀναμάρτητοι καὶ αὐτεξούσιοι· ταῦτα γὰρ σημαίνει
ἡ εἰκὼν καὶ ὁμοίωσις.

[2] *exp. in Lc.*, 7, 231.

in corde . . . Ergo unxit te Deus, signavit te Christus. Quomodo? Quia ad crucis ipsius signatus es formam, ad illius passionem accepisti signaculum, ad illius similitudinem et ad
ipsius formam resurgas, ad ipsius vivas figuram, qui peccato
crucifixus est et Deo vivit; et tuus homo vetus in fonte dimersus,
peccato crucifixus est, sed Deo resurrexit.'[1]

It is through the putting on of Christ who is the image of
God that man recovers the image in his own person; and the
putting on of Christ is the essential thing which Baptism denotes.
It is of the union with Christ that Baptism is the figure, the
sharing in Christ's own Baptism which transforms the believer
into the divine image by the formation of Christ within the
soul. This is very clearly explained by Cyril: 'We are transformed, as into the divine image, into Christ Jesus, not by
undergoing a bodily refashioning, but . . . by partaking of
the Holy Spirit, and possessing the riches of Christ Himself
within ourselves . . . for as many of you as were baptized into
Christ have put on Christ.'[2]

It is in the writings of the theologians of the Alexandrian
school that we should naturally expect to find the principal
examples of this theory of baptismal grace, for it is among them
that we see the clearest expression of the view that the 'image'
and 'likeness' consist in freedom from sin and from necessity.
This doctrine is by no means universally held in the Church
of the Fathers. The Antiochene theologians, for instance, tend
to identify the divine image in man with his status as lord over
the irrational creation. It is therefore not surprising that the
conception of Baptism as the means by which the image is
restored to man plays a relatively small part in their thought.
When Theodoret remarks that in Baptism the faithful receive
the τύπος of the resurrection,[3] he probably means that Baptism
is a symbol of resurrection, not that it conveys the stamp or
image of the future 'resurrection personality'. Epiphanius,
indeed, argues against the Audians that Baptism is not κατ'
εἰκόνα.[4] His meaning is hard to discover, however, and it
appears that this is an *argumentum ad homines*, which is not to be
pressed. In those writers, however, who, like Cyril, connect the

[1] 6, 2, 6–7.
[3] Heb. vi. 1 (3, 577).
[2] *Thds.*, 36 (5², 33D).
[4] *haer.*, 70, 5 (p. 237, 20; *PG.* 42, 348A).

regaining of the image with Baptism, there is a complete identification of the seal of the Spirit with the seal of the image. They are not introducing any new element into the doctrine of Baptism, any fresh theory of some extra gift of God additional to the bestowal of the Holy Spirit. Clement had described the indwelling Spirit as a 'shining *character*',[1] and Athanasius[2] explains that the Spirit is the seal by which the Logos seals all things. Those who are sealed are therefore made 'partakers of the divine nature'.

Two important points emerge from this interpretation of the 'seal' in terms of the restoration to man of the image of God. In the first place, the seal, conceived in this way, cannot be regarded (like the Gnostic and pagan sealings) as a quasi-magical sign or formula which automatically offers to the initiate a master-key to open the way to Heaven. It is a moral and spiritual character, and it can be lost; the baptismal robe, according to Cyril of Jerusalem, is, as we have seen, a character of the soul which must be preserved spotless if it is not, by its soiled condition, to reveal its wearer as a 'goat' at the Judgment. It may be renewed by repentance,[3] but the robe, or the presence of the divine image in the soul, presupposes the practice of virtue,[4] for it is only the purified soul which can become fashioned in the image of God.[5] The image is often equated with various aspects of the spiritual life, such as ἀπάθεια and kindred virtues,[6] and is indeed identified with perfection.[7] It is never fully formed in man while he is in his present imperfect state.[8] The Kingdom of Heaven, says pseudo-Maximus, is defined by some as 'the very form of the divine beauty of those who bear the image of the heavenly'.[9] It therefore follows—and this is the second point of importance for us to notice—that the seal of the Spirit, if it be identified with the 'stamp' of the divine image obtained through union with Christ, is not some-

---

[1] *str.*, 4, 18 (p. 299, 18; *PG.* 9, 1325A).
[2] *Serap.*, 1, 23 (*PG.* 26, 584-5).
[3] Cf. Or., *fr.* 14 *in Jer.* (p. 205, 1; *PG.* 13, 569C).
[4] Cf. Or., *hom.* 4. 3 *in Lev.* (p. 318, 4 ff.; *PG.* 12, 436B, C).
[5] Cf. Gr. Nyss., *anim. et res.* (*PG.* 46, 89C).
[6] e.g. id., *hom. opif.*, 5 (*PG.* 44, 137B).
[7] Clem. *str.*, 7, 16 (p. 71, 20; *PG.* 9, 540B).
[8] Mac. Aeg., *hom. spir.*, 25, 5 (*PG.* 34, 669D).
[9] *cap. theol.*, 2, 93 (*PG.* 90, 1169A).

thing which can be fully conferred upon the believer at a single moment, whether sacramentally or otherwise. The formation of Christ in the soul, the conformation of the Christian to the image of Christ, is a process whose completion—the ultimate goal of the spiritual life—is not to be perfectly realized under the conditions of a sinful world. We cannot maintain that a man receives the full imprint of the image of God at a single moment; it follows that he is not fully and perfectly sealed with the Spirit at any one moment of sacramental grace. The sealing is a process of growth and development corresponding to, and indeed identical with, the sanctification of the justified sinner.

It is in Baptism that the image begins to be portrayed in us, and it is completed by the process of spiritual illumination.[1] No sacrament except Baptism can be the medium of the seal when this is interpreted in terms of the divine image, for it must be through the sacrament of union with Christ that Christ begins to be 'formed' in the soul. It is difficult to see how Confirmation could be claimed as the sacramental sign of the seal when it is viewed in this light, although, of course, in the case of those baptized in infancy, Confirmation (as the completion of Baptism at which the conscious faith and instructed knowledge are supplied which were lacking at the actual Baptism) is a moment at which the union with Christ and 'sealing' which were potentially effected at Baptism are made real and significant.

At the same time, Baptism (and Confirmation too) is both actually and potentially effective. Its effect is present and proleptic. The faithful recipient of Baptism is in fact united with Christ in His death and resurrection at the moment of Baptism, and therefore receives the seal of the Spirit and of the image of God. It is also true that his realization of that spiritual union and his understanding of the indwelling presence of the Spirit develop gradually in the course of his Christian life, and will only be completed and perfected when the earthly life is transcended.

There may be many subsidiary moments of spiritual experience, whether mediated through rites and ceremonies of the Church or not, which effect, as it were, a sudden acceleration

[1] Diadoch., perf., 89.

in the slow process of growth, an abrupt upward leap in the gradual ascent towards the full realization of what has already been actually as well as potentially given in the sacrament of Baptism. Even in the case of those who are baptized as full believers, it may well be that Confirmation, viewed as a special blessing with prayer, and as a commissioning of the baptized to share in the missionary task of the apostolic Church, is one such moment—a renewing and increase of the Spirit, and a stage in the process of sealing with the *imago Dei*; but if Baptism is to retain its full significance, Confirmation cannot be regarded as the medium of that initial bestowal of the seal which is identical with becoming 'a member of Christ'. Nor is it the completion of the process of sealing. It is a defect in the teaching of the Fathers that they too often treat the gift of the Spirit as though it were both imparted and fully realized at one single moment. Their doctrine of the seal of the image does something to correct this deficiency and to remind us of the truth that conformation to the image of Christ, or sealing with the Spirit, sacramentally effected in Baptism, remains to be realized and perfected in the process of sanctification which leads to the 'day of redemption' when the seal becomes perfect conformity to the heavenly image.

CHAPTER THIRTEEN

THE SEAL OF THE CROSS

THE mystics and the theologians of the age of the Fathers tended to think of the seal imprinted upon the believer as the impress or stamp of the image of Christ set upon his soul by the agency of the indwelling Spirit of God. To the great mass of ordinary Christians, however, this conception was too profound to be properly understood. Yet it was precisely in the religion of the man in the street that the idea of the seal was strongest. The common believer looked for some plain token that he was really sealed for a day of redemption, branded as one of Christ's flock, marked with a sign of his membership of God's people, assured of a talisman against the powers of darkness, and given a password, as it were, which would ensure his reception by the angels into the gates of Paradise and his acceptance among the 'sheep' at the right hand of the heavenly Judge.

The old Israelite bore the outward sign of his membership of the chosen people, the covenant seal of circumcision. The Christian expected to receive a similar sign, and, like its forerunner in the old dispensation, it must be a visible token. The New Testament idea of the inward seal of the Spirit was scarcely adequate to meet his need. It was too refined and too deeply spiritual a conception to satisfy the superstitious and literal-minded convert from Hellenistic paganism, who wanted a tangible sign of his election and a quasi-magical talisman to protect him from the demons of Satan. Baptism in itself would hardly suffice; the symbolism of washing afforded no obvious token of Christ's ownership; and we may well believe that few converts had the necessary grasp of the fundamental principles of the Gospel to enable them to understand how they had become members of Christ through their Baptism. They needed a sign which could directly and unmistakably symbolize the fact that they had become the property of Christ.

10   261

There was one such *signaculum* which lay ready to hand, the sign of the Cross. We have noticed the evidence of Tertullian for the constant employment of this sign in daily life from a very early date. It served as a protection from evil demons, a sign of recognition among Christians, and a counter to the many gestures with which their pagan neighbours averted the evil eye, turned aside the malignant influence of hostile spirits, or invoked the aid of a beneficent deity. The words σφραγίζειν, *signare*, have as their commonest meaning the sense of 'to sign with the Cross'. This use begins in Greek at least as early as the *Acts of John*,[1] and it occurs in innumerable contexts. We find the practice of crossing oneself employed, for example, at 'grace' at table,[2] at the end of a service,[3] in the Liturgy,[4] and as a pious exercise so constantly practised in daily life that Christians tend to make the sign out of sheer force of habit,[5] and the moralist has to remind them to make it 'in the heart as well as on the brow'[6] in order that it may exert an inward effect upon the soul.[7] 'Sealing' with the Cross is a constant feature of miraculous cures,[8] blessings,[9] consecrations,[10] and ordinations,[11] and it is used in signing the Communion elements.[12] The Cross is depicted on walls and doors, or at least is 'signed' on them,[13] and Christians so constantly 'seal' their persons with this sign that Eusebius sees a fulfilment of the text καταλείψω ἐπ' αὐτῶν σημεῖον (Isa. lxvi. 18) in the fact that all those who have been converted to Christ make use of the saving 'seal'.[14]

References to σφραγίς in this sense, and similar passages on the sign of the Cross in the Latin Fathers, are too numerous to be classified here. For our present purpose it is sufficient to

---

[1] 115 (Lipsius-Bonnet, p. 215).
[2] Thdt., *h.e.*, 4, 18, 11; ps.-Ath., *virg.*, 13 (*PG.* 28, 265C); anon. ap. Cram., *cat. in* 1 Tim. iii. 9.
[3] *Test. Dom.*, 1, 26, 4 ps.-Germ. CP., *contempl.* (*PG.* 98, 409C).
[4] *Lit. Mc.* freq.; *Lit. Jac.* (Brightman, p. 45, 1); etc.
[5] Chrys., *hom.* 10. 5 *in Ac.* (9, 87C).
[6] *dial. Tim. et Aq.* (Conybeare, p. 66, 1; cf. Chrys., *hom.* 54. 4 *in Mt.* (7, 551).
[7] Chrys., *hom.* 87. 2 *in Mt.* (7, 820B).
[8] Pall., *apophth.* (*PG.* 65, 257A); Cass., *Coll.*, 15. 4; Thdt., *h. rel.*, 9 (3, 1188); *ibid.*, 13 (1210); Jo. Mosch., *prat.*, 56 (*PG.* 87, 2912A); Leont Neap. *v. Sym.*, 16, 20; etc.
[9] ps.-Germ. CP., *contempl.* (*PG.* 98, 409C).
[10] Epiph., *haer.*, 30, 12 (p. 348, 14; *PG.* 41, 428A).
[11] Chrys., *Jud. et gent.*, 9 (1, 571A).   [12] *A. Thom.*, 50 (p. 166).
[13] Chrys., *hom.* 54. 4 *in Mt.* (7, 551B).
[14] *d.e.*, 6, 25 (p. 295, 6; *PG.* 22, 484D).

observe two facts. First, that even so early as the latter years of the second century the commonest meaning of σφραγίς is the 'sign of the Cross', and secondly, that this seal connotes a potent weapon against the Devil and his agents. It is therefore a defence against evil of all kinds as well as an offensive instrument of great power. It is as a mighty protective force that the martyrs arm themselves with the 'seal', as countless martyr-acts testify. Dasius, for instance, when he boldly overthrew the apparatus of heathen sacrifice, 'armed his brow with the seal of the Cross of Christ, by whose power he contended mightily against the tyrant'.[1]

It was also a defence against evil influences of a more ordinary kind. Chrysostom attacks the practice, common among the women of his day, of smearing the foreheads of their babies with mud taken from the baths, which was thought to be a potent charm against the evil eye. 'How', he asks, 'could you rightly have the seal (i.e. the baptismal Cross) set by the priest's hand on the forehead where you smeared mud? Do not let this happen . . . but rather from their earliest infancy . . . train them to seal their brow with the hand; and until they are able to do this, make the sign of the Cross on them yourselves.'[2] Chrysostom also tells converts to Christianity that when they venture out of doors they ought not to follow the pagan custom of using lucky charms and incantations, or of 'binding bronze coins of Alexander on their hands or feet'. They must instead say, 'I renounce thee, Satan, and thy pomp and thy worship, and I give my allegiance to Thee, O Christ'. They should then make the sign of the Cross on their foreheads, for the devil cannot harm them when they have taken the seal as Christ's soldiers.[3] Here we find, once more, that military metaphor which is so often used by Christian writers when they seek to explain the idea of the 'seal', and we must return later to consider its implications for the use of consignation after Baptism. For the moment we will glance at one or two examples of the vast number of exceedingly interesting instances in the Fathers of the conception of the seal of the Cross as a prophylactic against

---

[1] *Mart. Dasii*, 11; cf. *Mart. Crispinae*, 4; *Mart. Cononis*, 6; *Mart. Eupli*, 2; *Mart Ariadnae* (*Studi e Testi*, 6, p. 131).
[2] *hom.* 12. 7 *in* 1 *Cor.* (10, 108A).   [3] *catech.*, 2, 5 (2, 244A–C).

demonic powers, for when we turn to the specifically baptismal use of the seal we shall find this idea of great value in helping us to understand why the sealing with the Cross came to acquire such importance in the theology and practice of Christian initiation.

An interesting example of the potency of the sign of the Cross is to be found in Chrysostom's advice to a Christian who enters a Jewish synagogue. 'If', he says, 'you seal your countenance, the evil power which inhabits the synagogue will immediately dash away.'[1] The seal of the Cross, used to consecrate holy water, enables that water to defeat the wizardry of Jews who try to obstruct Christian building operations.[2] It wards off the direct attacks of demons,[3] and the *signaculum crucis* was used for that purpose by Antony in the desert.[4] It is particularly effective for defeating demons when it is used in conjunction with the Name of Christ,[5] and a notable instance of this use of the seal is to be seen in its regular employment in the reception and exorcism of catechumens, to which there is a possible reference in the *Passio Pauli*,[6] and certain allusions in Hippolytus,[7] Ambrose,[8] and Augustine.[9] In all these cases the fundamental idea is that the sign of the Cross is a seal which, as the token of its wearer's status as Christ's own property, is effective to ward off the assaults of the enemy, and as the sign of Satan's ultimate defeat, to put to rout the powers of darkness.

It is not only in this world that the faithful need the protection of the seal which possesses this twofold property. 'Sealing' is primarily an eschatological concept, and the possession of the seal would be most necessary, so popular superstition believed, in the soul's journey to the final abode of the elect. The prayer which we have already noticed in the *Acta Philippi* well expresses the grand object of the semi-pagan convert's hopes and fears. He wants to be 'clothed in Christ's glorious robe, His bright seal . . . in order that he may pass by all the "cosmocratores"

[1] *Jud.*, 8, 7 (1, 687A).
[2] Epiph., *haer.*, 30, 12 (p. 348, 14; *PG.* 41, 428A).
[3] Evagr. Pont., *cap.*, 66.
[4] Cassian., *coll.*, 8, 18; cf. Ath. *v. Ant.*, 13.
[5] Gr. Nyss., *v. Gr. Thaum.* (*PG.* 46, 952C).   [6] 19.
[7] *trad. ap.*, 20, 8.   [8] *myst.*, 4, 20.
[9] *catech. rud.*, 20, 34; *tractat.*, 118, 5 in Jo.; *enarr. in Ps.* 141, 9.

and the evil dragon, our adversary'.[1] The sign of the Cross, marked on the forehead of the Christian was easily identified with the saving sign foreshadowed by Ezekiel,[2] preserving the recipient from the wrath and the adversary, and ensuring his recognition by God's angels when they should come to gather in His harvest and root out the tares for burning.

❧ It was inevitable that the signing of the convert with the Cross should come to be regarded as one of the most important, if not as *the* most important, of the various 'moments' of the ceremony of Christian initiation, for here was the permanent seal which would ensure acceptance for its possessor at the day of redemption. True, the outward signing represents and expresses the inward character conferred by Baptism, and therefore the Fathers are insistent that the seal is no automatic guarantee of salvation; it must be preserved intact.[3] Nevertheless, there can be little doubt that in the mind of the ordinary man the seal of the Cross, especially when conjoined with the mighty Name of the Trinity, was a powerful assurance of his election by God, and a potent defence against the hosts of Satan. ⸸

The Cross which seals the faithful will have its counterpart, when the final struggle begins, which is to usher in the times of the End, in the mark that Antichrist will set upon his own followers to brand them, like cattle, as his own possession.[4] This sign will be imprinted on their right hands or foreheads, so as to render it impossible for them thenceforth to make the Christian sign.[5] The saving seal is given to the believer in his initiation. At what period its administration began we cannot say, but it is undoubtedly early. It is to this sign that the acrostic probably

---

[1] 144.   [2] Tert., *Marc.*, 3, 22 (*CSEL.* p. 416, 1, 19).
[3] For Christian writers τηρεῖν τὴν σφραγῖδα has a different meaning from that which it bears in paganism; it has nothing, as a rule, to do with keeping the secret of a mystery.
[4] Hipp., *antichr.*, 6 (p. 8, 10; *PG.* 10, 733B); cf. Lact. *div. inst.*, 7, 17 (*CSEL.* p. 639, 10).
[5] Ephr., 3, 135F–136B; cf. id. 2, 224F; σκευάζει ὁ τύραννος, ἵνα πάντες τὴν σφραγῖδα τοῦ θηρίου βαστάζωσιν; *ibid.*, 225D: τὴν ἑαυτοῦ (sc. τοῦ δράκοντος) σφραγῖδα ἀντὶ τοῦ σταυροῦ. 3. 140B; δήμαρχοι γὰρ ἀπότομοι σταθήσονται κατὰ τόπον· κἄν τις φέρει μεθ' ἑαυτοῦ τὴν σφραγῖδα τοῦ τυράννου, ἀγοράζει βράχυ βρῶμα; ps.-Ephr. (ps. Isid. H.) *serm de fin. mund.*, 8: 'Nemo potest venundare vel emere . . . nisi qui serpentinum signum in fronte aut in manu habuerint.' The consequence of bearing this seal is to be cast into Gehenna with the Dragon (ps. Hipp., *consumm.*, mund., 28; Ephr. 2, 228D).

refers which is contained in the *Sibylline Oracles*.[1] We have met it in the Acts of Peter,[2] Tertullian (in his allusion to the 'Tau' of Ezekiel) and the *Apostolic Tradition* in which the bishop imparts the seal of the Cross as the concluding act of the baptismal rite.[3] References to the practice occur frequently in the *Acts of Thomas*,[4] and Cyril of Jerusalem describes the seal given in the post-baptismal consignation as a mark corresponding to the high-priest's consecration under the old Covenant.[5] In the *Apostolic Constitutions*, where the gift of the Spirit is associated with the unction administered before Baptism, the 'seal' is nevertheless held to be imparted in the consignation which takes place after the Baptism proper is over. Augustine alludes to the sign of the Cross in a punning reference to the phrase 'frontem non habet', which, as he points out, is equivalent to 'impudens est'. 'Non habeam nudam frontem, tegat eum crux Domini mei.'[6] The sign of the Cross is necessary in every sacramental action: Augustine goes so far as to maintain that, 'signum nisi adhibeatur, sive frontibus credentium, sive ipsi aquae ex qua regenerantur, sive oleo quo chrismate unguntur, sive sacrificio quo aluntur, nihil eorum rite perficitur'.[7]

The last quotation recalls in some measure the unusual idea found in a spurious work of Chrysostom, that the seal of the Cross is like the stamp of a royal signet which is applied to sacraments in order to guarantee the reality of the blessings received therein and confirm the promises of God which are attached to them.[8] The principal purpose of the baptismal seal of the Cross is, however, to afford the believer a permanent safeguard against the attacks of the devil and to enable him to be recognized by the angels as one of the elect. Its prophylactic character is often emphasized by ancient writers, especially, as we should expect, the popular writers of Christian romances. Thus we read in the *Acts of Andrew and Matthew*: 'Then the seven demons came and stood before Andrew wishing to slay him; and seeing the seal upon his brow which the Lord had given him, they were afraid, and could not draw near to him, but fled away.'[9] Hippolytus speaks of Christians who are en-

---

[1] 8, 244 ff.   [2] 5.   [3] 22, 3.   [4] 49, 54.
[5] *catech.*, 22, 7.   [6] *enarr. in Ps.* 141, 9.
[7] *tractat.* 18, 5 *in Jo.*   [8] *ador.*, 1, 2 (3, 822A).   [9] 27.

rolled in Christ's service 'bearing the trophy of victory over death on their foreheads',[1] and an interesting example of this conception of the power of the sign of the Cross occurs in Serapion's prayer for use in the consecration of chrism.[2] Gregory of Nyssa exhorts his readers to hasten as sheep to 'receive the seal and the sign of the Cross, the defence against all evils',[3] that is, they are not to delay in receiving the sign of the Cross at Baptism. The whole idea is well summed up in the Christian eclogue of Severus Rhetor who reproduces in verse the popular conception of the efficacy of the seal of the Cross:

Tityrus. Signum quod perhibent esse crucis Dei . . .
Hoc signum mediis frontibus additum,
Cunctorum pecudum certa salus fuit.

Aegon. . . . Nam cur addubitem, quin homini quoque
Signum prosit idem perpete saeculo,
Quo vis morbida vincitur?[4]

We find the same notion expressed in less lyrical terms in Isidore's reference to the 'crucis figura, quae fidelium frontes ad tutelam salutis praesignat'.[5]

It would be easy to multiply examples of this type of thought, but for our purpose it will be better to turn to a more satisfactory form of the idea of the seal of the Cross as a protecting influence. This is the conception of the seal as a fulfilment of the type of the Passover ritual of the smearing of the doorposts to 'seal' the elect from the wrath of God. We have met this idea already in connection with Baptism itself, and as it was applied to the signing of Christians with the Cross it provided a means whereby the crude popular notions of the branding of Christ's sheep could be transmuted into the thought of the external sign as a symbol of the genuine spiritual consecration of the faithful which is effected by the blood of Christ. Lactantius expresses this view of the baptismal mark of the Cross as follows: 'The Hebrews found safety in the sign of the blood alone, not because sheep's blood possessed such power in itself that it could procure men's safety, but because it was an image

---

[1] *Dan.*, 4, 9 (p. 208, 3).   [2] *euch.*, 25, 2.   [3] *bapt.* (*PG.* 46, 417B).
[4] *carm. bucol. de virtute signi crucis*, 105 ff. (*PL.* 19, 800B).
[5] Isid. H., *fid cath.*, 2, 26, 1–2 (*PL.* 83, 534).

of things to come. For the white lamb without blemish was Christ . . . who when he was sacrificed by these same Jews afforded salvation to all who should mark the sign of blood on their foreheads. Frons enim summum limen est hominis et lignum sanguine delibutum crucis significatio est . . . Quomodo autem vel in qua plaga tuti omnes sint futuri qui signum hoc veri et divini sanguinis in summo corporis sui notaverint, in novissimo libro docebo.'[1] Lactantius does not fulfil this promise to explain the efficacy of the sacred sign, but he has made it sufficiently clear to his readers not only that the ancient Passover ritual was a type of the application to the Christian of the saving blood of the Redeemer, but also that the believer's appropriation of the benefits of Christ's death (effected in Baptism) is visibly symbolized in his reception of the seal of the Cross. Here, therefore, the seal is no longer, as it so often is in popular literature, a magic passport to heaven like the Gnostic seals described in the Book of Jeu, but an outward and visible sign of a genuine spiritual reality. The reality is effected in Baptism, but the symbol which has come to be associated with it is the consignation which follows Baptism.

It is probable that a similar conception underlies the comparison drawn by Priscillian between the marking of the doorposts at the Passover and the sealing of the elect on their foreheads with the blood of Christ so that at the Judgment they may be numbered, not among those who bear the mark of the beast, but among the 'duodecim milia signatorum patriarcharum'.[2] It is, however, primarily to Baptism itself that this passage refers; the idea of consignation is present only by implication. A clearer comparison of the Passover sign with the seal of the Cross is made by Augustine[3] and by John Damascene,[4] who ascribes to the seal the effects of the original bloodsprinkling of the Passover. It is a protection against the destroyer, and it distinguishes the faithful from the general mass of the heathen.

This association of the seal of the Cross with the inward grace of Baptism naturally leads on to the theory that it symbolizes

---

[1] *div. inst.*, 4, 26 (*CSEL.* p. 383, 18 ff.).
[2] *tractat.*, 6, 110–111; cf. the use of *consignare* to describe the Passover smearing, Hil. *tract. myst.*, 2, 9 (*CSEL.* p. 35, 10).
[3] *catech. rud.*, 20, 34.   *f.o.*, 4, 11 (*PG.* 94, 1129B).

and represents the whole of the baptismal 'character' which the believer receives in the sacrament—that, in fact, it signifies his consecration to God. Cyril of Jerusalem explains that consignation gives the Christian a mark corresponding to the 'Holiness to the Lord' on the breastplate of the Aaronic high priest,[1] and in a very remarkable passage Ambrose[2] asserts that the sign of the Cross in the Christian's initiation signifies that conformation to the likeness of Christ in His Death and resurrection which is effected in him by the indwelling of the Holy Spirit. Here the sign of the Cross has actually come to symbolize the most profound spiritual effect of Baptism; it represents the reality of the mystical death and rising again with Christ which lies at the heart of the Biblical theology of Baptism. It is no doubt with a belief of this kind in his mind that the author of the treatise on the Passion included in the *spuria* of Athanasius can say that the 'Christ-bearing man (that is, the man who bears Christ's sign) is as God';[3] and it may be in a metaphor taken from this theory of the baptismal seal that Gregory of Nazianzus speaks of his pre-baptismal instruction branding a good mark upon the candidate, which he must keep inviolate by good living.[4] On the other hand, the external seal of the Cross is an empty and useless thing unless it does in fact represent the true Christian character. It can easily degenerate into a formal and vain pretence. Basil of Seleucia complains that there are those who retain their paganism under the guise of Christianity, 'that while they bear the seal of Christ they may follow in the devil's train'.[5]

From the view that the sign of the Cross is a symbol of the refashioning of the believer after Christ's image through the indwelling of the Holy Spirit, and that it signifies the essential status and character of the Christian, it is no long step to the belief that in the ceremony of sealing with the Cross the gift of the Spirit's indwelling presence is actually bestowed sacramentally. This development of thought was facilitated by the combination in the baptismal rite of the signing with the Cross and the anointing with chrism. The seal of the Cross was made with the chrism, and chrismation (itself a Messianic symbol)

[1] catech., 22, 7.   [2] sacr. 6, 2, 6–7.   [3] pass., 30 (PG. 28, 237A).
[4] or., 40, 44 (PG. 36, 421A).   [5] or., 27, 1 (PG. 85, 309B).

10*

was, as we have seen, frequently associated with the gift of the Spirit. Even without this association, however, the sign of the Cross was itself so potent a symbol that it would inevitably tend to be confused with the Pauline seal of the Spirit, or at least regarded as the means by which the latter was imparted. It was by a natural, albeit unfortunate, chain of ideas that the cruci-form sealing with consecrated chrism came to be regarded as the 'seal of the gift of the Holy Spirit' (the regular phrase by which it is described in the Eastern liturgies). We find this idea expressed in a popular form in the curious *Acts of S. Abdu'l Masich*[1] who was supposedly born in 390. In this story Asher, a Jewish boy, is converted and baptized by his young friends. After the baptism they perforate his ears, a thing forbidden to Jews, and insert in them gold earrings as a pledge (in fact, a 'seal') that he will remain a Christian all his life. On returning home to his mother Asher explains that he is now a bondslave who has had his ear 'bored through' at the door of the baptis-tery, and has sealed ('confirmavi') a covenant with his Lord for ever.[2] Later he meets a bishop and asks him to bless him, sign him with the sign of the Cross, and complete his Baptism. The bishop lays his hand upon him and gives him the *charisma* of the Holy Spirit.[3] Evidently it is the sealing with the Cross which is regarded as the completion of Baptism and the medium of the Spirit. The laying on of hands is for blessing, though it has to some extent become assimilated to consignation as a sign of the Spirit, and perhaps virtually identified with it.

The seal of the Cross, moreover, possesses a high eschato-logical importance such as St. Paul attached to the inward seal of the Spirit. It is a token by which the elect are to be recognized hereafter, and a sign which carries them safely to the abode of the blessed. The Christian upon whom the sign has been set is marked with his owner's brand, signifying his membership of Christ's flock; like a tattooed soldier, is immediately recognized and apprehended if he deserts his Lord's service.[4] The eschato-logical implications of this comparison of the 'sealed' Christian and the soldier are obvious enough. The man who bears the seal receives the due reward when his service is completed. One

---

[1] *Act. Boll.* 5, pp. 1–52.   [2] cap. 4.   [3] *Ibid.*, 9.
[4] Thdr. Mops., *catech.* (Mingana, p. 46).

of the most interesting comparisons between the seal of the Cross and the soldier's identification-mark is to be found in the *Acta Maximiliani*.[1] The young Christian pacifist, called up for service, refuses to the point of death to have the military mark imprinted on his person. To allow this to be done would be sacrilege, since he already bears the mark of Christ, the Cross which was signed upon him when he was sealed for the heavenly *militia*. This sealing had enrolled him in Christ's service: 'Nomen meum iam ad Dominum meum est'; and it is obvious from the very human and evidently authentic account of Maximilian's protest that his extreme and fanatical obstinacy is nourished and supported by the certainty that he has been sealed as one of the elect whom Christ will recognize and claim as His own.

With so many fundamentally important ideas attaching themselves to the use of the sign of the Cross at the close of the ceremony of initiation, it is not surprising that this practice comes to appropriate to itself the function of being the effective sign of the bestowal of the Spirit, and to overshadow both the laying on of hands and the actual unction with chrism as subsidiary rites in Baptism. *Consignatio* comes to stand for all that complex of post-baptismal ceremonies which was gradually separated from Baptism in the West and acquired an independent status as the sacramental rite later known as *confirmatio*. At a relatively early date inscriptions testify to the importance which was attached to 'consignatio',[2] and the word itself becomes the regular technical description of the rite of 'Confirmation' until the latter half of the fifth century when *confirmatio* begins to take its place. Innocent sets the tone for the mediaeval developments of the theory of Confirmation when he directs that the *consignatio* must be performed by bishops alone.[3] In the East, where the ceremonies of initiation retain their unity, it is the seal, in the sense of consignation, which is distinguished from Baptism as an element in the complex rite which bears its own weighty significance.[4] The general, though by no means absolute, reservation of the administration of consignation to

---

[1] Knopf, p. 86.
[2] Cf. 'D. P. Picentiae Legitimae Neophytae Die V Kal. Sep. Consignatae a Liberio Papa', Rossi, *Bull.*, 1869, p. 23, 26.
[3] *ep.*, 25, 3.   [4] e.g. Thdr. Stud., *epp.*, 2, 219 *qu.* 14 (*PG.* 99, 1665A).

bishops (so far as the West was concerned), and the Eastern practice of restricting to them the consecration of the chrism, represent a potent factor in the growth in importance of the seal of the Cross.

Normally, except perhaps in Syria, where sealing with the Cross tended to precede Baptism, the consignation was the last ceremony of a candidate's initiation. It marked his final acceptance into the Church as a baptized member entitled to all the privileges of Churchmanship, and, in particular to participate with his fellow believers in the Eucharist which immediately followed the initiation service. Originally the bishop was the minister of Baptism together with its subsidiary ceremonies as these came to be developed. It was fitting that the act which marked the completion of the baptismal rite should continue to be performed by the bishop in person even when the main ceremony of Baptism had perforce to be delegated to others, for not only was the candidate being signed with the sign of the Cross as a member of Christ's flock, but, in virtue of being stamped with the brand of Christ he was being received into the congregation of the local Christian community. It would inevitably fall to the lot of the bishop as the head of that community to administer the sealing which denoted the new member's complete acceptance as an initiated brother; the laying on of his hands in blessing would either take place at the same stage in the initiation, or the act of consignation would be identified with that of the laying on of hands—which in fact happened very frequently.

It should be observed that, if, as Thornton holds, the term σφραγίς had an 'unbroken ancestry reaching back into the New Testament' and always meant the application of the 'holy chrism' by the hand of a bishop, it would not be right to claim the unanimous witness of the Fathers for the view, also maintained by Thornton, that its administration was always confined to the apostles and their successors the bishops.[1] Basil of Seleucia describes a woman (Thecla) not only preaching the Word and catechizing, but also 'sealing many people and enlisting them for Christ'.[2] It is scarcely to be supposed that Thecla was sealing her converts with chrism consecrated for her

---

[1] *Confirmation Today*, p. 7, 10.   [2] *v. Thecl.* 1 (*PG.* 85, 557C).

by St. Paul, and it is to be doubted whether Thornton is prepared to recognize Thecla as an apostle, although she is given that title on at least one occasion in antiquity.[1] The answer, no doubt, is that Basil is here preserving the ancient and proper sense of the 'seal', that is, Baptism.

If, however, we accept the fact that the seal of the Spirit in Baptism is one thing and the seal of the Cross in the consignation is another, notwithstanding the unfortunate fact that the two were often confused, we shall recognize that it was fitting that consignation and the imposition of hands should be administered by the head of the local Christian community. At the same time it must be admitted that the retention of episcopal consignation inevitably tended to depreciate the importance of Baptism. It is by union with Christ and his consequent possession of the Spirit that the believer becomes a member of Christ's flock and can be received into the congregation of His people. It is in Baptism that union with Christ and the gift of His Spirit are sacramentally received. It is therefore to Baptism that the sealing with the sign of the Cross rightly belongs.[2] In the context of the actual Baptism it is an edifying piece of symbolism giving visible expression to a part of what has been effected at the font; but if it is administered apart from Baptism it tends to acquire an undue prominence and to come to be regarded as the outward sign of the inward seal of the Holy Spirit. The Gospel sacrament is thereby deprived of its positive significance and a minor, albeit impressive, symbolical action is exalted in its place. It is far more appropriate that the seal of the Cross should be given, as it is in the Anglican rite, during the actual service of Baptism, for it is when the candidate is baptized into Christ Jesus in the name of the Trinity that he becomes one of the covenant people, enrolled in Christ's service. The chief loss in symbolism which has occurred through the incorporation of the seal of the Cross in Baptism and its omission in the post-baptismal Confirmation

---

[1] *Act. Paul et Thecl.* (Grabe, *cod.*, G; Lipsius-Bonnet, p. 272, 20).
[2] It was by a duplication of the anointing and signing of the candidate, so that these ceremonies took place both immediately after Baptism and also at 'Confirmation'—a practice especially typical of Roman usage—and the latter was reserved for the bishop, that the separation of Confirmation from Baptism was rendered liturgically possible.

(or rather, perhaps, through the retention of the presbyteral signing which immediately followed Baptism and the omission of the episcopal signing which came later) is that the sign is no longer made with chrism, and is therefore deprived of its Messianic connotations; but that the sealing no longer demonstrates that the baptized has become a sharer in the royal and priestly character of the Christ is not a serious defect. It was the signing rather than the unction which came in ancient times to acquire so much significance; although the symbolism of chrismation was appreciated, and often expounded in homilies to the newly baptized, it was not the unction which was regarded with the most veneration as the seal for eternity; it was the potent sign of the Cross, the emblem before which the devils trembled.

Nor was it a grave loss that the signing of the candidate should no longer be performed, as a general rule, by the bishop. The change in the bishop's status from that of a 'parish priest' to that of a diocesan prelate might well suggest that the ceremony should be administered by the local head of the Church, no longer the bishop but the priest. It is proper that the bishop should administer Confirmation to those baptized in infancy, and that he should bless those baptized as adults and give them a token of their incorporation into the missionary and apostolic Church; but the seal of the Cross is properly baptismal. It should not be connected with Confirmation, and its association with the latter rite was due in large measure to the confusion which existed in the age of the Fathers between the different forms of 'sealing'—a confusion which was relatively harmless so long as the ceremonies of initiation were bound together as a unity, but which became intolerable when the rite had disintegrated.

The question arises whether the great and often superstitious value attached to the external seal of the Cross at Baptism led Christians to inscribe the sign visibly and permanently upon their persons. A case may be made for the view that the practice of tattooing the sign of the Cross upon the forehead was not unknown in Christian antiquity.[1] The analogy of pagan and

---

[1] Mr. R. H. Barrow treated this topic in a paper read to the Oxford Classical Association in June 1948, and kindly exchanged notes and references with me. He would maintain that the evidence for the existence of such a practice is more extensive than appears to me to be the case.

Hebrew practices of religious 'sealing' suggests the likelihood that Christians, too, may have sought to place themselves under the guardianship of Christ by wearing the permanent impress of the sign of His personal ownership. If the initiates in the mystery cults bore a visible sign that they had been sealed,[1] it is not improbable that the Christian converts, whose Baptism was so often described in terms of a mystery-initiation, may sometimes have worn a similar mark. Such a practice would make a strong appeal to the more literal-minded among those Christians whose eschatology included the idea that at the Judgment the elect would be distinguished by a visible mark such as that described by Ezekiel.

The actual evidence for such a practice is singularly hard to assess. There is the possibility that some modern examples of the painting or tattooing of the sign of the Cross may represent survivals of ancient Christian usage.[2] There is also a large array of passages in the ancient authors which appear at first sight to suggest that the mark of the Cross was actually so worn. On closer examination, however, the number must probably be drastically reduced, for the language used by the Fathers to describe the normal signing of the neophyte with chrism is so realistic, and so full of metaphors drawn from the tattooing of soldiers (metaphors which are applied both to consignation and to Baptism that it is very easy to be deceived into taking as a literal statement of fact what is really only the picturesque language of rhetorical preaching.

In the *Acts of Andrew and Matthew*, for example, the seven demons are deterred from attacking the Apostle, as we have already mentioned, by the sight of the seal of the Cross upon his forehead;[3] but whether we ought to suppose that St. Andrew really wore a visible Cross is extremely doubtful. The author probably thinks that the demons perceived Andrew's 'character' as one who had been signed with the Cross; the baptismal

[1] See above, pp. 24 ff.
[2] e.g. the practice current among the Copts of tattooing a cross on the forearm, and perhaps the custom, noticed by Bruce about the year 1765, which was followed by a fair-skinned tribe in the Aurez Mountains of Numidia; these people acknowledged that their ancestors had been Christians: 'Each individual of this tribe has a Greek cross marked with antimony between the eyes' (James Bruce, *Travels*, abridged edn., 1812, pp. 27–8).
[3] 27.

seal is still present, as it were, on his forehead, and capable of being seen by supernatural beings. Hippolytus makes a comparison between those who are enrolled in Christ's army, and those who are enlisted in the service of the emperor; he describes the former as those who 'bear the trophy on their brow';[1] but again the language is probably metaphorical. Other similar passages[2] exhibit the same use of exaggerated metaphor, which, if it were to be read as a sober statement of fact, would certainly suggest that the visible badge of the Cross was commonly worn in antiquity. Eusebius speaks of the Apostles as 'like us, sealed on their faces with the seal of Christ',[3] and Augustine, moralizing on the story of David and Goliath, remarks: 'Evacuata frons est quae habebat impudentiam superbiae suae; et vicit frons quae habebat humilitatem crucis Christi. Propterea et nos signum ipsum crucis in fronte portamus, qui illud intellegit . . . Factorem quaerit Deus signorum suorum, non pictorem. Si portas in fronte signum humilitatis Christi, porta in corde imitationem humilitatis Christi.'[4]

The language employed to describe the seal of the Cross often suggests that the seal was occasionally, at least, a physical mark. Such expressions as *conscribere*,[5] and *notare*[6] are rather startling and violent metaphors; one wonders whether they are sometimes intended to be taken literally. Even the use of the word *pingere* which so frequently denotes the making of the sign of the Cross is a little hard to understand unless the Cross was sometimes really painted on the person of the believer. The view that these expressions are not invariably used metaphorically might receive some support from the narrative of the conversion of Jews in Minorca contained in the *spuria* of Augustine. It is there stated that: 'Reversi itaque ad ecclesiam, et toto corde Domino gratias referentes, ilico in frontibus eorum signum salutis *impinximus*.'[7]

On the other hand, the word *pingere* is used quite generally of making the sign of the Cross, even as a gesture, and when, for instance, Jerome urges his readers: 'Ad omnem actum manus pingat Domini crucem', he does not really mean that

---

[1] *Dan.*, 4, 9 (p. 208, 3).
[2] e.g. Pontius, *v. Cypr.*, 7.
[3] *d.e.*, 9, 14 (p. 434, 28; *PG.* 22, 701A).
[4] *serm.*, 32, 12–13.
[5] e.g. Lact., *div. inst.*, 4, 26.
[6] *Ibid.*, cf. Prudent. *cathem.*, 9, 84.
[7] *ep. Sever.*, 12 (Aug., Ben. 8², 18D).

the Christian ought to be constantly *painting* the sign. Most of the examples which we have been considering refer to the baptismal consignation and its indelible character, not to any permanent physical marking. Thus, when Chrysostom says that the sign of the Cross is to be found everywhere, παρὰ ἄρχουσι, παρὰ ἀρχομένοις, παρὰ γυναιξί, παρὰ ἀνδράσι, παρὰ παρθένοις, παρὰ γεγαμημένοις, παρὰ δούλοις, παρὰ ἐλευθέροις· καὶ γὰρ συνεχῶς αὐτὸ ἅπαντες ἐγχαράττουσιν ἐπὶ τοῦ τῶν μελῶν ἡμῶν ἐπισημοτέρου μέρους, καὶ ὥσπερ ἐν στήλῃ ἐπὶ τοῦ μετώπου καθ' ἑκάστην ἡμέραν διατυπούμενον περιφέρουσιν,[1] he is not really telling us, in spite of his use of ἐγχαράττειν, that the sign is given any permanent form; he is merely talking about the ordinary custom of making the sign of the Cross with the hand. The same interpretation ought probably to be given to the rather more doubtful passage in which Chrysostom says that Christians 'inscribe' the Cross on their houses and on their doors, as well as on their foreheads, as a protection against demonic powers ;[2] the signing does not seem to have taken the form of a permanent visible mark. When Ambrose draws his rather extravagant analogy between the 'stamp' which marked Valentinian II and the tattoo mark on the imperial soldiers, he is comparing the soldier's sign with the inward seal of the image of Christ which Valentinian wore in his soul, not with any external mark which he might be supposed to have worn.[3] Even the picturesque language of Gregory of Tours gives us no more than a rhetorical allusion to the baptismal consignation when he writes, 'Quis est hic numinibus nostris contrarius, ac Christianae religionis socius qui frontem chrismatis inscriptione signatum ferat, lignumque crucis adoret?'[4]

There are, moreover, certain pieces of evidence which point directly away from the idea that Christians were actually sealed with a visible sign. Minucius Felix, it must not be forgotten, declares: 'Nos denique, non notaculo corporis, ut putatis, sed innocentiae ac modestiae signo facile dinoscimus.'[5] The pseudo-Athanasian treatise on the Pascha speaks of the Christian's 'hidden seal' which forms the γνωρίσματα τῆς στρατίας.[6]

---

[1] *Jud. et gent.*, 9 (1, 571A).
[3] *obit Valent.*, 58.
[5] *Oct.*, 31.

[2] *hom.* 54. 4 *in Mt.* (7, 551B-D).
[4] *glor. mart.*, 40 (*PL.* 71, 742).
[6] *pasch.*, 5 (*PG.* 28, 1085D).

Nevertheless, there must have been some reason for the pre-
valence of the idea which Minucius Felix contradicts, and the
fact that the Christian seal is an invisible thing does not necessarily compel us to hold that no Christians at any time wore an
external badge. It was certainly expected that in the hereafter
the elect would bear a visible token of their salvation,[1] and
some individuals may well have thought it desirable to antici-
pate that time. There were, too, plenty of pagan and Jewish
precedents for such a practice, and similar customs prevailed
in some heretical or quasi-Christian circles. We read, for instance, of a Manichaean monk named Clementianus, who had
'written on his thigh' the inscription 'Manichaeus discipulus
Christi Jesu',[2] and some such custom, prevailing in Gnostic
quarters, may possibly underlie the obscure account given by
Epiphanius of an image at Alexandria, borne in procession at
the temple of Kore on the night corresponding to Epiphany,
which had a golden 'seal' of a cross upon the forehead, on
either hand, and on the knees.[3]

Further, even when we have discarded the ambiguous passages which probably refer metaphorically to the baptismal
consignation there remain a few instances where the language
of the writer is scarcely intelligible unless he is alluding to a
literal marking of the seal of the Cross upon a believer. There
is, for example, the curious statement in the pseudo-Pionian
Life of Polycarp that πιστὴ παρθένος . . . εἶδεν . . . τὸν τράχηλον
αὐτοῦ λαμπρὸν ὡς χιόνα καὶ σφραγῖδα ἐπάνω,[4] with which we
may compare Lucian's reference to the wearing of a religious
tattoo mark on the neck.[5] It is not entirely clear that Chrysostom
is speaking metaphorically when he says that Christian
emperors 'bear the Cross on their brows above their diadems'.[6]
There is at least one piece of positive evidence that some
Christians did mark themselves with a visible and permanent
badge of the Cross. At the outbreak of a persecution the martyr
Glyceria[7] addressed her fellow Christians, exhorting them to
remain faithful: ἀδελφοὶ . . . ὁρᾶτε ποίου βασιλέως τὸν χαρακτῆρα
ἔχομεν, καὶ ποίῳ τύπῳ ἐν τῷ μετώπῳ ἐσφραγίσθημεν καὶ ποίου

[1] Cf. Ephr., 3, 135F–136B.   [2] Vict. Vit., *persec. Vand.*, 2 (*PL.* 58, 201).
[3] *haer.*, 51, 22 (p. 285, 18).   [4] 21.
[5] *De Dea Syr.*, 59.   [6] *exp. in Ps.* 109, 6 (5, 259B).
[7] *Act. SS.*, May 3rd, pp. 12 ff.

νομίσματος τὴν ἐπιγραφὴν παρειλήφαμεν . . . σπεύσωμεν διὰ τοῦ δεσποτικοῦ νομίσματος σῶοι εὑρεθῆναι παρὰ τῷ αἰωνίῳ βασιλεῖ, ἔχοντες τὸν χαρακτῆρα ἄσπιλον.¹ This is the normal rhetorical imagery which was so frequently applied to the baptismal seal of consignation. Then, however, we read: ἐξῆλθεν οὖν καὶ ἡ ἁγία Γλυκερία, ἐπιγράψασα ἐπὶ τὸ μέτωπον αὐτῆς τὸ σημεῖον τοῦ σταυροῦ τοῦ χριστοῦ μέσον τοῦ προσώπου πρός φωτισμὸν τῆς ψυχῆς . . . σείσασα τὴν χεῖρα τῷ ὄχλῳ λέγει· βλέπετε τὴν ἐπὶ τοῦ μετώπου μου γραφεῖσαν φωτεινὴν λαμπάδα; καὶ εἰποῦσα ταῦτα, ἔδειξε τὸν σταυρὸν τοῦ χριστοῦ.² It would hardly be reasonable, even in the picturesque exaggeration of highly coloured rhetoric, to ask a group of people whether they *saw* the invisible seal of consignation; there is nothing to suggest that the crowd was given miraculous insight to perceive it, as St. Paul's 'shining seal' was revealed to Xanthippe; and we may therefore conclude that Glyceria did actually paint a cross on her forehead in some way or other. It would be unsafe to generalize from a single dramatic action performed in the stress of an emergency; but, taken together with the less unambiguous pieces of evidence cited above, it may reasonably suggest to us that there were Christians, at least occasionally, who translated the idea of the seal of the Cross into outward and visible form. That such a practice could be followed, even if only by a very few Christians, suffices in itself to demonstrate the importance of the seal in the popular mind.

In the sense of a visible badge of Christianity, and as a protection against evil powers, the seal of the Cross does not differ greatly, so far as the underlying theory of it is concerned, from the Carpocratian 'sealing' of the tip of the right ear as a talisman against the demons and a sign of recognition for the elect of God. This conception of the seal is liable to degenerate into a kind of fetichism, and it is to the credit of the early Church that the evidence for the wearing of a tangible external sign which should serve as a passport to salvation is no stronger than in fact we have seen it to be. The association of the Scriptural conception of the Covenant-seal of the elect with external signs and ceremonies was developed fully enough in many quarters to cause much theological and liturgical

¹ *Act. SS.*, May 3rd, 2. ² *Ibid.*, 3.

confusion, for such ideas do not readily adapt themselves to the New Covenant of the Spirit; but the exaggerated and often superstitious reverence which was paid by popular piety to the seal of consignation at least stopped short of the introduction into orthodox Catholicism either of the use of such physical 'seals' as those employed by Heracleon and the Carpocratians, or of the revival of something like the circumcision seal of the Old Covenant of Israel.

Note: The anointing of the neophyte with chrism is, as we have seen, often regarded by patristic authors as the sacramental medium of the gift of the Spirit. It follows that for those writers who hold this view the actual ceremony of unction is closely connected with the reception of the 'seal'.[1] Nevertheless, in the consignation administered by the bishop with chrism, it is generally the sign of the Cross and not the anointing *per se* which constitutes the outward sealing. Though the sealing with the Cross is accompanied by unction, the one being the stamp of Christ's ownership and the other the sign of participation in His Messianic character, yet they are not identical, and it is to the former that the term 'seal' is usually reserved.

It is in the popular literature, especially when it is coloured by Gnostic beliefs, that we find the greatest importance attached to the ceremony of anointing in relation to the sealing of initiates. According to the *Acts of Thomas*, the Apostle prepared for the administration of a baptism by ordering oil to be brought, 'in order that through the oil they might receive the seal'.[2] This is one case where something like the 'baptism in oil' of which Dix speaks really takes place. The Gnostics' fondness for oil, and their readiness to allow it a degree of respectability which they often denied to mere water, are very odd features of their practice. Certainly the seal in the *Acts of Thomas* is more than a signing of the Cross with chrism; it derives its efficacy from being connected, or identified, with the unction by which the Name, the Power of Christ, and the Holy Spirit were brought down upon the initiate.[3] The Manichaeans appear to have followed the example of the Gnostics, and to

---

[1] Cf. Ath., *Ar.*, 1, 47 (*PG.* 26, 109B); *Serap.*, 1, 23 (584C); Cyr. H., *catech.*, 22, 7.
[2] 26 (Lipsius-Bonnet, p. 142, 4).   [3] *Ibid.*, 121 (p. 230, 22).

have been willing enough to employ a sealing with oil when they refused at the same time to admit the use of Baptism in water.[1] The probability is that it was chiefly on the fringes of Christian orthodoxy, or beyond them, that the symbol of chrismation (which may have been employed from an early date as a visible sign of the believer's participation in the priesthood and royalty of Christ) was exalted into a sacrament of salvation or of the gift of the Spirit, overshadowing Baptism in importance even when it did not entirely extrude it from its rightful esteem, and was recognized as the means by which the convert was sealed for eternity.

This is not to say that the idea that unction, as distinct from the sign of the Cross, constitutes the seal is absent from orthodox writings. When Origen describes the oil as the symbol of the gift of the Spirit, and explains that by receiving the Spirit the convert regains his 'robe and ring', he approaches closely to the conception of the unction as the medium of the believer's seal, for the Prodigal's ring stands for the seal of the Spirit or of the *imago Dei*. The strongest evidence, however, for the fact that in some orthodox quarters the seal was virtually identified with chrismation itself comes from the Syrian writers. Ephrem ascribes to unction the eschatological function of the Christian seal: it conveys a distinguishing 'character' which marks off Christ's people; it is the 'olei obsignatio' which turns men from wolves into Christ's sheep.[2] It must, however, be observed that an allusion to the sign of the Cross immediately follows this statement, and it is hard to say whether Ephrem ascribes the virtue of the seal primarily to the anointing or to the signing with the Cross. Although the oil is said to represent the blood of Christ,[3] and the descent of the Trinity to abide in the anointed is mediated through unction,[4] it is nevertheless the Cross which constitutes the 'signum vivificum' and 'vexillum regale' which Christ's flock receives as its brand. In the *Liturgical Homilies* of Narsai, although the idea of a sealing with oil is inextricably bound up with that of the brand of the Cross, the oil of anointing is spoken of as the seal (*rushmâ*), and we are told that, 'an armour is the oil with which the earth-born are anointed, that

[1] *Disp. Phot.*, 45 (*PG.* 88, 572C).   [2] *hymn. Epiph.*, 3, 7 (Lamy, 1, p. 32).
[3] *Ibid.*, 10 (p. 34).   [4] *Ibid.*, 16 (p. 36).

they may not be captured by the evil spirits in the hidden warfare. It is the great brand of the King of Kings with which they
are stamped . . . He marks their faces with the brand of the
oil.'[1] A good deal more importance is attributed here to the
anointing than we normally find in the orthodox Fathers.
Ephrem, again, compares the 'oleum Christi' with circumcision
under the old Covenant,[2] which implies that the anointing is a
seal. The *Apostolic Constitutions*, somewhat hard put to it to find
a good reason for the addition of the bishop's unction, administered after Baptism, to the pre-baptismal anointing which,
as in the *Didascalia*, confers the Spirit, maintain that it is a seal
of the covenants entered into at Baptism;[3] but this is a very
different conception of the seal from that of the mark singling
out the elect for salvation.

The symbolism of unction is, of course, always connected
very closely with that of the bestowal of the seal of the Cross.
This is true of every form of the initiatory rite, from Hippolytus
onwards—though even in the *Apostolic Tradition* it is not the
anointing as such, but the signing with the Cross which is
described as a 'seal'. This intimate connection of the two is
particularly noticeable in Innocent's claim for the bishop of the
sole right 'frontem ex eodem oleo signare'.[4] Nevertheless, the
unction itself is not often regarded as the medium of sealing
except in so far as chrism is the material with which the seal of
the Cross is 'painted'. The allusion of Didymus to 'the saving
seal and the divine chrism'[5] is probably metaphorical, and
denotes the inward seal or unction of the Spirit conferred in
Baptism. When Leo says that 'renati per aquam et Spiritum
sanctum, accepistis chrisma salutis et signaculum vitae
aeternae',[6] he certainly has in mind the external rite of unction,
but it is probably the sign of the Cross which constitutes the
seal. Occasionally, however, the influence of typology leads to a
clearer identification of sealing with anointing; thus Theodoret
says that the baptized 'receive as a royal seal the unction of
the πνευματικὸν μύρον which symbolizes the unseen grace of
the Holy Spirit'.[7]

---

[1] *hom.* 22 (B), Connolly, *TS.* 8, pp. 40, 43–4.
[2] *hymn. Epiph.*, 3, 1–7 (Lamy, 1, pp. 28 ff.).
[3] 7, 22, 2.
[4] *ep.*, 25, 3 (*PL.* 56, 515C).
[5] *Trin.*, 2, 1 (*PG.* 39, 452C).
[6] *serm.*, 24, 6.
[7] *Cant.* i. 2 (2, 30).

A passage in the Areopagite which is often quoted as an example of the idea of the seal of chrismation almost certainly refers to the practice of signing new converts with the Cross upon entering the catechumenate.[1] We are on much surer ground when we turn to the famous 'canon' falsely assigned to the Council of Constantinople (381) as its seventh canon. This enactment, dated about 465 and reproduced in canon 95 of the Council in Trullo, explicitly identifies unction with sealing and declares that through it the gift of the Spirit is bestowed. It contains the standard formula of the Greek Confirmation rite, 'The seal of the gift of Holy Spirit', which in the liturgies is recited at the moment of consignation with chrism.

It may be observed that σφραγίζειν is occasionally used to describe the admission of heretics into the Church when no explicit account is given of what the outward rite of sealing actually comprises. We read in Mark the Deacon of an Arian ship's captain who was 're-sealed' at sea during a violent storm. His admission into the Church took place at the urgent request of the passengers who attributed their peril to the presence of the heretic on board; but we are not told anything of the way in which the 'sealing' took place. Probably we should understand consignation with chrism.

Unction with chrism, we may conclude, signified participation in Christ's priesthood and Messianic character, and, according to some writers, it conveyed the gift of the Spirit. It was therefore accorded a high degree of importance, but it has relatively little to do with the actual sealing of the initiate, except in so far as it was thought to be the medium of the activity of the Spirit who seals the believer inwardly.

We do not find the laying on of hands explicitly equated with the seal, and an implicit connection between them exists only in so far as consignation and the laying on of hands were virtually identified, so that what is properly the function of the one could be attributed to the other.

[1] e.h., 2, 3, 4 (PG. 3, 400D).

CHAPTER FOURTEEN

THE SEAL OF THE NAME

CLOSELY allied to the conception of the baptized Christian as one who is sealed for salvation with the sign of the Cross there is the idea that he is 'stamped' at his baptism with the name of Christ or of the Trinity. The seal is then no longer a visible mark, like the Cross 'painted' with chrism on the forehead of the candidate, but it is the invisible imprint of the potent and tremendous Name of God which marks the believer as God's property and protects him against the assaults of the devil.

For this line of thought there were many pre-Christian precedents. The awe with which the Hebrew of the Old Testament contemplated the ineffable and majestic Name is too often displayed in the biblical writings to make it necessary for us to dwell here upon this familiar aspect of Jewish theology. In blessing and in cursing the utterance of the divine Name has an independent power, a living force, which must inevitably achieve the purpose with which it was pronounced. It stands for and represents God Himself. The Temple is the place where the Lord would place His Name; it is as dwellers in far-off lands call upon the Name of the Lord that they are enabled to realize His presence.[1] The covenant people of Israel are those upon whom the Lord has placed His name.[2] The sacred tetragrammaton is a 'seal' worn by the high priest, and it was to this mighty and potent emblem that Alexander paid humble adoration when he visited Jerusalem.[3] Hebrew legend held that it was the seal of the Name of Yahweh (according to one account, engraved upon a stone)[4] which held back the imprisoned waters of the primal abyss; thus Manasses addresses God, 'who hast shut up the deep and sealed it by thy terrible and glorious name'.[5] The Name of Yahweh is both a sign given

[1] Cf. 1 Kings viii. 43.
[2] Pss. Sal. ix. 18.
[3] Jos., Ant., 11, 8, 5.
[4] Targ. Jon. Ex. xxviii. 30.
[5] Prayer of Manasses.

to the people of the Covenant to distinguish them from the outside world, and a powerful weapon against their adversaries. In both respects, the Name exhibits the character and function of the 'seal'.

The mark or sign which in the Apocalypse distinguishes the elect of God from the servants and followers of Antichrist is the seal set upon their foreheads,[1] and this seal is described as the name of God.[2] Since, according to Deissmann,[3] the 'mark of the beast' borne by the apostates probably consists of a χάραγμα which included the emperor's name and the year of his reign (such stamps are found on commercial documents in papyri of the first and second century), it is fairly certain that the writer of the Apocalypse is imagining that the elect in Heaven are visibly sealed with the divine name actually marked upon their persons. There is, however, no evidence that orthodox Christians at any time inscribed the name of God or Christ on their foreheads, despite the obvious analogy of pagan religious practice and the influence of secular tattooing, for it must presumably have been with some form of imperial monogram that the employees of certain government undertakings,[4] and perhaps soldiers as well, were marked.

Nevertheless, early Christian literature, especially popular romances, are full of examples of the high importance which was attached to the utterance of the tremendous name of God or the potent name of Jesus. The name is a powerful defence against the forces of the devil; when it is uttered over a person it consecrates him to God, and, indeed, unites him with God; it is the power of God, and in certain aspects it can almost be equated with the Holy Spirit.

Heitmüller[5] argues that the Christian belief in the tremendous potency of the Name is the clue to the understanding of the 'seal'. He believes that the 'seal', both in the New Testament and in the Fathers, means primarily the Name of God, of Christ, or of the Trinity, by which the believer is, as it were, stamped with his master's brand. Just as a sheep is branded with the name of its owner, so the Christian who has had the sacred

---

[1] i. 2; ix. 4.
[2] xiv. 1; xxii. 4.
[3] *Bible Studies*, pp. 240–7.
[4] See p. 11 above.
[5] *Im Namen Jesu*, 1902; etc. (see bibliography).

Name invoked over him at Baptism is metaphorically branded with Christ's sign and marked out as His property which will be claimed by Him at the Judgment. Bousset[1] argues along similar lines and maintains that when the terms 'seal' and 'sealing' are applied to Christian initiation they denote neither the inward stamping of the soul with the presence of the Holy Spirit, nor the external rite of Baptism in water, but that solemn invocation of the Name by which the candidate is assured that he belongs to God and is placed under special divine protection against the powers of evil. Bousset goes so far as to suggest that the pronouncement of the Name in the sacrament is a survival in a less crude form of an early practice of marking the candidate physically with the Name under which he had been enrolled, and that it was on this account that the term 'seal' continued to be used for some time very inappropriately to mean the utterance of the Holy Name in Baptism.

These theories are not satisfactory. Both Bousset and Heitmüller are trying to find in the conception of the seal of the divine Name a single master key to the interpretation of every instance of 'sealing' in the Bible or the Fathers; but to attempt to do this is to fall into the error of over-simplification. The conception of the seal is a focal point at which many different lines of thought converge; it is susceptible of many very varied interpretations, and no single idea, whether it be of the application to the believer of the power of the Name, the sign of the Cross, Baptism itself, Confirmation, or even the indwelling presence of the Spirit, is capable of exhausting its full implications. Much theological confusion has been caused by attempts to use a single principle of interpretation in order to explain the significance of the idea of 'sealing', and to employ the conception of the Name as such a principle is especially unsatisfactory, for in only a relatively few instances is it of paramount importance.

At the same time, the idea of the seal of the Name deserves attention. As in the case of the seal of the Cross, this is a notion which receives the greatest amount of emphasis in Christian literature of the popular type, and the apocryphal Acts are full of examples of the tremendous and awe-inspiring consequences

[1] *Kyrios Christos*, p. 278.

which the superstition of the vulgar attached to the utterance of the divine Name. The Name is 'great and terrible',[1] through its power marvels are performed,[2] and miracles of healing are accomplished.[3] In particular, it is the great and potent weapon against demons, which wards off their assaults and drives them out of the souls which they possess. The Christian use of the Name in exorcism is actually compared by Origen with the 'philosophy concerning names' of the Hebrews, Egyptians, Persians, and other peoples,[4] and much superstition undoubtedly attached itself to the idea that the uttered Name exercised a mysterious power; a considerable potency was evidently believed to reside in the names of demons, that is, pagan deities, for to make mention of them, even in the singing of heathen songs, was thought to make a man subject to the powers of evil.[5] At times the popular Christian use of the Name approximates closely to the manner in which the magical papyri prescribe the employment of uncouth, half-Hellenized, barbarous names of God for the purpose of casting spells. On the other hand, a vitally important distinction is drawn between the idols with their fictitious names and the true and sovereign Name of the Christian God.[6] It is in the power of this Name that the heathen gods are put to flight, the force of magic is overthrown, and demons are exorcized.

The Old Testament titles, 'God of Abraham, God of Isaac, God of Jacob', are mighty names by which the demons are defeated;[7] but it is chiefly in the power of the Name of Jesus Christ that cures are wrought and the devils reduced to subjection, so that 'the mighty works that are even now performed by His Name' are a manifest proof of His Messiahship.[8] Justin declares that τὰ δαιμόνια ὑποτάσσεσθαι τῷ ὀνόματι αὐτοῦ καὶ τῇ τοῦ γενομένου πάθους αὐτοῦ οἰκονομίᾳ.[9] It is through the Name of Jesus—here follows a brief credal statement about His Person and saving work which may have formed part of the actual formula of exorcism—that 'every demon is exorcized, conquered, and placed in subjection', and 'many Christians heal

---

[1] *Mart. Mt.*, 14, 15.
[2] *A. Phil.*, 11, 12; *Mart. Andr.*, 3.
[3] *A. Jo.*, 22, 25; Or., *Cels.*, 3, 24 (p. 220, 29; *PG.* 11, 948C).
[4] *Cels.*, 1, 25 (p. 76, 13; *PG.* 708A).
[5] *Const. App.*, 5, 10, 2.
[6] Or., *mart.*, 46.
[7] id., *Cels.*, 5, 45.
[8] *Just. dial.*, 35.
[9] *Ibid.*, 30.

those who could not be cured by any other exorcists and casters of spells, defeating and chasing away the demons who possess them'.[1] The Name of Christ gives power to His followers to triumph over the gods of paganism,[2] and Athanasius declares that, 'where Christ is named and faith in Him, all idolatry is destroyed, every deceit of demons is confuted, πᾶς δὲ δαίμων οὐδὲ τὸ ὄνομα ὑποφέρει· ἀλλὰ καὶ μόνον ἀκούσας φυγὰς οἴχεται.[3]

The Name of Christ and the seal of the Cross are linked together by Epiphanius as the sovereign remedy against sorcery: it has no power where there are the name of Christ and the seal of the Cross.[4] The efficacy of the Name and the Cross as means of averting and destroying the power of the devil arises, of course, from the fact that in their more positive aspect both are signs which denote consecration to God or Christ and mark a person or thing as His property over which He alone can exercise sovereign rights. The Name accordingly receives much emphasis in the ritual of consecration. A striking instance of this use of the Name occurs in the *Excerpta Theodoti*,[5] and in the *Acts of Thomas* the invocation of the Holy Name for the consecration of oil is closely connected with the idea that the power of Christ enters into and dwells in the dedicated offering.[6] In Serapion's blessing of water and oil the formula runs: 'We bless these creatures through the name of thine only-begotten Son Jesus Christ; we name the name of Him who suffered and was crucified and rose and is seated on the right hand of the Uncreate upon this water and this oil; grant healing power to these creatures'.[7] In the *Apostolic Constitutions* it is by the invocation of the Name of Jesus that the oil is consecrated for the pre-baptismal unction of the candidates,[8] and it is one of Augustine's familiar arguments against the Donatists that the Name of God in consecration, even when it is pronounced by the unworthy, has an independent efficacy of its own: 'Non est autem aqua profana et adultera super quam Dei nomen invocatur, etiamsi a profanis et adulteris invocetur.'[9]

---

[1] *Just. dial.*, 85; 2 *apol.*, 6.   [2] Tert., *apol.*, 23.
[3] *inc.*, 30, 6.   [4] *haer.*, 30, 8 (p. 344, 7; *PG.* 41, 420B).
[5] καὶ ὁ ἄρτος καὶ τὸ ἔλαιον ἁγιάζεται τῇ δυνάμει τοῦ ὀνόματος, οὐ τὰ αὐτὰ ὄντα κατὰ τὸ φαινόμενον οἷα ἐλήφθη, ἀλλὰ δυνάμει εἰς δύναμιν πνευματικὴν μεταβέβληται, 82, 1.
[6] 157 (p. 267, 6).   [7] *euch.*, 17.   [8] 7, 42, 3.   [9] *bapt.*, 3, 10, 15.

The idea of consecration by the utterance of the Name over the person or thing to be dedicated, the parallel notion of the Name as a mighty agency by which the power of the devil is destroyed, and the connection between the Name and the indwelling Presence, all have an obvious bearing upon Baptism, and we find in fact that the Name in Baptism is sometimes closely connected with the seal. This connection is particularly marked in Hermas, where in at least one passage the seal appears to be identical with the Name invoked over the baptized.[1] The same idea, though without the specific mention of the seal, occurs in two of his other baptismal passages, where we are told that, 'whoever does not receive (an expression frequently used of the seal) His name shall not enter into the Kingdom of God',[2] and where the name is closely linked with the spiritual garment of the virtues of Christ which the convert assumes at his Baptism.[3]

It is interesting to find in an early Roman document so strong an emphasis upon the invocation of the Name of the Lord. If this type of teaching was in fact widely current in the Roman Church in the second century, it may possibly form the background of the Roman attitude to schismatic baptisms in the time of Stephen. Whereas Cyprian's thought is dominated by the conception of the Church as the sphere of the Spirit and the complex of baptismal ceremonies as a unified rite by which the Spirit is bestowed within the fold of the Church, the mind of Stephen, and the traditional doctrine which he is following, attach supreme importance to the Name in which the baptisms even of schismatics have been administered. Whatever we may think of the outlook of the *De Rebaptismate*, it does not appear that it was the intention of Stephen to depreciate the importance of Baptism. On the contrary, it is a rite of so high a significance that even when it has been administered by the unworthy or by those in schism, it must be treated as valid and on no account regarded as null and void. The reason for this insistence, so far as we can infer it from the writings of the opposite party, is that the baptism had been administered in the Name of Jesus Christ.[4] We must not forget that Stephen claimed to be following *consuetudo*, and in the high importance which Hermas

---

[1] *sim.*, 8, 6, 3-4.   [2] *Ibid.*, 9, 12, 8.   [3] *Ibid.*, 9, 13, 2.   [4] Cypr., *ep.*, 73, 4.

attaches to the invocation of the Name at Baptism we have a strong hint of the way in which this *consuetudo* had been formed and handed down in the Church at Rome.

Unlike Hermas, however, Stephen's party evidently did not directly connect the Name with the seal; the letter of Cornelius to Fabius shows that the seal meant something else in third century Rome; but the association of the two is not really far from their minds. Stephen's party could logically have maintained that the schismatics' converts had received the 'seal' in their Baptism, which for that reason could not be repeated; but the identification of the seal with the outward sign of consignation, and the further connection of that sign with the gift of the Spirit, prevented them from making that assertion and involved them in the difficult doctrine that the Name was effective even on the lips of schismatics, and yet that Baptism in the Name, when administered clinically, was insufficient to give the candidate the full grace of Baptism unless it were completed by a further 'sealing'.

A very high degree of importance was attached to the baptismal use of the Name by the Marcosian Gnostics, who in some cases completed their baptisms with quasi-magical formulae expressed in barbarous and half-understood tongues. In these pieces of mysterious abracadabra the divine Name plays a great part. That the convert is sealed by the power of the Threefold Name is a belief which we meet in the *Excerpta Theodoti*, where it occurs in one or two passages which bring the reception of the seal of the Name into close connection with the idea of the stamp of the image of God.[1] The idea that the Name constitutes the baptismal seal is, however, not prominent in the patristic literature as a whole. Heitmüller endeavours to wrest an allusion to the Name out of almost every instance of the occurrence of the term 'seal' in a baptismal context; but many of the examples which he cites prove on examination to have no direct connection with the Name; they refer in many cases to consignation or to Baptism.

Nevertheless, it is true to say that, where the ceremony of initiation remains intact as a unity, there are some who tend to

---

[1] 86, 2. The Name is virtually identified by Theodotus with the Spirit (*ibid.*, 22, 6: τοῦ ὀνόματος τοῦ . . . ἐν τῇ περιστερᾷ κατελθόντος).

associate the particular moment of the reception of the seal with the utterance of the Name of the Trinity in the baptismal formula. Thus Gregory Nazianzen urges parents not to be afraid to let infants receive the seal. They must not fear the weakness of their nature; instead of using amulets and incantations as good-luck charms for the child, the mother is exhorted to 'give him the Trinity, the great and good phylactery'.[1] Similarly, Epiphanius recalls the command given to the Apostles: 'Baptize . . . into the . . . Name of the Trinity, the holy and royal seal.'[2] The conception of the seal of the Name represents an adaptation to Christian practice of the secular idea of 'sealing' soldiers with the name of the emperor,[3] and it is therefore not surprising to find that the Name is often brought into close connection with the sign of the Cross as the distinguishing badge of the Christian soldier. Ephrem speaks of the Christian 'signing on his brow the holy Name of the Lord or the glorious Cross of the Saviour'.[4] The Name is also associated in the *Liturgical Homilies of Narsai* both with unction (the '*rushmâ*' of the oil) and with a threefold signing with the Cross: 'The three names the priest casts upon the oil, and consecrates it that it may sanctify the uncleanness of men by its holiness. With the name hidden in it he signs the visible body: and the sharp power of the name enters even unto the soul. . . . With the name of the Father and of the Son and of the Spirit he seals his words; and he confirms him that is being baptized with their names. The three names he traces upon his face as a shield; that the tyrant may see the image of the Divinity on the head of a man. . . . He calls the King's servants by their name. . . . "Such a one", he says, "is the servant of the King of Kings that are on high and below; and with His name he is branded, that he may serve as a soldier according to His will. The name of the Divinity he mixes in his hands with the oil."'[5]

On the whole, however, it is but rarely that the Fathers apply to the Name the idea of the seal in its full significance as an eschatological marking for future redemption, a sign of the

---

[1] *or.*, 40, 17 (*PG.* 36, 380–1).
[2] *inc. ap haer.*, 20, 3 (p. 231, 12; *PG.* 41, 277C).
[3] Ambr., *obit. Valent.*, 58. [4] 3, 135F–136B.
[5] *hom.* 22 (B) tr. Connolly, *TS.* 8, pp. 40 ff.

Covenant-people, and a protection against hostile powers.[1] It is, moreover, easy to exaggerate the value of the idea of the consecrating power of the Name as a key to the interpretation of the conception of 'sealing'. The invocation of the Name is certainly at times linked closely with the activity of the Spirit or of the 'power' which is, as it were, brought down by the utterance of the sacred Name upon the offering that is to be dedicated. This theory of consecration is, as we have implied, especially strong in Gnostic circles. We can observe a close association of the seal with the Name in the *Acts of Thomas*, where the unction which precedes or even replaces Baptism is accompanied by the prayer, 'Come holy name of Christ that is above every name; come power of the Most High; . . . come most high gift of grace; come Holy Spirit and . . . seal them in the name of the Father and Son and Holy Spirit'.[2] The semimagical invocations of which this prayer is composed are exceedingly obscure and difficult to interpret, but it seems fairly clear that the Holy Name, the power of the Most High (cf. Luke i. 35), and the Spirit are virtually identified with each other, so that the Name is a dynamic medium of God's activity in relation to men, conveying to them His presence and charismatic gifts. Together with, or as identical with, the Spirit, the Name may perhaps constitute the ἐπισφράγισμα τῆς σφραγῖδος (to which the same passage refers), whose reception enables the neophyte to see that vision of the Lord as a young man bearing a light which is a recurrent feature in several of the baptismal narratives of the apocryphal Acts. An early liturgical fragment from a Vienna papyrus may perhaps be cited as an example of the same type of thought about the Name.[3] Yet in most orthodox writers there is little trace of any direct connection of thought between the utterance of the Name in Baptism and the idea that the baptized Christian is Χριστοφόρος. The seal of the indwelling Spirit, mediating the risen life of Christ to the believer is certainly bestowed through the sacrament, but there is no general disposition to associate this sealing with the parti-

---

[1] In a curious passage, Zeno of Verona appears to combine the notions of the seal of the Name and the seal of the Image, when he likens the baptized to a 'golden denarius, sealed *triplicis numismatis unione, tractat.*, 2, 35 (*PL.* 11, 481A).

[2] 27 (Lipsius-Bonnet, pp. 142-3).

[3] *P. Vind.*, 19896 vo., 16 (*PO.* 18, 446).

cular moment in the rite of initiation when the sacred Name is pronounced.

As regards the idea that the elect will be sealed with the Name in the hereafter, it is true that apocalyptic literature suggested that the Name of Christ would actually be worn inscribed on the foreheads of the saints; the Apocalypse of St. John was apparently quite explicit on this point.[1] Nevertheless, commentators on the Apocalypse tended to interpret figuratively the wearing of the seal of the Name which is there described. Arethas, for instance, explains that it really means that the elect are sealed with the holy light of the divine countenance, and so become an object of terror to the demons.[2]

Along another line of reasoning, the notion of the Name as a seal for the redeemed passes over quite naturally into the conception of the Trinitarian Name in Baptism as a seal of the convert's faith. The Name is now no longer thought of as a mysterious power which actually conveys, through its own independent potency, the presence and activity of God to consecrate and bring under His personal ownership the person or object over which it is pronounced. It is no longer regarded as constituting or conveying the seal by which the elect are marked for a day of redemption. The idea that the Name is in some sense the power of God has given place to the thought that the Name of the Trinity enshrined in the baptismal formula, or the credal summary to which the candidate has assented is a seal. It is not a seal in the sense of a brand set upon God's sheep; it is a seal in the sense that it is a token and guarantee of faith and orthodoxy. It is a proof or ratification, rather than a sacramental sign. In this respect the threefold Name fulfils the same function as circumcision under the Old Covenant. That was, as Severian of Gabala points out, given by God, not as effecting righteousness but as a seal and sign of Abraham's faith.[3] The naming of the Trinity, on this view, does not effect any change in the spiritual state of the believer; it ratifies and confirms the faith which he has already come to possess.

---

[1] It may be the seal of the Name which Commodian has in mind when he says of Elijah's preparation of the elect for the Judgment: 'Et signo signat populum in nomine Christi'—*carm. apol.*, 840; cf. *instruct.*, 1, 41, 8.

[2] *Apoc.* 39 (*PG.* 106, 684B) ap. Cram., *cat. in Apoc.*, xiv. 3.

[3] Rom. iv. 11 (Staab, p. 217, 11).

It is faith, says Tertullian, which procures the washing away of sin, and the faith which obtains that grace is 'fides obsignata in Patre et Filio et Spiritu sancto'.[1] It is in this sense of the term 'seal' that the same author speaks in a somewhat obscure metaphor of 'obsignatio baptismi, vestimentum quodammodo fidei',[2] and uses the phrase 'the sealing of faith' as a straightforward synonym for Baptism.[3] The writer of the *De Consummatione Mundi* included in the spurious works of Hippolytus, speaks of the need to preserve intact the 'seal of faith',[4] that is, the orthodox belief into which the convert had been baptized. He has, as it were, had his orthodox faith ratified by his acceptance of Baptism, and, though in these passages there is no explicit allusion to the Trinitarian Name, it is made clear elsewhere that it is the credal formula with its mention of the threefold Name that constitutes the particular moment in Baptism at which the candidate's true faith is sealed and attested. Eunomius' heresy is ruled out, declares Basil, by the baptismal experience of every Christian, for in Baptism we are 'sealed into Father and Son, not into creator and thing created'.[5] The thought of the baptismal creed (in this case the Creed of Nicaea) was in the mind of Eutyches when he maintained in his declaration of faith: 'In this faith was I sealed and baptized, and until this day I have lived in it, praying also to die in it.'[6]

The seal of faith is sometimes brought into a close relationship with other conceptions of the seal. This is notably the case in Ambrose's exegesis of the Prodigal Son's ring—that favourite text with which the Fathers so often illustrated their teaching about the seal. 'Anulus quid est aliud nisi sincerae fidei signaculum, et expressio veritatis? . . . Qui autem anulum habet, et Patrem habet et Filium et Spiritum sanctum, quia signavit nos Deus, cuius imago Christus, et dedit pignus Spiritum in cordibus nostris; et sciamus hoc anuli istius qui in manu datur esse signaculum, quo cordis interiora, factorumque nostrorum ministeria signantur. Ergo signati sumus, sicut et legimus: Cre-

---

[1] *bapt.*, 6.　　　　　　　　　　[2] *Ibid.*, 13.
[3] '. . . si post fidem obsignatam dicimus, non habeo quo vivam', *idol.*, 12.
[4] *consumm.* 42 (p. 306, 29; *PG.* 10, 945A).
[5] *Eun.*, 2, 22 (1, 258B; *PG.* 29, 620C).
[6] C. Chalc., *act.*, 1 (*ACO.* 2, 1, 1; p. 91, 7).

dentes, inquit, signati estis Spiritu sancto.'[1] Eulogius, in one of the fragments preserved by Photius of his work against the Novatianists, argues that the fallen must be rescued. The seal which the sinner received at Baptism must be saved from the devouring jaws of the devil, lest his pastors be charged with the total loss of a 'rational sheep'. Irrational beasts are 'sealed' on the ear or the leg. The shepherd's duty is, as Amos pointed out, to rescue at least the ear or the leg from the beast of prey and present it to the owner when he makes up his reckoning. The rational animals who comprise the flock of the spiritual pastor must therefore make every effort to save their souls from the devil, in order that the seal of the faith with which they were signed on the soul in Baptism may be saved and presented to the Master when he makes his inspection.[2] The eschatological seal which marks Christ's servant for the life to come is again connected with allegiance to the faith in the liturgical commemoration of those who have departed in 'the faith and seal of Christ'.

This eschatological significance, however, is not the primary connotation of the 'seal of faith'. It is, as we have remarked, a ratification or token rather than a brand which stamps the soul for eternity. In very many cases it is identified with the Creed, that is to say, the credal interrogations at Baptism; it is at any rate always synonymous with the essential Christian belief in the Trinity. Irenaeus, for example, says of Trinitarian heresy that 'in respect of the three points of our seal error has strayed widely from the truth',[3] and in very similar language the treatise against the Sabellians ascribed wrongly to Athanasius speaks of the Christian 'having the summary of the faith in Baptism, and in the three holy seals, through which he is regenerated to salvation'.[4] In the latter passage the eschatological conception of the seal has to some extent returned; it is interesting to observe that regeneration itself is ascribed to the efficacy of the 'seals' of the threefold Name. A more normal association of the seal with credal orthodoxy occurs in the somewhat laboured exposition given by Optatus of the 'fons signatus':

---

[1] *exp. in Lc.*, 7, 231 (*PL.* 15, 853B, C).
[2] *fr. Novat.*, 3 ap. Phot., *cod.*, 280 (*PG.* 104, 342D ff.).
[3] *dem.*, 100.   [4] 8 (*PG.* 28, 109C).

'fontem constat unum esse . . . unde haeretici non possunt vel ipsi bibere vel alios potare, quia soli sigillum integrum, id est symbolum catholicum, non habentes, ad fontem verum aperire non possunt.'[1] Orthodox faith is summed up, as we have seen, in the use of the threefold Name. The faith, says Epiphanius, is proclaimed to those who receive Baptism 'in one seal of the names of the Father, Son, and Holy Spirit'.[2] Hence we later find 'The seal of Faith' as the title of a credal document.[3]

This development of the conception of the seal of the Name is interesting and important. It illustrates how closely two very different ideas of sealing can approach each other when they are brought into connection with Christian initiation. The eschatological pledge of redemption and the formal ratification of faith find a common meeting-point in the use of the Trinitarian Name in Baptism and in the candidate's profession of faith. Yet in this line of thought the idea that the Trinitarian Name is a ratification of belief and a guarantee of orthodoxy is always uppermost, and the use of the term 'seal' in this connection is therefore of comparatively little significance for our purpose of investigating the ancient conceptions of the 'branding' of the Christian believer 'for a day of redemption'.

---

[1] 2, 8 (*CSEL.* p. 44, 14).
[2] *haer.*, 76, 20 (p. 367, 14; *PG.* 42, 557A).
[3] See Lebon, *R.H.E.*, 25 (1929), pp. 1 ff.).

CHAPTER FIFTEEN

CONSIGNATION AND
CONFIRMATION

THE history of the doctrine of 'sealing', as we have traced its development in the Fathers, is full of confusions and contradictions which long remained unresolved. The fundamental idea that by his reception of the gift of the Spirit (or the renewal in him of the image of God) the Christian is given a sign or seal which marks him as one of the elect was often obscured by the conception that the sign of the Cross was itself such a seal. In the ceremony of initiation, where the actual rite of Baptism, including the utterance of the sacred Name, anointing, signing with the Cross, and to some extent the laying on of hands as well, were all combined in a single dramatic action, the various theories of what constituted the seal could all find expression and in some measure be harmonized. Yet the really important theological problem demanded an answer: was the believer sealed with the gift of the Spirit by virtue of his sacramental incorporation into Christ in Baptism, or did he receive that gift independently of water-baptism? Is the reception of the essential Christian endowment of the 'earnest' of the Spirit separable from the membership of Christ and His Church effected, according to the New Testament (assuming that we have interpreted its evidence rightly) in Baptism itself? If the answer be made that the gift and sealing of the Spirit are not conferred in water-baptism itself, the further question remains whether the consignation of the sign of the Cross imparts such a seal (either as itself constituting an indelible brand, or as being the medium of the inward gift of the Spirit), or whether the seal is to be sought elsewhere, perhaps in the imposition of hands.

The majority of the patristic authors, as we have seen, do not try to answer these questions; they are content to ascribe the gift of the Spirit indiscriminately to Baptism, consignation, the laying on of hands, and sometimes to anointing as such, in so far as it can be distinguished at all from the signing with the Cross in chrism. The inconsistency of these theories was not strikingly apparent so long as the initiation rite remained a complex whole, and the confusion of opinions at least had the merit that it helped to preserve the truth that the operation of the Spirit is free and manifold; it is not tied to any rite or rites. When, however, the unity of the baptismal procedure breaks up, and the subsidiary ceremonies which had been, so far as we can judge, attached to Baptism in the second century, became established as an independent rite, it became an increasingly urgent necessity to define the relation between it and Baptism and to find some solution to the problem of what constituted the sacramental medium of the gift of the Spirit and the 'seal' of the believer.

Foreshadowings of such a solution are to be found as early as Clement, who speaks of regeneration as the thing peculiarly signified by the water of Baptism, and of 'increase' as the special grace given by the baptismal reception of the Spirit.[1] Clement, of course, is referring to the external and inward parts of Baptism itself; there is no question here of distinct rites; but we shall find that the idea that the Spirit bestows 'growth' or 'increase' is one which exercises a profound influence on the later solution to the problem of the sacramental gift of the Spirit. It might naturally suggest that a giving of 'increase' would be the peculiar function of the Spirit in the rite of consignation or of the imposition of hands when these became detached from Baptism proper. Another conception which played a great part in the development of the doctrine that a special gift of the Spirit as opposed to the initial bestowal of His indwelling presence, is received in Confirmation, is hinted at by Serapion when he refers to the effect of sealing with the Spirit as 'strengthening', and 'establishing'.[2] That the Spirit is the strengthener and confirmer, not only of men's souls, but of the universe, is a prominent part of the patristic doctrine of His work. It is this aspect of the gift of the Spirit which is emphasized by Didymus;[3] later, when theologians are seeking a

[1] *paed.*, 1, 12 (p. 148, 19; *PG.* 8, 368A).
[2] *euch.*, 25, 2.   [3] *Trin.*, 2, 14 (*PG.* 39, 712A).

satisfactory rationale of the separate rite of chrismation and imposition of hands, this conception is so strongly asserted that *confirmatio* becomes the technical term for the rite.

Along a parallel line of thought, the gift of the Spirit is regarded as consisting primarily in a 'perfecting'.[1] The bestowal of perfection is another of the chief functions attributed to the Spirit by the Fathers, both in respect of Creation and of sanctification.

All these developments of thought suggest the view that, as the New Testament already implied, there are different modes of the bestowal of the Spirit, and various ways in which His grace makes an approach to men. Thus, Eusebius infers from the apparent double gift of the Spirit to the Apostles[2] that there are distinctions in the manner of the Spirit's approach; he speaks of a partial bestowal, effecting remission of sins, at the 'insufflation' and another, fuller, gift 'in more perfect power' at Pentecost.[3] Hilary, too, hints at the idea of degrees of progress in man's reception of the Spirit, or at least of the gift of the Spirit as partly proleptic, like the sowing of a seed whose fruit grows gradually, remains for the present invisible, and will be fully manifested hereafter.[4] Theodore of Mopsuestia compares the stages in the Christian's reception of the Spirit with the experience of Jesus. Our regeneration by the Spirit is effected in the water of Baptism when we are born again in the font as in a womb; the subsequent unction with chrism corresponds to the descent of the Dove.[5]

The *De Sacramentis*, following the early liturgies, distinguishes the regenerating activity of the Spirit in Baptism from the bestowal of the seven-fold gifts in the subsequent consignation;[6] in later writers this becomes a common doctrine, reflecting a liturgical practice which has remained constant. Of equally great importance is the idea that the peculiar function of the consignation and the imposition of hands is to convey a 'strengthening' of the Spirit, corresponding to some extent to the physical strengthening of a child when he begins to grow up. It is this conception which is partly responsible for the general

[1] Cyr., *Joel*, 2, 32 (3, 224E).   [2] John xx. 22; Acts ii. 4.
[3] *eccl. theol.*, 3, 5 (p. 162, 3 ff.; *PG*. 24, 1009C).
[4] Cf. *tractat. in Ps.* 64, 15.   [5] *catech.* (Mingana, pp. 54–5; 66; 68).
[6] 3, 2, 8, 10; 6, 2, 6, 7.

substitution of the term *confirmatio* for *consignatio*, as we observed above in our discussion of an early instance of this type of thought. The former title appears in canon 2 of the First Council of Orange (441), and soon becomes common. We must not exaggerate the difference between the two words. Their lexicographical histories run on lines which converge on at least one point: each comes to possess, though along a different line of development from the other, the meaning 'attestation' or 'authentication'. At the same time the substitution of the one term for the other has a very real theological significance. The rite of consignation still takes place; indeed it is generally regarded as the primary external symbol in *confirmatio*, so that 'unction' and 'confirmation' can be treated as virtually synonymous, and the laying on of hands is relegated to the status of a merely incidental process in the ceremony of consignation;[1] but the use of the word *confirmatio* suggests that, although the external seal of the Cross remains, the notion of the seal which is marked on the elect 'for a day of redemption' is being to some extent detached from the signing with chrism, and perhaps by implication is being restored to Baptism where it properly belongs.

Certainly the change in terminology implies that the vivid eschatology of the rite of consignation (when considered as a sealing of the elect) has been replaced by a totally different complex of ideas. The fundamental conceptions associated with the word *confirmatio* are not eschatological at all—a fact which is clearly brought out in the very important and influential Gallican homily on Pentecost which was once attributed to Eusebius of Emesa, and is ascribed by Dom. G. Morin to Faustus of Riez.[2] 'Ac sic', the writer says, 'continuo transituris sufficiunt regenerationis beneficia; victuris autem necessaria sunt confirmationis auxilia. Regeneratio per se salvat mox in pace beati saeculi recipiendos, confirmatio armat et instruit ad agones

---

[1] Cf. Ps.-Bede, *comm. in Ps.* 26 (*PL.* 93, 611A), and see Coppens, *L'Imposition des Mains*, p. 312, n. 2.

[2] Dix points out the interesting history of this homily, which, through its incorporation in the False Decretals under the name of Melchiades, exercised a profound influence on mediaeval and Reformed thought on Confirmation (*The Theology of Confirmation in Relation to Baptism*, pp. 21 ff.). The homily is discussed, together with the rest of the collection attributed to Eusebius, by G. Morin, who ascribes them to Faustus, in *ZNTW*. 34 (1935), pp. 92-115.

mundi huius et praelia reservandos. Qui autem post baptismum cum acquisita innocentia immaculatus pervenit ad mortem, confirmatur morte: quia iam non potest peccare post mortem.' The Holy Spirit, already given in Baptism, strengthens the faithful in Confirmation for the trials and combats of this mortal life. The eschatological seal of the Spirit is by implication rightly assigned in this author to Baptism in which the indwelling presence which is the earnest of redemption is bestowed upon the new Christian. At Pentecost itself there was such a strengthening. The Apostles were fitted for active service in Christ's cause. Before Pentecost an Apostle could deny Christ; after it there were martyrs. 'Per Spiritum sanctum dono sapientiae spiritalis illuminamur, aedificamur, erudimur, instruimur, consummamur.'

The preacher is trying to answer the question, 'Quid mihi prodest post mysterium baptismatis ministerium confirmationis?' His answer is that the latter is a *benedictio*. It is the means whereby the Spirit arms and strengthens Christ's soldiers, and the medium through which an 'increase' is bestowed for the active life of the mature believer. 'Sic enim exigit militaris ordo ut cum imperator quemcumque in militum receperit numerum, non solum signet receptum (that is, bestows the seal connoting ownership), sed etiam armis competentibus instruat pugnaturum. Ita in baptizato benedictio illa munitio est. Dedisti militem, da et adiumenta militiae. Numquid prodest si quisquam parentum magnam parvulo conferat facultatem, nisi providere studeat et tutorem. Ita paracletus regeneratis in Christo et consolator at tutor est . . . Ergo Spritus sanctus, qui super aquas baptismi salutifero descendit illapsu, in fonte plenitudinem tribuit ad innocentiam, in confirmatione augmentum praestat ad gratiam . . . In baptismo regeneramur ad vitam, post baptismum confirmamur ad pugnam: in baptismo alimur, post baptismum roboramur.'[1]

There is no better or more precise statement than this of the doctrine of Confirmation (and, by implication, of sealing with the Spirit) which emerged out of the confusion which had beset patristic thought on Baptism, sealing, and the gift of the Spirit from the late second century onwards. Each element in the

[1] *hom. in Pent.* (Gaigneus, 1547, pp. 77-9).

theory of 'pseudo-Eusebius' is developed by other writers. The 'strengthening' aspect of the Spirit's activity is emphasized by Gennadius of Marseilles when he says of heretics received into the Church: 'Purgati iam fidei integritate confirmentur manus impositione. Si vero parvuli sunt, vel hebetes, qui doctrinam non capiant, respondeant pro illis qui eos offerunt iuxta morem baptizandi; et sic manus impositione et chrismate communiti eucharistiae mysteriis admittantur.'[1] The idea that the gift of the Spirit in Confirmation is a gift of His power is found in Paschasius (d. 512), who rather curiously connects it with the working of miracles. In Baptism, he says, there is bestowed remission of sins; in the coming of the Holy Spirit (Paschasius, unlike 'pseudo-Eusebius' seems to reserve the Spirit's activity to Confirmation) gifts of supernatural power are conferred, and miraculous signs are performed by the confirmed—an early instance of the absolute use of the verb *confirmare*.[2] The view that in Confirmation the Christian is armed for combat is hinted at by Augustine in his comparison of chrismation with the anointing of a wrestler,[3] a simile which was taken up and developed by Prosper.[4]

That Confirmation is a sacramental rite of growth and increase in the spiritual life, a symbol and pledge of the sanctifying work of the Spirit, is emphasized, not only by the 'pseudo-Eusebius', but by many writers throughout the Middle Ages. As early as the end of the fifth century, John the Deacon sets out to answer the question, 'Is it of any real disadvantage to a man who has been baptized if he die without receiving the anointing with chrism and the bishop's *benedictio*?' His reply is that Baptism and Confirmation are analogous to stages in the progress of our natural life. Baptism is equivalent to birth. When a man is born, 'perfectum hominem natum esse dicimus'; his *substantia* is already defined, and, 'si ergo accidunt adiumenta ad aetatis provectum, numquid adiectum est aliquid definitioni substantiae? Absit . . .'.[5] The complete renewal of life, with the bestowal of the Spirit, and therefore presumably the sealing for eternity, are given in Baptism, to some extent proleptically and potentially.   All is then given, but the gift has to unfold

---

[1] *eccl. dogm.*, 52 (*PL.* 58, 993C).   [2] *Spir.*, 2, 4 (*PL.* 62, 31B, C).
[3] *tractat.* 33. 3 *in Jo.*   [4] *sent. Aug.*, 346.   [5] *ep. Senar.*, 14.

itself and reveal its nature gradually as the new life expands and develops. It is given, as it were, in germ, and the *adiumenta* of the same Spirit are required for growth into the Christian life. From the eschatological standpoint, however, it is Baptism alone which is of ultimate significance. The ideas of John the Deacon on this matter are not dissimilar from those of Aquinas when he speaks of Confirmation as the sacrament of growth in new life,[1] as, 'aetas perfecta vitae spiritualis', and 'spirituale augmentum'.[2]

In the East, where presbyters administered chrismation, and Baptism and its associated rites were never separated from each other, the need of finding a satisfactory definition of the Spirit's work in consignation was never so acute as in the West. There, however, the view that in chrismation the special gift of the Spirit is for 'perfection' bears some resemblance to the general Western theory of Confirmation, and the idea that 'strengthening' is received in this rite is also present in the later Greek theologians. The former conception is particularly prominent in the Nestorian baptismal rite.[3]

These developments, however, do not spell the end of theological difficulties and confusion. The theory still persists that the gift of the Spirit in the full sense, as distinct from *a* gift, is received in Confirmation alone;[4] and even where a rationalized theory of the relation of Confirmation to Baptism has been evolved on the lines which we have been tracing, the solution of the problem is still far from satisfactory. Certain gains have been achieved. The totally unscriptural tendency to divorce 'baptism of the Spirit' from 'baptism in water' has been arrested, and there is now less inclination to confuse an external sign or seal with the inward seal of the indwelling Spirit which is received by faith in Baptism; but there is a grave danger of treating the Holy Spirit impersonally and His dealings with the soul as a quantitatively measurable gift of which one may receive more or less, or a series of instalments. The idea that

[1] *S.T.*, 3, 72, 1.
[2] *Ibid.*, 3, 72, 5; cf. Aquinas' view that Confirmation bestows the power of the Spirit 'ad pugnam spiritualem contra hostes fidei', *ibid.*
[3] Denzinger, *Rit. Orient.*, 1, p. 49.
[4] Cf. *v. Faronis Meldensis*, 103 (*MGH.* 5, p. 195): 'In ministerio confirmationis, in quo animae corporum baptizatorum donum sancti Spiritus accipiunt ... Dum per chrisma unctionis a beato Farone donum sancti Spiritus percipit.'

man's spiritual life is strengthened, equipped, and developed to maturity by the continued activity towards him of the Holy Spirit, is highly valuable and contains much truth; but the conception of Confirmation which was developed along these lines was essentially connected with the Baptism of infants, and, indeed, owed its origin to the process of reflection upon the peculiarly difficult problem of relating consignation to *infant* Baptism: So far as the Confirmation of those who were baptized as believers was concerned, the answer given by these later Latin Fathers to the question, 'Why Confirmation?', was not wholly satisfactory. Scriptural precedent, if we have interpreted rightly the meaning of the laying on of hands in the New Testament, might have suggested that in the case of those baptized as adult believers, the episcopal *benedictio* had as one of its chief functions the association of the converts in the Church's apostolic mission, and their commissioning as participants in the missionary enterprise. Rabanus Maurus does in fact indicate this aspect of Confirmation when he remarks that the confirmed are strengthened with the Holy Spirit 'ad praedicandum aliis'.[1] This, it should be noted, is a different conception from the view that Confirmation constitutes the layman a priest, in the sense that it is a kind of ordination to the priesthood of all believers. As Jerome explained: 'Sacerdotium laici, id est baptisma. Scriptum est enim, "Regnum quippe nos et sacerdotes Deo et Patri suo fecit". Et iterum, "Gentem sanctam, regale sacerdotium".'[2] On the whole, however, the theory of Confirmation worked out by such writers as 'pseudo-Eusebius' was hardly applicable to the Confirmation of converts baptized as full believers; in their case it implied an artificial separation of aspects of the bestowal of the Spirit which are really indissolubly connected.

In the immediate background of the problem, as it confronted the later authors, there lay, as we have remarked, the whole question of the theology of infant Baptism, and it is of this that they are primarily thinking when they try to elucidate the theory of Confirmation. Their ideas of the 'sacrament of

---

[1] *inst cleric.*, 1, 30 (*PL.* 107, 314A): 'ad praedicandum aliis idem donum quod ipse in baptismate consecutus est.'
[2] *Lucif.*, 4 (*PL.* 23, 166A).

growth', 'augmentum', 'robur', and the rest, are valuable when they are related to infant Baptism. They suggest that the seal of the indwelling Spirit, bestowed proleptically in Baptism, is made fully realizable through a further act of the Spirit's grace. They could not, however, provide a genuinely satisfactory solution along the line of that suggestion until they had been related to a regular system of catechetical instruction for the baptized children, such as the Reformers made it their business to establish, and to the conscious completion and fulfilment of their Baptism on the part of the children through a response of faith expressed in the confirmation of their baptismal vows.

CONCLUSION

IT is not within our present scope to discuss the pressing contemporary problems of the importance to be assigned to Confirmation, the relation which it bears to the Christian's reception of the gift of the Spirit, and the status of those Christians who are unconfirmed. It is, however, proper to consider whether our study can be said to have any bearing on these weighty matters; and the answer which we must give is primarily a negative one, namely, that the patristic teaching on 'sealing' is inconclusive and can afford no adequate ground upon which to base a precise doctrine of the bestowal of the Holy Spirit in relation to Baptism and Confirmation.

Nevertheless, certain positive conclusions emerge from a consideration of the New Testament and the Fathers. In the first place, we find that there is no foundation in the New Testament, nor any clear testimony in the early Fathers, for the view that in the Christian dispensation God's people are sealed as His own possession by undergoing an outward and visible ceremony, other than Baptism in water, analogous to the external seal of circumcision in the old Covenant and standing in the same relationship to Baptism as circumcision stood to the proselyte-baptism of the Jews. We must not therefore argue from the Jewish system of initiation to a supposed parallel series of rites in primitive Christianity; to do so would be in a real sense to undermine the Gospel and bring ourselves into the bondage of the Law. Hence we reject as unscriptural the view advanced by Thornton[1] that 'the promise of the Spirit, which, according to St. Peter's Pentecostal sermon, the ascended Christ "received from the Father", is implemented for us only when through the apostolic ministry' (i.e. through the bishop in Confirmation) 'we are sealed by that same Spirit "unto the day of redemption"'—a theory which implies that no unconfirmed person is a true Christian. Such teaching would rightly incur the criticism which Calvin's baptismal rite directed

[1] *Confirmation Today*, p. 9.

against the late mediaeval abuses of Confirmation: 'Atqui non dubium est quin luminaria, unguenta (quae chrismata nominantur) aliaeque pompae generis eiusdem a Deo numquam institutae sint, sed ab hominibus introductae, sensimque eo progressa superstitio sit, ut maiore in pretio atque honore haberentur quam ipsum Christi institutum';[1] for in the New Testament the 'seal' is the inward mark or stamp of the indwelling Spirit of God which is received by the convert who is justified by faith in Christ and through Baptism is sacramentally made a partaker of Him in His death and resurrection. In some second-century Fathers the connection of this spiritual sealing and the sacrament of Baptism has become so close that the seal and the rite are regarded as identical. The identification was natural (though none the less regrettable) for the seal was received by the believer in Baptism because his Baptism re-enacted Christ's own Baptism, so that he was enabled to participate symbolically in the Spirit's descent at the Jordan, and, through the mediation of the Son of God, to hear, as it were, the divine declaration of his own adoptive sonship.

Secondly, we conclude that there is little convincing evidence in the New Testament for the view that Baptism regularly involved or included any other rite than the Baptism in water which was practised from the earliest days of the Church. There was no special sacrament of 'Spirit-baptism'. Laying on of hands was certainly practised on certain special occasions, and this ceremony, symbolizing fellowship, 'solidarity', and the incorporation into a single unit of those who performed it and those who received it, was regarded by St. Luke as the means whereby special *charismata* of the Spirit, appropriate to the missionary enterprise, were bestowed upon certain converts, so that the apostolic character of the missionary Church was transferred from the original Apostles to some recruits to its evangelistic task. Less certainly, the writer to the Hebrews suggests that in some quarters this rite may have been performed on all converts and associated closely with the regular practice of Baptism. It is not, however, implied that this constituted a 'Spirit-baptism' for which the normal water-baptism was simply a preliminary purification.

[1] Kidd, *Documents*, 305 (p. 624).

Unction was probably not practised in connection with Christian initiation in the apostolic age. The Christian's anointing was his participation in the Messiah's 'unction' with the Holy Spirit.

Thirdly, the tremendous and mysterious ceremony of Baptism was at a relatively early date embellished with various other symbolical actions. With some of these, such as the preliminary exorcisms, we are not here concerned. Chrismation, and sometimes the solemn imposition of hands, the one denoting participation in Christ the other (probably derived from the narrative of Acts rather than from a continuous tradition, though the evidence of Heb. vi. 2 leaves us in doubt on this point) signifying the gift of the Spirit, acquired a steadily growing importance. We hear of the former for the first time in Gnostic circles, but both usages spread rapidly, and were regarded as ancient and traditional in orthodox quarters by the time that the *Apostolic Tradition* of Hippolytus made its appearance.

Chrismation and consignation with the sign of the Cross formed the regular conclusion of the ceremony of initiation from that time onwards until it was discarded in the sixteenth century by the Reformed churches. This edifying practice signified by a visible sign one aspect of what had been sacramentally effected in Baptism. It translated into dramatic form the New Testament teaching that in Baptism the believer is made a member of Christ and a sharer in His Messianic character so that the Church can be described in later times by Theophilus of Antioch as the 'anointed people'. It marked the convert as one who had been claimed by Christ as His own property, and it constituted an outward 'sealing' which signed the Christian with His Master's token. The growing importance which was attached to the consignation in the late second and third centuries was partly, no doubt, due to the materialistic outlook of many half-converted pagans who joined the Church; such people would easily fail to appreciate the deep spiritual significance of the Pauline 'seal of the Spirit', and would tend to look for physical and semi-magical tokens to give them a safe passage through the spheres of the *cosmocratores* into the divine pleroma. The seal of the Cross therefore came very readily to be identified with the inward seal of the Spirit, or to be regarded as the means of the latter's bestowal; and this confusion was often accompanied by a tendency to identify the consignation with the scriptural laying on of hands.

The theory that the seal of the Spirit was received in the final consignation, and not in water-baptism, was not, however, so far as the relatively scanty evidence allows us to draw a firm conclusion, the teaching of the early Fathers, and it never wins universal acceptance. Apart from the various other conceptions of the 'seal' which were entertained by patristic writers, such as the idea of the Name invoked in Baptism as the means by which the believer was sealed, and despite the confused and inconsistent theories of many of the Fathers on this matter, it remains true, as Pusey remarked, that, 'It is unquestionable that the primary use of the word 'seal', both among the Fathers and in the Liturgies, relates to Baptism',[1] and not to any of its subsidiary rites.

It is when the rite of initiation breaks into two separate parts (as it did in the West on account of the growth of the Church and the rise of presbyteral Baptism, the practice of baptizing infants very soon after birth, and the reservation to the bishop of his ancient function of signing the newly baptized with the Cross, or laying hands upon them in blessing as they entered on their new duties and privileges) that consignation and the imposition of hands acquire an independent significance. As we have seen, a doctrine of Confirmation is developed to rationalize the division of the rite of initiation, and the initial gift of the Spirit tends to be assigned to Baptism while in Confirmation there is believed to .be a gift of the Spirit for strengthening and equipping for spiritual warfare, or of the sevenfold gifts as a special endowment.

It is on these lines that the practice of Confirmation is defended by St. Thomas: 'Hoc enim sacramentum est perfectio baptismi.'[2] The grace of Baptism is positive, and not merely negative—a washing away of sin and nothing more,[3] but Confirmation is the sacrament of growth and spiritual maturity, whereas Baptism is the beginning, the new birth:

---

[1] *Scriptural Views of Holy Baptism* (Tract 67), p. 153.
[2] *S.T.*, 3, 72, 9. [3] *Ibid.*, 3, 69, 4.

'Sic igitur vitam spiritualem homo accipit per baptismum, qui est spiritualis regeneratio. In confirmatione autem homo accipit quasi quandam aetatem perfectam spiritualis vitae.'[1] Confirmation is not said to be a sealing with the Spirit; but the sign of the Cross, conferred at Confirmation, is an outward badge or sign of the Christian soldier. He is marked with the stamp of his leader: 'Ideo in fronte signatur chrismate, ut neque propter timorem neque propter erubescentiam nomen Christi confiteri praetermittat.'[2] Aquinas is faithfully reproducing what we judge to have been the original significance of consignation, except that the thought of the Cross as a sign of recognition for the day of Judgment is largely replaced by the idea that it is, as it were, the coat of arms borne by the Christian soldier during his time of active service in the Church militant on earth.

At the Reformation all the Protestant Churches rejected Confirmation as a sacrament, on the ground that it lacked Dominical institution. Alone in the West, the Church of Rome maintained its status as a sacrament, on the warrant of apostolic rather than Dominical institution. The Church of England preserved the Catholic doctrine of Baptism as an effective sign— a theory which was rejected by Zwingli and the Anabaptists (for whom Baptism was a seal in the sense that it was *cognitio* and not *causa salutis*), and which was in the last resort scarcely consistent with Calvin's theology. Yet it denied the right of Confirmation to be termed a sacrament of the Gospel,[3] and in some quarters there was a strong reaction against the mediaeval theory and practice of Confirmation. Thus, taking the crudest popular view of the 'seal' as representative of the general theory of Confirmation in the unreformed Church, Tyndale declared: 'They think that if the bishop butter the child in the forehead that it is safe.'[4] His condemnation might have been advantageously levelled against popular notions of 'sealing' at any time from the later second century onwards to his own day; for what he is attacking is the ultimate degradation of the Biblical 'seal of the Spirit' which had been brought about by the fatal confusion between the spiritual seal and an

---

[1] *S.T.*, 3, 72, 1.   [2] *Ibid.*, 3, 72, 9.   [3] Cf. Article XXV.
[4] 'Obedience of a Christian Man' (*Works*, Parker Soc., vol. 1, p. 277).

outward consignation. Cranmer maintained that: 'The Church useth chrism for the exterior sign, but the Scripture maketh no mention thereof,'[1] and Thomas Rogers holds that 'It is an error to ascribe salvation unto chrism and not only unto Christ. ... It is an error to maintain that any bishop can give heavenly graces to any creature. ... It is an error that by Confirmation the Holy Ghost is given to the full.'[2] He also holds that the Popish doctrine of Confirmation of baptismal grace and strengthening by the seven gifts of the Holy Ghost is a 'dangerous and very damnable doctrine'.[3]

Much of this criticism has as its real object the gross superstition of the ignorant. Jewel, however, raises a more serious objection to the mediaeval theory when he attacks the view that without Confirmation Christian initiation is essentially incomplete; 'More, they said he was no perfect Christian, that was not anointed by the bishop with this holy oil. This was another abuse. For whosoever is baptized receiveth thereby the full name of a perfect Christian, and hath the full and perfect covenant and assurance of salvation: he is perfitly buried with Christ, doth perfitly put on Christ, and is perfitly made partaker of his resurrection. Therefore they are deceived, that say no man is a perfit Christian that is not marked with this oil. Else the apostles and holy martyrs were but half Christians because they lacked this oil.'[4]

This protest was largely justified. It was also true that, although the emphasis laid in the Middle Ages upon Confirmation as a sacrament of growth might have led to its association with the baptized person's conscious and spontaneous profession of faith (whose postponement, together with the disappearance of the catechumenate, was the gravest disadvantage of infant Baptism), the habit of administering the rite at too young an age, and the lax practice of the mediaeval Church, had rendered it impossible so to use Confirmation as a means of rectifying the deficiencies of infant Baptism and making Baptism and Confirmation (considered as two parts of one whole) a real equivalent to the Baptism of the primitive Church. Moreover,

---

[1] *Works*, Parker Soc., p. 80.
[2] *The Catholic Doctrine of the Church of England* (Parker Soc., p. 255).
[3] *Ibid.*, pp. 253-4.
[4] 'A Treatise of the Sacraments' (*Works*, Parker Soc., vol. 2, p. 1126).

Confirmation had sometimes been exalted into a sacrament of equal, or even greater, value than Baptism itself. 'They say Confirmation is more honourable than Baptism because any priest may baptize, but Confirmation is given only to a bishop or a suffragan. So do they give a greater pre-eminence to Confirmation, which is devised by man, than to the holy sacrament of Baptism, which Christ himself ordained. I need not speak more hereof; the error is so gross, so thick, so sensible and palpable.'[1]

The first achievement of the Reformers was to restore in full and unequivocally the ancient and proper significance of Baptism in its positive aspect as the sacrament of the bestowal of the Spirit. Thus Jewel insists that 'Baptized infants are the temples and tabernacles of the Holy Ghost'.[2] Hooker implies the same doctrine;[3] and among later writers Barrow maintains that 'In Baptism the gift of God's Holy Spirit is conferred',[4] and Beveridge rightly says that, 'as baptizing necessarily implies the use of water, so our being made thereby disciples of Christ as necessarily implies our partaking of His Spirit; for all that are baptized and so made the disciples of Christ are thereby made the members of His Body and are therefore said to be baptized into Christ. But they who are in Christ . . . must needs partake of the Spirit that is in Him, their Head. Neither doth the Spirit of Christ only follow upon, but certainly accompanies the Sacrament of Baptism.'[5]

This teaching is not incompatible with the doctrine that the baptized may receive further endowments of the Holy Spirit in Confirmation; but at times Anglican thought has exhibited as much confusion as that of the Fathers in its attempt to answer the question by what sacramental medium the essential Christian possession of the Spirit is received. Jeremy Taylor's *Discourse of Confirmation*, for example, which significantly borrows its alternative title, Χρῖσις τελειωτική, from the Areopagite, suggests that the gift of the Spirit is specially mediated in Confirmation; and sometimes we meet a theory of a partial and a fuller gift of the Spirit, as when Beveridge asserts that the uni-

---

[1] 'A Treatise of the Sacraments' (*Works*, Parker Soc., vol. 2, p. 1126).
[2] *Ibid.*, p. 1128.   [3] *Eccl. Pol.*, 5, 64, 4.
[4] *The Doctrine of the Sacraments: Of Baptism*, § 2 (ed. Napier, vol. 7, p. 507).
[5] *serm.*, 35 (*Works, Lib. of Anglo-Cath. Theol.*, vol. 2, p. 183).

versal practice of the Church was to administer the laying on of hands, 'it being by this that they were always believed to receive the Holy Ghost, by which alone they are made complete Christians, capable of all the privileges of the Gospel'.[1]

Nevertheless, despite the tendency in Anglicanism to postulate a repeated gift of the Spirit, or a 'fuller measure' bestowed in Confirmation after an initial gift in Baptism, it is broadly true that in the sixteenth-century writers there is little or no assertion that a specific gift is received through the imposition of hands. Even Hooker who in general follows the teaching of Aquinas on confirmation tends to speak of what is therein bestowed as 'the illumination of God's . . . Spirit' rather than as a 'gift'.[2]

The second, and more successful, reform was the relating of Confirmation to infant Baptism in such a way as to make it the means of supplying the response of faith which is required in Baptism but cannot be made in the case of infants. The emphasis came to be laid increasingly upon the catechetical rather than the sacramental aspect of Confirmation, that is, upon the preparation of the candidate (by means of a revival in a new guise, adapted to infant Baptism, of the ancient catechumenate), and upon his confirmation in his own person of the baptismal vows made on his behalf by the godparents. This was not an entirely new development; before the Reformation young children had commonly received some catechetical instruction in preparation for Confirmation. The great stress, however, that was now laid upon this aspect of Confirmation was entirely novel, and of great theological importance. The rite itself gained a new balance, such as it had never possessed since its isolation from the other ceremonies of initiation to stand by itself as a truncated ceremony, the detached finale of the Baptism service. It now comprised, on the one side, the candidate's public profession of faith, completing his Baptism by the addition to it of what had been an essential part of the adult Baptism of the early Church; on the other side there was prayer for the strengthening of the candidate with the Holy Ghost the Comforter, the increase in him (but not the initial

---

[1] *Thes. Theol.* (*Works, Lib. of Anglo-Cath. Theol.*, vol. 9, pp. 45-6).
[2] *Op. cit.*, 5, 66, 1.

bestowal) of the Spirit's gifts of grace, and his perseverance and increase in the Spirit until he shall come to the Lord's Kingdom; the prayer was accompanied by the imposition of hands by the bishop, so that the primitive symbol of fellowship and benediction was appropriately extended to the baptized person who had now professed his faith and entered fully into the status, privileges, and duties potentially conferred upon him in Baptism.

Some Reformers evidently went so far as to suppose that in securing this change of emphasis they were restoring the original significance of the rite: 'Touching Confirmation', says Rogers, 'the sentence and judgment of the true Church is that rightly used, as it was in the primitive Church, it is no sacrament, but a part of Christian discipline, profitable for the whole Church of God. . . . The bishop by sound doctrine, grave advice, and godly exhortation, confirmed them in that good profession, and laying his hands upon them, prayed for the increase of God's gifts and graces in their minds.'[1] This is, of course, historically absurd; Confirmation, as envisaged by the Reformers and as practised in accordance with the Prayer Books of 1552 and thereafter, has little in common with the rite that was performed, either as a part of the baptismal service or as a separate act, in the Church of the early centuries, and it has no direct Scriptural precedent. Theologically, however, the Reformers were right. Their development of Confirmation made it possible to retain infant Baptism along with the doctrine of justification *sola fide*. The Christian who was baptized in infancy was now able to make his necessary profession of faith after due instruction, and, on so supplying the deficiency which infant Baptism would otherwise suffer, to receive the blessing of the representative leader of the Christian society with prayer for his strengthening and increase in the Holy Spirit.

In the Prayer Book the chief emphasis is not laid upon the reception of the gift of the Spirit, nor is anything said about sealing with the Spirit; indeed, the thought is primarily of the believer's reception of a renewed and more perfect apprehension, comparable with that bestowed in Ordination, of the Spirit already given, as the Baptism service clearly states, in Baptism

[1] *Op. cit.* (p. 253).

itself for regeneration and for sanctification. That the purpose of the Anglican service is primarily to enable the baptized to ratify their vows seems to be indicated by its use of the verb 'confirm'. In the service itself (as distinct from the opening and closing rubrics), it is twice used of the confirming by the candidates of their baptismal promises, and only once (in the Preface) is it used passively of the confirmation of the candidates themselves: '. . . that none hereafter shall be confirmed.'

The difference of outlook in the services of 1662 and 1928 in this respect is striking. In the latter, with its unfortunate preface which adduces Acts viii. 14–17 as Scriptural authority for the expectation of a special gift of the Spirit through the laying on of hands with prayer, the thought of an endowment of the Spirit has been brought to the forefront once again; happily, however, it is nowhere suggested in the 1928 rite that the candidate is to receive the indwelling presence of the Spirit for the first time.

As we have already remarked, the concept of sealing is absent from the Anglican Confirmation service. The seal of the Spirit is implicitly associated with Baptism, and the outward seal of the Cross, the mark, as Aquinas expressed it, of the Christian soldier, has already been received at Baptism. The only seal in our Confirmation rite is the candidate's ratification of his baptismal profession and the sealing to him of God's promises. That the bishop should be its minister is obviously highly fitting and appropriate, although, as the history of Confirmation compels us to believe, it is in no way essential.

It is by no means clear what attitude the English Reformers would assume towards the question of the significance of Confirmation when administered to those baptized as adult believers, or, indeed, whether they would hold it to be necessary. In relating Confirmation to infant Baptism in the way which we have described, they had achieved a theological reunion of the sundered elements of the ancient initiatory rite, and at the same time given a fuller meaning to the 'Confirmation' part of it than it had ever hitherto possessed. On the other hand, the provision in the Prayer Book of 1662 that 'it is expedient that every person thus baptized (sc. as an adult believer) should be confirmed by the Bishop so soon after his Baptism as conveniently may be' appears at first sight to represent a retrograde step. Where Confirmation might have been restored as an integral part of a single baptismal rite, it is still sundered from Baptism as a separate service. However soon after Baptism it may be administered, it is still not part of the same rite of initiation. Episcopal administration of Confirmation, or the presbyteral administration of Baptism, has serious disadvantages in the case of adult Baptism.

It is an open question whether Cranmer would have recognized any need for Confirmation in the case of an adult who had made his own personal confession of faith and undertaken his own vows at Baptism; but we may well hold that the 1662 Book was right in prescribing Confirmation for those baptized as believers, though it is regrettable that it was not incorporated in the service of Baptism. It is this separation of the two in the case of adults which upsets the entire balance of Christian initiation and leads to the highly erroneous notion that Baptism is but a part of 'Confirmation preparation'.

If it were included in the Baptism service, the Confirmation of adults would not, of course, possess exactly the same meaning as the Confirmation of those baptized in infancy. It would not include a renewal of those vows which the candidates would just have undertaken, or a new declaration of the faith they would have just professed. The fact that such things do at present take place when a separate Confirmation follows shortly after an adult Baptism creates an unpleasant atmosphere of unreality and not unnaturally gives rise to the mistaken opinion that in such circumstances Baptism is no more than a preliminary formality which must be undertaken in order to qualify for Confirmation.

If Confirmation were restored to its ancient place as an integral part of an adult believer's initiation, its purpose would be primarily to convey the blessing of the bishop to a new member of his flock, and a commission to take his place as an active partner in the Church's apostolic task. This will involve and necessitate the bringing of the baptized person into a new and special relationship to the Holy Spirit whose indwelling presence has been mediated to him by virtue of his membership of Christ which has been bestowed on him sacramentally by faith in Baptism; but there should be no thought of the gift or seal of the Spirit as a grace of Confirmation. It is possible, indeed, that even the use of such a phrase as 'a gift of the Spirit' should be avoided in the case of the Confirmation of those who are being baptized as adults. It is by the use of such language that the modern theology of Baptism and Confirmation, like that of the ancients, has often been led astray. It has, for example, produced the artificial attempt of Puller to distinguish the indwelling of the Spirit, bestowed in Confirmation, from His regenerating influence in Baptism, and to maintain that in Baptism we receive gifts of grace, whereas in Confirmation the Spirit Himself is given. In fact, the reverse appears to be true; the Spirit is received in Baptism, since we are there incorporated into Christ and His Church, and gifts of grace in Confirmation. In any case, we must avoid the attempt to isolate the workings of the Spirit from each other; otherwise we shall be in danger of depersonalizing the Holy Spirit. We are concerned not with 'fuller' or 'lesser' 'outpourings', but with the gracious dealings of a Person. It is therefore impossible to accept Mason's distinction of the Spirit's operation *ab extra* from His personal indwelling. It is difficult, if not impossible, to understand how there can be remission of sins, adoption, or regeneration, without His indwelling presence. As Dr. Bright remarked in reply to the views of Pullen and Mason: 'A theory which admits that baptism involves regeneration and the "quickening touch" of the Spirit, and "in a sense" a reception of Him by reason of "incorporation into Christ" yet denies to the baptized, as such, that personal indwelling of the Spirit which is the "great prerogative of the Gospel dispensation", forbids them to consider themselves as "temples of the Holy Ghost", confines the "baptism of the Holy Ghost" to confirmation . . . can hardly be said to commend itself by consistency, and would seem to require a serious alteration in the pastoral teaching of the clergy, in the practice of the Church, and in the text of the Prayer-book offices and catechism.'[1]

We may sum up the matter thus. The convert to faith in Christ receives the indwelling presence of the Holy Spirit by virtue of his participation (through faith responding to the

[1] *Morality in Doctrine*, p. 91 n.

grace of God in Christ) in the status of sonship to God and freedom of access to the Father which is the gift of God the Son to redeemed humanity. This union with Christ and sharing in His Sonship (so far as that is possible for those who receive it by grace and not by nature) is symbolized and sacramentally effected by Baptism which re-enacts the Baptism of Jesus in which the Spirit descended upon Him, and He was proclaimed the Son of the divine Father. In so far as that Baptism pre-figured and symbolized the redemptive purpose of Christ's mission as the 'Servant of Yahweh', and was fulfilled in His death and resurrection, the convert can himself share sacra-mentally in that death and rising to new life. The resurrection life which is entered upon at Baptism is life in the Spirit; and the indwelling presence of the Spirit is simply one aspect of the sharing of the resurrection life of Christ which is begun in Baptism. By that presence the Christian believer is, so to speak, identified and marked out as a member of Christ's Body and an heir to His covenant promises. It is therefore the 'seal' of the New Covenant, and it follows that it is in Baptism that the believer is sealed.

The benefits of the sacrament are, however, conferred to some extent proleptically, for in the single action there is sum-med up an experience of Christ which is gradually realized throughout the whole course of the Christian's life. It expresses in a moment what can in fact be realized only step by step. The process of sanctification, as well as the decisive act of justifica-tion, is foreshadowed and proleptically summed up, so that the effects of the sacrament are partly actual and partly potential. It is therefore only at the end of the Christian's life, or perhaps only after his earthly life is over, that he can enter into a full understanding of what he has received in Baptism. The in-dwelling presence of the Spirit, a Person and not a *donum gratiae*, is mediated to the believer through Baptism as the sacrament of conversion; but that personal presence comes to be appre-hended more fully, and more deeply experienced, as the Christian proceeds on the course of his life in the Spirit. 'Baptism', says Dr. Quick, 'in any case only effects the begin-ning of the process of which it symbolizes the whole. Christ treats the baptized as already risen to sonship, and thereby elicits from him through His fatherly care that actuality of sonship which in present fact is very imperfectly his. Baptism symbolizes more than it effects and yet what it leaves to effect afterwards is only the consequence of a reality which it has effectively symbolized already.'[1]

In the case of an infant the effect of Baptism is primarily potential rather than actual, but it remains true that in Baptism he is made 'a member of Christ, the child of God, and an inheritor of the kingdom of Heaven', even though these phrases have in his case to be used in a somewhat different sense from that in which they are applied to one who is baptized as a believer. He receives a new status and is brought into a covenant relationship to God; he is admitted a member of the society which is Christ's Body; and he enters the community of God's sons, the special sphere of the operation of the Holy Spirit. These are facts with eschatological consequences of supreme importance.

If, then, it is true that in this sense the baptized infant has been made a member of Christ and an inheritor of the Kingdom, it follows that it is true in the same sense that he has received the Spirit's presence which is one aspect of membership of Christ and adoptive sonship in relation to the Father. He is therefore sealed with the earnest of the Spirit 'for a day of redemption'. His realization of the indwelling of the Spirit comes gradually, or perhaps in a decisive moment of conversion. A vitally significant moment in this realization is that of Confirmation, when the obligations of his baptismal profession are confirmed, and the benefits of Baptism are in turn confirmed to him on the level of full consciousness. There is no fresh 'gift', and no fresh undertakings on his part; there is a fuller realization and actualizing of what has already been given and undertaken proleptically. A new and fuller apprehension of the Spirit is granted in answer to prayer, following the completion of Baptism by the actual making of the response of faith to God's grace which was vicariously offered at Baptism. Together with the other effects of Baptism, the seal of the Spirit is confirmed to the believer in Confirmation; he enters upon a fuller apprehension of the sealing he already possesses; but it is not bestowed

[1] *The Christian Sacraments*, p. 173; cf. p. 179.

in this rite, for the seal is 'Christ within', dwelling in the soul through the Holy Spirit. This seal can be sacramentally received only in Baptism, but its realization is decisively advanced in Confirmation.

When a man has been baptized as an adult believer, his Confirmation, most fittingly administered, as we have suggested, as part of a single service of initiation, may properly be believed to set him in a new relationship to the Holy Spirit whose presence has been mediated to him through his incorporation into Christ in the actual Baptism. His membership of Christ and his consequent participation in the Spirit are not conferred upon him as an individual in isolation from the society of the Church. On the contrary, they are effected by the activity of Christ in His Body, and it is as a member of that Body that he enters into union with Christ and enjoys the fellowship of the Holy Ghost. Confirmation emphasizes these truths, and it is as a member of the Church that in Confirmation the believer receives the blessing of God through the representative leader of the Church and is commissioned for service in the Church's spiritual warfare. His experience of the indwelling Spirit will inevitably become deeper, and his apprehension of Him clearer and fuller, as a result of his participation in the Church's service to its Lord. He does not receive 'more of the Spirit' in Confirmation, nor is a special gift of the Spirit bestowed upon him; but he is given an active commission to be carried out in the strength of the Spirit, and in executing it he will more fully apprehend and realize the Spirit who is already present to him.

An analogy may perhaps be found in the case of a military recruit. He becomes a soldier as soon as he enlists, and as such possesses a certain status and particular functions, duties, and privileges; but it is not until he goes on active service that he arrives at a full realization of what has always in fact been his character and work as a soldier. The difference in the case of the adult Christian soldier is that he is always on active service and never possesses a status without the exercise of the functions which it involves. We may find a further illustration in the deeper and fuller experience of friendship which often resltus from the sharing of a particular task by two men who are already friends. The new circumstance of their work together does not of itself create their friendship, but it transforms and enlarges it. In a not dissimilar fashion, Confirmation may be said to initiate a deeper and enlarged experience of the fellowship of the Holy Spirit in a person who is charged with a share in the Church's apostolic task to be performed, as it were, in the company of the Spirit's personal presence. Ordination is another such moment in which the Christian may receive a status and commission which may be said to alter and enlarge his relationship to the Holy Spirit; but, again, in the case of Confirmation it is most appropriate that the moment of this experience should follow the Baptism of an adult believer immediately; there is no time at which such a person is not really engaged in the work which he is to carry out in the strength of the Spirit.

Confirmation therefore appears to be a valuable and highly significant part of the initiation of the person who is baptized as a believer, though it loses much force by being separated from Baptism; it must not, however, be regarded as a rite by which such a person becomes in the full sense a Christian; for this Baptism is entirely sufficient; nor must it be considered as a sacrament in the true and full sense of a 'sacrament of the Gospel', for to do this would be to depreciate those which are rightly so described—Baptism in which by virtue of our union with Christ in His death and resurrection we are sealed with the Spirit for a day of redemption, and the Eucharist by which we sacramentally feed on Christ and 'shew forth the Lord's death till He come'.

The Reformers were probably wise in their abandonment of the practice of chrismation. The outward sealing with the Cross, which occupied so prominent a place in the thought of the Church of the Fathers, has already taken place in Baptism, and the symbolism of the use of chrism in effecting the consignation serves only to illustrate what has also been done in Baptism—namely, that the candidate has received the priestly and kingly status which belongs to the Church as the people of the Christ. It is an edifying symbol, comparable with the ancient practice of giving milk and honey to the neophytes to illustrate their entrance into the land of promise; but it has at best no more than a relatively minor importance, and it is not appropriate to the Confirmation of those whose Baptism took place long before, since it relates to what was then done rather than to what is being performed in Confirmation.

The imposition of hands, however, is highly appropriate. What is symbolized in the rite, apart from the confirmation to the candidate of the benefits of Baptism, is perhaps his ordination to an 'apostolate' in the sense of a commission for service in the Church's mission to the world. This is well symbolized by his reception of the ancient sign of blessing and of 'solidarity' from the bishop as the representative of the apostolic Church, while prayer is made that he may grow in the strength of the Spirit and receive the daily increase of the gifts which the indwelling Spirit bestows upon him.

It may be that in this ceremony we have a real link in theory and practice with the laying on of apostolic hands recorded in the New Testament; but the link is admittedly fragile. Confirmation as practised in the Church of England today may have little direct historical connection with what was done by Peter and John in Samaria. To say this is in no way to disparage Confirmation, or to deny that it preserves and maintains important elements in Apostolic doctrine and practice. It is to be acknowledged that under the guidance of the Spirit the ratification of the baptismal profession and the blessing and commissioning which follow it have become the means by which the apparent inconsistencies and theological difficulties attaching to infant Baptism have, at least hitherto, been satisfactorily remedied. At the same time, if we keep in mind the implications of the teaching of the New Testament and the early Church, we shall refuse to accept the doctrine that it is in this rite alone that a man can receive the seal of the Spirit by which he is signed for eternity; we shall not see in it the means by which alone one can be made a full Christian; and we shall recognize the force of Dr. Rawlinson's warning that 'it would be a mistake . . . not only in tactics but in theology to insist on the acceptance of Confirmation as an indispensable prerequisite to reunion . . . or to place the obligatoriness of Confirmation upon the same level with that of Baptism itself'.[1]

---

[1] *The Theology of Christian Initiation*, p. 27.

BIBLIOGRAPHY

ABRAHAMS, I., *Studies in Pharisaism and the Gospels*, 1917.

ANRICH, G., *Das antike Mysterienwesen in seinem Einfluss auf das Christentum*, 1894.

ANZ, W., 'Zur Frage nach dem Ursprung des Gnostizismus' (*T.U.* 15, 4, 1897).

BAER, H. VON, *Der heilige Geist in den Lukasschriften* (Beitrage zur Wissenschaft vom A. und N. Testament, 3 folge, heft 3, 1926).

Baptism Today (Second Interim Report of the Joint Committee of the Convocations of Canterbury and York on Baptism, Confirmation, and Holy Communion, 1949).

BARRETT, C. K., *The Holy Spirit and the Gospel Tradition*, 1947.

BARTH, K., 'The Teaching of the Church regarding Baptism' (*E.T.*, Payne, E. A., 1948).

BEHM, J., *Die Handauflegung im Urchristentum*, 1911.

BELSER, J., *Das Zeugnis des 4. Evangelisten für die Taufe, Eucharistie und Geistessendung*, 1912.

BERNARD, J. S., 'The Odes of Solomon' (*Journal of Theological Studies*, 12 (1911), pp. 1 ff.).

BONNETAIN, P., 'Le Baptême de Notre Seigneur' (*Rev. Apolog*, 48, pp. 27–35; 50, pp. 51–63, 1929–30).

BORNEMANN, J., *Die Taufe Christi durch Johannes in der dogmatischen Beurteilung der Christlichen Theologen der 4 ersten Jahrhunderten*, 1896.

BOTTE, B., 'Hippolyte, La Tradition Apostolique' (*Sources chrétiennes*), 1946.

BOUSSET, W., *Kyrios-Christos*, 1913.

—, *Hauptprobleme der Gnosis*, 1907.

—, *Die Religion des Judentums*, 1903.

BRANDT, W., 'Die jüdischen Baptismen', *Z.A.T.W.*, Beiheft 18, 1910.

BRIGHT, W., 'Morality in Doctrine' (Sermon 8, *Divine Sealing*), 1892.

BRÜCKNER, W., 'Geist und Geistesgaben im N.T.' (*Religion in Geschichte und Gegenwart*, ii, pp. 1200–1213).

BÜCHSEL, F., *Der Geist Gottes im N.T.*, 1926.

BURKITT, F. C., *Christian Beginnings*, 1912.

—, *Early Eastern Christianity*, 1904.

CARPENTER, J. ESTLIN, *Phases of Early Christianity*, 1916.

CARRINGTON, P. (Archbishop of Quebec), 'Confirmation and St. Justin' (*Theology*, Dec. 1949, pp. 448–52).

CHASE, F., *Confirmation in the Apostolic Age*, 1909.

Confirmation or the Laying on of Hands vol. 1, Historical and Doctrinal, S.P.C.K., 1926.

Confirmation Today (Report of the Joint Committees of the Convocations of Canterbury and York, 1944).

COPPENS, J., *L'Imposition des Mains*, 1925.

CORBLET, J., *Histoire dogmatique, liturgique, et archéologique du Sacrement de Baptême*, 1881–2.

CULLMANN, O., 'La Signification du Baptême dans le N.T.' (*Rev. de Theol. et Phil.* 30 (1942), pp. 121 ff.).

—, *Die Tauflehre des Neuen-Testaments Erwachsenen- und Kindertaufe*, 1948.

CUMONT, F., *Les Mystères de Mithra*, 1902.

—, *Religions orientales dans le Paganisme romain*, 1929.

D'ALÉS, A., *Baptism and Confirmation*, 1929.

DAVIES, J. G., 'The Disintegration of the Christian Initiation Rite' (*Theology*, No. v. 1947).

DEISSMANN, G. A. 'Bible Studies' (*E.T.*, Grieve, A.), 1901.

DEY, J., Παλιγγενεσία, 1937.

DIX, G., 'Confirmation or the Laying on of Hands?' (*Theology Occasional Papers*, 5, 1936).

—, *The Apostolic Tradition of Hippolytus*, 1937.

—, *The Theology of Confirmation in Relation to Baptism*, 1946.

—, 'The Seal in the Second Century' (*Theology*, Jan. 1948; reviewed by Botte, B., *Bull. de Théol. Anc. et Med.*, Louvain, V, Jan.–Apr. 1949, no. 1279).

DÖLGER, F. J., 'Die Firmung in den Denkmalen des Christlichen Altertums (*Rom. Quartalschr.*, 19, 1905, pp. 1–41).

—, *Das Sakrament der Firmung historisch-dogmatisch dargestellt*, 1906.

—, *Sphragis*, 1911.

DRESIG, S. F., *De Usu Stigmatum apud Veteres ad Gal.* 6: 17, 1733.

DUCHESNE, L., *Les Origines du Culte chrétien*, 1903.

EASTON, B. S., 'Self-Baptism' (*American Journal of Theology*, 24 (1920), pp. 513–18).

—, *The Apostolic Tradition of Hippolytus*, 1934.

—, 'The Purpose of Acts' (*Theology Occasional Papers*, 6, 1936).

EDSMAN, C.-M., 'Le Baptême de Feu' (*Acta Seminarii Neotestamenti Upsalensis*, IX), 1940.

EISLER, R., 'Das Qainzeichen und die Qeniten' (*Le Monde oriental*, 23 (1929), pp. 48–112).

EISLER, R., 'The Messiah Jesus and John the Baptist' (*E.T.*, 1931).
FLEMINGTON, W. F., *The N.T. Doctrine of Baptism*, 1948.
FULLER, R. H., 'Baptism and Confirmation' (*Theology*, Apr. 1946).
GALTIER, R., 'La Consignation à Carthage et à Rome (*Recherches de Science Religieuse*, 1911, pp. 369–83).
—, 'La Consignation dans les Eglises de l'Occident' (*Rev. de l'Histoire ecclesiastique*, 13 (1912), pp. 257 ff.).
GAVIN, F., *The Jewish Antecedents of the Christian Sacraments*, 1928.
GUNKEL, H., *Die Wirkungen des heiligen Geistes*, 1888.
HARNACK, A., *Militia Christi*, 1905.
HEINEMANN, A., 'Die Lehre vom hl. Geist im Judentum und in den Evangelien' (*Monatschr. für Gesch. und Wissenschaft des Judentums*, 66 (1922), pp. 169–80, 268–79; 67 (1923), pp. 26–35).
HEITMÜLLER, W., *Im Namen Jesu*, 1903.
—, Article, 'Taufe' (*R.G.G.*, V, pp. 1086–1102).
—, *Taufe und Abendmahl im Urchristentum*, 1911.
—, *ΣΦΡΑΓΙΣ* (*Neutest. Studien für Georg Heinrici*, 1914).
HOOKE, S. H., 'The Way of the Initiate', and 'Christianity and the Mystery Religions' (*Judaism and Christianity*, vol. 1, 1937).
HOSKYNS, E. C., and DAVEY, F. N., *The Fourth Gospel*, 1940.
HUTCHINGS, W. H., *The Person and Work of the Holy Ghost* (4th edn.), 1893.
'Infant Baptism' (*Theology Occasional Papers*, New Series, 1, 1939).
JACKSON, F., and LAKE, K., *The Beginnings of Christianity*, vol. 5 (1933): Additional note on *The Name, Baptism, etc.*, by S. New.
JEREMIAS, J., 'Der Ursprung der Johannestaufe' (*Z.N.T.W.*, 28 (1929), pp. 312–20).
JURGENSMEIER, F., *Der mystische Leib Christi*, 1933.
KIRK, K. E., Criticism of the Report of the Joint Committee of the Convocations on Confirmation in *Oxford Diocesan Magazine*, Nov.–Dec. 1944.
KNOX, W. L., *Some Hellenistic Elements in Primitive Christianity* (Schweich Lectures, 1942).
KOCH, H., 'Zeit und Heimat des Liber de Rebaptismate' (*Z.N.T.W.*, 8 (1907), pp. 190–220).
—, 'Taufe und Askese in der alten ostsyrischen Kirche' (*Z.N.T.W.*, 12 (1911), pp. 37–69).
KÖNIG, E., *Die Messianische Weissagungen*, 1923.
KOSNETTER, J., *Die Taufe Jesu*, 1936.
KOSTER, D., *Die Firmung im Glaubensinn der Kirche*, 1948.
KUBITSCHEK, J. W., article, 'Signum' (Paully-Wissowa, *Real-Encyclopaedie*, 1923, cols. 2361–2455.
LAMBERT, J. C., *The Sacraments in the New Testament*, 1903.

LAROS, M., *Confirmation in the Modern World*, 1938.
LEENHARDT, F. J., *Le Baptême chrétien*, 1945.
LEISEGANG, H., *Der Heilige Geist*, 1919.
—, *Pneuma Hagion*, 1922.
LOHMEYER, E., 'Johannes der Taüfer' (*J.B.L.* 51 (1932), pp. 300–19.
LUNDBERG, P., *La Typologie baptismale dans l'ancienne Eglise* (Act. Semin. Neotast. Upsal. X) 1942.
MAASS, E., 'Segnen, Weihen, Taufen' (*Archiv für Religionswissenschaft*, 21 (1922), pp. 241–86).
MACDONALD, F. C., *A History of Confirmation*, 1925.
MANSON, T. W., 'Entry into Membership of the Early Church' (*Journal of Theological Studies*, 48 (1947), pp. 25 ff.).
MANSON, W., *Jesus the Messiah*, 1943.
MARSH, H. G., *The Origin and Significance of the N.T. Baptism*, 1941.
MASKELL, W., *Holy Baptism, A Dissertation*, 1848.
MASON, A. J., *The Relation of Confirmation to Baptism*, 1890, 1891.
MICHAELIS, W., *Reich Gottes und Geist Gottes nach dem N.T.* (Basel, *n.d.*).
MOORE, G. F., *Judaism*, 1927.
MUNDLE, W., *Der Glaubensbegriff bei Paulus*, 1932.
NOLLOTH, C. F., *The Rise of the Christian Religion* (chapter 24: 'The Sacraments'), 1917.
O'DWYER, M., *Confirmation: A Study in the Development of Sacramental Theology*, 1915.
O'LEARY, DE L., *The Sacrament of Holy Baptism*, 1912.
OEPKE, A., Articles, βάπτω, βαπτίζω, βάπτισμα, βαπτισμός, βαπτιστής in Kittel, *Theologisches Wörterbuch zum N.T.*, 1933.
OULTON, J. E. L., 'Second-Century Teaching on Holy Baptism' (*Theology*, March 1947).
PERDRIZET, P., 'La miraculeuse Histoire de Pandare et d'Echédore,' etc. (*Archiv. für Religionswissenschaft*, 14 (1911), pp. 54–129).
PLOOIJ, D., *The Baptism of Jesus* (*Amicitiae corolla*, ed. Wood, H. C.), 1933.
POSTER, G., 'Tractate Gerim', Text, Transl., Notes, *Angelos*, 2 (1926), pp. 1–38).
PREISKER, H., 'Die Vikariatstaufe (1 Cor. xv. 29)', *Z.N.T.W.*, 23 (1924), pp. 298–304).
—, 'Apollos und die Johannesjünger in Act. xviii. 24–xix. 6' (*Z.N.T.W.*, 30, 1931, pp. 301–4).
PREUSCHEN, E., 'Valentinus, Gnostiker' (*Realencyc. für Prot. Theol. u. Kirche* 20, pp. 395 ff.).
PROCKSCH, O. 'Wiederkehr und Wiedergeburt' (*Festschrift für L. Ihmels*, 1928, pp. 1–18).

PULLER, F. W., *What is the Distinctive Grace of Confirmation?* 1880.

PUSEY, E. B., *Scriptural Views of Holy Baptism* (Tract 67), 3rd edn., 1840.

QUICK, O. C., *The Christian Sacraments*, 1927.

RAHNER, H., 'Taufe und geistliches Leben bei Origenes' (*Zeitschr. für Askese und Mystik*, 1932, pp. 205–23).

RAMSEY, A. M., 'The Doctrine of Confirmation' (*Theology*, Sept. 1945).

RATCLIFF, E. C., 'The Relation of Confirmation to Baptism in the Early Roman and Byzantine Liturgies' (*Theology*, Sept.–Oct. 1946).

—, 'Justin Martyr and Confirmation' (*Theology*, April 1948).

RAWLINSON, A. E. J., *Christian Initiation*, 1947.

REITZENSTEIN, R., *Die hellenistischen Mysterienreligionen*, 1910.

—, *Die Vorgeschichte der Christlichen Taufe*, 1929.

RENDTORFF, F. M., *Die Taufe im Urchristentum im Lichte der neuen Forschungen*, 1905.

RICHARDS, G. C., *Baptism and Confirmation*, 1942.

ROBINSON, H. WHEELER, *The Christian Experience of the Holy Spirit*, 1928.

ROGERS, C. F., 'Baptism and Christian Archaeology' (*Studia Biblica*, 5, pp. 301 ff.).

—, 'How did the Jews Baptize?' (*Journal of Theological Studies*, 12 (1911), p. 437.

SAGNARD, F., 'Clément d'Alexandrie, Extraits de Théodote' (*Sources chrétiennes*), 1948.

SAHLIN, H., *Studien zum dritten Kapital des Lukasevangeliums*, 1949.

SCHEIDT, H. (ed.), *Die Taufwasserweihegebete* (Liturgiegeschichtliche Quellen und Forschungen, Münster, 29), 1935.

SCOTT, E. F., *The Spirit in the New Testament*, 1923.

—, *The Kingdom and the Messiah*, 1910.

SEEBERG, A., *Der Katechismus der Urchristenheit*, 1903.

SLADDEN, J. C., 'Baptism and the Gift of the Holy Spirit' (*Church Quarterly Review*, 146 (1948)).

SPICQ, C., *Les Epîtres pastorales*, 1947.

STADE, B., 'Das Kainzeichen' (*Z.A.T.W.*, 14 (1894), partly based on Dresig, q.v.).

STARK, A., *Der Taufritus in der Griechisch-Russischen Kirche*, 1903.

STOFFELS, J., *Die mystische Theologie Makarius des Ägyptiens*, 1908.

STONE, D., 'The Relation of Confirmation to Baptism' (*Church Quarterly Review*, 45 (1898), reviewing Puller, Mason, and Wirgman).

—, *Holy Baptism*, 1912.

STROMBERG, A. VON, *Studien zur Theorie und Praxis der Taufe*, 1913.
SWETE, H. B., *The Holy Spirit in the N.T.*, 1910.
—, *The Holy Spirit in the Ancient Church*, 1912.
SYNGE, F. C., 'The Spirit in the Pauline Epistles' (*Church Quarterly Review*, 237 (1934)).
TAYLOR, J. R. S., and others, *Baptism and Confirmation*, 1945.
The Theology of Christian Initiation (Report of the Archbishops' Theological Committee on the Relations between Baptism, Confirmation, and Holy Communion, 1948).
THOMPSON, J., *Offices of Baptism and Confirmation*, 1914.
THORNTON, L. S., *The Common Life in the Body of Christ*, 1941.
—, *Confirmation Today*, 1946 (Address to St. Alban's Diocesan Synod).
UMBERG, J.-B., *Die Schriftlehre vom Sakrament der Firmung*, 1920.
VILLIAN, A., *Les Sacraments, Histoire et Liturgie*, 1931.
WARREN, F. E., *Liturgy and Ritual of the Ante-Nicene Church*, 1897.
WILLIAMS, G. O., 'The Baptism in Luke's Gospel' (*J.T.S.*, 45 (1944), pp. 31–8).
WINDISCH, H., *Taufe und Sünde im ältesten Christentum*, 1908.
WIRGMAN, A. T., *The Doctrine of Confirmation*, 1897.
WOBBERMIN, G., *Religionsgeschichtliche Studien zur Frage der Beeinflussung des Urchristentums durch das antike Mysterienwesen*, 1896.
WOTHERSPOON, H. J., *Religious Values in the Sacraments*, 1927.

ADDITIONAL BIBLIOGRAPHY

Books and articles relevant to this discussion which have been published since the above bibliography was compiled include the following:

ADLER, N., *Taufe und Handauflegung*, 1953.
ALAND, K., 'Did the Early Church Baptize Infants?' (*E. T.*, 1963).
ATKINSON, J., 'Confirmation: The Teaching of the Anglican Divines' (*The Churchman*, 77, 2, 1963).
BAILLIE, D. M., *The Theology of the Sacraments and Other Papers*, 1957.
BAILLIE, J., *Baptism and Conversion*, 1964.
Baptism and Confirmation Today (The Schedule attached to the Final Reports of the Joint Committees on Baptism, Confirmation, and Holy Communion, as presented to the Convocations of Canterbury and York), 1954.
Baptism, Confirmation and Communion (The Schedule attached to the Minority Reports of the Joint Committees), 1954.
Baptism and Confirmation (A Report submitted by the Church of England Liturgical Commission to the Archbishops of Canterbury and York), 1958.
BARTH, M., *Die Taufe ein Sakrament?*, 1951.
BEASLEY-MURRAY, G. R., *Baptism in the New Testament*, 1962.
BENOIT, A., *Le Baptême chrétien au deuxième Siècle*, 1953.
BOUYER, L., 'La Signification de la Confirmation' (*La Vie Spirituelle* (suppl.), 29, 1954).
—, 'Christian Initiation' (*E.T.*, 1960).
BROMILEY, G. W., *Baptism and the Anglican Reformers*, 1953.
CAMELOT, T., 'Sur la Théologie de la Confirmation' (*Révue des Sciences Philosophiques et Théologiques*, 38, 1954).
CHURCH OF SCOTLAND, Interim Reports of the Special Commission on Baptism, 1955–9.
—, *The Biblical Doctrine of Baptism* (A Study Document issued by the Special Commission on Baptism), 1958.
CLARK, N., *An Approach to the Theology of the Sacraments*, 1956.
CRANFIELD, C. E. B., 'The Baptism of our Lord—A Study of St Mark 1 : 9–11' (*Scottish Journal of Theology*, 8, 1955).
CROSS, F. L., *I Peter, A Paschal Liturgy*, 1954.
CULLY, K. B. (ed.), *Confirmation : History, Doctrine and Practice*, 1962.

DAHL, N. A., 'The Origin of Baptism' (*Norsk Teologisk Tidsskrift*, 56, 1–2, 1960).

DANIELOU, J., 'Le Symbolisme de l'Eau vive' (*Révue des Sciences Réligieuses*, 32, 1958).

DAVIES, J. G., *The Spirit, the Church, and the Sacraments*, 1954.

DE LA POTTERIE, I., 'L'Onction du Christ' (*Nouvelle Révue Théologique*, 80, 1958).

DELLING, G., βάπτισμα βαπτισθῆναι (*Novum Testamentum*, 2, 1957).

DEWAR, L., *The Holy Spirit and Modern Thought*, 1959.

EVANS, P. W., 'Sealing a Term for Baptism' (*Baptist Quarterly*, 16, 1955–6).

EVERY, G., *The Baptismal Sacrifice*, 1959.

FISHER, J. D. C., *Christian Initiation : Baptism in the Medieval West*, 1965.

GILMORE, A. (ed.), *Christian Baptism*, 1959.

—, *Baptism and Christian Unity*, 1966.

HANSSENS, J. M., *La Liturgie d'Hippolyte*, 1959.

HERON, J., 'The Theology of Baptism' (*Scottish Journal of Theology*, 8, 1955).

HICKINBOTHAM, J. P., 'Confirmation in the Early Centuries' (*The Churchman*, 77, 2, 1963).

HINDLEY, J. C., 'The Seal and the First Instalment' (*Indian Journal of Theology*, 9, 3, 1960).

HUGHES, P. E., 'Confirmation : Recent Theological Trends' (*The Churchman*, 77, 2, 1963).

JEREMIAS, J., 'Infant Baptism in the First Four Centuries' (*E.T.*, 1960).

—, 'The Origins of Infant Baptism' (*E.T.*, 1963).

LAMPE, G. W. H., '*Baptisma* in the New Testament' (*Scottish Journal of Theology*, 5, 1952).

—, 'Theological Issues in the Baptism–Confirmation Controversy' (*The Modern Churchman*, n.s. 1, 1, 1957).

—, 'The Relation of Baptism and Confirmation' in K. B. Cully, *Confirmation : History, Doctrine and Practice*, 1962.

LEEMING, B., *Principles of Sacramental Theology*, 1956.

MARCEL, P. C., *The Biblical Doctrine of Infant Baptism*, 1953.

MINCHIN, B. (ed.), *Becoming a Christian*, 1954.

MOLLAND, E., 'La Circoncision, le Baptême et l'Autorité du Decret apostolique (Actes xv. 28 sq.) dans les milieux judéochrétiens des Pseudo-Clementines' (*Studia Theologica*, 9, 1, 1955).

MOULE, C. F. D., 'The Nature and Purpose of I Peter' (*New Testament Studies*, 3, 1, 1956).

NEUNHEUSER, B., 'Baptism and Confirmation' (*E.T.*, 1964).

OULTON, J. E. L., 'The Holy Spirit, Baptism and Laying on of Hands in Acts' (*Expository Times*, 66, 1954–5).

PAYNE, E. A., 'Baptism and the Laying on of Hands' (*Baptist Quarterly*, 14, 1953–4).

POCKNEE, C. E., *The Rites of Christian Initiation*, 1962.

—, 'Confirmation in the Anglican Tradition' (*Church Quarterly Review*, 1966).

RAWLINSON, A. E. J., *Current Problems of the Church*, 1956.

SCHNACKENBURG, R., 'Baptism in the Thought of St Paul' (*E.T.*, 1964).

SCHNEIDER, J., 'Baptism and Church in the New Testament (*E.T.*, 1957).

SYNGE, F. C., 'The Holy Spirit and the Sacraments' (*Scottish Journal of Theology*, 6, 1953).

THURIAN, M., 'Consecration of the Layman' (*E.T.*, 1963).

THORNTON, L. S., *Confirmation : Its Place in the Baptismal Mystery*, 1954.

TORRANCE, T. F., 'The Origins of Baptism' (*Scottish Journal of Theology*, 11, 1958).

VISCHER, L., *Ye are Baptized*, 1961.

WHITAKER, E. C., *Documents of the Baptismal Liturgy*, 1960.

—, *The Baptismal Liturgy*, 1965.

WHITE, R. E. O., *The Biblical Doctrine of Initiation*, 1960.

WORLD COUNCIL OF CHURCHES, FAITH AND ORDER COMMISSION, *One Lord, One Baptism* (Report of the Theological Commission on Christ and the Church), 1960.

ZEDDA, S., *L'adozione a figli di Dio e lo Spirito Santo*, 1952.

GENERAL INDEX

INDEX OF SCRIPTURAL REFERENCES